Old modes of production and capitalist encroachment

Old modes of production and capitalist encroachment

Anthropological explorations in Africa

Edited by Wim van Binsbergen and
Peter Geschiere

KPI

London, Boston, Melbourne and Henley

First published in 1985
by KPI Limited

Routledge and Kegan Paul plc
14 Leicester Square, London WC2H 7PH,

Routledge and Kegan Paul
9 Park Street, Boston, Mass. 02108, USA,

Routledge and Kegan Paul
464 St Kilda Road, Melbourne,
Victoria 3004, Australia and

Routledge and Kegan Paul plc
Broadway House, Newtown Road,
Henley-on-Thames, Oxon RG9 1EN

Set in Times Roman
by Hope Services, Abingdon, Oxon
and printed in Great Britain by
Redwood Burn Ltd, Trowbridge, Wiltshire

Library of Congress Cataloging in Publication Data

Old modes of production and capitalist encroachment.
(Monographs from the African Studies Centre, Leiden)
Includes bibliographies and index.
1. Economic anthropology — Africa — Addresses, essays,
lectures. 2. Communism and anthropology — Africa — Addresses,
essays, lectures. 3. Communism and anthropology — France —
Addresses, essays, lectures. 4. Economic anthropology —
France — Addresses, essays, lectures. 5. Africa —
Economic conditions — Addresses, essays, lectures.
I. Binsbergen, Wim M. J. van. II. Geschiere, Peter.
III. Series.
GN645.039 1984   306'.3   84-12236

British Library CIP Data also available

ISBN 0–7103–0089–1

To Gerrit Grootenhuis

Contents

Contents

Contents

Figures

Notes on contributors

Wim van Binsbergen (1947) read social and cultural anthropology and Third World sociology at the Municipal University of Amsterdam. He conducted field-work in Tunisia, Zambia, and Guinea-Bissau, and received a doctorate from the Free University of Amsterdam. He taught at the University of Zambia, the University of Leiden and the University of Manchester, and is now Head of the Department of Political Science and History, African Studies Centre, Leiden.

Peter Geschiere (1941) read history and social-cultural anthropology at the Free University, Amsterdam, where he also received his doctorate. He conducted field-work in Tunisia and Cameroon. He taught at the University of Kisangani, Zaïre, and is now Senior Lecturer in Social Anthropology at the Free University, Amsterdam.

Klaas de Jonge (1937) read social sciences and Third World demography at the Municipal University of Amsterdam and the Ecole Pratique des Hautes Etudes, Paris. He conducted field-work in Paris, Tanzania and Senegal. He was a Research Officer at the African Studies Centre, Leiden, and now combines social research and political practice in Mozambique.

Jos M. van der Klei (1942) read social and cultural anthropology and Third World sociology at the Municipal University of Amsterdam. He conducted field-work in Tunisia and Senegal. He was a Research Officer at the African Studies Centre, Leiden, and now teaches methods of anthropological field-work at the Free University, Amsterdam.

Reini Raatgever (1946) read Third World sociology at the Free

University, Amsterdam. Already as a student she developed an expertise on Marxist theory, in combination with active political practice. At the African Studies Centre, Leiden, she did library research into women and rural development in Africa. She taught at the Free University, Amsterdam, and now lives in Paris.

Simon Simonse (1943) read social and cultural anthropology at the University of Utrecht and the University of Leiden. He held research appointments at the Municipal University of Amsterdam and the African Studies Centre, Leiden. He taught at a teacher-training college, Zaïre, at Makerere University, Uganda, and at a College for Social Work, Amsterdam. He is now Senior Lecturer in Anthropology, University of Juba, Sudan.

Preface

Wim van Binsbergen and Peter Geschiere

This book is the result of a long series of meetings of the Amsterdam Work-group for Marxist Anthropology, extending over a number of years. Early in 1977, the initiative to found this work-group was taken by Simon Simonse. His interest in French Marxism had already resulted in his Dutch translation of Nikos Poulantzas's *Les Classes sociales devant le capitalisme aujourd'hui*, published with Socialistiese Uitgeverij Nijmegen (SUN). The members of the work-group were recruited according to the time-honoured anthropological principle of the personal network. The first to be enlisted were Wim van Binsbergen, Klaas de Jonge and Jos van der Klei; at the time, all were attached to the African Studies Centre, Leiden, some fifty kilometres from Amsterdam, where all work-group members lived and where meetings invariably took place. Soon Johan van der Walle joined the work-group. He was then working on a Dutch translation, commissioned by SUN, of Emmanuel Terray's *Le Marxisme devant les sociétés primitives*; regrettably, this translation was never published. Finally, Reini Raatgever and Peter Geschiere joined the work-group; they were then in the process of discovering French Marxist anthropology in the context of a seminar led by Geschiere at the Free University, Amsterdam.

By 1977, the work of Meillassoux, Godelier, Rey, Terray and other French Marxist anthropologists had hardly met with any recognition in the Netherlands. For the members of our work-group, getting acquainted with the ideas of these anthropologists was a rewarding and thrilling experience. Often the discussions went on well into the small hours, and our enthusiasm increased as our glasses were emptied. From the outset our discussions were focused on concrete matters: time and again the more general insights offered by the French School were tested in the light of our own field-work experiences — which basically meant Africa (except for van der Walle, whose research had been on the Dutch and German peasantry). Reini Raatgever had not yet herself done any field-work, but she more than made up for this by a profounder knowledge of the works of Marx and Althusser. In this way, she increasingly came to function as the Marxist conscience of our group. It became apparent that the French School had certainly not yet managed to propound a fully-fledged theoretical scheme. None the less, its general insights turned out to open up new and unexpected perspectives upon our own field-work materials. Moreover, we found that precisely the confrontation with our empirical data, collected from a different theoretical perspective, afforded all sorts of opportunities to criticize and further develop the French theories. In this respect the French School's body of ideas represented for us no less than a breakthrough in anthropological theory, as is clear from the publications of the members of our work-group since 1977, in this volume and elsewhere. In 1980 the work-group, in association with the African Studies Centre and the Free University, invited Claude Meillassoux to the Netherlands for a series of lectures. Similarly, in 1981 Terray came to Amsterdam and Leiden. Both occasions confirmed that the work of these anthropologists can lead to stimulating discussion — precisely because of the open, non-dogmatic character of its theorizing.

In the course of 1978 the group began to contemplate the idea of a collective volume to emerge from our group discussions. The first phases of this process of intellectual production passed fairly swiftly: the application of the French School's general ideas soon resulted in a number of interesting papers. But, as was to be expected, turning these papers into a collective volume was a much more time-consuming and arduous process. Wim van Binsbergen and Peter Geschiere were entrusted with the editorship. In their insistence on uniformity and precision of presentation, style and theorizing they proposed alterations which only after further group discussions — now of a pragmatic, rather than theoretical nature — led to the Dutch version of this book. It was published as *Oude produktiewijzen en binnendringend kapitalisme* by the Free University, Amsterdam, in association with the African Studies Centre, Leiden (1982) — the first volume in

Matthew Schoffeleers's new anthropological series. Each member of the work-group wrote his or her own contribution; however, the many successive versions of each chapter have been subjected to group discussions of such frequency and incisiveness that as far as general content is concerned, the book can only be regarded as a collective product of the work-group as a whole.

However, the present English version of this book differs substantially from the Dutch one. It was prepared when our work-group had virtually ceased to exist, its members having dispersed over Amsterdam, Leiden, Paris, Senegal, Southern Sudan and Maputo. For better or worse, this meant that for our editorial work we had to do without such guidance as the work-group discussions might have offered. Bonno Thoden van Velzen and Joel Kahn made helpful criticism of earlier drafts. Translation offered us the opportunity to correct such slight imperfections of style, terminology and bibliography as the original Dutch edition contained. Inclusion in the series of Monographs from the African Studies Centre meant that van der Walle's contribution on the articulation of modes of production in the history of the Dutch province of Drenthe had to be omitted. This has had the unfortunate effect that van der Walle is no longer manifestly present in this book, to which he contributed as participant in our work-group discussions. Likewise, van Binsbergen's chapter in the Dutch edition could not be included here: it has already been published as chapter 7 of his *Religious Change in Zambia*, in this same series of Monographs. However, his work on the ideological dimensions of the articulation of modes of production is here represented by an analysis of ethnicity in Western Zambia, first published in the *Journal of Southern African Studies* (1981), and rewritten for the present book. New, in this edition, is also Wim van Binsbergen's and Peter Geschiere's chapter on anthropological field-work from the perspective of the French School. Originally prepared as a discussion paper in the context of Meillassoux's visit in 1980, this piece was extensively rewritten partly on the basis of work-group discussions and of Meillassoux's personal reaction. The Introduction, by Peter Geschiere and Reini Raatgever, was expanded, e.g. by a discussion of the reception of the French School's leading ideas in the Anglo-Saxon academic world. Considering the patchiness of this reception so far, it would appear as though, along with the application to a specific body of empirical data, the translation of French ideas for an English audience constituted the main *raison d'être* of the present English edition.

Sheila Gogol Vuisje translated chapter 3, most of chapter 2, and (with Peter Geschiere) chapters 1 and 4; Wim van Binsbergen translated chapters 5 and 6, 7 (with Peter Geschiere) and 8 (with Don Bloch), and supervised the translation of the other chapters.

Neither the Dutch nor the English edition could have been accomplished but for the great material and moral support from the African Studies Centre, and notably its General Secretary, Gerrit Grootenhuis, (to whom we dedicate this book). Wilma Keijzer, Adriënne van Wijngaarden, Ria van Hal and Mieke Brouwer typed and retyped the successive versions with great accuracy and displayed the most incredible patience in the face of the editors' correction mania. Inevitably, translation and production of this book have taken a considerable amount of time; the contributions in it therefore reflect the international scholarly discussion up to 1982.

After the work-group members' present diaspora and current researches, they hope to resume their stormy and stimulating discussions within a few years' time. Meanwhile the present book is the provisional result of scholarly and friendly exchanges which over five years have taken place between academic petty-commodity producers. Aware of the pitfalls of exchange-value even in intellectual production, the authors have waived their royalties in a vain attempt to hang on to the use-value they hope their product possesses.

Chapter 1

Introduction: Emerging insights and issues in French Marxist anthropology

Peter Geschiere and Reini Raatgever[1]

Current events and the relevance of current theories in Third World studies

In the social sciences theories seem always to lag behind current events. In the African continent, for instance, each new development seems to illustrate the inadequacy of the generally accepted insights of anthropologists, political scientists, economists or historians. Of course, it has become a commonplace to direct criticism of this nature to Parsonian modernization sociology, which prevailed in the field of African studies in the 1950s and 1960s. In contrast with the ambitious blueprints advanced by this type of sociology, the African states in their practical developments did not all tend to conform to modern — i.e. western — ideal types. In almost all the countries of Africa, within a few years after independence, democratic systems modelled on western examples made way for one-party systems or military dictatorships. And the relevance of a concept like nation-building to the understanding of, for instance, the complicated struggle between factions in the national politics of these countries has become increasingly questionable.

However, similar objections may even be raised with regard to the newer theories on imperialism, 'dependencia' and international centre–periphery relations — all of them concepts which came to play an important role in African studies since the late 1960s. It is becoming equally difficult to explain current developments in the African continent as a direct consequence of the interests of a few capitalist core countries. The view, for instance, of post-colonial governments as mere puppets of international capitalist interests has clearly fallen through as too easy a simplification. From the threatening words of the Nigerian leaders addressed to the English government in 1979 during the conflict over Zimbabwe, it is clear that under certain circumstances an ex-colony is perfectly capable of exerting pressure on the former metropole. In this case, moreover, the pressure exerted by Nigeria was effective: it seems to have brought the Thatcher government to a drastic reversal of policy, which helped to achieve the independence of Zimbabwe sooner than expected. Moreover, the bold intervention on the part of the very same Nigeria — and, even more so, on the part of Libya — in the internal affairs of Chad only went to show that nowadays young states may become dependent not only on capitalist core countries. The same holds true for the recent conflicts involving Western Sahara, Ethiopia and Uganda. Since independence, the old relations of dependence between the colonies and the metropoles have developed into increasingly complicated chains of international power relations.

The economic dependence of the poor countries on the rich has always been interpreted as being essentially based on the exchange of raw materials from the ex-colonies for industrial products from the capitalist core countries. But this is also becoming more and more of a simplification. African countries like Senegal, Upper Volta or Mozambique are now most acutely dependent on the world market for the import of food. On the other hand, the oil crisis did much to increase, albeit temporarily, the international influence of Nigeria as an important supplier of this raw material. However, for most of the African countries the oil crisis meant a drastic intensification of their economic dependence, although not so much on the capitalist core countries as on the oil states and international financial agencies such as the International Monetary Fund, the World Bank and the OPEC funds. Thus, in recent years, the relations of economic dependence have also become more complex: there has been a shift from the levels of trade and production to the monetary level. Too little attention has been devoted to the study of these developments and their societal effects.

However, the limitations of 'dependencia'-theory are especially evident in the analysis of national politics and of the increasing differences, in this field, between the various African countries. In such countries as Tanzania and Mozambique the state has tried to gain direct control over industry and agriculture by way of the nationalization of western companies and a drastic reorganization of the old rural production communities. In Kenya and the Ivory Coast, the government has thrown open the national economy to western business. Again, countries like Guinea-Bissau and Cameroon seem to grant high priority to the development of production by independent peasants who cultivate food and market crops within the existing village communities. To put it in more general terms: the ruling classes in the post-colonial African states certainly have in common that they hold an intermediary position between the international capitalist interests and the African producers. But, from examples like the ones cited above, it can be concluded that this intermediary role allows African leaders of state enough leeway to follow their own options in drawing up their national and international policies.

Confronted with this confusing diversity and the inadequacy of general explanatory models, social scientists may easily react by turning away from verbose theories on development or under-development and by concentrating on empirical studies of local or regional problems. And studies of this kind are more and more in demand, certainly on the part of African governments who base their development plans upon such studies. There is a very real danger that social scientists will come to function as pure technocrats who draw up short-term recommendations without much insight into the broader context and the implications of the problems they study. Of course, even for the most practical and problem-oriented research, a broader interpretative framework is indispensable; but where is a general framework to be found that leaves enough room for the diversity of developments in Africa?

For the authors of this book, most of whom have conducted prolonged anthropological field-work in Africa, a very real problem lay in this tension between general theories, on the one hand, and the confusing diversity of the field situations we had studied so intensively, on the other. Anthropological field-work requires a lengthy period of living in and with a community, usually quite a small one. It creates fascinating opportunities for intensively experiencing a different social reality. But after the termination of field-work, the problem is usually how to relate the data gathered at a local or regional level to broader historical developments: to the gradual incorporation of the community into larger political and economic frameworks, to the expansion of the market economy, to the establishment of the colonial state, to the growth of new types of inequality within the old communities, and so forth. To solve this problem of how to relate field-work and wider developments, anthropologists certainly need general explanatory models. But, in anthropology especially, such models should never be so rigid or so dogmatic as to detract from the specific relationships that the anthropologist has studied and experienced as an observer in the course of his or her field-work. For the authors of this book, faced with this dilemma, it was extremely stimulating to become acquainted with the theories of a few French anthropologists — notably Meillassoux, Terray, Rey and Godelier — who are strongly influenced by the work of Karl Marx. Ever since 1977 we have been meeting regularly — sometimes once a week, sometimes once a month — to discuss these theories, trying in particular to re-analyse our own field-work data in the light of this new perspective.

Possibilities and limitations of the model of an articulation of modes of production

It is not the purpose of this Introduction to elaborate upon the theoretical and socio-political background of Marxist — or historical–materialist — anthropology in France. Other authors have already done so.[2] Our aim here is more limited: to introduce a few central concepts and themes from the work of the French anthropologists, in so far as these have played an important role in our work-group discussions and in the analyses of field-work material to be presented in the following chapters of this book. Somewhat wider issues are taken up again towards the end of this book: the relevance of these theories for anthropological field-work in general (chapter 7), and a critical evaluation of the 'modes of production debate' between the French anthropologists (chapter 8).

In our work-group discussions one key concept of the French Marxist anthropologists proved to be particularly inspiring: the now quite common idea of an articulation of modes of production. To summarize briefly: in their view, modes of production do not replace each other in the development of a society; instead, a new mode of production can develop — can 'establish its dominance' — on the basis of the continued functioning of older, 'subordinate' modes of production.[3] To put it more concretely, in this view the modern history of Africa can be characterized as a process during which the dominance of the capitalist mode of production was established all over the continent. But this capitalist expansion certainly did not bring about the immediate demolition of the old modes of production in Africa. On the contrary, the old relations of production were 'used', as it were, for the further expansion of capitalism. It is precisely because of the continuing cohesion of the old production communities (no matter how transformed) that specific forms of capitalist exploitation are possible — notably the withdrawal of relatively cheap labour and market products from the village economy.

Meillassoux's *Femmes, greniers et capitaux* (1975) elaborates on this idea very clearly. In his view, the wages in the capitalist sectors of African societies can remain relatively low because a large part of the labourer's needs are still met by the food production of the old village community. In practice, the wages have to cover the labourer's living expenses only during his productive period. As soon as the labourer is too ill or too old to work, he returns to his village, where he lives off the food crops cultivated by his family. His wife and children — the future generation of labourers — can remain in the village and live off their own food gardens as well. As long as the food production in the village continues to function, the African migrant worker provides cheaper labour for the capitalist entrepreneur than the 'real' proletarian; the latter is of course completely dependent on his wage, and thus on the capitalist sector, for his own maintenance — during his unproductive periods as well as his productive periods — and for the support of his wife and children. In the case of the peasant migrant worker an 'over-exploitation' of labour takes place:

> he produces both labour-rent and surplus-value. The first derives from the free transfer of labour-power produced in the domestic economy to the capitalist sector of production; the second from exploiting the producer's labour-power bought by the capitalist   (Meillassoux 1981: 115).

In other words, as a wage-labourer the migrant worker produces surplus-value for the capitalist entrepreneur. But at the same time the entrepreneur extracts a labour-rent from the domestic community where the migrant worker has been raised and where his labour is being reproduced (cf. Gerold-Scheepers and van Binsbergen 1978: 25–6).

The same holds true for the cultivation of market crops by African peasants within the framework of the old production communities: the prices of these market products can be kept down because the peasants provide for their own maintenance by cultivating food crops at the same time. As Rey put it, 'Capitalism expands at the expense of the village community, but at the same time thanks to that village community' (1971: 519). On the one hand this model suggests a general line in modern African developments: the increasing dominance of capitalism. But, on the other, this increasing dominance can never be viewed as an all-explaining factor. The old relations of production — whether transformed or mutilated — do retain their own significance for the specific forms in which capitalist dominance could be established and expanded. Therefore the model assumes considerable diversity: in each social formation the articulation of old and new relations has to follow its own path. Ultimately, it is a matter of research to assess just how this articulation took place in a given region. The most important questions are: how exactly was the dominance of capitalism established, what footholds for this dominance were to be found in the old relations of production, and in what sense did the latter become transformed so as to fit in with specific requirements of capitalist interests? There are no standard answers to these questions, as in each region the process departed from specific preconditions.

Following Marx's footsteps, these French anthropologists stress the fact that the expansion of capitalism was never an easy, automatic process. On the contrary, it called for experiments, improvisation, and often the most bizarre coercive measures, especially in the first stages of the articulation. In some regions, the expansion of European trade could be superimposed on old trade networks or forms of tribute; there, European entrepreneurs could enter into 'class alliances', often with the most unexpected partners: with Muslim marabouts in Senegal, or with polygamous local chiefs in Cameroon, who expanded their harems to include hundreds of wives in order to put them to work on the cultivation of market crops (see chapter 4). In other regions, however, drastic intervention on the part of the colonial state was called for to 'break open' the old village communities and force them towards surplus production for colonial trade.

Moreover, capitalist exploitation did not have one and the same aim in the various parts of Africa. In the colonial economy, certain regions (such as Upper Volta) were to serve as labour reserves; colonial authorities there devoted the brunt of their efforts to the recruitment of labour migrants who were sent to cultivate cash-crops on plantations in the more accessible parts of Africa. Elsewhere, for example along the west coast of Africa, the development of the colonial economy was mainly based on the production of independent African peasants, without any abrupt alterations in the old systems of land management and labour organization. In other regions again, for example in Kenya, the dominance of capitalism resulted in the large-scale expropriation of land for the benefit of white planters. All these variations were essential to the development of both the old and the new contradictions within African societies. And it is this complicated intertwining of old and new contradictions that has shaped the confusing diversity in present-day power relations and in the performance of the ruling classes in contemporary Africa. In this sense, the model of an articulation of modes of production may provide a general perspective by which to analyse the complexity and variability of present-day politico-economic developments on the African continent.

At the same time this model can serve as a new stimulus for anthropological studies. The traditional anthropological preoccupation with such subjects as kinship, bridewealth, witchcraft or prophetic movements does not necessarily betray, in this view, an antiquarian interest in phenomena doomed to disappear. On the contrary, these phenomena derive from the old relations of production which have still retained some of their force and which can even generate new forms during their inevitable transformation under capitalist dominance. Therefore the study of these old structures and their modern transformations continues to be indispensable if social scientists are to gain insight into contemporary power relations and into the wide range of effects of capitalist expansion in Africa. In this perspective, for example, it is easy to understand why, along with the anthropologists, virtually all the segments of the African population, including the westernized élite, are still preoccupied with 'traditional' — in fact often 'neo-traditional' — ideas about kinship, bridewealth, witchcraft and so forth.

Moreover, a historical–materialist perspective may not only help towards the understanding of the survival of these old organizational principles; at the same time this approach enables anthropologists to look for explanations of why these principles played such a dominant role in the old African societies. Meillassoux, for example, has tried to explain the dominant role of kinship — and related traits like the authority of the elders and the importance of bridewealth — in these societies by referring to specific consequences of the relations of production and reproduction (linked with a certain level of the productive forces — see Meillassoux 1975). The debate about Meillassoux's explanation is certainly not closed yet. But, at any rate, it is striking that this was one of the first anthropological attempts at explaining kinship — rather than accepting it as an institution that simply happens to play a large role in this type of society. At the same time such explanations of the dominant role of kinship on the basis of the inherent logic of the relations of production and reproduction may help to analyse transformations of the old kinship organization in modern conditions. To some extent following in Meillassoux's footsteps, Rey tries to show how changes in the old African forms of organization — for instance in the authority of the elders and in the payment of bridewealth — furthered capitalist expansion in that continent. In particular he emphasizes the monetarization, and the subsequent 'inflation', of the bride-'prices' which in many parts of Africa functioned as a kind of lever, forcing young men to go and earn money outside the village, or to cultivate new cash-crops. Thus, in his view, the transformation *and* the continuing significance of the old relations of exploitation were (and still are) crucial for the solution of the problems inherent in capitalism: its demands for wage-labour and for new market products (Rey 1971, 1976; see chapters 2, 4 and 7 below).

The work of the French Marxist anthropologists does clearly open up new perspectives. But it would be false to suggest here that they already offer a complete and well-balanced theory. On the contrary, there is even some doubt as to whether one can speak of a single paradigm here. There is certainly no consensus among these anthropologists. Godelier strongly disagrees on many points with Meillassoux, Rey and Terray. These three authors have also carried out fervent polemics between each other, but they do share a common background. All three have been influenced by Balandier; all three have conducted prolonged field-work in Africa, and their subsequent theoretical publications clearly bear the mark of their experiences in the field. Godelier did field-work in Papua New Guinea, but his theoretical analyses are mainly based on research data gathered by others, particularly on Latin America: the old Inca and Aztec societies. A major difference from Meillassoux, Rey and Terray is, moreover, that Godelier was much more influenced by Lévi-Strauss. He has been characterized by the others as a 'pseudo-Marxist structuralist', and whatever the truth of this epithet, it does point out real differences. According to the others, Godelier's analyses are marked by an a-historical outlook. He seems in any case to be less interested in modern transformations of pre-capitalist relations, and their articulation with capitalism.[4]

Marxist anthropology and general theoretical developments within Marxism

What precisely is the meaning of Marx's theories for the work of these French anthropologists, and what positions do the latter take in the general debates within Marxism? An important issue among these anthropologists has been the extent to which their own analyses are based upon a correct interpretation of the Marxian concepts and theories. They all reject a dogmatic application of Marx's theories. Their aim is rather to elaborate upon the concepts and methods Marx developed for the analysis of capitalism, so that these tools can equally be utilized for the analysis of pre-capitalist modes of production and their articulation with capitalism. But, in doing so, they have the intention of continuing along Marx's line of thought. On this subject, they have been strongly influenced by the philosopher Althusser and his followers Balibar and Poulantzas in their interpretation of Marx. But it is often difficult to assess what exact effect Althusser's influence has had on these French anthropologists. Althusser's explorations did not concern anthropology directly, but in many respects they formed a necessary preliminary for the development of a historical–materialist anthropology. An important factor was his rejection of the Stalinist version of Marxism, in which the theory was no more than a simplified outline backing certain political practices. Althusser emphasized that it was justified to develop a philosophical approach to the ideas of Marx, complementary to — and not directly instrumental to — Marxism as a political theory and practice. Especially in his earlier works there was a definite over-emphasis on theory, which he himself later referred to as 'theoreticist deviation'.

This 'theoreticist' emphasis was one of the reasons why Althusser's influence on other fields initially remained rather diffuse. His work functioned more as a general source of inspiration than as a clearly delineated paradigm. In the 1960s, his influence was felt in various fields (particularly in political science, economics and psychology, but also in social geography, theory of literature, and even in theology). But no integrated and shared scientific practice emerged. The boundaries between the various disciplines were hardly affected, and the Althusserian ideas were mainly evaluated in relation to their applicability within each distinct discipline.

This is certainly true for anthropology. The French anthropologists who, in the 1960s, began to develop a historical-materialist anthropology rarely arrived at an explicit application, elaboration or criticism of the ideas of Althusser. In other respects, as well, these anthropologists made few contributions to the central issues of the theory of historical materialism itself. With the exception of Godelier, none of them made an attempt to deal with dialectics in a sophisticated manner. Nor did these anthropologists write about problems of freedom and necessity, evolution, consciousness and alienation — all of which were issues in heated discussions with and among Marxists at the time (cf. the discussions of the work of Sartre, Habermas, Adorno, Popper, Kolakovski, etc.).

Indeed, the abstract theoretical nature of Althusser's work, up until the 1970s, failed to provide much support for the development of a historical-materialist *method* within the field of anthropology. In research practice, Althusser's contributions have largely been used as 'Grand Theory', supplemented by the customary methods and techniques of the anthropological discipline. Consequently, a central issue came to be how concepts from this abstract Marxist theory were to be related to research data gathered in accordance with customary methods. The methodologies which had come to be common practice in the social sciences continued to exert a great amount of influence on the work of the French Marxist anthropologists — for example those for logically verifying the propounded relations between general and specific theories and those for the empirical falsification of relationships between data as propounded by specific theories (operationalization and the construction of indicators). Thus, these anthropologists mainly concentrated on the operationalization of the concepts. Terray's attempts to find a standard formula for operationalizing the mode of production concept made it clear how great the problems are in this field. He developed a model to operationalize the concept for pre-capitalist African societies, based on the assumption of a non-problematic relation between reality and theoretical concepts. Subsequently, however, he had to recognize that such operational-izing of the concept could lead to considerable confusion in anthropological analysis, and had to correct his formulations on substantial points (see p. 14 below).

At the end of the 1960s, Althusser more or less abandoned the idea that internal scientific testing (within the 'theoretical practice' itself) was possible. Then he tended to prefer again the idea of testing scientific interpretations through the practice of the class struggle. But this viewpoint also confronts social scientists with very real problems. The so-called 'primacy' of the class struggle continues to be a rather vague, and often hard to digest, part of Marxist theory. The slogan 'no revolutionary theory without a revolutionary practice' obliges intellectuals to an all-out devotion to that practice before they have a right to follow up their theoretical interests, and this has driven many left-wing intellec-tuals to their wits' end. It would be wiser to apply the criterion of practice in a less rigid, more flexible, manner. Moreover, in this respect, anthropologists are faced with very specific problems since, in their field of research — mostly outside their own society — political action is usually out of bounds for the researcher, and rightly so. Moreover, in the study of African situations, the requirement that the deeper contradictions of the society have to be completely dissected before one can go on to draw conclusions and publish the data is absolutely untenable. Quite apart from the problem that social scientists are still hardly capable of a definite analysis of the politico-economic structures, there are also practical problems involved. In Africa, a too obvious attention to social contradictions would lead to a kind of scientific shifting cultivation, because the anthropologist would become a *persona non grata* in any region he had written about. This holds true for the socialist African countries as well as for the military dictator-ships.

The utilization of central Marxist concepts in anthropology

In view of all these problems and the lack of clarity as to what historical-materialist anthropology really is, one can hardly expect the French anthropologists to use central Marxian concepts such as productive forces, relations of production and modes of production in an identical or unequivocal sense. Therefore, rigid and simple definitions of these concepts would hardly be in place in an Introduction like this; it would only simplify or even vulgarize the theories involved. Nevertheless, these terms are used again and again in the following chapters of this book, so that some discussion is called for as to how these concepts function in the work of French Marxist anthropologists.

One thing these anthropologists all have in common is their opposition to a dogmatic interpretation of historical materialism, notably of a Stalinist conception. Rather simple and unequivocal definitions of the central concepts of Marx were in keeping with this conception. A *mode of production*, for example, defined as a specific manner in which the means needed to provide maintenance are produced, was viewed as consisting of two separate parts: the productive forces and the relations of production. The *productive forces* were defined as the relations between the producers and the objects or natural resources needed for the production; often this notion was even further simplified as referring to the relation between man and nature as a purely technical relation. The *relations of production* were defined as mutual relations between people involved in the production process. This social relation could be either one of co-operation and assistance, or one of dominance and subordination. In the Stalinist conception, these technical and social relations were supposed to be identified by fairly direct observations. Thus the mode of production could be deduced directly from the results of empirical research. Moreover, in this conception the level of productive forces was thought to determine the nature of the relations of production, following Marx's view that the development of the productive forces necessitated revolutionary transformations of the relations of production.

To some, an incisive criticism of this Stalinist position may appear as intellectual affectation. However, the issues involved here are very crucial ones. In practice, this theoretical position served as the legitimation for certain developments and specific social practices under Stalinism. This is why, later on, the critique of the Stalinist interpretation of Marxian theory has been so fierce. French Marxists such as Althusser, Balibar and Poulantzas protested against the rigid nature of Stalinist theory, which reduced the entire social formation to the economic basis in which, moreover, the technological component was viewed as being dominant. They see the Marxian concepts as *theoretical* concepts, and consequently as the basic elements of a theory that draws certain links between phenomena. According to them, the acknowledgment of the determination 'in the last instance' of society by the economic level should never lead one to overlook the specific causality of elements on other levels (political or ideological institutions), or to deny the complex intertwining of causal connections between the various levels. In the work of these French Marxists, the definition of central Marxian concepts has become a much more complicated matter, precisely because their main interest is in the *relations* between the various elements.

In their view a mode of production is not something to be constructed on the basis of empirical evidence, but a complex to be reconstructed along theoretical lines. Productive forces and relations of production are two different types of relations between the elements in production, *viz.* the worker (producer), the means of production (to be subdivided into labour instruments and labour objects) and the non-worker (non-producer). The term *productive forces* refers to the relations between the producer and the means of production, from the viewpoint of the real production process (the non-producer is not directly involved here). The term *relations of production* refers to the relations between the producer, the means of production and the non-producer, from the viewpoint of the social process of control over production. The manifestation of all these relations and of their combinations forms the complex structure referred to as *mode of production*. It may be clear by now how complicated the Althusserian definitions can become, even in a very simplified version.

On the one hand, this kind of interpretation of the Marxian concepts does have a clear advantage: it allows more room for the complexity and infinite diversity of social processes. But, on the other, the high theoretical level of the formulations creates new problems. In research practice, it has not proved easy to apply such formulations, and considerable confusion has sometimes been the consequence. This is clearly illustrated by the difficulties the French Marxist anthropologists experienced in operationalizing the mode of production concept. These problems also provide a good starting-point for a further exploration of the perspective within which these anthropologists work, and of the ways in which they differ from each other.

Terray's difficulties with the mode of production concept have been briefly mentioned above. In his 1969 study, in which he repeatedly cited Althusser, he proposed to distinguish modes of production on the basis of different forms of co-operation. Working from this criterion he concluded that, in Meillassoux's material on the Guro, two modes of production can be distinguished: one based on hunting with extensive co-operation, and the other based on agriculture with limited co-operation (Terray 1969: 97–107).

This operationalization of the mode of production concept — which Terray himself re-formulated later (1975, 1979) — met with strong criticism. Godelier, for instance, objected that Terray's formulation amounted to a simple bracketing of the mode of production concept with any form of production, leading to a disastrous proliferation of the number of modes of production. In practice, anthropological researchers, inspired by Terray's interpretation, returned from the field with long lists of newly invented modes of production. Due to the all too simple linking of the mode of production concept to one single criterion, the concept could become rather shallow, losing much of its analytical value. Godelier's own views on how to apply this concept became clear from his remark that a general model of a mode of production should never be formulated on the basis of data from one society; anthropologists, he claims, are still far from capable of formulating the theoretical model of the mode of production for 'tribal' societies; much more extensive and detailed data will have to be gathered about a larger number of societies of this type (Godelier 1979: 17).

Meillassoux hardly uses the mode of production concept in his general analyses of African village society. According to him, this concept did not have 'a truly scientific status', not even in Marx's own works (1975: 146). In his earlier publications he used more global terms to denote the old village societies, such as 'les sociétés traditionnelles d'autosubsistance' (Meillassoux 1960). But he later introduced a more specific term, 'la communauté domestique', in order to distinguish the simple agricultural societies in Africa from the 'horde' of hunters and food-gatherers (1975). Essential features of this 'domestic community' are the following: it is barely possible to exercise control over the means of production, the agricultural tools are simple, and there often is an abundance of land. Control over production is possible only by way of direct control over persons, *viz.* the producers themselves. In this kind of society, hierarchic relations can develop only within small politico-economic units, and these hierarchic relations are mainly based on control over reproduction (*viz.* the biological reproduction of new producers). Within the villages, the family elders can control the circulation of wives and bridewealth between the small exogamous units. This also secures their control over the labour of the younger men within their own community: a young man can pay bridewealth and marry a wife only through the intermediary of his elder.[5]

In Meillassoux's view, the relations between the elders and the younger men within the domestic community are ultimately based on reciprocity. The elders use the surplus labour of the younger men so as to accumulate certain prestige goods (iron, salt, trade commodities). But, finally, these prestige goods are used to pay for wives for the younger men — in other words, surplus labour is remunerated after all. Meillassoux's interpretations differ sharply from Rey's on this point. In Rey's general analyses of African village society, the mode of production concept — in the specific form of a 'lineage mode of production' — does play a central role. But Rey handles the concept in a very different manner from Terray in his 1969 study (Terray's subsequent re-formulations corresponded more or less to Rey's — see Terray 1975). To Rey, the essential relationship in every mode of production is the 'relation of exploitation'. Every mode of production is character-ized by a specific form of surplus labour. In Rey's view, the form of surplus labour determines the class contradiction which is essential to the mode of production in question. The capitalist mode of production is based on surplus labour in the form of wage-labour, so that entrepreneurs and proletarians come to form the opposing classes. The feudal mode was characterized by surplus labour in the form of the land-rent paid by serfs to landlords, and thus the essential class contradiction was one between serfs and landlords (see Rey 1973: 100; Rey 1979).

According to Rey, the notion of exploitation is particularly relevant in situations where the surplus labour expropriated from the direct producers serves as a means whereby the ruling class retains its control over the producers. He concludes that there is every reason to speak of exploitation in the old African village societies as well. For there, the surplus labour of the young men was transformed into prestige goods, which were controlled by the elders. And it was precisely due to their control over these prestige goods, often used for bridewealth, that the elders could maintain their monopoly over the circulation of women, which again served to perpetuate their authority over the younger men. Thus, in Rey's view, elders and the younger men (as social and not as biological categories) should be characterized as two opposing classes. Moreover, he emphasizes that this old class contradiction still plays a large role in present-day African relations under capitalist dominance. Reacting to these interpretations, Meillassoux has again sharply objected to the use of the term 'class' in this connection. In accordance with the general emphasis in Meillassoux's work on the importance of the relations of (biological) reproduction, he wants to speak of classes only if separate modes of (biological) reproduction can be distinguished. According to him, elders can never be viewed as a dominant class because — unlike feudal landlords or capitalist entrepreneurs — they can never independently reproduce themselves as a group (Meillassoux 1975: 123).

It may have become clear by now that French Marxist anthropology has not yet produced a finished, ready-made theory. The differences of opinion, only briefly indicated above, and the problems in the operationalization of central concepts are still very great indeed. In this Introduction, it is not our aim to elaborate on these polemics, and even less to define our own position with regard to the issues concerned (but see chapters 7 and 8 below). This collection of studies, rather, demonstrates the relevance and the limitations of these theoretical explorations through their application to anthropological field-work data (notably chapters 2–6). However, in the present English version of our book, it may be relevant to add a brief discussion of some reactions the ideas of the French Marxist anthropologists have prompted in the Anglo-Saxon literature.

Some Anglo-Saxon reactions to the French theories

In British anthropology it has become more or less commonplace

— especially when new influences from outside are evaluated — to refer to Ardener's Malinowski lecture of 1971 and to his comments on the crisis in British (and international) anthropology.[6] According to Ardener, a new trend in this crisis was that France is replacing England and the USA as 'a source of new or fashionable theory'; in this context he pointed to the influence of Lévi-Strauss, but also to the growing interest in French Marxists. In the same vein, Bloch noted in 1975 'a renewed interest in fundamental Marxist concerns among British anthropologists' and he also referred to the growing influence of French anthropologists in particular.[7] Since then Anglo-Saxon reactions — from anthropologists, but also from historians, sociologists of development and others — to the work of Terray, Godelier, Meillassoux and (to a lesser degree) Rey have become so numerous that it is impossible to discuss them in a few pages.[8] Here, selected issues can only briefly be indicated, in order to give some impression of the way the French theories have been accommodated in Anglo-Saxon discussions.

A survey of these reactions conveys the impression that in many respects the Channel is still very wide and deep. Of course, some of the French anthropologists, notably Godelier, Meillassoux and Terray, have benefited from their thorough knowledge of classical British anthropology. Yet the Anglo-Saxon reactions to their own work have hardly, as yet, played a role in the debates among the French Marxist anthropologists themselves (exceptions are, e.g., a few references to the work of Goody — see Terray 1973). But it is particularly remarkable that many Anglo-Saxon reactions seem to be based on only a partial knowledge of the work of these French Marxist anthropologists. This may have a very practical reason. English translations of the main French publications have been long in coming out, and several important studies have still not been translated.[9] Yet it remains somewhat surprising that certain Anglo-Saxon writers deem themselves capable of criticising their French colleagues fairly severely even when they have not been able, apparently, to consult major publications of direct relevance to their criticism.[10]

Another peculiarity is that Anglo-Saxon comments have been expressed mainly in theoretical discussions; this was possible because of some over-reaction against the much-abused Anglo-Saxon empiricist tradition. Anglo-Saxon critics have scarcely tried to assess the French theories by applying them to empirical data;

yet Meillassoux and Terray have emphasized that the test of the relevance of their ideas lies in the practice of research.

In these Anglo-Saxon reactions to French Marxist anthropology, so far two focal points have emerged. Reactions from anthropologists came especially from the circle round the review *Critique of Anthropology*.[11] Another forum has been the review *Economy and Society*, where the French theories were regularly quoted in the context of debates on underdevelopment, modes of production and capitalist expansion.[12]

In this latter debate one turned to French Marxist anthropology in the expectation that the theories of the French School might serve to counterbalance the all too global analysis *à la* Wallerstein and Frank — notably by doing more justice to the multifarious role of pre- or non-capitalist forms of organization as existing on the periphery of the capitalist system. In this context Rey's theories are of special interest, but unfortunately very little of his work has yet been translated.[13] This may explain certain oddities. For instance, Foster-Carter (1978), one of the few authors trying to expound Rey's theories in English, hardly refers to Rey's monograph (1971) and, possibly because of that, gives a very partial rendering of these theories. Rightly he characterizes Rey's 'project' as an attempt to analyse how capitalism can 'take root' in new social formations. But he (1978: 60–1) completely neglects a mechanism which Rey particularly emphasizes in his monograph: the monetarization of the old relations of exploitation, which thus can serve as a kind of lever forcing the producers out of the old communities and towards the capitalist labour market. It is in this perspective that Rey sees a parallel, despite numerous differences, between the role of the feudal land-rent and African bridewealth in the expansion of capitalism. In both cases the monetarization *and* the continuing significance of the old relations of exploitation offered a welcome solution to the capitalist demands for wage-labourers and surplus products (see p. 8 above; Rey 1971:21, 121, 416f., 1973: 161). Therefore Foster-Carter seems to miss the point when he objects that Rey's theory does not clarify the variations in capitalist expansion. To Rey, a vital question is how capitalist interests could 'make use' of the old relations of exploitation. Thus, depending on the variety of forms of the old modes of production and of the capitalist presence within the social formation concerned, various possibilities for class alliances emerged, leading to specific patterns of articulation of capitalist and subordinate modes of production (see Geschiere in press, a).[14]

Wolpe, too, seems to make only a very partial use of Rey's, Terray's and Meillassoux's insights in his discussion of theories on the articulation of modes of production (an introduction to a collection of articles from *Economy and Society*), although he cites these authors at the beginning of his argument (Wolpe 1980a). Distinguishing between 'restricted and extended concepts of the mode of production' — viz. modes *with* and *without* their own 'mechanism of reproduction' or 'laws of motion' — Wolpe arrives at somewhat mechanical conclusions. Apparently, he wants to maintain this distinction fairly strictly in order to derive from it different types of articulation: an articulation of two 'extended modes of production', each with its own 'mechanisms of reproduction', and an articulation of a dominant 'extended' mode with a subordinate 'restricted' mode, which, because of the destruction of its own mechanisms of reproduction, has become subservient to the former's mechanisms of reproduction.

It may be clear from the above that the theories of the French Marxist anthropologists suggest a far more subtle relation between the dominance and the reproduction of a mode of production (see Rey 1971; Terray 1975; Meillassoux 1975: part II). After all, Wolpe's contrast between modes of production with and without their own mechanisms of reproduction seems far too absolute. The French anthropologists try to demonstrate, on the basis of an analysis of historical processes, how and to what extent the reproduction of the subordinate mode of production is made subservient to the participation of the producers in the productive processes of the dominant mode, usually capitalism. But this does not imply that the specific forms ensuring the reproduction of the old relations are completely destroyed. On the contrary, Rey for instance emphasizes the continuing significance of the old relations of exploitation despite their modern transformations (such as their monetarization). At the same time French anthropologists stress that the subordinate relations of production serve a major function for the reproduction and the expansion of capitalist relations within the social formation concerned. In Meillassoux's view the 'cheap' reproduction of labour within the 'domestic' communities, through the 'over-exploitation' of labour which it entails, is vital to capitalist expansion. Rey's idea of the old relations of exploitation serving as a lever in the articulation with capitalism has the same purport: although subordinate, the old forms of organization do retain a certain dynamic of their own. The crucial question is how, in each case, the mechanisms of reproduction of the subordinate and the dominant mode have become intertwined (in chapter 3, below, Jos van der Klei presents an example of such a process of intertwining). Therefore it makes little sense to speak of subordinate modes of production having lost their own mechanisms of reproduction; nor is it analytically enlightening to conceive of an articulation of two 'extended' modes of production when these have supposedly no mutual impact on their respective mechanisms of reproduction.

None the less Wolpe's exposé has the merit of indicating indirectly how necessary it is to attempt a further clarification of the concept of reproduction — a concept which is clearly 'undertheorized' in French Marxist anthropology also. In a different context the difficulties attending the use of this concept became particularly manifest — namely in the critique of Anglo-Saxon feminist anthropologists on the work of Meillassoux.[15] The main issue in this discussion was Meillassoux's attempt to explain the crucial role of reproduction — used mainly in the sense of biological reproduction — within the 'domestic' community, and its consequences for the subordination of women (see p. 15 above). Harris and Young (1981) in particular show that Meillassoux's use of the term 'reproduction' is somewhat loose and sometimes even confusing (cf. also Edholm, Harris & Young 1977). But this critique leads them to a long exposé on the notion of reproduction in general, ignoring the differences between modes of production. They propose a distinction of three types of reproduction without tackling the question as to what extent these types of reproduction may be differently related in the various modes of production. And without further comment they lump together examples from very different modes of production (e.g. Harris and Young 1981: 138). One of the merits of French Marxist anthropologists is surely that, on the basis of anthropological and historical material, they have at least *tried* to identify specific modes of production and to make explicit the specific logic underlying each mode.[16] This still seems the best starting-point also for further theorizing on the notion of reproduction: each mode of production poses its own problems of reproduction, and it is in such a perspective that the notion of reproduction can best be operationalized (see chapter 2, below, by Klaas de Jonge, on the relation between biological reproduction and the class contradictions specific to the lineage mode of production; see also Meillassoux 1979).

The most sophisticated reactions to French Marxist anthropology are doubtless to be found in *Critique of Anthropology* and connected publications. In particular the analytic exposé by Kahn and Llobera (1981b) on the development of Marxist anthropology in France raises interesting points of critique.[17] As anthropologists, Kahn and Llobera are aware of the variety, specificity and complexity of human societies. This leads them to the question: has the ever more subtle re-formulation of the 'Marxist hypothesis' — the determination by the economy in the last instance — indeed averted the danger of economism from French Marxist anthropology? In other words, have these French anthropologists really liberated themselves from the idea of 'a category of economy which purports to be general to all societies?' (Kahn and Llobera 1981b: 307). According to Kahn and Llobera, it is especially by the continuing vagueness on this point that important debates among these French anthropologists have remained without solution — notably the debate on the existence of 'exploitation' in 'primitive' societies. In the last chapter of this book Reini Raatgever returns to this issue.[18] Here we can only remark that Kahn and Llobera too have limited their critique, as yet, mainly to the theoretical level. They are certainly right in concluding that problems in the application of the concept of exploitation are

> inherent in the very attempt to define exploitation in some purely objective, that is, economic, sense based on some absolute and eternal distinction between productive and unproductive labour . . . The problem can only be resolved in the context of a theory which refuses to separate the notion of surplus and its distribution on the one hand from the social constitution of the categories of productive and unproductive labour on the other (Kahn & Llobera 1983b: 313).

In a more familiar anthropological idiom: whatever constitutes exploitation cannot be determined exclusively by us anthropologists, but should also take into account the culture-specific notions and perceptions of the participants. The implications of such a critique, however, can become manifest only in the analysis of empirical material derived from some specific society or societies.[19] Therefore the obvious continuation of this theoretical critique would be a collection of empirical studies to test the insights of French Marxist anthropologists into the specific logic of pre-capitalist modes of production — just as in this collection their insights into the articulation of old modes of production with capitalism are applied.

The 'reception' of French Marxist anthropology in the Netherlands

Reactions to the French theories in Dutch anthropological publications were not primarily expressed in the form of theoretical debates, as in Anglo-Saxon countries, but were more directly connected with empirical analysis. The practical reasons for this may be self-evident. Within the much smaller Dutch-language area there is hardly room for a Dutch equivalent of reviews like *Critique of Anthropology* or *Economy and Society*, which could have served as a forum for a general theoretical discussion.[20] Of course, extensive theoretical discussion did take place in Holland as well, but mainly at conferences and/or seminars.[21] References to French Marxist anthropology in Dutch publications are primarily to be found in dissertations and other studies dealing directly with anthropological field-work material: consequently critical evaluations of these French theories were formulated mainly on the basis of their application in empirical studies.[22] In retrospect, this closer link with the practice of research may not have been a disadvantage. It corresponded in any case to the tenor of the discussions in our work-group which led to the present collection built primarily around our own field-work material.

The way these French anthropological theories were 'received' in the Netherlands should be seen against the somewhat specific background of general theoretical developments in Dutch anthropology. In contrast to the French situation, the growing interest in the use of Marxist concepts in anthropology in the Netherlands during the 1970s did not directly stem from a reaction against idealist versions of structuralism. It is true that of old the position of structuralism in Dutch anthropology (the so-called Leiden School) has been very strong; the emergence of 'symbolic anthropology' as an important field of specialization can be considered as a continuation of this tradition up to the present day. However, especially in the course of the 1960s, other theoretical orientations rapidly gained influence: first Köbben's version of comparative structural-functionalism (Köbben 1964), and later Gluckman's Manchester School and other approaches derived from it. In Holland it was not the latent Marxist strand of the Manchester School (see note 8) which had much influence, but rather the emphasis on the social process and extended case analysis (van Velsen, Turner), particularly as leading on to a very different derivation from this school: the 'transactionalist' theories of anthropologists such as Bailey, Barth and Boissevain.[23] Around 1970 these theories, introduced by Boissevain in particular, seemed to become the dominant paradigm in Dutch anthropology.[24] And it was especially those anthropologists influenced by this transactionalist approach who eventually became interested in the relevance of Marxist insights for anthropological analysis.[25]

Against this background specific questions were posed to French theory. In France, Marxist anthropology originated from a reaction against a-historical and idealist tendencies in structuralism — notably against the structuralist tendency to ignore contradictions and change. Dutch anthropologists were much more interested in the possibilities of a Marxist approach for surpassing the limitations of the 'transactionalist' paradigm (see van Binsbergen 1977, Geschiere 1978a). In that paradigm the focus on conflict and entrepreneurial activities of individual leaders had certainly led to an interest in change and inequalities wihtin local communities. The problem was, however, that the transactionalist approach seemed to inspire only narrow analyses of 'micropolitics' — of conflicts and competition between local leaders. Therefore a number of Dutch anthropologists quoted above (note 22) looked to Marxist theories mainly for a solution of how to relate these micro-political and micro-economic processes to wider historical developments, such as state formation and the expansion of the market economy or colonization and decolonization.[26]

All this should not create the impression that Marxist anthropology has become really popular among Dutch anthropologists. On the contrary, the French theories especially still meet with considerable suspicion, possibly due to their complexity and abstract formulations.[27] It is true that terms such as exploitation, articulation and mode of production have suddenly become very much *en vogue* in professional circles in the Netherlands as well. But an incidental borrowing of terms means inevitably that the underlying theories are distorted. No wonder that a certain disappointment with the explanatory value of the Marxist concepts in anthropology is setting in already. Of course it is only by respecting the coherence and the complexity of a theory that its application in empirical studies can yield new insights. The reader may judge to what extent the following contributions constitute a case in point.

The contributions in this collection

The preceding sketch of the Dutch anthropological context indicated only a part of the backgrounds to the discussion within our work-group. In reality very different motivations played a role. For some of us the interest in French Marxist anthropology derived primarily from intellectual curiosity and from the expectation to find there conceptual tools with which to improve the analytical apparatus of anthropologists. Others became interested in these anthropological theories by way of their participation in the student movement from 1968, and in the debates on imperialism and on Althusser (in the Netherlands, stimulated especially by the group around Socialistische Uitgeverij Nijmegen (SUN) — a Marxist publishing house). However, a common motivation was our growing involvement, by anthropological field-work in Africa or by political activities in Holland, with the problems of under-development and capitalist expansion — the shocking experience of the *Verelendung* of the African countryside, the growing loss of autonomy by the peasants and the disintegration of their social institutions. As a work-group we set out to assess whether French Marxist anthropology could help us to gain a deeper understanding of these world-wide problems.

These differing motivations are clearly present in the following contributions. The first three studies (chapters 2, 3. and 4) concentrate especially on politico-economic problems in African rural areas and on the relevance in this context of the ideas of French Marxist anthropologists.

Klaas de Jonge (chapter 2) analyses demographic developments among the nineteenth-century Nyakyusa of Tanzania in relation to the old 'domestic' contradictions. Using his own field-work material and Monica Wilson's data he argues that demographic processes are not independent causes — as older demographers supposed — but that they are determined by politico-economic contradictions. In this respect de Jonge goes even further than Meillassoux: among the Nyakyusa demographic reproduction proves to be determined by the old 'domestic' power-relations rather than by the 'objective' prerequisites of the optimal reproduction of the communities. He demonstrates that the Nyakyusa elders succeed in manipulating the reproduction of their group primarily in order to strengthen their own position.

Jos van der Klei (chapter 3) applies Meillassoux's analysis of the articulation of 'domestic' and capitalist relationships to developments among the Diola (southern Senegal). But he too arrives at a somewhat different interpretation from Meillassoux, notably concerning the role of trade and of prestige goods in the relation between elders and juniors. Among the Diola the authority of the elders was based not on bridewealth but on initiation rites and on their control over prestige goods needed for those rites. Of old, the Diola acquired these prestige goods by trade with neighbouring groups. This had specific consequences for the establishment of capitalist dominance under colonial rule among the Diola — notably leading to an extremely rapid development of migrant labour and the emergence of new forms of exploitation of the juniors by their elders.

In the next contribution (chapter 4) Peter Geschiere uses Rey's and Meillassoux's general interpretations of the imposition of capitalist dominance in Africa in a bid to explore the role of the colonial state and its remarkable variability. Starting from the example of the Maka (southeastern Cameroon), where the old, 'tribal' patterns of organization hardly offered any foothold to expanding capitalism, he demonstrates that in such a situation particularly drastic forms of coercion were applied by the colonial authorities — violent labour-raids and harsh enforcement of surplus production — in order to mobilize producers for the capitalist economy. In other regions of Africa, however, the old patterns of organization — pre-existing forms of surplus labour or trade networks — did facilitate capitalist expansion much more than was the case among the Maka; there, state intervention took a very different form: it was directed instead towards forming and controlling all kinds of alliances with pre- or non-capitalist exploiting classes. Geschiere argues that the colonial patterns of articulation are still of direct consequence in the variations in the present-day power-relations and class contradictions within post-colonial African states.

In the following contributions, Simon Simonse and Wim van Binsbergen deal with topics less frequently explored in historical-materialist analysis. Simonse (chapter 5) applies theories of the articulation of capitalist and pre-capitalist modes of production to the analysis of modern African fiction: modern classics by Achebe and Laye, and more recent novels by Ouologuem, Bessie Head, Sembène Ousmane and Armah. He argues that a reading of these novels in terms of the tensions between the old and new modes of production *and* their intertwining yields new insights into the work of these writers. Rejecting current, more idealistic, interpretations of African literature, he proposes to distinguish three phases in the development of modern African fiction: first a nostalgic and romanticizing phase, followed by a period in which a sceptical attitude towards the pre-capitalist modes of production dominated, and finally the current phase of the complete break-through of capitalism which relegates the old African forms to the status of a utopian caricature.

Wim van Binsbergen (chapter 6) tackles from another angle the difficult problem of the relation between politico-economic trans-formations and ideological interpretations. He discusses the meaning of a tribal ideology among the Nkoya in western Zambia, where he conducted field-work. This brings to the fore a crucial issue in all anthropological research: the methodological problem of how to define the unit of study. Contrasting the Nkoya's lopsided view of their collective historical experience (the basis of their ethnic awareness) with the picture that would emerge were that history analysed from the modes of production perpective, van Binsbergen attempts to disentangle the dialectics of conscious-ness underlying both the participants' ethnic constructions and our own analytical stance as anthropologists.

In the last two chapters the relationship between Marxist theory and anthropological research is discussed in a more general perspective. Chapter 7 by Wim van Binsbergen and Peter Geschiere concerns the relevance of the theories of French Marxist anthropologists to the practice of anthropological field-work. Until now, in the literature, surprisingly little attention has been paid to the specific implications of the theoretical explorations of these French anthropologists for field-work. These anthropol-ogists themselves have written very little on their own field-work experiences, and the reactions to their work have been mainly on a theoretical level — that is, the discussion has been mainly about the relevance of these theories for interpreting data rather than for collecting data. Yet, for the further development of a Marxist anthropology, the relation to field-work does seem very important. There is a danger that the discussion will begin to turn in theoretical circles. New research seems vital for once more stimulating the theoretical discussion. But, then, such research should be directly related to these theories. The question is therefore in which respects does French Marxist anthropology offer really new starting-points and methods for the anthropologist doing field-work. van Binsbergen and Geschiere discuss some problems and possibilities in this context, referring to their own field-work and to the monographs of the French anthropologists. They concentrate notably on the relevance of the concept of a 'lineage' mode of production in anthropological field-work, and on the problem of how to relate the levels of production, politics and ideology while carrying out research.

The last chapter (8) is related to the wider discussion within Marxism on the work of Althusser and its relevance in the different disciplines; here, the focus is, of course, on anthropology. Reini Raatgever deals with some general issues and ambiguities in the theoretical analyses of the French Marxist anthropologists. She starts from theoretical premises formulated by Althusser and Godelier. But her main interest is in the application of these premises in the study of African 'lineage' societies: the operationalization of the concept of mode of production and the use of the notion of exploitation in this context. Her discussion of the differing viewpoints of Meillassoux, Rey and Terray shows that especially the application of the notion of exploitation raises important theoretical issues for the further development of a Marxist anthropology. However, she emphasizes that in this respect as well theoretical progress depends primarily on further anthropological and historical field-work: without such empirical input, there is a danger that the flow of discussion among Marxist anthropologists may stagnate in sterile polemics on premises and interpretations.

A warning like this may be opportune for other reasons as well. In the Netherlands, as in other parts of the western world, the general interest in Third World problems is clearly waning. Thus the marked *practical* relevance of the theories discussed above may be relegated to the background, leaving only the relation of these theories to an intellectual practice. In any case it is clear that, in the Netherlands also, Marxist anthropology is developing into a respectable academic speciality — leading on, perhaps, to intellectualism not related to any practice. But whether Marxist anthropology is taken to be a form of political action or a purely academic discipline, to anthropologists it must be clear that theory is to be developed only in close interaction with empirical research. That is indeed the tenor of this collection. Cut-and-dried Marxist prescriptions for research or analysis are not offered here. Our concern has rather been to understand African situations with the help of historical materialism — to relate Marxist theory to the practice of research, in an attempt to grasp real problems of present-day Africa.

Notes

1 Like all other chapters of this book, this Introduction has been extensively discussed by all members of our work-group. For the English version of this text, Wim van Binsbergen, in particular, offered very valuable suggestions concerning both contents and form.
2 Cf. e.g. Copans & Seddon (1978) and, in particular, Kahn & Llobera (1981b).
3 Terray (1975: 91) has given a clear definition of when a mode of production is to be viewed as dominant: 'a mode of production is "dominant" within a social formation if and when it imposes the requirements of its own reproduction, upon the other modes of production present within that social formation'. Terray referred in this context especially to the work of P.-P. Rey. The idea that different modes of production can be found side by side (or rather on top of each other) within one and the same society/social formation has certainly not met with general acceptance. Immanuel Wallerstein, among others, resolutely rejects this idea; in his view it is confusing to speak of the survival of older modes of production as subordinate modes under, for instance, capitalist dominance because this can easily blur the fact that these old relations undergo drastic transformation precisely because of the establishment of capitalist dominance (see 1974a: 127; 1974b: 390).
4 See for further information on the work of these French Marxist anthropologists: Copans & Seddon (1978), and Kahn & Llobera (1981b). Here a brief summary may suffice. Meillassoux conducted field-work among the Guro of the Ivory Coast in the late 1950s (see his monograph of 1964); later he worked in Mali and Senegal. Since 1960 he has published a number of general theoretical articles (collected in

Meillassoux 1977). As yet, his most important theoretical work is certainly *Femmes, greniers et capitaux* (1975) — a general analysis of the 'domestic' community and the changes it has undergone under capitalist dominance. Rey conducted field-work in Congo-Brazzaville in the area around Mossendjo (see his monograph of 1971), and subsequently in northern Togo. His monograph of 1971 was already particularly rich in theoretical discussions. These were complemented by *Les Alliances de classes*, his main theoretical work until now (written in the late 1960s, but published in 1973), in which he attempted to formulate a general theory of the establishment of capitalist dominance over pre-capitalist modes of production. In this work, Rey followed closely Marx's own analysis of the birth of capitalism from feudalism in western Europe. Publication is eagerly awaited of Rey's *thèse d'état*, exploring further the possibilities and problems for applying the Marxian concepts to anthropological material. Terray conducted field-work among the Dida and the Abron, both in the Ivory Coast (see Terray 1975). His first theoretical work was *Le Marxisme devant les sociétés 'primitives'*, which contained a materialist 'reading' of Morgan and an interpretation of Meillassoux's material on the Guro. Subsequently Terray himself re-formulated his theoretical views on important issues (see 1975 and 1979). He is now working on a *thèse d'état* on the Abron kingdom. Godelier has published a large number of theoretical studies in the course of the 1960s and 1970s (see especially 1973). In 1982 he published a book on the Baruya (Papua New Guinea) where he conducted field-work for several shorter periods in the late 1960s and during the 1970s. The studies collected in the present volume were mainly inspired by the work of Meillassoux, Rey, Terray and, to a lesser degree, Godelier. These are as yet the most prominent authors in French Marxist anthropology. In addition, other French anthro-pologists, such as J. -L. Amselle, J. Copans, P. Bonte and M. Augé may be mentioned, who work more or less along the same lines.

5 See Meillassoux (1975: 58 and 70), where he further defines his conception of the 'domestic community'. On the level of the productive forces, he mentions the following features: 'All other subsistence activities are complementary to agriculture: they are never undertaken at the expense of agricultural activities . . . the use of land as an instrument of labour . . . the use of "individual" agricultural implements . . . the use of human strength as the major source of energy in agriculture and craft-work' (in more concrete terms, the last two characteristics imply that the hoe — and not a plough drawn by animal traction — will be the most important technical implement; since the hoe is a simple tool that is usually easy to acquire, it is often more difficult to gain control over the producers, by way of control over the means of production, in hoe-farming than in plough-farming). On the level of the relations of production the most important feature is that these relations 'support a hierarchic structure based on anteriority (or "age"); in other words the domestic community is a gerontocracy' (quotations from the English translation

(1981: 34, 42) of Meillassoux's *Femmes, greniers et capitaux*, 1975). It is striking that, in other parts of the same book, Meillassoux himself uses the term 'domestic community' much more loosely. Here, the term seems to refer to any familiar unit, without assuming a special level of the productive forces or special relations of production. Meillassoux then seems to view the 'domestic community' as a subordinate form of organization, everywhere under capitalism — even in areas where the simple forms of agriculture, referred to in his definitions of the 'domestic community', have since long ceased to exist (cf. e.g., Meillassoux 1975: 11, 216).

6 Cf. e.g. Clammer (1978a: 1) and Copans & Seddon (1978: 4), who both began their discussion on the influence of French Marxist anthropology in England by referring to Ardener (1971: 449).

7 Bloch 1975a: xi. Cf. also Crummey & Stewart (1981: 13), who, in the same vein, refer to the theories of Meillassoux, Terray and Rey as some sort of way out from the deadlock in the study of African history.

8 Cf. also notes 11 and 12 below; see further Kahn & Llobera (1981b: 285) and especially Copans & Seddon (1978: 9). The latter refer also to Marxist tendencies in the work of older British anthropologists like Worsley, Firth, Lloyd and Goody who are not directly influenced by the French theories. In this context one could also mention the — somewhat latent — Marxist strand in the Manchester School (Gluckman, Turner, van Velsen, Frankenberg, Watson, and Worsley's earliest work) which was maybe less inspired by theoretical interests than by political affiliations and which found expression in the attention devoted to specific topics (conflict, labour relations) rather than in overtly Marxian theoretical explorations. Cf., however, recent work by Frankenberg (e.g. 1978) where he re-analyses Gluckman's work within a consistent Marxist framework.

9 The first study from French Marxist anthropology to be translated into English was Terray's *Marxism and 'Primitive' Societies* (1972). Consequently it received considerable attention in Anglo-Saxon discussions. This created a certain confusion because the study happened to be severely criticized by Terray's colleagues in France; subsequently even Terray himself proposed important reformulations of central notions in this publication (see Terray 1975, 1979; and pp. 14–15 above). In the 1970s some of Godelier's studies were translated (cf. 1972, 1977). A translation of Meillassoux's main theoretical work *Femmes, greniers et capitaux* became available only in 1981, but his monograph on the Guro (1964) has still not been translated into English. From Rey's work neither his monograph (1971) nor his main theoretical study (1973) has been translated. Important collections of articles by French Marxist anthropologists, translated into English, are Seddon (1978a) and *Critique of Anthropology* (1979; 13–14). Cf. also *Critique of Anthropology* (1974, 1 and 1975, 3); Kahn & Llobera (1981a); Friedman & Rowlands (1978) and Diamond (1980).

10 A clear illustration is R. G. Cooper's rash critique (1978). According to him, French Marxist anthropology has not even surpassed the

ancient debate in economic anthropology between 'formalists' and 'substantivists'. He qualifies Rey's theory as 'silly' while he refers — in 1978! — only to an English translation of one early article. Likewise Clammer, in his Introduction to the collection of articles in which also Cooper's appeared (Clammer 1978a), bases his critical evaluation of French Marxist anthropology only on early publications (for instance in 1978 he does not seem to have consulted Meillassoux's *Femmes, greniers et capitaux* from 1975); cf. also Clammer (1975) for a critique of Rey which does not take into account important publications such as Rey (1971 and 1973). A similar partial, or even defective, knowledge seems to be the base for Foster-Carter's (1978) and Bradby's (1975) critical comments on Rey's work and for Wolpe's analysis of the debate concerning the articulation of modes of production (see pp. 18–19). Crummey & Stewart (1981) defend a Marxist interpretation of African history by invoking Meillassoux, Terray and Rey, but in the rest of their argument they completely ignore relevant debates in French Marxist anthropology (for instance on the issue of class contradictions in African 'stateless' societies).

11 Cf. e.g. *Critique of Anthropology* (1979, 13–14, 'French Issue'), Kahn & Llobera 1981a, and Taylor in *Critique of Anthropology* (1975 and 1976 (6). But cf. also the collections by Bloch (1975), Clammer (1978b) and Diamond (1980) and the review *Dialectical Anthropology* (for instance Eric Wolf's review of Godelier's work in *Dialectical Anthropology*, 1975, 1). Of course studies like Hindess & Hirst (1975) and Friedman (1976; Ekholm & Friedman 1980) have also been directly influenced by French Marxist theories, but they seem of less relevance in this context. The Hindess and Hirst argument is so abstract that it seems difficult to apply in concrete anthropological research. Neither does Friedman's interest in the analysis of global systems — cf. Wallerstein — seem to be of direct significance to specific anthropological research. More directly related to our interests as anthropologists and Africanists are the numerous references to French Marxist anthropology in studies on African history (Cf. e.g. Palmer & Parsons 1977, Papstein 1978, Law 1978, Crummey & Stewart 1981). However it here concerns somewhat occasional references. For the most consistent theoretical reaction to the French theories in the study of African history, *see* Jewsiewicki (*inter alia* 1981).

12 Several contributions, related to this debate, appeared in the *New Left Review*. Cf. e.g. Wolpe (1980b — a collection of articles from *Economy and Society*), Taylor (1972); Foster-Carter (1978). Parallel discussions, especially concerning Africa, have been conducted in the *Review of African Political Economy*, but here hardly any systematic attention has been paid to French Marxist anthropology (cf. Geschiere in press, a). Cf. also Saul (1979).

13 From Rey's work, only articles dealing mainly with the analysis of the 'lineage mode of production' have been translated (Dupré & Rey 1973, Rey 1975 and 1979). But as noted above, his main works on the articulation of capitalism and subordinate modes of production (Rey

1971, 1973 and 1976) were not available in English, prior to the translation of Rey (1973) in *International Journal of Sociology*, Summer 1982, 12, 2: 1–120.

14 Foster-Carter may have neglected this aspect of Rey's analysis because in his rendering of Rey's 'project', he leans heavily on an article by Bradby (1975), the first résumé of Rey's theories in English. Bradby does not refer at all to Rey's monograph (1971); consequently she deals even more superficially than Foster-Carter does with Rey's analysis of the mechanisms enabling capitalism 'to take root' in the old forms of organization — such as the monetarization of the old relations of exploitation. Neither does she refer to Rey's point that, as long as the village communities can withdraw in some kind of autarky, violence by the (colonial) state (as distinct from market mechanisms) is needed in order to enforce participation by the villagers in the money economy (see Rey on the 'colonial mode of production' characterized by a forced labour régime — 1971: 321, 338, 342ff.). Since she ignores this last aspect, Bradby's rendering of Rey's theory on violence and her criticism of it are equally unconvincing (cf. Bradby 1975: 145 and 150). Very brief but better balanced résumés of Rey's theories are to be found in Cliffe (1977) and Soiffer & Howe (1982). Neither article refers to Rey's monograph. But Cliffe does at least show how, in Rey's perspective, different patterns of articulation of capitalist and pre-capitalist modes of production can be distinguished within one region (East Africa — cf. also Saul 1979). And Soiffer & Howe are the only ones to pay due attention to the importance, in Rey's theory, of the intertwinement of old and new relations of exploitation. However, their application of Rey's theory to developments in northeastern Brazil is somewhat chaotic because they concentrate on the role of local patrons, instead of starting from a concrete analysis of the local mode of production and its economic articulation with capitalism.

15 E.g. Harris & Young (1981), O'Laughlin (1977), Mackintosh (1977) and Molyneux (1977). This feminist critique was partly connected with the debates in *Critique of Anthropology*.

16 Of course the attempts in French Marxist anthropology, to recognize and distinguish several pre-capitalist modes of production have not yet yielded definitive results (see p. 14 above on the differences of opinion in this respect). But despite all the problems involved, it seems that especially this aspect of the French theories should be further developed and applied (see ch. 7 below). For instance, if a clearer survey of the old modes of production in Africa were available, it would be possible to analyse and compare their respective modes of reproduction, just as it would be possible to distinguish their respective forms of articulation with capitalism.

17 The first part of this study sketches the social and intellectual background of the development of Marxist anthropology in France. That section contains many interesting data which could be further analysed in a wider perspective of *Ideeëngeschichte* — for instance by relating this development more clearly to the pressure exerted by

Stalinism and to the impact of the events in Hungary and Algeria (cf. e.g. Le Roy Ladurie 1982).

18 Cf. Raatgever (in press) for an attempt to construe a specific 'economic region' for the lineage mode of production on the basis of the internal logic of that mode.

19 Cf. Seddon's analysis of the pre-colonial social formation in the Maghreb (1978b), and Jewsiewicki's study of the lineage mode of production in Zaïre (1981); both articles offer interesting applications of some of the ideas of French Marxist anthropologists in the analysis of empirical data, and, thus, do suggest novel insights; see also Kahn (1980).

20 Cf., however, *Ter Elfder Ure* (in press) and a few articles in *Antropologische Verkenningen* (Geschiere 1982b and the issue 1982, 2).

21 Cf. also the Introductions to collections of conference papers: van Binsbergen & Meilink (1978a), Buijtenhuijs & Geschiere (1978a), van Binsbergen & Schoffeleers (in press), as well as the review article by Gerold-Scheepers & van Binsbergen (1978).

22 Cf. the monographs by van Binsbergen (1981a) and Geschiere (1982a); and also articles by de Jonge (1979), Schoffeleers (1978 and 1982), Konings (in press) and Geschiere (1982c; in press, a; in press, b).

23 A clear résumé of developments in Dutch anthropology is to be found in the collection by Kloos and Claessen (1981); compare, notably, the contribution by van Binsbergen (1981b).

24 Cf. e.g. Mitchell & Boissevain (1973), Blok (1974), Boissevain (1974), van Hekken & Thoden van Velzen (1972) and Bax (1976). See for a critique on this 'transactionalist' approach with some Marxist overtones Thoden van Velzen (1973).

25 Cf. van Binsbergen (1970), van der Klei (1971), Thoden van Velzen (1973) and Geschiere (1978a: ch. 11a).

26 Other Dutch anthropologists have tried to escape from the transactionalist cul-de-sac with the help of the theories of Norbert Elias, using notably his concept of (con)figuration for the analysis of regional processes in relation to wider historical developments (cf. e.g. Blok 1974 and Bax, forthcoming). A somewhat surprising consequence has been that, while Elias himself formulated his theories especially in reaction against Parsons's structural-functionalism, the Dutch 'Eliasians' threw themselves in a somewhat quichotic polemic with Marxism (cf. e.g. *Amsterdams Sociologisch Tijdschrift*, 1980, 7, 2).

27 In this respect the recent critiques of Althusser by Kolakowski (1978) and Thompson (1978) played a certain role. In informal discussions some Dutch anthropologists are apt to refer to these critiques as being so fundamental that it is no longer worth while to take the trouble of trying to understand Althusser's work. However, Kolakowski's critique is part of a general study of the development of Marxist theory, and his conclusion — Althusser has nothing new to say — is hardly relevant to anthropological theorizing: Althusser happened to be the main channel through which the Marxist tradition could reach

French anthropology. Thompson's lengthy critique of Althusser's theory of history leads to the opposite conclusion — Althusser is guilty of idealist theorizing by using theological 'attributes' and therefore, his methods are inimical to historical materialism *per se* (Thompson 1978: 196). We share Thompson's critique on certain points — notably concerning the problematic status of the concept of class struggle (see p. 11 above). But, at least for the time being, we do not share Thompson's bitterness (Thompson 1978: 383).

References

Amsterdams Sociologisch Tijdschrift (1980), 7, 2: 117–82.

Antropologische Verkenningen (1982), 1, 2, special issue 'Religie en machtspolitiek'.

Ardener, E. (1971), 'The New Anthropology and its critics', *Man*, 6: 449–67.

Bax, M. G. (1976), *Harpstrings and Confessions*, Assen: van Gorcum.

Bax, M. G. (forthcoming), *Peasants, Priests and the Politics of Polarization*.

van Binsbergen, W. M. J. (1970), 'Verwantschap en territorialiteit in de sociale structuur van het bergland van Noordwest Tunesië', doctoraalscriptie, University of Amsterdam.

van Binsbergen, W. M. J. (1977), 'Occam, Francis Bacon, and the transformation of Zambian society', *Cultures et développement*, 9: 489–520.

van Binsbergen, W. M. J. (1981a), *Religious Change in Zambia*, London: Kegan Paul International.

van Binsbergen, W. M. J. (1981b), 'Dutch anthropology of sub-Saharan Africa in the 1970s', in Kloos & Claessen (1981): 45–85.

van Binsbergen, W M. J. & Hesseling, G. (eds) (in press), *Aspecten van Staat en Maatschappij in Afrika: Recent Nederlands en Belgisch Onderzoek*, Leiden: African Studies Centre.

van Binsbergen, W. M. J. & Meilink, H. A. (1978a), 'Migration and the transformation of modern African society: Introduction', in van Binsbergen & Meilink (1978b): 7–21.

van Binsbergen, W. M. J. & Meilink, H. A. (eds) (1978b), *Migration and the Transformation of Modern African Society, African Perspectives 1976/2*, Leiden: African Studies Centre.

van Binsbergen, W. M. J. & Schoffeleers, J. M. (eds) (in press), *Theoretical Explorations in African Religion*, London: Kegan Paul International.

Bloch, M. (1975a), Introduction, in Bloch (1975b): xi–xiv.

Bloch, M. (ed.) (1975b), *Marxist Analyses and Social Anthropology*, London: Malaby Press.

Blok, A. (1974), *The Mafia of a Sicilian Village 1860–1960*, Oxford: Blackwell.

Boissevain, J. (1974), *Friends of Friends: Networks, Manipulators and Coalitions*, Oxford: Blackwell.

Bradby, B. (1975), 'The destruction of natural economy', *Economy and*

Society, 4: 128–61.

Buijtenhuijs, R. & Geschiere, P. (1978a), Introduction, in Buijtenhuijs and Geschiere (1978b): 7–19.

Buijtenhuijs, R. & Geschiere, P. (eds) (1978b), *Social Stratification and Class Formation, African Perspectives 1978/2*, Leiden: African Studies Centre.

Clammer, J. (1975), 'Economic anthropology and the sociology of development: "liberal" anthropology and its French critics', in Oxaal, Barnett & Booth (1975): 208–29.

Clammer, J. (1978a), 'Concepts and objects in economic anthropology', in Clammer (1978b): 1–21.

Clammer, J. (ed.) (1978b), *The New Economic Anthropology*, London: Macmillan.

Cliffe, L. (1977), 'Rural class formation in East Africa', *Journal of Peasant Studies*, 4: 195–224.

Cooper, R. G. (1978), 'Dynamic tensions: symbiosis and contradiction in Hmong social relations' in Clammer (1978b).

Copans, J. and Seddon, D. (1978), 'Marxism and anthropology: a preliminary survey', in Seddon (1978a): 1–46.

Critique of Anthropology (1979), 13–14, 'French Issue'.

Crummey, D. and Stewart, C. C. (eds) (1981), *Modes of Production in Africa: The Precolonial Era*, Beverley Hills: Sage.

Diamond, S. (ed.) (1980), *Toward a Marxist Anthropology*, The Hague: Mouton.

Dupré, G. and Rey, P. -P. (1973), 'Reflections on the pertinence of a theory of exchange', *Economy and Society*, 2: 131–63.

Edholm, F., Harris, O. and Young, K. (1977), 'Conceptualising women', *Critique of Anthropology*, 9–10: 101–31.

Ekholm, K. and Friedman, J. (1980), 'Towards a global anthropology', *Itinerario* 1980–1: 61–77.

Foster-Carter, A. (1978), 'The modes of production controversy', *New Left Review* 107: 47–79.

Frankenberg, R. (1978), 'Economic anthropology or political economy? (I): The Barotse social formation', in Clammer (1978b): 31–61.

Friedman, J. (1976), 'Marxist theory and systems of total reproduction', *Critique of Anthropology*, 7: 3–16.

Friedman, J. and Rowlands, M. (eds) (1978), *The Evolution of Social Systems*, London: Duckworth.

Gerold-Scheepers, T. J. F. A. & van Binsbergen, W. M. J. (1978), 'Marxist and non-Marxist approaches to migration in Africa', in van Binsbergen & Meilink (1978b): 21–35.

Geschiere, P. (1978a), 'Stamgemeenschappen onder staatsgezag, veranderende verhoudingen in de Maka Dorpen in Zuidoost Cameroun sinds 1900', dissertation, Free University, Amsterdam.

Geschiere, P. (1978b), 'The articulation of different modes of production, old and new inequalities in Maka villages (Southeast Cameroon)' in Buijtenhuijs & Geschiere (1978b): 45–69.

Geschiere, P. (1982a), *Village Communities and the State*, London: Kegan Paul International.

Geschiere, P. (1982b), 'Produktiewijzen en verandering: enkele themas in het werk van Franse marxistische antropologen', *Antropologische Verkenningen*, 1(1): 45–75.

Geschiere, P. (1982c), 'L'agriculture de subsistance, l'autonomie de la femme et l'autorité des aînés chez les Maka (Cameroun)', *Journal d'agriculture traditionelle et de botanique appliquée*, 29, 3–4: 307–21.

Geschiere, P. (in press, a), 'Marxistische visies op de post-koloniale staat in Afrika — de discussie in *RAPE* en de historische benadering van Rey', in van Binsbergen & Hesseling (in press).

Geschiere, P. (in press, b), 'European planters, African peasants and the colonial state, alternatives in the "mise en valeur" of Makaland during the interbellum', *African Economic History*, (papers SOAS workshop 'Business Empires in West Central Africa', London, May 1982).

Godelier, M. (1972), *Rationality and Irrationality in Economics*, New York: Monthly Review Press (first published as *Rationalité et irrationalité en économie*, 1966, Paris: Maspero).

Godelier, M. (1973), *Horizon, trajets marxistes en anthropologie*, Paris: Maspero.

Godelier, M. (1977), *Perspectives in Marxist Anthropology*, Cambridge University Press (translation of Godelier 1973).

Godelier, M. (1979), 'The appropriation of nature', *Critique of Anthropology*, 13–14: 17–29.

Godelier, M. (1982), *La Production des grands hommes*, Paris: Fayard.

Harris, O. & Young, K. (1981), 'Engendered structures: some problems in the analysis of reproduction', in Kahn & Llobera (1981b): 109–48.

van Hekken, N. & Thoden van Velzen, H. U. E. (1972), *Land Scarcity and Rural Inequality in Tanzania*, The Hague: Mouton.

Hindess, B. & Hirst, P. (1975), *Pre-capitalist Modes of Production*, London: Routledge & Kegan Paul.

Jewsiewicki, B. (1981), 'Lineage mode of production: social inequalities in Equatorial Central Africa', in Crummey & Stewart (1981): 93–115.

de Jonge, K. (1979), 'Peasant fishermen and capitalists: development in Senegal', *Review of African Political Economy*, 15–16: 105–23.

Kahn, J. S. (1980), *Minangkabau Social Formations, Indonesian Peasants Economy*, Cambridge University Press.

Kahn, J. S. & Llobera, J. R. (eds) (1981a), *The Anthropology of Pre-capitalist Societies*, London: Macmillan.

Kahn, J. S. & Llobera, J. R. (1981b), 'Towards a new Marxism or a new anthropology?' in Kahn and Llobera (1981a): 263–329.

van der Klei, J. M. (1971), 'De relatie specialist/klant, bezien binnen het normatieve raamwerk van sociale verhoudingen en zijn organisatie in 1969 (N.W. Tunesië)', doctoraal scriptie, University of Amsterdam.

Kloos, P. and Claessen, H. J. M. (eds) (1981), *Current Issues in Anthropology: The Netherlands*, Rotterdam: Netherlands Sociological and Anthropological Association (NSAV).

Köbben, A. J. F. (1964), *Van Primitievan tot Medeburgers*, Assen: van Gorcum.

Kolakowski, L. (1978), *Main Currents of Marxism*, Oxford University Press.

Konings, P. (in press), 'Peasantry and the state in Ghana', in van Binsbergen & Hesseling (in press).

Law, R. (1978), 'In search of a Marxist perspective on pre-colonial tropical Africa', *Journal of African History*, 19: 441–52.

Le Roy Ladurie, E. (1982), *Paris-Montpellier, P.C.-P.S.U. 1945–1963*, Paris: Gallimard.

Mackintosh, M. (1977), 'Reproduction and patriarchy: a critique of Meillassoux's *Femmes, greniers et capitaux*', *Capital and Class*, 2: 119–28.

Meillassoux, C. (1960), 'Essai d'interprétation du phénomène économique dans les sociétés traditionelle d'autosubsistance', *Cahiers d'Etudes Africaines*, 1: 38–67.

Meillassoux, C. (1964), *Anthropologie économique des Gouro de Côte d'Ivoire*, Paris/The Hague: Mouton.

Meillassoux, C. (1975), *Femmes, greniers et capitaux*, Paris: Maspero.

Meillassoux, C. (1977), *Terrains et théories*, Paris: Anthropos.

Meillassoux, C. (1979), 'Historical modalities of the exploitation and over-exploitation of labour', *Critique of Anthropology*, 13–14: 7–17.

Meillassoux, C. (1981), *Maidens, Meal and Money*, Cambridge University Press (translation of Meillassoux 1975).

Mitchell, J. C. & Boussevain, J. (eds) (1973), *Network Analysis*, Paris/The Hague: Mouton.

Molyneux, M. (1977), 'Androcentrism in Marxist anthropology', *Critique of Anthropology*, 9–10: 55–83.

O'Laughlin, B. (1977), 'Production and reproduction: Meillassoux's *Femmes, greniers et capitaux*', *Critique of Anthropology*, 8: 3–33

Oxaal, J., Barnett, T., & Booth, D. (eds) (1975), *Beyond the Sociology of Development*, London: Routledge & Kegan Paul.

Palmer, R. & Parsons, N. (eds) (1977), *The Roots of Rural Poverty in Central and Southern Africa*, London: Heinemann.

Papstein, R. J. (1978), 'The Upper Zambezi: a History of the Luvale People 1000–1900', PhD thesis, University of California, Los Angeles.

Raatgever, R. (in press), 'Geëchte arbeid: uitbuiting onder de dominantie van de verwantschap', *Te Elfder Ure*, 32.

Rey, P.-P. (1971), *Colonialisme, néo-colonialisme et transition au capitalisme*, Paris: Maspero.

Rey, P.-P. (1973), *Les Alliances de classes*, Paris: Maspero.

Rey, P.-P. (1975), 'The lineage mode of production', *Critique of Anthropology*, 3: 27–79.

Rey, P.-P. (1976), *Capitalisme négrier: la marche des paysans vers le prolétariat* (together with E. le Bris and M. Samuel), Paris: Maspero.

Rey, P.-P. (1979), 'Class contradiction in lineage societies', *Critique of Anthropology*, 13–14: 41–61.

Saul, J. (1979), *The State and Revolution in Eastern Africa: Essays*, New York: Monthly Review Press.

Schoffeleers, J. M. (1978), 'A martyr cult as a reflection on changes in production: The case of the lower Shire Valley 1590–1622 AD', in Buijtenhuijs & Geschiere (1978b): 19–33.

Schoffeleers, J. M. (1982), 'Nowadays they spit at Jesus: The religious proletarization of an African rural district', Paper, Xth World Congress of Sociology, Mexico, 1982.

Seddon, D. (ed.) (1978a), *Relations of Production, Marxist Approaches to Economic Anthropology*, London: Cass.

Seddon, D. (1978b), 'Economic anthropology or political economy? (II): Approaches to the analysis of pre-capitalist formations in the Maghreb', in Clammer (1978b): 61–110.

Soiffer, S. M. and Howe, G. N. (1982), 'Patrons, clients and the articulation of modes of production', *Journal of Peasant Studies*, 9: 176–206.

Taylor, J. (1972), 'Marxism and anthropology', *Economy and Society*, 1: 339–50.

Taylor, J. (1975), 'Pre-capitalist modes of production (I)', *Critique of Anthropology*, 4–5: 127–56.

Taylor, J. (1976), 'Pre-capitalist modes of production (II)', *Critique of Anthropology*, 6: 56–69.

Te Elfder Ure (in press) 32, special issue on Marxism and Anthropology.

Terray, E. (1969), *Le Marxisme devant les sociétés 'primitives'*, Paris: Maspero.

Terray, E. (1972), *Marxism and 'Primitive' Societies*, New York: Monthly Review Press (translation of Terray 1969).

Terray, E. (1973), 'Technologie, état et tradition en Afrique: Note critique', *Annales, Economies, Sociétiés et Civilisations*, 28: 1331–8.

Terray, E. (1975), 'Classes and class consciousness in the Abron kingdom of Gyaman', in Bloch (1975b): 85–137.

Terray, E. (1979), 'On exploitation: elements of an autocritique', *Critique of Anthropology*, 13–14: 29–41.

Thoden van Velzen, H. U. E. (1973), 'Robinson Crusoe and Friday: strength and weakness of the big man paradigm', *Man*, 8: 592–612.

Thompson, E. P. (1978), *The Poverty of Theory and Other Essays*, London: Merlin.

Wallerstein, I. (1974a), *The Modern World System: Capitalist Agriculture and the Origins of the European World Economy in the Sixteenth Century*, New York: Academic Press.

Wallerstein, I. (1974b), 'The rise and future demise of the world capitalist system, concepts for comparative analysis', *Comparative Studies in History and Society*, 16: 387–415.

Wolpe, H. (1980a), Introduction, in Wolpe (1980b): 1–45.

Wolpe, H. (ed.) (1980b), *The Articulation of Modes of Production: Essays from 'Economy and Society'*, London: Routledge & Kegan Paul.

Chapter 2

Demographic developments and class contradictions in a 'domestic' community: The Nyakyusa (Tanzania) before the colonial conquest [1]

Klaas de Jonge

Introduction

The aim of this chapter is to analyse the specific features of reproduction in a pre-capitalist society, i.e. in the old 'domestic' community of the Nyakyusa. In this context, biological (or demographic) reproduction is taken to refer in particular to the reproduction of labour. [2]

The basic assumption is that, in the domestic community, biological reproduction should be viewed not as a 'natural process' (in the line of Malthus), but rather as a political-economic process (in the line of Marx). A new and rather original elaboration upon Marx's view on demographic developments is to be found in Meillassoux's recent theories on the 'domestic' community (a model based on the old African agricultural communities). According to Meillassoux, biological reproduction played an essential part in the functioning of communities of this type. But, in several aspects, Meillassoux did not appear to be fully consistent in his application of Marx's premise to domestic organizational patterns. The example of the Nyakyusa, to be analysed here, suggests that, in this type of community also, demographic reproduction was not directly determined by the objective requirements of the production process (as Meillassoux sometimes seems to think), but rather by the political interests of the 'domestic' authorities — the elders.

The reproduction of labour

Demography is usually defined as the study of the size, structure and distribution of human population and the changes in these variables (see e.g. Monsted & Walji 1978: 34). The central question here is to what extent a given community can safeguard the replacement of generations, or, formulated in a different way, to what extent can the reproduction of labour be assured? According to Malthus (1960), this depends on food production. Since food production increases in an arithmetic progression: 1, 2, 3, 4, 5, 6 . . . while the population expands in a geometric progression: 1, 2, 4, 8, 16, 32 . . . the growth of food production would lag behind population growth. Assuming this to be the case, Malthus could not help being pessimistic. Only as a result of famine, epidemics and wars (the positive checks) would population pressure decrease again and the balance be restored. Malthus also considered the possibility that such natural checks could be replaced or supplemented by voluntary population control, e.g. by means of 'preventive checks' such as sexual abstinence, the postponement of marriage, etc. But his opinion was that the poor would never apply such checks and therefore he advocated the abolition of social legislation which provided the poor with some degree of security. According to Malthus, any support of the poor would lead to early marriages and even more children, whose upkeep would become a burden to the richer citizens.

Marxists also have studied the conditions under which the reproduction of labour takes place. Marx and Engels did this with respect to the capitalist mode of production and Meillassoux with respect to the pre-capitalist African communities, which he referred to as 'domestic communities'. But, as noted above, these Marxists reach conclusions totally different from those of Malthus. The basic assumption of Marx and Engels was that there was no 'natural population law' in the sense that Malthus meant. In his foreword to the second edition of *Das Kapital*, vol. 1, Marx cited with favour the following quotation:

> Marx e.g. denies that the law of population is the same at all times and in all places. He asserts on the contrary that every stage of development has its own law of population . . . With the varying degree of development of productive power, social conditions and the laws governing them vary too (cf. Marx 1912: xxix, quotation from the *European Messenger*, St Petersburg, May number, 1872: 427–36).

The essential difference from Malthus is that Marx and Engels linked biological reproduction to the political-economic organization of the community.

> It would seem to be the proper thing to start with the real and concrete elements, with the actual pre-conditions, e.g. to start in the sphere of economy with population, which forms the basis and the subject of the whole social process of production. Closer consideration shows, however, that this is wrong. Population is an abstraction if, for instance, one disregards the classes of which it is composed. These classes in turn remain empty terms if one does not know the factors on which they depend e.g. wage-labour, capital, and so on (Marx 1977: 205).

Marx and Engels did not view demographic factors such as fertility and population growth as independent causes. To them, a central question was that of the significance of a surplus of labour (unemployment) within the context of the capitalist system. Only against that background were questions such as why the population increased or decreased during a specific period in capitalist development to be analysed.

> The labouring population therefore produces, along with the accumulation of capital produced by it, the means by which itself is made relatively superfluous, is turned into a relative surplus population; and it does this to an always increasing extent. This is a law of population peculiar to the capitalist mode of production . . .
> . . . But if a surplus labouring population is a necessary product of accumulation or of the development of wealth on a capitalist basis, this surplus population becomes, conversely, the lever of capitalist accumulation, or a condition of existence of the capitalist mode of production. It forms a disposable industrial reserve army, that belongs to capital quite as absolutely as if the latter had bred it at its own cost. Independently of the limits of the actual increase of the population, it creates, for the changing needs of the self-expansion of capital, a mass of human material always ready for exploitation (Marx 1912: 645–6).

After Marx and Engels, hardly any further efforts were made to develop these theoretical assumptions in Marxist circles (an exception may be Chayanov — see Kerblay 1971). At most, the old debate between Malthus and Marx became relevant again in modern discussions about the population problem in underdeveloped areas.[3] But it was not until the 1970s that really new insights were formulated, when several French Marxist anthropologists — Meillassoux (1975, 1979) and Godelier (1975) — tried to elaborate further upon Marx's assumption that every mode of production has its own population law, and to apply this assumption also to pre-capitalist modes of production.

Especially in Meillassoux's writings, demographic reproduction plays a central role. For Africa, his views were applied by Gregory and Piché, among others, but they were particularly concerned with demographic developments after the penetration of capitalism (Gregory and Piché 1979). In this chapter I want to confine myself to the pre-capitalist period. Meillassoux emphasizes that the old domestic relations of production continued to play a specific role for a long time, even after capitalism had become the dominant mode of production. Therefore, even in order to analyse the present relations, it remains necessary to understand the individual specific 'logic' which stems from the old domestic relations of production.

What does Meillassoux have to say about demographic reproduction in a domestic community? One of the most important implications of his theory is that in this type of community biological reproduction is of particular importance. He tries to define the domestic community on the basis of the productive forces and the relations of production. In these communities agriculture is the most important activity. Land, which is rarely scarce, is held by kinship groups, often of a patrilineal composition. The major part of the food needed for consumption is produced within the community. Trade is of minor importance. Human labour is the most important source of energy and the implements utilized are simple. Social relations are of a personal nature and create a hierarchic structure based on age ('antériorité') — i.e. on the authority of the elders over the younger people.

Of crucial importance is the fact that the authority of the elders in these domestic communities is based not so much on control over the material means of production as on control over the producers or, more specifically, over the production of the producers — i.e. over the fertile women. The technical requirements for domestic agricultural production can be controlled by the elders only to a very limited extent. As has been noted above, the tools (hoe, cleaver) are usually simple and readily available;

42

moreover, land is rarely a scarce resource. In Meillassoux's view, the authority of the elders is mainly based on their 'anteriority' in the production processes; the elders — 'who came earlier' — actually gave the younger men 'advances' (seeds and sufficient food until the next harvest), and only because of these advances can these younger men acquire their own position as independent producers in the successive agricultural cycles. Moreover, the elders have the technical and social knowledge that is needed to organize production. Because of this, they are entitled to a certain functional authority in the organization and in the management of the agricultural production of their community.

However, such factors provide at best a rather unstable economic basis for the authority of the elders. A younger man can acquire the necessary technical knowledge quite easily, and once he has a place in the agricultural cycle of production he is, in principle, no longer dependent on advances (of food and seeds) from his elders. A much more important restriction on the younger men's drive for independence is that they need to have a wife before they can lay claim to the position of an independent head of family. Only when he has control over a wife, and especially over her children, can a man expect to have enough labour-power in the future to continue the agricultural cycle year after year. Thus, in practice, the authority of the elders in this type of community appears to be based on their control over the nubile women (in Meillassoux's terms, the means of reproduction) and over the circulation of women and bridewealth between the communities.[4]

According to Meillassoux, the conditions of production determine that it is not control over the means of production but control over the biological reproduction (and the safeguarding of reproduction) which is the most important basis for relations of dependency in the domestic community. In his view, the production is of course the 'determining instance', but the specific disposition of domestic production makes biological reproduction the 'dominant' preoccupation. This is evident, for example, from the emphasis put on marriage, from the function of bridewealth which gives a man control over his descendants but at the same time makes the younger men dependent on their elders; also from the fertility rites, the norms for classifying women in accordance with their reproductory cycle, the tensions with respect to adultery and the various sexual prohibitions; and, more generally, from the role of kinship, which Meillassoux considers to be a juridical-ideological expression of production and reproduction relations, which are of course again linked to the level of the productive forces.

The biological reproduction within this type of community is often complicated because the domestic communities are usually rather small. This is why great imbalances can occur in the demographic structure, and the development of the local communities is due to more or less haphazard differences in birth-rates (within one group, for example, more boys may be born and in another group more girls, etc.). As a result, relations between the communities may become unstable or even bellicose, if a group tries to deal with its shortage of fertile women by kidnapping daughters from other groups. But, often, all sorts of institutions are developed to cope with the imbalances of demographic reproduction in a more peaceful way. According to Meillassoux, the real function of the system of the circulation of marriageable women and bridewealth between the various communities is to guarantee an even distribution of women over the different communities which thus together constitute a 'matrimonial area'.

In the same vein, extensive possibilities and rules for adoption would guarantee, within this type of community, an equal division of (future) producers over the production units (by way of adoption, families threatened by a shortage of adult producers in the future because of a low birth-rate or a high death-rate of children, could take in children from families where, because of a high number of births, the balance between productive persons and non-productive ones — children — threatened to dip to the other side). In Meillassoux's view, these institutions were used by the authorities of the communities in order to attain a better distribution of the producers, between the communities as well as within them. In this way, the various production units would have sufficient labour at their disposal to continue the agricultural cycle year after year.

Even this extremely brief summary of Meillassoux's ideas gives rise to a number of questions. It is striking, for example, that he focused most of his attention on the procreative role of the woman (as producer of new labour-power); he hardly devoted any attention at all to the productive role that the woman herself played as labourer. This is all the more surprising since the productive role played by women in domestic farming was such a large one. Another question is whether Meillassoux did not draw too direct a link between the redistribution of the labour of young men and women over the various production units and the demands made by production. In my opinion, his analysis was based on the assumption of a kind of harmony model of reciprocity between different communities and between the younger and older people within one and the same group; under this assumption, irregularities in the reproduction of labour would automatically be corrected by way of all kinds of intervening institutions.

The question remains, however, whether this continual attempt to arrive at a 'better' redistribution of labour was not much more closely related to attempts on the part of elders to maintain their power; i.e. whether the actual practice of biological reproduction was not more directly determined by internal power relations in the community than by the 'objective' need to strike a balance between the irregular demographic development and the demands of production.

In this article, the usefulness of Meillassoux's model will be examined on the basis of one concrete case: the Nyakyusa of southern Tanzania. First some general information about the Nyakyusa and their agricultural production will be presented. Then the old organizational principles of their society will be dealt with, as will the most important contradictions they entail. Lastly, attention will be devoted to the consequences of the old principles and contradictions for demographic reproduction among the Nyakyusa.

The Nyakyusa

The Nyakyusa (approx. 250,000 in 1967) constitute the majority of the population of Rungwe, a district in the southern highlands of Tanzania, just to the north of Lake Malawi.[5] The Nyakyusa consist of a cluster of different peoples who bear linguistic and social similarities. Most of them live in the Rungwe valley and in the mountainous region to the north of it. The area they live in is characterized by great natural contrasts: the lake shore is a flat region with a large amount of rainfall, and rice is one of the main crops cultivated there. Central and northern Rungwe, on the other hand, are hilly and even mountainous in some parts, and there is somewhat less rainfall there. This is where the most important

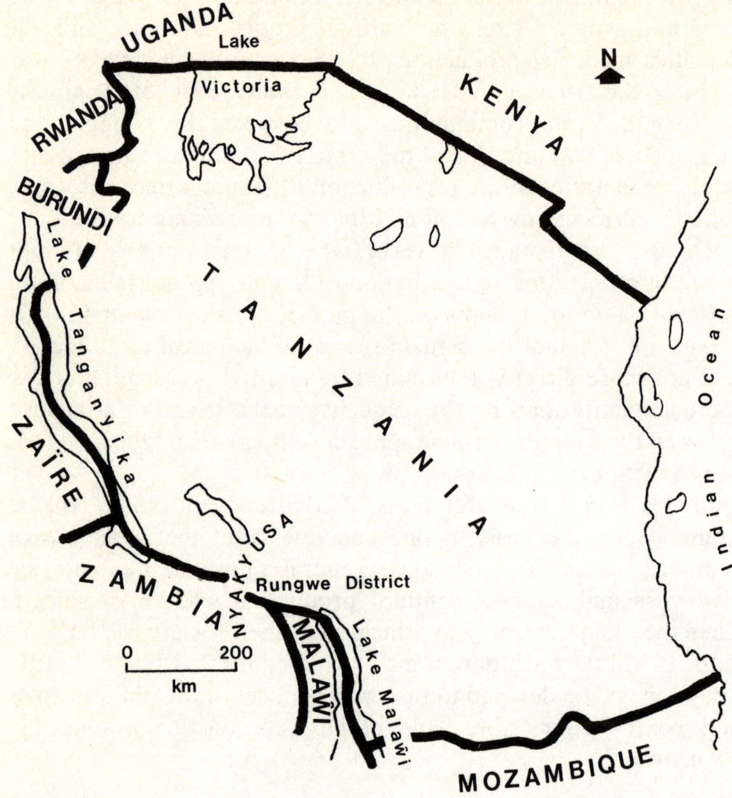

Figure 2.1 The Nyakyusa in their environment

farming regions are situated, and nowadays export crops such as coffee and tea are cultivated.

In all probability the Nyakyusa chiefs came to the Rungwe valley with their followers in the early sixteenth century. Other smaller groups were already living there and these were subjugated and mixed with the Nyakyusa. In many of the old Nyakyusa stories, the point is stressed that these chiefs brought 'civilization' to the valley, and by this mainly cattle is meant.

Farming was (and is) the most important form of production for the Nyakyusa. A striking aspect of their farming system — and a rather unusual one in Africa — is that in Rungwe it was possible to cultivate vast stretches of land permanently. The soil was so fertile and the rainfall so regular that long fallow periods were seldom

46

necessary. Crop alternation was all that was needed in order to prevent the soil from becoming exhausted. The most important crops in pre-colonial times were bananas, millet and beans. In addition to the crops, animal husbandry was of some importance. The Nyakyusa also hunted and fished. Due to its location between chains of high mountains, and also because of the warlike attitude of the population, the Nyakyusa remained extremely isolated for a long time. This enabled the Nyakyusa to develop the Rungwe valley into a prosperous and relatively densely populated area. Thus the first white men to visit Rungwe (in 1877) described it as a land overflowing with milk and honey.

In fact this region was not completely isolated. There were small-scale trade contacts with other peoples. In return for grain, mats and other products, the Nyakyusa received copper (for jewellery or ornaments), iron (for weapons), earthenware, salt and probably cattle. Yet it is striking that these trade contacts remained so restricted, since Rungwe is part of what is referred to as the 'corridor', a region between Lake Malawi and Lake Tanganyika which has always been characterized by continual waves of migration, and by extensive long-distance trade (including traffic in ivory and slaves). Particularly in the nineteenth century, Arab slave-traders penetrated more and more deeply into this region on their forays from the coast. But, as has been noted above, for a long time the mountain ranges — and possibly the warlike attitude of the Nyakyusa as well — protected the Rungwe region from the unsettling impact of this plundering. The Nyakyusa did not start to have more regular contact with the Arab traders until the end of the nineteenth century, at the same time as Europeans (at first missionaries, then German government officials) penetrated the area so as to establish their authority there. As a result of joint efforts on the part of the Nyakyusa and Europeans, the slave-traders were soon defeated. The hunt for slaves, which had such drastic demographic consequences in other parts of Tanzania — the depopulation of entire regions, particularly in the nineteenth century — had very little effect on demographic developments in Rungwe.

Agricultural production and relations of production

From accounts by the first European explorers of the prosperity of the Nyakyusa, we can conclude that at the end of the nineteenth century (before the colonial conquest), their agricultural production must have been sufficient to meet the vital needs of the members of their society. The production of the Nyakyusa communities was primarily oriented towards 'use-value': consumption within their own group, while surplus products were sometimes bartered. For example, part of the production of the kin-groups was exchanged for prestige goods such as spears, iron-capped hoes, or cattle: the main component of bridewealth.

The most important source of energy was human labour (hardly any use was made of draught-animals, let alone mechanical energy). The most important implements were simple ones: a hoe for the men and a dibble for the women, and with such tools the fields were cultivated intensively all the year round. Under conditions like these, it was logical that the wealth and the power of the head of a household mainly depended on the number of labourers he had under his control. The more wives and children he had, and the more labour services he could demand from other relatives, the greater his prestige. The size of the households and the number of productive persons they included were of decisive importance in the organization of production.

The adult men not only regulated the organization of the work in the fields but also had the land itself under their control. Simply because he was a member of an age-village, or -ward, a man could exercise his right to a plot of land, and the extremely fertile crater land (only a very small percentage of the total amount of land) was inherited by one man from another within the patrilineal kin-groups.

A man often kept a few small plots of land and part of the banana crop for himself, and distributed the rest among his wives. But this was more a kind of division of labour, because the man still maintained his control over the harvesting of the most important crops such as millet and rice. The women could do whatever they wanted with the other crops (maize, sweet potatoes, beans, cassava, etc.) of the fields allotted to them, but this did not strengthen their economic position very much, because the food surplus available to the women was often little and economically without much value for the reason that these products were accessible to everybody (van Hekken, personal communication).[6]

The basic economic unit — the group that worked together so as to perpetuate the production cycle — was the household, consisting of a man, his wife or wives (if it was a polygamous household) and the unmarried children. An unusual feature of the old Nyakyusa organization was that the households frequently did not constitute a group of co-residing people, since some of the unmarried children might live elsewhere. Occasionally, particularly in the peak periods, a household could call in the help of outside labourers; for example, teams of workers could be invited consisting of relatives from the father's or the mother's family or of age-mates.

Although the Nyakyusa were very much a society of agriculturalists, there was also some degree of specialization. A few of the men were smiths, diviners or healers, and some of the women also were priestesses or healers. But the most important division of labour was along the lines of sex and age. The men built the houses, planted the banana trees and did the harder farmwork like tilling the fields with their hoes. They also went out hunting and war-making. The unmarried men between the ages of fifteen and thirty-five were the warriors. Small wars between the chiefdoms, and later (at the end of the nineteenth century) with the slave-traders and the Germans as well, were quite a common phenomenon. The old men above the age of fifty were responsible for organizing the martial expeditions and for seeing to other village affairs — festivities, marriages and so forth. Boys between the age of six and ten tended the cattle of their elders. Unmarried sons above the age of ten cultivated the land belonging to their fathers, often assisted by age-mates. When he became betrothed, a young man was also expected to work on his father-in-law's fields. After his marriage, a man was allotted his own fields, which he cultivated together with his wife. But even then, he still had to help his parents and his wife's parents in their fields. Once he was married, however, a man could also expect his mother and sisters to help him.

The women did the sowing, weeding and harvesting. In addition, they were responsible for all the daily household tasks such as the maintenance of the house, fetching water and wood, cooking the meals, making beer and taking care of the children. They also made mats. Starting very young (between four and six), the girls had to help their mothers. The married adult women controlled the food supplies.

Kinship organization and age-villages

Ever since the Wilsons, the well-known ethnographers who studied the Nyakyusa, the generally accepted image of the old Nyakyusa organizational system has been that it was defined by two principles. As can be expected with this type of society, kinship was (and is) an important organizational principle. But the unusual aspect of the Nyakyusa was thought to be that, in addition, a second principle played an equally important role: the formation of age-groups (or even age-villages), usually consisting of non-related men of approximately the same age and their wives and children (see e.g. G. Wilson 1959; M. Wilson 1963).

The kinship system was patrilineal, and in the first instance inheritance was adelphic. This means that the property of one man was always inherited by another man and, if possible, a younger brother would inherit the property of his older brother. The generation of the sons did not inherit any property until the generation of the fathers had been exhausted. The property inherited in this manner mainly consisted of cattle and crater land, which was valuable because it was so scarce. The women were handed down in accordance with the same principles by way of the system of levirate: a widow was expected to marry her deceased husband's brother, but her later children were viewed as the children of her deceased husband. Consequently, in the first instance, the control over all the scarce means of production and reproduction (cattle, crater land and women) was determined by the relations within the patrilineal sublineage. In addition, the wider group of bilateral relatives — which also included relatives in the female line — was important in the organization system of the Nyakyusa: work was regularly done in co-operation with these relatives, and cattle and gifts were also exchanged with them.

To the Nyakyusa, kinship mainly had to do with cattle. In addition to the cattle inherited from one man by another, cattle also circulated at funerals and weddings: when a son got married, the entire lineage would give cattle to the lineage of the bride; they would also receive cattle at the marriage of a daughter. Although the general rules were fixed, in practice this kinship system allowed for numerous opportunities to manipulate lineage relations. In this chapter I shall show that it was mainly the older men who were in a position to build up an extensive network of obligations by means of the exchange of cattle (within the lineage itself as well

50

as between the different lineages) and thus strengthen their own positions. Usually kinship relations of this type were corroborated by all kinds of moral coercion ('occult' sanctions).

According to the Wilsons, the age-villages played no less important a role than the kinship organization referred to above. This is the aspect that the Nyakyusa are mainly known for in anthropological literature. The Wilsons saw Nyakyusa society as consisting of a large number of small more or less independent chiefdoms without any kind of central authority. A chiefdom consisted in turn of a number of villages (age-villages).

How did these age-villages come into being, in the Wilsons' view? The age-villages would be founded next to the village of the parents, as a separate neighbourhood inhabited by boys above the age of ten. When the oldest boys reached the age of seventeen or eighteen, the neighbourhood would stop accepting new boys. Consequently, brothers often lived in different neighbourhoods. Most of the men got married when they were about thirty years old, and their wives came to live with them (virilocal marriage). The neighbourhood would thus develop into an almost independent village. The territorial boundaries between the age-groups were articulated by an entire body of ideas and values. A neighbourhood did not attain complete independence until after the age-group's 'coming out' (*ubusoka*) had taken place; this ritual event took place only once per generation, when the men of the neighbourhood were in their late thirties. Then the older generation had to make way for the younger one, and the young men who were 'coming out' would settle at a new location.[7]

On the grounds of what has been said above, we can conclude that Nyakyusa society exhibited most of the features of a domestic community. But there are also several deviations from this model. In the first place, there was the beginning of a centralizing process. The Nyakyusa already had chiefs who bore a hereditary title and, moreover, who exercised authority over a number of villages. In the Wilsons' opinion the Nyakyusa chief was not an autocrat; in order to carry out his public functions, he usually needed the approval of the old notables (but this did not hold true with respect to his religious functions, which were precisely those that were of such great importance). Meillassoux's model of the domestic community, however, involved the kind of small kin-groups between which clear authority relations were not supposed to exist. Another deviation from Meillassoux's model is the fact that in Nyakyusa society, in addition to the kinship units, age-villages played an important role. Yet the question remains whether this difference was the basis for the development of power relations that were truly different from those stipulated by Meillassoux's model.

Another aspect seems to be of greater significance — namely the fact that some of the Nyakyusa land (crater land) was scarce and was inherited within a restricted circle of kinsmen, whereas most of the other land was in the hands of what was mainly a territorial group (age-village). Meillassoux, in contrast, stressed the fact, in his definition of the domestic community, that land was not scarce and was solely under the control of kin-groups. In addition, it appears from the available material on the Nyakyusa that women fulfilled an unusually important productive role, indispensable to the economic system as a whole; they were responsible for the daily reproduction of the system (the food supply). Although Meillassoux was not unaware of the exploitation of women within the domestic community, he concentrated his attention upon the control over the reproductive role of women, and overlooked the role of women in agricultural production.

With respect to the internal contradictions within the system, Meillassoux's model is certainly valid. But in the following section it will become clear that what was involved here was a hierarchic variant of the domestic community. The Nyakyusa elders had control not only over reproduction, but also over certain lands, and consequently had a more stable power base than the seniors in the communities Meillassoux referred to.

The power of the elders over the young men and the women

There were two important contradictions in Nyakyusa society; one between the generations and one between the sexes. In addition to their control over agricultural production (land, the labour of women, the labour of work-teams of young men, etc.), the older men also had control over biological reproduction through their monopoly of the access to marriageable women. In this society, a marriage contract was settled by the husband's lineage giving cattle to the wife's lineage.[8] These marriage cattle were mainly kept and exchanged by the older men. Usually this type of marriage relation between certain lineages was continued through a number of generations. Thus the organization of reproduction created cohesion on a broader scale than the social units needed for production.

Up to the time he got married, a man had to work for his father, without any control over the products of his own labour. Of course a father had the obligation to feed his children, and also to procure wives for his sons. But he often tried to postpone doing so for as long as possible. First, he could use the cattle that he got after marrying off his daughter, for example, in order to marry a second or third wife himself. There was all the more reason for a father to postpone his son's marriage since, due to an avoidance taboo, his daughter-in-law would have to live in a different neighbourhood or village and would consequently not be able to be much help to him as far as the household chores were concerned.

There was also direct competition between fathers and sons for marriage cattle and wives. A man could try to postpone the marriage of his son by arguing that the lad did not yet deserve a wife since he had not worked enough, or had not shown a sufficient amount of respect. This power position of the older men was strengthened by a wide range of notions, particularly about the 'breath of people'. The elders were viewed as intermediaries between the ancestors and their own living descendants; this is why it was thought that a young man who did not behave properly towards his father could be punished by his ancestors by way of a disease, etc.[9]

Thus the elders could command control over various women and, consequently, over numerous children. Their network of relatives would expand, giving them control over more labour. This, in turn, meant a strengthening of their political position and their prestige: labour could be transformed into food and beer, so that it was mainly the older generation who could afford to receive their own age-mates with generous hospitality. Therefore polygamy was the ideal of all the Nyakyusa men. In addition to the reasons referred to above, the Nyakyusa men also believed that a man needed several wives in order to lead a more satisfying sexual life. Having several wives was also the most significant symbol of the status of a chief; some chiefs had even dozens of wives. Polygamy on such a large scale was feasible because the average age of the husbands was higher than that of the wives (a fact that will be dealt with below).

The status of the women was even lower than that of the young men. A boy still had the chance of one day attaining the status of adult man, if only he lived long enough. But a woman was destined to be in a position subordinate to that of an adult man for the rest of her life. Although the position of women in the production process was relatively strong, in other spheres of life it was much weaker. A woman was usually married off before she had reached puberty, without her having any say in the matter. Sometimes she had to act as a replacement for her sister who had died or who had proved unable to bear children (sororate marriage). The man had exclusive sexual rights over his wife. She had no right to a lover, whereas the man could conclude a second marriage without informing his first wife. In a levirate marriage — whereby after the death of her husband a woman would be 'taken over' by his heir — a woman similarly had very little say in the matter. Formally, a Nyakyusa woman had no control at all over her own children. Women had to behave respectfully, they had to observe the avoidance taboos, and kneel when greeting an adult man. The inequality between men and women was also strengthened by the belief in the 'breath of people': a woman who did not show the proper respect for her male relatives ran the risk of becoming sterile or of giving birth to sick children. Women were also attributed with certain supernatural powers (witchcraft), but these powers were viewed as being impermissible. Among the Nyakyusa, it was completely permissible to use violence against women (or children) if they misbehaved in any way, but it was severely looked down upon if a woman hit a man. Moreover, in daily practice, the Nyakyusa women had to work much harder than the men. There was a division between the generations of women, but it was less marked than that between the generations of men. It was very feasible that the various wives of one and the same man might be of different generations.

How can the old Nyakyusa power relations be characterized in the framework of the theories of the French Marxist anthropologists dealt with in this book? Meillassoux stressed that the power of the elders was mainly dependent on the control they exercised over the access to marriageable women. The power of the Nyakyusa elders was indeed mainly based on their control of cattle and its circulation in the form of bridewealth; their power was also strengthened by the kinship system. The custom of adelphic inheritance, for instance, strengthened the position of the elders as compared to that of the younger men in that, after his death, the father's cattle remained under the control of one of his brothers rather than his son.

There seems to be every reason to assume that the Nyakyusa valued cattle so highly because of its role with respect to bridewealth. Indeed, the economic significance of cattle was not all that great among the Nyakyusa. The control of the elders and the chiefs over the cattle was also ideologically based on all kinds of beliefs. G. Wilson described the following train of thought among the Nyakyusa (1959: 287):

> the ancestors of a chief influence the prosperity of entire
> chiefdoms. Rain and good crops, the fertility of women and
> cattle are dependent on their good will, which in turn is
> dependent on the regular sacrificing of cows. And the chiefs,
> their living descendants, are responsible for these sacrifices.

It goes without saying that the chiefs had more cattle than other people; their power and influence were closely linked to the extent of their control over cattle. A chief could expand his herd by means of inheritance, by marrying off women, or by way of cattle raids carried out by the men of his chiefdom. Thus it was mainly the chiefs who were in a position to marry many wives. For the ordinary man, the possession of cattle was also of great importance. A man could start an independent household only after he had got married, and he remained completely dependent upon his father until his father gave him cattle for his marriage. Thus the power position of the older men was clearly based on a flow of goods and services from the younger men and women to the seniors (cf. also Caldwell's idea of an 'inter-generational flow of wealth').[10] Among the Nyakyusa, the appropriation of surplus labour by the elders assumed such large proportions that their example is actually more in keeping with Rey's conception of the old African village society than with Meillassoux's version of the domestic community.[11] Rey used much stronger terms than Meillassoux to describe the old inequality within these societies. In Rey's view, the elders (not as a 'biological' but more as a 'social' category) were a dominant class that exploited the rest of the community — the young men, the women and the children.[12] The information available about pre-colonial Nyakyusa society does indeed justify the use of the term 'exploitation'. I take this term to mean that neither the young men nor the women, as direct producers, were in a position to have any control over either the extent or the appropriation of their own labour surplus (cf. also Terray 1979: 36). Among the Nyakyusa, this exploitation did not take place by way of economic coercion, but through the institution of bridewealth and various ideological sanctions. With the surplus that the young men and the women produced, some of which was transformed into marriage cattle, they themselves contributed (and still contribute) towards the perpetuation of their own dependence on the seniors.

Biological reproduction among the Nyakyusa

Now that we have dealt with the factors responsible for the specific form of class relations within the domestic community, we can approach our main subject, biological reproduction among the Nyakyusa. To what extent was biological reproduction among the Nyakyusa determined or influenced by these old class relations?

According to Meillassoux, the safeguarding of biological reproduction is a predominant obsession in every community. This is a logical consequence of Meillassoux's analysis of the domestic mode of production. As was indicated above, Meillassoux stressed that human labour is the only important form of energy used in 'domestic' agriculture, whereas other means of production, such as land or simple tools, are hardly ever scarce. Therefore the continual availability of human labour was the most important condition for the continuation of the annual agricultural cycle.

In this chapter I hope to go further than Meillassoux in my analysis of biological reproduction among the Nyakyusa. It is to Meillassoux's credit that (contrary to the Malthusian analysis) he did show that — at least in the domestic community — more human labour meant greater production. But — as said above — the question remains whether Meillassoux did devote a sufficient amount of attention to the role of the internal contradictions characteristic of the domestic community. In Meillassoux's line of thought (i.e. assuming the 'objective' requirement that above all biological reproduction had to be safeguarded), in the domestic community men as well as women would be expected to marry at as early an age as possible. There would be only a limited amount of polygamy, and a negligible difference in marital ages needed to compensate for the higher mortality-rate among men. This kind of system would indeed mean a maximization of the number of children born, and would offer the greatest safeguard for the biological reproduction of a domestic community as a whole.

However, in reality it was the fixed strategy of the Nyakyusa seniors to marry polygamously, and to have as many wives as possible. They monopolized the women and thus certainly strengthened their own position. But, at the same time, their behaviour had a negative effect on the biological reproduction of the community as a whole. We shall show this on the basis of the demographic conditions of the Nyakyusa by the end of the nineteenth century.

About 1890–1900, the Rungwe region made an impression of prosperity, and the Nyakyusa were expanding their territory. Consequently we can assume that, just before the onset of the colonial period, the population growth was positive. On the other hand, the overall mortality-rate — strongly fluctuating as a result of famines and epidemics — must have been high, and consequently there was at most a very slight population growth. On the basis of these assumptions, utilizing the demographic data which I collected in the 1960s (de Jonge 1971 and 1974) and the data collected by Monica Wilson in the 1930s (M. Wilson 1977), I have drawn up a reconstruction of various aspects of the Nyakyusa population just before the colonial period; in so far as relevant to the present argument, this reconstruction is summarized in Tables 2.1 and 2.2.[13]

Before the colonial conquest, the demographic reproduction of the Nyakyusa must have been based upon 'natural fertility'; this only means that they did not use any effective means of birth control (Henry 1972: 121). The average number of children that a woman had had by the end of her fertile period was high (5.6 children per woman). But the mortality-rate was so high that a man needed to father at least five children if he was to have a reasonable chance of at least one son surviving by the time he was sixty-five.[14] Table 2.1 makes it clear that, even with an average birth-rate of 5.6 children born to each woman in her fertile period, there was quite a considerable percentage of households with one wife with either no daughters (21%) or no sons (28%) who had reached marriageable age. This meant that a father either had no son to work for him or no daughter to bring in marriage cattle.

These figures make it clear that in spite of the high fertility rate, there was a precarious demographic situation on the community level as well as on the household level. Does this mean that

Table 2.1 *Percentage distribution of Nyakyusa households with one wife, with respect to the number of surviving daughters (up to the age of 15) and the number of surviving sons (up to the age of 30), at the end of the nineteenth century[a]*

No. of surviving children	Percentage of households with that number of surviving	
	daughters (<15 yrs)	sons (<30 yrs)
0	21	28
1	38	40
2	28	24
3	11	7
4	2	1
5	–	–
6	–	–
	100	100

[a] Distribution calculated by Ruben Huele.

demographic reproduction among the Nyakyusa was determined by unhampered fertility, solely kept in check by a high mortality-rate? This would more or less coincide with Malthus's view, for he was of the opinion that poor or underdeveloped peoples reproduced more extensively than the development of food production allowed for, so that such calamities as famines, epidemics and wars became inevitable. The Nyakyusa certainly did have their famines, epidemics and wars, but Malthus's view is still not applicable to them. In the old relations of production in Rungwe, the expansion of biological reproduction was the most important means of increasing production. It has been noted above that there was no general land scarcity among the Nyakyusa, so that a community with a larger and more rapidly increasing population (which means more labour) probably would have greater opportunities to increase its food production than one where population growth stagnated or decreased (cf. Boserup 1965). There was thus a good reason why the chiefs tried to expand their chiefdoms and get more followers, and why a large number of wives and children was the Nyakyusa ideal.

Moreover, it was certainly not the case that fertility went completely unchecked. It may be true that no effective type of birth control was utilized, but there were a number of different social and political-economic factors that created a situation in which the actual fertility-rate was considerably lower than was biologically possible. In the appendix (p. 62f.), the factors are dealt with that formed, in the old Nyakyusa society, a link between the socio-economic structure (particularly the nature of social relations of production) on the one hand, and fertility on the other. In the rest of this section, I shall deal more extensively with a more general background factor: the significance of the old class relations and, in particular, of the power position of the seniors with respect to demographic reproduction.

Nyakyusa men and women wanted numerous offspring, not only for the sake of having children, but also for prestige and wealth. However, young men had to wait a long time before they could get married, whereas the older men with various wives and many children had a privileged position. Table 2.1 showed that the demographic reproduction of a household remained precarious if the husband had only one wife, even if we assume that she lived until the end of her fertile period. Consequently polygamy was the best strategy to safeguard the reproduction (and the production) of a household. But polygamy is feasible only if, to a certain extent, a small group of men can monopolize the women. This does not necessarily mean that some men have to stay unmarried all their life, but it does mean that a difference has to be maintained between the marital ages of men and of women. Table 2.2, which gives an estimation of the age distribution of the Nyakyusa at the end of the nineteenth century, shows the extent and the effects of this marriage-age difference.

On the grounds of the material gathered by the Wilsons, we can assume that practically all the women above the age of fifteen were married, either to monogamous or polygamous men. In pre-colonial times, divorce is thought to have been more infrequent than was the case later; if a divorce did take place, then the woman did not remain single for long. Similarly, a widow was usually incorporated into the household of her husband's heir. He was under the obligation to take care of her as he took care of his wife, even if she had long passed the fertile age (thus in Nyakyusa society, older women did not go to live with their sons, as was often the case elsewhere). It has been noted above that men married when they were about thirty; they then generally remained married until they died, and most of the older men were polygamous. So, for our calculations, it would not distort the

Table 2.2 *Age distribution of Nyakyusa men and women at the end of the nineteenth century (see note 13)*

Age	Men	Women	Total
0– 4	6,920	6,885	13,805
5– 9	5,380	5,395	10,775
10–14	4,975	4,995	9,970
15–19	4,645	4,660	9,305
20–24	4,275	4,290	8,565
25–29	3,905	3,920	7,825
30–34	3,555	3,555	7,090
35–39	3,200	3,320	6,430
40–44	2,860	2,910	5,770
45–49	2,540	2,620	5,160
50–54	2,200	2,320	4,520
55–59	1,820	1,990	3,810
60–64	1,400	1,595	2,995
65+	1,745	2,235	3,980
Total	49,420	50,690	100,000

actual proportions simply to assume that all the women above the age of fifteen and all the men above the age of thirty were married, and that all the men above the age of fifty were polygamous.

Table 2.2 shows that the male population above the age of fifty constituted only 7.2% of the total population. This small class of seniors held a highly privileged position, but there were also considerable differences within this class. The chiefs, the head-men, the senior members of the wealthier lineages and, as a result of the system of adelphic inheritance, the elder brothers, had more power than the other older men. In this connection, it must be noted that by no means all the 'younger' men ever became 'older' men. For if we consider the mortality-rate during the period in question — for the man, life expectancy at birth was twenty-seven — we can calculate that of every hundred living boys born, only twenty-nine were ever to attain the status of 'elder'; only a few of those twenty-nine were ever to become privileged seniors. Table 2.2 also shows that there were 33,325 married women and 19,300 married men; in other words, 1.73 wives per husband. It can also be calculated that 37% of the married men were polygamous, and that these older polygamous men had an average of three wives.[15] These are extremely high figures, but they are still not improbable;

in Guinea, for example, polygamy on a similar scale was still prevalent in the 1950s. One certainty is that this unequal distribution amply enabled a small class of elders to safeguard the reproduction of their own families. With an average of three wives, they must have had an average of fourteen children, and with the mortality-rate of the time being as it was, an average of six children were still alive when their father was sixty-five.

Of course the situation was much more favourable for the wealthier lineages. This is evident from the data gathered by Monica Wilson about a number of wealthy family elders who had an average of 4.4 wives and 7.8 surviving children, so that their lineages rapidly increased in size, and consequently in power and wealth as well (see Wilson 1977: 84 n. 11). She raised the question whether this type of group could be viewed as being representative of the total population, but it will become clear below that, in a demographic sense, this definitely was not the case.

Whether the fertility rate of the women in polygamous households was equal to or higher or lower than that of the women in monogamous households was not, in itself, of primary import-ance with respect to the privileged demographic position of the elders. But with regard to the demographic reproduction of the society as a whole, this question was of great importance. It can be assumed that, in fact, in all the age categories, the fertility rate of the women married to polygamous men was about 20% lower than that of the women married to monogamous men (van der Walle 1968: 232). This was the result of a combination of factors whose relative importance is unfortunately difficult to ascertain. As a result of the rotation system prevalent in polygamous marriages (a husband had to spend an equal number of nights with each of his wives), the coition frequency per wife was lower; the age of the polygamous men was higher (decreased potency); in polygamous marriages, numerous rules regarding sexual intercourse (absti-nence, etc.) were adhered to more strictly; moreover, women whose fertility could be expected to be very low or nil were more likely to marry polygamous men (de Jonge 1974: 68–9).

By the end of her fertile period, a Nyakyusa woman had given birth to an average of 5.6 children. This meant that the community as a whole could just about reproduce (NRR = 1.15; this index is explained in note 13). On the basis of the differential fertility rates of women married to monogamous and polygamous men, we have been able to calculate that the women married to monogamous men gave birth to an average of 6.0 children and the women married to polygamous men an average of 4.8 children. Thus the reproduction rate of the women married to monogamous men was amply sufficient (NRR = 1.23), but the demographic reproduction rate of the women married to polygamous men was below the level necessary in order to safeguard the reproduction of labour (NRR = 0.98).[16]

In view of the nature of the relations of production in Nyakyusa society, and in view of the precarious demographic situation in the pre-colonial period — the high and fluctuating mortality-rate — it is no wonder that the Nyakyusa were so preoccupied with reproduction and the promotion of fertility. This is entirely in keeping with the model of the domestic community presented by Meillassoux. But Meillassoux's analysis of demographic reproduction was overly focused upon the community as a whole and upon the 'objective' demands made by reproduction: the fact that, for greater production, in the domestic economy the main demand is for more people. He failed to devote a sufficient amount of attention to the social classes within the domestic community. The example of the Nyakyusa shows that, in order to safeguard their own position with respect to the young men and women, the seniors adopted a marriage strategy (polygamy) which increased the precariousness of the community's demographic situation and endangered the reproduction of labour.

In Nyakyusa society, as was the case elsewhere, demographic development was influenced by the relations of production, in particular by the power position of the seniors. So even in this pre-capitalist society, biological reproduction was directly influenced by political relations.

Appendix: The fertility of Nyakyusa women

In the calculations pertaining to the fertility of Nyakyusa women, I made use of the variables of Davis & Blake (1956); I added the distinction between desirable and undesirable factors and an indication of their positive or negative influence on fertility.

The first three 'structural' factors influenced fertility positively and had effects that were viewed as desirable: (1) the low marriage age of the women; they were betrothed at the age of 8 or 9 and married right after menarche; (2) the universal nature of marriage: only some disabled or mentally disturbed women did not get married; and (3) the short period between the termination of a marital relationship (due to divorce or the death of the husband and the start of a new relationship). The combination of these three factors meant that, for virtually her entire fertile period, a woman was in either a monogamous or a polygamous marital situation.

The following factors had a negative influence on fertility and were viewed as undesirable. (4) Sterility among women, which could not have been very high (it was uncommon in the 1960s). (5) Induced abortion does not seem to have been practised. (6) Miscarriages, however, were quite common (at least ¼ of the pregnancies are thought to have ended in miscarriages — see Henry 1972: 130).

In addition, there were a number of practices common among the Nyakyusa that restricted fertility. In the first place, there was (7) the practice of voluntary abstention from sexual intercourse, especially immediately after confinement (post-natal abstinence for 6 to 8 months). It was also prohibited for a woman to have sexual intercourse during her menstruation, for a mother to have any more babies after her son's marriage, or for a woman to become pregnant in the period between her daughter's menarche and the birth of her daughter's first child. These last two prohibitions, which were based on the feeling that the sexual activities of successive generations should be kept separate, were not likely to have had much effect on the level of fertility.

Another factor was (8) coition frequency: the higher the coition frequency, the greater the chance of a woman becoming pregnant, though in general a frequency of 2 or 3 times a week is sufficient to lead to pregnancy within 7 months (Henry 1972: 132). We have noted the possibility that, for women in polygamous marriages, the coition frequency was lower. In the post-natal period, after the period of complete abstinence a low coition frequency was still deemed necessary; if it was adhered to, this practice can have had some influence. It has been noted that the Nyakyusa did not have any effective means of birth control. However, they did practise (9) *coitus interruptus*, especially when a woman was still nursing a baby.

Very little is known about the following two factors: (10) involuntary abstinence due to impotence, ill-health or temporary separation, and (11) the use of medicine or operations to promote fertility/infertility. Of course involuntary abstinence could not have failed to have an effect, though it is highly unlikely that the 'medicinal' measures did. The aim of most of the practices referred to here (post-natal abstinence, *coitus interruptus* and reduced coition frequency) was not so much to decrease fertility as to increase the newborn baby's survival chances. This concern also underlay the fear involving the birth of twins, which required a special ritual.

The combination of a long nursing period (according to the Wilsons, infants used to be nursed until they were 2 or 3 years old) and post-natal taboos is thought to have resulted in a normal period of 4 to 5 years between two successive births. Shorter intervals between births were imputed to a lack of self-control on the part of the parents and were viewed as a manifestation of 'beastly' behaviour. It was generally believed that the violation of these taboos would endanger the husband (impotence), the wife (sterility) or the children (diseases, death). The Wilsons also mentioned another reason, besides increasing the survival chances of babies, for the long interval between two births: in case of war, the second youngest child would have to be able to run, holding his mother's hand, while she carried his younger sibling.

Notes

1 I wish to acknowledge with thanks the suggestions and criticisms by the other members of our work-group, and by Henk de Gans, Ruben Huele and Anton Kuijsten. Also, this chapter could never have been written but for the inspiration and data to be found in Monica Wilson's works. In a later article I hope to discuss the changes that took place in reproduction among the Nyakyusa as a result of the introduction of the capitalist market economy.

2 The general term 'reproduction' refers not only to the biological (= demographic) reproduction of the members of a community (the population factor), but also to the reproduction of relations, so that the continuation of a community is safeguarded.

3 More than a hundred and fifty years later, neo-Malthusians wrote about the population problems of poor countries in much the same vein: these recent authors attribute the fact that there is little or no rise in the standard of living to rapid population growth, which therefore should be restricted — now, however, not by way of all kinds of moral preventive measures, or by simply not doing anything to prevent death among the poor, but by way of birth-control programmes.

4 This still does not explain why men were granted this control over women. According to Aaby (1977: 49), this had to do with irregularities in demographic reproduction, constituting a threat to the perpetuation of the group. Control over more reproducers (women) became a prerequisite for the further expansion of the group. Since women were the object of this expansion, in Aaby's view, they could not simultaneously exercise this control themselves. Thus, by kidnapping them and at the same time by protecting them, the men came to 'rule' over the women.

5 The description of the Nyakyusa is based on extensive literature; most importantly, the work of Monica and Godfrey Wilson. Other authors include Konter (1979), van Hekken (n.d.), McKenny (1973), Wright (1971), Carsley (1969), Iliffe (1979) and de Jonge (1974). No efforts were made to refer to all these sources in the course of this chapter. I made the most use of the recent book by Monica Wilson (1977) dealing with the Nyakyusa in the period from 1875 to 1971 and incorporating most of the findings of the literature referred to above.

6 This is in line with what Goody (1976) wrote about African hoe cultures (extensive agriculture), where there is no shortage of land and where bridewealth constitutes an important institution. The position of women is thought to be stronger there than in agricultural societies where ploughs are used.

64

7 The Wilsons probably over-estimated the importance of age-villages as an organizational principle. Such authors as McKenny (1973) have suggested that, due to certain theoretical convictions, the Wilsons devoted too much attention to the 'rules' and too little attention to the social reality of the situation. This view is corroborated by the results of van Hekken's field-work; according to her, age-villages not recruited on a kinship basis were very much of an exception (cf. van Hekken n.d.).

8 There were two other types of marriages that did not involve any payment in the form of cattle: the service marriage and the elopement marriage. The service marriage was viewed as being inferior, since the children would belong to the wife's family. The service marriage, as the name indicates, also meant that the husband had to work for his father-in-law for years (bride-service). The elopement marriage was viewed as improper.

9 The 'breath of people' was a legitimate and defensive form of witchcraft directed against anyone who violated certain generally accepted norms (Wilson 1963: 102).

10 It is with some hesitation that I quote from the work of Caldwell (1976) here. This demographer does not adhere to clear Marxist points of view, but ever since 1978 he has made use of such terms as 'mode of production' and 'relations of production'. He has tried to formulate a sociological theory that on certain points coincides with Meillassoux's. When writing about the social and economic advantages and disadvantages (assets and liabilities) of large families, he is of the opinion that it is the social conditions that determine whether a high or a low fertility rate was economically rational; to be more specific, the fertility rate is determined by the direction of what he refers to as 'the inter-generational flow of wealth'. In 'traditional' societies, this flow of goods, money, labour, services, protection, political support and so forth goes from the younger to the older generation. So in societies where the main flow goes from the children to the parents, a high fertility rate is rational, whereas in societies where the flow goes from the parents to the children, a low fertility rate is rational. Caldwell views this difference as a social phenomenon rather than as being determined by economic conditions. He mainly analyses the effects of the growing influence of European cultural traditions in the Third World on the 'inter-generational flow of wealth'. But he devotes hardly any attention to the question why there is 'traditionally' a flow of goods and services from young people to older people, whereas this is precisely the point that Marxist anthropologists such as Rey and Meillassoux tried to explain. Caldwell appears to take the power of the elders for granted, especially in his 1976 article. In his 1978 publication, he turns out to be somewhat 'Marxized'; there he draws a link between the influence of cultural traditions and changes in the production sphere, but with respect to the basis of the elders' power, he does not do much more than emphasize the role of 'gossip' in order to affirm their control over their dependants.

11 Cf. Rey (1979: 51–2). Marx used the term 'surplus labour' to refer to a

general social phenomenon that takes place as soon as the productivity of human labour-power exceeds immediate vital needs; such surplus labour manifests itself in a wide range of different ways, depending on the mode of production. In the capitalist mode of production, the characteristic form of surplus labour is the 'surplus value' of the wage-labourer; in the feudal mode of production, it was the land-rent paid by the serf. In pre-capitalist modes of production, there was also surplus labour in the form of tribute, military service or communal activities for the benefit of the group (or its leaders). One difference between the pre-capitalist and the capitalist mode of production is that in the pre-capitalist mode, surplus labour was usually extracted by means of non-economic coercion. But, in general, it can be said that surplus labour and the product it produces are utilized for the maintenance of social relations as well as for the expansion of the means of production (Bottomore 1979: 127, 153 and 161; Marx 1965).

12 Meillassoux (1975: 123, 124) did not agree with Rey on this point. Meillassoux refused to speak of classes here, since young men eventually became elders and elders voluntarily handed down their power. Rightly, in my opinion, Rey repudiated this by pointing out that only very few young men — and no women at all — were ever to achieve the status of senior, and also by showing that within the lineage groups themselves, there was also very clear evidence of exploitation (Rey 1979). For further references to this debate, see ch. 1 and ch. 8 of the present book.

13 For this reconstruction, I used the population models of Coale & Demeny (1965). In 1968, the South model (level 9) was most applicable to the Nyakyusa; I used the South tables to reconstruct the pre-colonial situation. Assumption for that period: low positive growth. One might compare this with the general United Nations estimates on Africa: for the period from 1800 to 1850, a birth-rate of 42 and a mortality-rate of 36 (cf. United Nations 1968).
At $r = 0.005$, South model, level 4 (women) gives a birth-rate of 41.9 and a mortality-rate of 36.9. For the total population, a birth-rate of 41 and a mortality-rate of 36 can be assumed. At the same time, there was a GRR (29) of 2.77, a TFR of 5.6 (2.77 × 2.03) and a NRR of 1.15 (2.77 × 0.415). On the basis of the mortality table selected, the probability that a man would reach the age of 50 was $l_{50}/l_0 = 0.292$ and the probability that a woman would reach the age of 29 was $l_{29}/l_0 = 0.415$. Table 2.2, the distribution of the Nyakyusa population according to age and sex at the end of the nineteenth century, was drawn up by applying a sex ratio model for Africa to the distribution of women according to the South table (level 4). Although the size of the population is not all that important for our line of argument, I should like to note that a total of 100,000 seems to be a reasonable estimate of the Nyakyusa population around the year 1890 (in 1934 the total population was also approx. 100,000).
Explanation of the demographic abbreviations and terms used above:

GRR (gross reproduction rate): at the prevailing birth-rate, the total number of female children that a woman could have, specified according to age.

TFR (*total fertility rate*): the number of children that a fictive cohort of 1,000 women would have if, in their reproductive years, they all adhered to the fertility rate, specified according to age, prevailing at a given moment.

NRR (*net reproduction rate*): at the prevailing birth-rate, specified according to age, and the prevailing mortality-rate, specified according to age, the total number of female children that a newborn woman could have. If NRR < 1, then the population has the tendency to increase; if NRR > 1, it has the tendency to decrease, and if NRR = 1, then zero growth is to be expected.

l_x = (a mortality table measurement): the number of surviving persons at age x, based on a cohort of 100,000.

gross birth-rate: number of births in a given year in each thousand of the total population.

gross mortality-rate: number of deaths in a given year in each thousand of the total population.

14 On the basis of the probability calculation:

$$\sum_{k=0}^{n} \binom{n}{k} p^k \ q^{n-k} \ (1 - l_x/l_0)^k = 1 - \text{pr} \quad \ldots (1)$$

In which n = number of children
k = number of boys (girls)
p = q = 0.5 probability of a boy or girl
l_x/l_0 = probability of survival from 0 to x years of age (for example l_{20}/l_0 = 0.47 means a 47% probability that a boy will survive until the age of 20. If a woman is on average 29 years old when giving birth and the father is on average 44 years old, then the probability that the father will have one surviving son when he is 64 years old is l_{20}/l_0).
pr = probability that a boy will survive (assume 75%).
Now, since

$$(1 - l_{20}/l_0)^k \ = \ 0.53^k, \text{ and } p^k(0.53)^k \ = \ (0.53p)^k,$$
substitution in (1) yields:

$$\sum_{k=0}^{n} \binom{n}{k} (0.53p)^k \ q^{n-k} \ = \ (0.53p + q)^n \quad \ldots (2)$$

For a probability of 75% that a boy will survive . . . 1 − pr = 0.25, and consequently

$$n \ = \ \frac{\log(1 - \text{pr})}{\log(0.53p + q)} \ = \ \frac{\log 0.25}{\log 0.76} \ = \ 5.2 \quad \ldots (3)$$

which means that if a household is to have a good probability (75%) that one son is to survive, then a man has to father at least 5.2 children.

15. Table 2.2 shows that 37.1% of the married men were polygamous (7,165/19,300) and 62.9% were monogamous (12,135/19,300); that these men had an average of 2.96 (rounded off to 3) wives ((33,325–12,315)/7,165). A polygamous man had an average of 2.96 × 4.8 = 14.2 children, of whom 5.9 survived (see also note 16).

16. In these calculations, the figures on the marriage situation pertained to men, the figures on reproduction pertained to women, and the figures on the probability of survival pertained to children. With respect to the married men, 63% were monogamous and 37% were polygamous. This means that if a young woman married a monogamous man, it could be assumed that she would be in a monogamous marriage situation for at most twenty years, and that if a young woman married a polygamous man she would never be in a monogamous marriage situation. It was much more difficult to draw up these figures (% monogamous/polygamous) pertaining to women. On the basis of this distribution, I calculated the average number of children born to monogamous and polygamous women (an average of 5.6 children per woman at the end of her fertile period) with the formula $0.63 \times K + 0.37 \times (0.8K) = 5.6$, resulting in 6.0 children born to monogamous women and 4.8 children born to polygamous women. Thus the NRR of monogamous women was $1.23 = 6.0/2.03 \times 0.415$ and the NRR of polygamous women was $0.98 + 4.8/2.03 \times 0.415$. If the survival probability of children in polygamous (richer) families was not equal to that of children in monogamous families, then this would only lead to even greater differences in reproduction between the two groups. (For the calculation and the definition of NRR, see also note 13.)

References

Aaby, P. (1977), 'Engels and women', *Critique of Anthropology*, 3, 9–10: 25–53.

Bloch, M. (ed.) (1975), *Marxist Analyses and Social Anthropology*. London: Malaby Press.

Boserup, E. (1965), *The Economics of Agrarian Change under Population Pressure*, London: Allen & Unwin.

Bottomore, T. (ed.) (1979), *Karl Marx*, Oxford: Blackwell.

Brass, W., Coale, A. J., Demery, P., Heisel, D. F., Lorimer, F., Romaniuk, A., van der Walle, E., (1968), *The Demography of Tropical Africa*, Princeton University Press.

Caldwell, J. C. (1976), 'Toward a restatement of demographic transition theory', *Population and Development Review*, 2, 3–4: 321–66.

Caldwell, J. C. (1978), 'A theory of fertility: from high plateau to destabilization', *Population and Development Review*, 4, 4: 553–77.

Carsley, S. R. (1969), *The Princes of Nyakyusa*, Nairobi: English press.
Chojnacka, H. (1980), 'Polygamy and the rate of population growth', *Population Studies*, 34, 1: 91–105.
Coale, A. J. and Demeny, P. (1965), *Regional Model Life Tables and Stable Populations*, Princeton University Press.
Colson, E. & Gluckman, M. (1959), (ed.) *Seven Tribes of British Central Africa*, Manchester University Press.
Davis, K. & Blake, J. (1956), 'Social structure and fertility: an analytic framework', *Economic Development and Cultural Change*, 4, 2: 221–35.
Godelier, M. (1975), 'Modes of production, kinship and demographic structures', in Bloch (1975): 3–27.
Goody, J. (1976), *Production and Reproduction: a Comparative Study of the Domestic Domain*, Cambridge University Press.
Gregory, J. W. & Piché, V. (1979), *The Demographic Regime of Peripheral Capitalism: Illustrated with African Examples*, Montreal: Université de Montreal, Département de Démographie.
van Hekken, P. M. (n.d.), 'Nyakyusa without age-villages', unpublished.
Henry, L. (1972), *Démographie, analyse et modèles*, Paris: Larousse.
Iliffe, J. (1979), *A Modern History of Tanganyika*, Cambridge University Press.
de Jonge, K. (1971), *Fécondité chez les Nyakyusa du Rungwe (Tanzanie): étude socio-démographique*, Mémoire, École Pratique des Hautes Études (Démographie du Tiers Monde), Paris.
de Jonge, K. (1974), 'Fertility: a dependent variable', in Sterkenburg & de Jonge (1974): 61–74.
Kerblay, B. (1971), 'Chayanov and the theory of peasantry as a specific type of economy', in Shanin (1971): 150–60.
Konter, J. H. (1979), *Traditie en Armoede: een Case-study van de Nyakyusa, Tanzania*, Leiden: Institute of Cultural Anthropology.
McKenny, N. (1973), 'The social structure of the Nyakyusa: a re-evaluation', *Africa*, 43, 2: 91–107.
Malthus, T. (1960), 'A summary view of the principle of population', in *Three Essays on Population: Thomas Malthus, Julian Huxley, Frederick Osborn*, New York: Mentor Books, pp. 13–59; first published 1830.
Marx, K. (1912), *Capital: a Critical Analysis of Capitalist Production*, vol. I, London: Glaisher (trans. S. Moore, E. Aveling and F. Engels), 1967 repr.
Marx, K. (1965), *Pre-capitalist Economic Formations* (1858), New York: International Publishers.
Marx, K. (1977), *A Contribution to the Critique of Political Economy* (1859), Moscow: Progress Publ., second printing.
Meillassoux, C. (1975), *Femmes, greniers et capitaux*, Paris: Maspero.
Meillassoux, C. (1979), 'Historical modalities of the exploitation and over-exploitation of labour', *Critique of Anthropology*, 13–14: 7–16.
Monsted, M. & Walji, P. (1978), *A Demographic Analysis of East Africa: A Sociological Interpretation*, Uppsala: Scandinavian Institute of African Studies.

Radcliffe-Brown, A. R. & Forde, D. (eds) (1965), *African Systems of Kinship and Marriage*, Oxford University Press.

Rey, P. -P. (1979), 'Class contradiction in lineage societies', *Critique of Anthropology*, 13, 4: 41–60.

Shanin, T. (ed.) (1971), *Peasants and Peasant Societies*, Harmondsworth: Penguin Books.

Sterkenburg, J. & de Jonge, K. (eds) (1974), *Population Growth and Economic Development in Africa*. Special Issue *Kroniek van Afrika*, New Series, Leiden: African Studies Centre.

Terray, E. (1979), 'On exploitation: elements of an autocritique', *Critique of Anthropology*, 13–14: 29–39.

United Nations (1968), *Age Data in African Censuses and Surveys*, E.C.A., Addis Ababa, paper.

van de Walle, E. (1968), 'Marriage in African censuses and inquiries', in Brass *et al.* (1968): 183–238.

Wilson, G. (1938), *The Land Rights of Individuals among the Nyakyusa*, Oxford University Press.

Wilson, G. (1959), 'The Nyakyusa of south-western Tanganyika', in Colson & Gluckman (1959): 253–91.

Wilson, M. (1963), *Good Company: a Study of Nyakyusa Age Villages*, Boston: Beacon Press.

Wilson, M. (1965), 'Nyakyusa kinship', in Radcliffe-Browne & Forde (1965): 111–39.

Wilson, M. (1977), *For Men and Elders: Change in the Relations of Generations and of Man and Woman among the Nyakyusa-Ngonde People 1875–1971*, London: International African Institute.

Wright, M. (1971), *German Missions in Tanganyika 1891–1941*, Oxford: Clarendon Press.

Chapter 3

Articulation of modes of production and the beginning of labour migration among the Diola of Senegal[1]

Jos M. van der Klei

Introduction

The Diola inhabit the larger part of the abundantly watered Lower Casamance region in southwest Senegal. They are proud and capable farmers with a strong sedentary tradition. Their villages are large and predominantly endogamous. In the nineteenth century, on the eve of the imposition of colonial rule, the villages had a high degree of political and social independence. There was no political organization above the level of the individual villages. Relations between neighbouring villages were sometimes marked by outright hostility. Consequently, the Diola preferred not to venture outside the territory of their own villages for fear of being captured and sold as slaves. But the Diola villages did have trade relations with the outside world. These relations were maintained by traders belonging to the ethnic groups surrounding the Diola, mainly the Islamic Malinke; these travelled to the Diola villages with their wares.

The area was subjected to a military pacification campaign in 1917, particularly at the insistence of French trading companies which had established themselves in the region at the end of the nineteenth century but had managed to gain only very little grip on the Diola. In subsequent years, rapidly increasing numbers of young Diola went to work as seasonal migrant labourers in the cash crop regions of the Gambia and Central Casamance.

Many writers have viewed colonialism in Black Africa, and the developments that have taken place since, within the framework of the expansion of capitalism throughout the African continent. They have stressed the fact that ever since the arrival of colonialism, Africans have increasingly applied their labour-power in production processes centred on the capitalist world market. This often necessitated migration. Modern labour migrations as generated in this context differ from traditional migrations in Africa in that the traditional migrations tended to constitute a geographical expansion of one and the same type of society and mode of production, whereas modern migrations are characterized by the fact that the migrant enters into a totally different mode of production, i.e. the capitalist one.

The question remains as to just exactly how this incorporation into the world market, now so widespread in Africa, came about at the time. It is clear that the opening up of the African labour market for capitalist market production was one of the principal aims of colonial government policies. This opening up, and the consequent start of labour migration, can be explained primarily as the result of certain policies deliberately carried out by the colonial authorities. Amin (1974b) and many other authors have been very explicit on this point. The methods used by colonial officials to further a policy of capitalist penetration in various parts of Africa included levying taxes in money, periodic forced labour for the colonial government (*corvée*), porter duties and so forth. Sometimes the incorporation into the capitalist system took place more indirectly. For example, Meillassoux (1962) showed how the suppression of African commercial trade by the colonial government led to the same result.

Although Meillassoux (1965, 1977a, 1977b) and Rey (1971, 1976) both saw this opening up of the African labour market as primarily a result of the policies carried out by the colonial government, they also noted a number of other factors. They made it clear that the developments were not solely the result of government intervention, but that internal contradictions within the African social formations could also have contributed. Rey (1971) argued that as soon as the dominant group of elders within the pre-capitalist mode of production started to demand that brideprices be paid in money, the younger people were forced to go out and earn money by selling their labour-power outside their community, i.e. in the capitalist sector. So here we find that pre-capitalist contradictions characteristic of the domestic African mode of production could serve to promote the expansion of capitalism.

In this chapter, the rapid rise of labour migration among the

Diola will be explained on the basis of the specific historic combination of these two factors (government policies and internal contradictions within the pre-capitalist mode of production). Immediately after the military pacification of the region in 1917, labour migration began among the young Diola. This was not due to direct coercion on the part of the colonial government, nor was it brought about by the brideprice mechanism. The Diola did not pay bridewealth. The function fulfilled by the brideprice elsewhere in Africa with respect to the articulation of the domestic and the capitalist modes of production is here discharged by initiation ceremonies. At these ceremonies, and on the occasion of the death of a family elder, prestige goods — notably cattle — are ostentatiously slaughtered in large numbers. In the pre-colonial period, these prestige goods were obtained from the neighbouring Malinke by trade. At the end of the nineteenth century this form of trade lost much of its importance, causing a subsequent fall in the supply of prestige goods. The reasons for the decline of cattle can be sought in the reduced demand for the products traditionally supplied by the Diola (mainly rice and slaves), and in the fact that during this period the colonial government, struggling to impose itself, made every effort to restrict internal African trade. Therefore, when we devote this chapter to the incorporation of the Diola into the market economy, special attention will have to be focused on the development of internal African trade.

First a description will be given of Lower Casamance and the Diola. Then a general account will be presented of the functioning of their mode of production as it still existed around 1900. The external trade relations that the Diola maintained with neighbouring peoples played a central role within their social formation. What did these trade relations consist of? With whom were they maintained? How did they change under the influence of the imposition of colonial rule upon the Diola and their traditional trade partners? In what way did this contribute to labour migration among the Diola, and how can the specific features of that migration (its being seasonal and confined to youth) be accounted for? These are the questions we hope to answer in the course of this chapter.

Lower Casamance and the Diola

Lower Casamance covers an area of about 100 by 100 kilometres

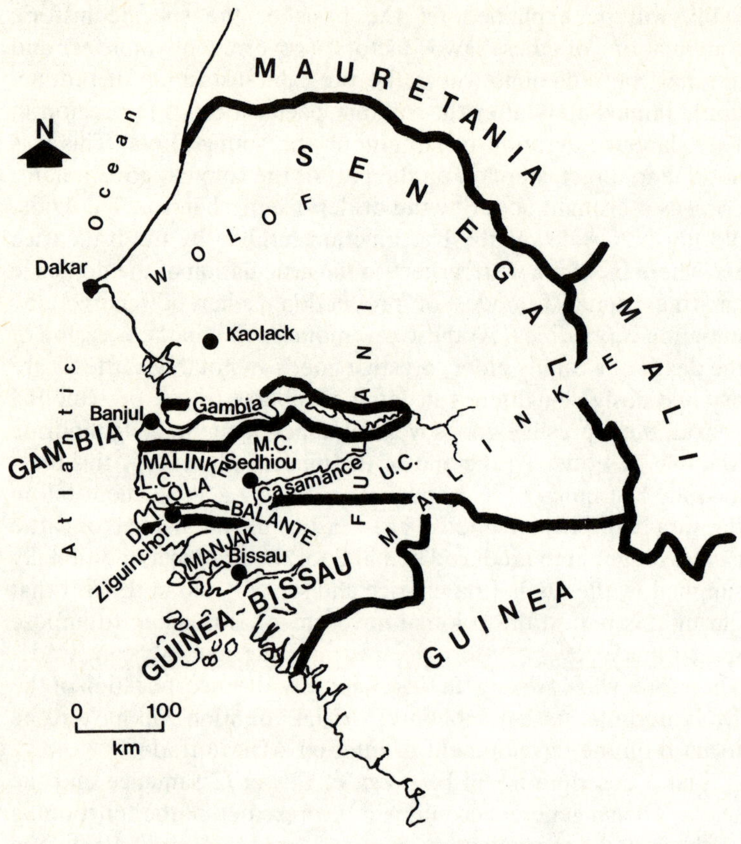

Figure 3.1   The Diola in their environment

L.C. = Lower Casamance;   M.C. = Middle Casamance;   U.C. = Upper Casamance

around the mouth of the Casamance River (see Figure 3.1). It is in
the transitional zone between the savannah and the tropical forest.
Vegetation is abundant and there is an extensive network of
waterways and creeks, all connected with the Casamance River
which here runs into the Atlantic Ocean. To the north, Lower
Casamance borders on the Gambia, a former British colony, and
to the south on Guinea-Bissau, which was formerly Portuguese:
two of the first centres of European trade in West Africa. The
Malinke live to the north and the east of the Diola region, and a
number of smaller ethnic groups, most important among whom
are the Balante and the Mandjak, live to the south.

Before the military pacification of Lower Casamance, the main occupation of the Diola was growing rice. Portuguese travellers who visited the region around 1450 noted the intensive and ingenious nature of their farming methods. The Diola grow rice on the gently sloping banks of the many tributaries of the Casamance River. The clearing of these fields required a great deal of work. The most favourably situated fields have been cultivated for centuries. A system of small dikes catches the rainwater during the rainy season (July–October), so that every year rice can be grown on the same fields.

The agricultural implements used are simple but efficient: a long arched wooden spade (*kajendo*) to cultivate the rice-fields, and knives to cut off the ears.

In farming, there is a clear division of labour between men and women: the men work the land and the women sow and harvest the crops. The cattle, constituting a considerable herd, are not commonly used as beasts of burden or as draught animals. Instead, they function as prestige objects and are ostentatiously slaughtered on special occasions.

In addition to growing rice, the Diola also hunt, fish, and gather forest produce. Since the beginning of the colonial period, fields all over the higher plateaux round the villages have been cultivated for groundnuts. Unlike rice, this crop has always been sold. In the course of the present century, many of the rice-fields that were relatively difficult to cultivate ceased to be used and very few, if any, new rice-fields were started, so that there was a fall in the production of rice. The clearing of large parts of the forest for the cultivation of groundnuts reduced the importance of hunting and gathering as a means of subsistence.

The Diola mode of production in pre-colonial times, and the importance of external trade relations

Up to 1900, before the imposition of colonial rule, the Diola villages were quite autonomous in many ways. Their contact with the outside world consisted of wars with neighbouring villages or trade with the Malinke. Therefore, as far as the characteristic features and the functioning of the pre-capitalist Diola mode of production are concerned, a description of the socio-economic structure of one village will suffice.[2]

If we try to imagine ourselves in a Diola village at the time, we would see the following picture.[3] The Diola village is a predominantly endogamous community consisting of at least two exogamous wards. Each ward (*kolole*) has its own meeting-place and sacred forest, where the ward's most important shrine (*bukin*) is located. There is a clear dividing line between the different wards of the village, and in many ways they are completely separate units. The first Frenchmen to visit the region regarded these units as individual villages, and referred to what we now call a village as a 'groupe de villages'.[4] The various wards of a village are linked to each other by marriage. Once in every twenty to twenty-five years, all the boys from the various wards of the village are initiated together in the sacred forest of one of the wards, the one recognized as being the most important. About the time of these initiation rites (*bukut*), the neighbouring villages are often raided and captives and cattle are brought back.

The population of a ward consists of the members of one or more patrilineal descent groups. These descent groups are organized in extended families (*elup*) which each inhabits its own compound (*fank*). The extended families are the most important socio-economic units. Each extended family consists of a group of close patrilineal relatives of about three or four generations with a family elder as leader. This group has a certain amount of inherited or recently cleared rice-fields, which are divided among the married male members of the group. Upon his marriage, which cannot take place until after he has been initiated, a man is apportioned a piece of his father's land to provide for his family. Polygamous marriages are rare. Women do not inherit any land. When they marry, they take up residence in their husband's ward and compound. If necessary and if available, a man can borrow rice-fields from his mother's relatives.

The captives (*amikel*) taken during the raids on neighbouring villages are not locally kept as slaves: they are either incorporated in the community or sold to the Malinke.

Each nuclear household within this patrilineal extended family has its own share of the family land. The family elder is in charge of the livestock and acts as the group's main representative to the outside world. He has the best fields and his household has the largest number of productive members.

Each nuclear household eats the rice produced on its own fields. The fields are cultivated by members of the household, but the various households in one extended family also take turns in helping in each other's fields.

Labour is organized not only on the level of the nuclear family and the extended family but also on the ward level: unmarried young men and girls are organized into age-groups which do farming work for various households in other wards of the village as well as in their own. When these groups work in their own ward, they are 'paid' with food. When they work outside their ward, they usually work for the prospective father-in-law of one of the members of the group. This labour is not remunerated since it is part of the bride-service the father-in-law is entitled to. If we draw a distinction between the elders on the one hand (who control the production factors), and the unmarried younger people (who by definition do not), then it can be said that the rice surplus controlled by the elders is mainly produced by the younger people. This rice surplus can be quite sizeable. It is a source of prestige, and it is not unusual for rice to be saved for decades.

What do the elders do with this rice surplus? Some of it is to be eaten on special occasions such as weddings, funerals and initiation ceremonies, and some of it is traded for articles that come from outside the Diola region and cannot be locally produced. In addition to iron (for weapons and tools), the main articles in this respect are prestige goods such as loincloths and, even more important, cattle.

These cattle constitute a scarce resource which has to be replenished constantly for two reasons: environmental conditions in the Diola region are not conducive to the natural reproduction of livestock (Pélissier 1966: 762); and moreover the Diola slaughter their cattle in large numbers on two occasions — at the death of a family elder, and at initiation ceremonies.

Rice is not the only means of acquiring cattle. In addition to other products such as beeswax, captives taken in the wars with other Diola villages are traded with the Malinke for cattle. These inter-village wars mainly take place when a village holds its initiation rites. The initiates have to prove their courage, usually by attacking a neighbouring village and bringing back cattle and captives.

Death of a family elder

The death of a family elder represents a situation of crisis and of transition. It means that the descent group has lost its central figure. But when the relatives of the deceased slaughter all the group's cattle on this occasion, the unity of the group is confirmed and the centrifugal forces that might lead to the segmentation of the group are countered. This communal tie acquires a very concrete form when the relatives jointly lease part of their family land to a different descent group in order to secure cattle to be slaughtered at the funeral of the family elder. For this leased land will be returned to the descent group only if, at some future time, they have amassed enough cattle to 'buy' it back.

The amount of cattle slaughtered on this kind of occasion is a public manifestation of the manpower the deceased family elder used to control when still alive: the more dependants, the more surplus production and the more prestige goods such as cattle. Thus the massive cattle-killing serves as a source of prestige for the deceased and his surviving relatives.

Initiation rites (*bukut*)

Only once in about every twenty to twenty-five years, each village holds its own initiation rites for all the young men who have not yet been circumcised. Once a man has gone through the rites, he can marry and thus gain access to the main production factors: land and labour. And in fact we see that immediately after the initiation, an entire age group of young people gets married, bringing about a village-wide redistribution of land and labour. The initiation rites are one elaborate social drama lasting about a year and reaching its climax in the circumcision of the young men in the village's central sacred forest. They then spend about two months in isolation there, and under the harshest of conditions are initiated into the secrets which are known only to initiated men. It is a part of the rites that the initiates have to fight their way into the group of initiated men. The symbol of this 'fighting their way in' is an actual fight between the older men and the initiates, which is won by the latter. The initiation also means that the young men no longer belong to the group of women and non-initiates. So before they are circumcised in the sacred forest, the prospective initiates bid farewell to their mothers. It is on the occasion of these rites that we witness the reproduction of the Diola mode of production (characterized by the dominance of a small group of married men, and within this group the elders particularly, over the unmarried

78

men and the women). The biologically reduced ranks of the group of married men are filled again by the younger men. The initiation rites take place only once in every two decades; a father and a son cannot be initiated at the same time and ideally there even has to be one *bukut* between a father's and his son's. These conditions result in the fact that Diola men marry at a relatively late age (thirty or older). Therefore the dominant group of married men remains small, and the group of dependent young men large.

On the day the initiates enter the sacred forest, large numbers of cattle are slaughtered by each descent group in the village. The meat is divided among the members of the descent group, and the relatives of the initiates' mothers also have a right to a share. During one *bukut*, most of the village's cattle are thus slaughtered altogether.

So, among the Diola, livestock proves to serve an essential function in the reproduction of the relations of production. A large group of dependent young men produces a surplus which is then controlled by a small group monopolizing the means of production. Some of this surplus is converted into cattle. On two occasions (major funerals and initiation), the killing of these cattle is an indispensable step in the process through which the descent group, and the dominant position of the elders within it, is to reproduce.

The external trade relations enabling the Diola to acquire this livestock are closely linked to the Diola mode of production. The following section will describe the development of these trade relations.

The external trade relations of the Diola over time

The period up to 1850

In the period immediately preceding the arrival of the first Europeans (1450), a considerable part of West Africa belonged to the Mali empire, which was dominated by the Malinke. The Diola were on the periphery of this empire, but most probably were never politically a part of it (Curtin 1975: 8–9). Around 1500, this empire broke up into a number of more or less autonomous states.

The fact that they occupied junctions of the internal African trade routes largely provided the economic basis for the Malinke states. The Diola were surrounded by several of these states: those along the Gambia River to the north, and the Gaabu state to the east. All the trade contacts of the Diola with the outside world took place through the intermediary of the Malinke, some of whom had by then been converted to Islam. The Diola traded prisoners, beeswax, salt and rice for cattle, iron and textiles. Starting in the fifteenth century, Europeans began to participate in West African trade, and in this region they had trading-posts on the Gambia River and (to a lesser degree) in Guinea-Bissau. Malinke traders brought various commodities from the hinterland (including the Diola region) to these 'factories', and then returned inland with European articles. Thus until the beginning of the twentieth century, the Diola were never in direct contact with European traders; at first the Malinke, and later the Afro-Portuguese as well, acted as intermediaries. Mungo Park, the explorer who visited the region at the end of the eighteenth century, described the Diola as 'a wild and unpleasant tribe', and noted this intermediary trade role of the Malinke (Park 1969: 4).[5]

The participation of Europeans in West African trade did not bring about any essential alteration in the transactions of the Diola with the outside world. However, there was a change in the provenance of some imported goods: African iron was replaced by European iron. Exported goods such as captives and beeswax were now also supplied to the European merchants by the Malinke. The import of firearms probably did much to enlarge the scale of the inter-village wars and subsequently the number of captives who were sold as slaves. The Europeans were not interested in purchasing rice, nor did they have any interest in cattle transactions. Trade in these commodities remained completely African, as did much of the slave trade. The livestock that the Diola got from the Malinke had been obtained in turn by the Malinke from the Fulani in Upper Casamance. To the north of these various ethnic groups (Diola, Malinke and Fulani), the basin of the Gambia served as a trade route.

Until the beginning of the nineteenth century, trade conducted by Europeans on these coasts was limited and irregular. The rulers of the Malinke states on the Gambia River regulated the supply of African commodities and stored them until the European ships arrived. In the eighteenth century, the slaves brought to the shores of the Gambia River to wait for transportation to America were put to productive work: they cultivated groundnuts for their masters (Curtin 1975: 230). Others, who had come there as free men with the trade caravans from the east, seeking their fortune in this trade centre while waiting for the European ships, also used their time productively by cultivating groundnuts on leased land in the area (Curtin 1975: 231). Were these groundnuts perhaps purchased by the European slave-ships as food for the slaves during the voyage?[6] Anyway, the groundnut producers on the shores of the Gambia River were the forerunners of the 'strange farmers', immigrants who made the Gambia the first groundnut-exporting region of West Africa about 1850, after the trans-Atlantic slave trade had largely subsided. By then, however, a period had begun which differed fundamentally from the previous one in which European trade was still irregular, in which the European traders had to pay the Malinke rulers toll-money for the right to conduct trade, and in which it was ultimately the Africans who set the prices. The European forts along the coasts at this period were built more to ward off the ships of other competing European nations than to impose European conditions of exchange on the Africans. However, there was a fundamental change in these relations in the course of the nineteenth century, and the middle of the century can be viewed as the turning-point.

The period from 1850 to 1917

Until the beginning of the nineteenth century, Europeans had only conducted trade with Africa and had not played any direct role in actual production there. Slaves had been the most important African export. This changed when the trans-Atlantic slave trade was formally prohibited (England 1807 and France 1816); a few decades later the European powers put an end to slavery and the slave trade in their spheres of influence in Africa (England 1833 and France 1848). These spheres of influence still only covered a very small part of the African continent, and internal African slavery and the slave trade there continued to exist up until the beginning of the twentieth century, when European control became effective throughout Africa.[7]

After the suppression of the trans-Atlantic slave trade, there was an increasing interest on the part of the Europeans in other African products. The growing industries in Europe created a need for a larger and more continuous supply of raw materials, and at the same time European technological and industrial developments (arms, steamships, railways, etc.) made it possible for a larger part of Africa to play (voluntarily or involuntarily) an active role in production for the European market. Europeans, who until then had confined themselves to their trading-posts on the coast, now made their way inland, often accompanied by military troops, in order to establish relationships with the local rulers and to make formal trade agreements.

One of the side-effects of the Europeans' conducting trade direct with the African producers was that the intermediary role played by the African rulers gradually came to be viewed as an obstacle. When the colonial powers started to make capital investments (railways, ports, roads, telegraph facilities, etc.) in order to facilitate and augment trade in manufactured commodities, the days of the political and economic autonomy of the local states were numbered, and European colonial rule was instituted. Initially the Diola were unaffected by all these developments, but the adjacent regions to the north (the Gambia and Central Senegal) and to the east (Central Casamance) were very deeply concerned. The Gambia, which had formerly been one of the most important regions exporting slaves from the interior, now became one of the foremost groundnut-producing and -exporting regions of West Africa. The same held true for the neighbouring region of Central Casamance (Curtin 1975: 141).

Who produced these groundnuts? As has already been noted, it was the 'strange farmers' or *navétanes*, seasonal migrants who had come mainly from western Mali to Senegal and the Gambia, and who either leased a plot of land there and cultivated groundnuts on it, or came to live on a farmer's property where, in exchange for food and lodgings, they worked a few days a week in their host's fields and spent the rest of the week growing groundnuts on a plot of borrowed land. The Diola did not engage in this kind of 'free' contract labour in the Gambia or anywhere else, although the Gambia did border on their region. However, it is very possible that until the beginning of the twentieth century, Diola captives were bought up by Malinke traders and put to work as slaves on the groundnut fields in the Malinke area (Central Casamance and large parts of the Gambia).

It was not until the last quarter of the nineteenth century that French trading companies were established in the Diola region itself.[8] For their trade with the Diola, they used the services of the Malinke traders, who had been playing this kind of intermediary role for centuries. Following the Conference of Berlin in 1885, Lower Casamance was allocated to France. This meant that from then on the French were to have a monopoly on trade there and could refuse to allow entry to traders from other European countries. First, the French tried to take over the existing African trade. Military expeditions were sent out to draw up an inventory of the products and the labour supply in the region. Lieutenant Noury, who headed a small military party traversing the Diola region in 1902, stated in his report:[9] 'The region is extremely rich; the plains bordering the arms of the river are fertile and produce a great deal of rice [. . .], the region has many rubber trees [. . .], they are hard workers and they have large herds of livestock.'

The French traders were not very successful. The existing flow of trade through the intermediary of the Malinke continued to be mainly directed towards the English colony of the Gambia, and the goods involved (rice, prisoners and cattle) were not for the European market. Time after time, French attempts to force the Diola villages into maintaining fixed trade relations with them proved to be in vain because the region was so inaccessible and because there were no local political leaders.[10] The villages may have formally put themselves under French 'protection' and promised to pay taxes, but as soon as the military party left the village, the Diola forgot all the agreements that had been made: 'The inhabitants do not refuse to engage in trade, but they want no part of fixed relations with the administration' (Villard 1943: 172).

The levying of taxes proved to be a sorry affair. If a village did pay taxes, it was because the French sent armed men to collect them, and even then they had to accept payment in kind (rice, cattle, rubber, etc.). As an excuse, the villagers said that they could not possibly come to the administrative posts to deliver their taxes because the neighbouring villages would not let them pass but would take them captive, which was actually the case.

In the meantime, this situation did work to the advantage of the Malinke traders, and they duly exploited it. They were the real authorities in the region, and often the people who maintained relations with the French commercial companies. They used this position to threaten the Diola with French military intervention if they were not willing to engage in trade with the Malinke on the latter's terms. Often it was also the Malinke who collected the taxes, claiming to be acting on behalf of the French. There was a gradual change in the traditional trade between the Diola and the

Malinke: such products as rubber and palm kernels came to be included, and rice ceased to be important (Roche 1975: 368).

Around 1890, the French tried to gain more direct control over the villages by appointing Malinke (who were then actually the real authorities in the region) as representatives of the colonial administration. This more or less formalized the exploiting position which the Malinke had built up on the basis of their intermediary role. In each village these new colonial representatives appointed a headman. These headmen were usually people who were part of the Malinke trade network; sanctioned by the colonial authorities, they did not hesitate to appropriate cattle and other goods for their own use under the guise of levying taxes. The French policy was a complete failure and led to rebellion among the Diola, so it was soon abandoned. All attempts to gain more control over the Diola, and particularly over their production, proved to be in vain. The French trading companies in the region lodged a complaint with the Governor in St Louis, the colonial capital, demanding that punitive expeditions be sent to the 'disobedient' Diola villages (Roche 1975: 381). However, there were not enough soldiers in Lower Casamance to undertake such a mission, and the colonial government shrank for the time being from the expenses involved in a once-for-all military pacification of the Diola. Moreover, the French troops had their hands full trying to deal with the militant Muslim leaders (*marabouts*) from Central Casamance and the Gambia who had declared war on the Diola 'heathen' at the end of the nineteenth century.

In a renewed attempt to gain economic control over the area, the Malinke traders were tackled. They were made to report for registration. The advanced trading-posts of the European companies, largely staffed by Malinke, were withdrawn so that the Diola had to emerge from their forest if they wanted to engage in trade. Payment in kind was no longer accepted. Customs posts were set up on the borders with the Gambia and Portuguese Guinea in order to restrict the existing flow of trade to those regions, and to channel it to the French trading companies (Roche 1975: 265–6). So the traditional trade-routes now formally became routes for contraband traffic. It did not have much effect, as the products still did not end up in the hands of the French trading companies. These companies even had a great deal of difficulty finding enough labourers to load the ships in Ziguinchor, the regional capital of Casamance (Roche 1976: 315).

The resistance on the part of the Diola around the turn of the century, and their refusal to adapt to and participate in production for the European market, contrasted with the attitude of the Malinke at the time. In the second half of the nineteenth century, the Malinke region was already producing groundnuts for export. This took place within relations of production that were based either on slavery or on its more contractual derivations (Pélissier 1966: 553). Unlike the Diola, the Malinke wanted to be paid in cash (Roche 1976: 316), and they purchased rice from the Europeans. In 1906, rice was, in terms of money, the most important article imported by the European traders into the Casamance region (Roche 1976: 317). This imported rice was sold not to the Diola (who produced a surplus of rice), but to the Malinke. The Malinke had increasingly replaced their food production of millet by the cultivation of groundnuts. The money they received for their groundnuts they now used to buy rice from Indo-China instead of getting it from the Diola region, as they used to do (Pélissier 1966: 762). This is sign enough that the external trade relations of the Diola significantly altered during this period. The Malinke, who had traditionally absorbed part of the Diola rice surplus in exchange for cattle and other commodities, now bought rice from the Europeans, to whom they sold their groundnuts.

It was not until France became involved in World War I in 1914, and came to be in increasingly urgent need of its colonies' products and labour, that the Diola region was firmly confronted. As late as 1917 van Vollenhoven, the Governor-General of French West Africa, lamented: 'We still do not have Lower Casamance under our control [. . .] We can no longer accept the fact that this region is a tumour in the colony while it should be its show-piece' (Roche 1975: 483).

The military pacification of Lower Casamance took place in the course of the next year, and in the following years there was a rapid growth in the direct participation of the Diola in the capitalist market economy. After that, the seasonal migration began of young Diola men to the groundnut fields of the Gambia and Central Casamance.

The military pacification of Lower Casamance and the beginning of Diola labour migration

One might assume that the start of Diola labour migration was related to the pacification of their region. Let us therefore examine just exactly what this pacification implied and see to what degree it can account for the subsequent migration.

The pacification consisted of the following aspects:

a. the periodic levying of poll-tax;
b. the enlistment of periodic forced labour for the colonial administration (*corvée*);
c. the recruitment of soldiers for the French army;
d. the disarmament of the population;
e. the appointment of village headmen;
f. instituting effective control of the borders with the Gambia and Portuguese Guinea;
g. the suppression of inter-village wars and raids;
h. the elimination of the relative trade autonomy of the Malinke.

Let us discuss these points in the order in which they are listed here.

The levying of taxes was seen by the French as well as by the Africans as the symbol of subjugation, but the French also viewed it as a means of forcing the Diola to use their labour-power for market production: 'The obligation to pay taxes will promote trade, because once they [the Diola — JvdK] are forced to have money, this will force them to work for it.' (Leprince 1905: 324).

Thus labour migration to the cash-crop regions of the Gambia and Central Casamance could be interpreted as something the Diola were compelled to do in order to earn the money they needed to pay taxes. But what happened in reality was that the migrants did not return with money. They either used their wages to buy goods on the spot, or they made a détour of some two hundred kilometres to buy cattle from the Fulani in Upper Casamance and bring them home with them (Pélissier 1966: 541, 762).

Unlike the case in many other regions of French colonial Africa, here the forced labour instituted by the French did not mean that Africans were taken from their villages to work in distant places as porters or otherwise. In Lower Casamance, forced labour was restricted to the construction and maintenance of local roads. Each village was responsible only for the stretch of road in its own territory. If the work had to be done more than 5 kilometres away from the village, meals were provided.

In the war years 1917 and 1918, the recruitment of soldiers was initially a very frightening affair for the villagers, and many of the young men fled into the forest when the recruiters approached, but in the end only a few hundred men were recruited out of a total population of approximately 100,000 (Roche 1975: 450).

When the population was disarmed, numerous rifles and other firearms did turn up, but probably an even larger number remained concealed. Moreover, new arms were smuggled in from the Gambia. Nevertheless, this disarmament contributed towards the termination of the inter-village wars and raids for which the region was notorious in earlier years.

The appointment of village headmen by the French aroused a great deal of opposition on the part of the Diola. Traditionally, the Diola villages did not have any formal leaders. In each village, the only political authority was a council of family elders or a 'big man'. The French often had a difficult time finding someone who wanted to be village chief, because the person chosen would then live in great fear of being punished by his fellow-villagers. The French gave the village headman who was finally appointed 'carte blanche' in carrying out his responsibilities, which frequently led to large-scale abuses of power (Suret-Canale 1964: 439). The village headman was the lowest rank in the French colonial administrative hierarchy, but he had a very important say in matters involving the levying of taxes, the organization of forced labour and the recruitment of soldiers.

The increased supervision of the borders with the Gambia and Portuguese Guinea did make the traditional African trade-routes more difficult — but not altogether impossible — to use.

The suppression of the raids and wars between the various Diola villages was effective. This had two significant effects on subsequent developments. In the first place, captives were no longer taken, so that this means of attaining prestige goods was eliminated. In the second place, the cessation of hostilities made it possible for the Diola to move freely outside the territory of their own village. This had previously been impossible, as is evident from written accounts and oral statements. The greater freedom of movement was a first prerequisite for the beginning of migration.

Finally, an effect of the French pacification was that the Malinke traders who, for centuries, had served as the only link between the Diola and the outside world, had to surrender this position to the French colonial authorities and the French commercial companies. They were either incorporated into the colonial trade system, where they merely served as a link, or they disappeared altogether from the scene, together with the flow of trade they had controlled for centuries (rice and slaves in exchange for cattle and other prestige goods).

No single one of all these effects of the military pacification of the Diola region can be viewed as the sole direct cause of the labour migration that began at the time. Only a combination of a number of these factors, brought to bear upon the features of the traditional Diola mode of production, and the fundamental role played by external trade relations, would enable us to fit together the separate pieces of the jigsaw puzzle in such a way as to explain the beginning of labour migration. This would lead to the following reconstruction.

In the traditional Diola mode of production, where the elders controlled the means of production, the younger people produced a surplus which the elders appropriated. Production was organized on the basis of descent groups. The elders exchanged part of the surplus for prestige goods such as cattle, which were brought in from outside the area by Malinke traders. The amount of prestige goods in the hands of a family elder reflected the number of dependants in the descent group and was thus an expression of his manpower and strength. On two occasions, which were both inevitable crisis situations in the life of the descent group, this wealth and power were publicly displayed and at the same time destroyed. Consequently, the constant supply of these prestige goods was an essential condition for the continued existence of the Diola mode of production, and thus for the power relations between the older and younger generations. About the turn of the century this supply of prestige goods was endangered, as rice (in exchange for which the Diola traditionally got their prestige goods from the Malinke) came to be less in demand. This decline began in the middle of the nineteenth century when in Central Casamance the Malinke started cultivating groundnuts for the market, using the money they got for their crops to buy Indo-Chinese rice from the European traders.

Captives, another important export product which the Diola

traditionally exchanged for prestige goods, did not cease to play this role until the time of the French pacification. Due to the eclipse of slave-raiding, the disappearance of the Malinke inter-mediary trade, and the fact that the French trading system did not take over the traditional trade flow of rice and captives in exchange for cattle and other prestige goods, the supply of prestige goods was greatly endangered.

However, this supply was re-established when young Diola, instead of using their labour-power for producing a surplus within the traditional mode of production, were sent out by the elders to work as migrant labourers within the capitalist mode of production in the groundnut fields of the Gambia and Central Casamance, both of which were Malinke regions. They either used the money they earned there to buy such goods as loincloths on the spot, or went by foot to the Fulani who lived about two hundred kilometres to the east and bought cattle from them. When they returned to their villages, these goods were handed over to the elders. Thus the supply of prestige goods was re-established.

This line of reasoning also provides an explanation for various other phenomena. When young Diola went away to work as migrant labourers, the most labour-intensive paddy fields fell into disuse; a surplus of rice for external trade purposes was no longer necessary, and the production of rice was now confined to direct food production. This also makes it clear why migration did not start until after the pacification of the Diola region. Before then, travel was too dangerous and external transactions always took place through the intermediary of the Malinke. Moreover, this also explains why it was precisely the young unmarried Diola men who went away to work as migrant labourers, why the money they earned was so often spent on prestige goods, and why this labour migration was largely confined to a specific season: a few weeks in October and November when the groundnuts were harvested (Suret-Canale 1964: 313). This migration period did not have a detrimental effect on the rice production in the Diola villages, which mainly required the men's labour in the months from July to September.

The period (immediately following the pacification of the region) during which the Diola mode of production was articulated with the capitalist one without this altering the internal relations of production of the former, was a very short one and can be viewed as transitional. For the internal relations of production were soon to undergo very drastic changes as a result of labour migration, and even more so as a result of groundnut farming, which was introduced in the Diola region by the returning migrants in the 1920s. The descent group as a production unit was to split up into separate households.

Conclusion

In this chapter I have attempted to show how and why the Diola came to participate in the capitalist market economy. This process of integration started all over West Africa at the time of the establishment and expansion of European colonialism: at the end of the nineteenth century. Amin and other authors view this integration as a direct result of colonial government policies specifically designed to promote market production among the African population. They refer in this respect to the levying of taxes, forced labour for market production, and other forms of government coercion. With the model of the domestic community or the domestic mode of production, and even more specifically with the idea of the articulation of this mode of production with the capitalist one, French Marxist anthropologists such as Meillassoux and Rey offer a new approach to this question. This enables us to see this integration process as the result not only of external coercion but also of internal contradictions (older generation versus younger generation) within the relations of production of the domestic community. Rey stressed that, in various parts of Africa, the older generation more or less forced the younger generation to go out and work in the capitalist sector by demanding that brideprices be paid in money. A similar development, however, did not occur among the Diola, among whom the function fulfilled by the brideprice elsewhere in Africa was performed by the prestige goods necessary for the initiation rites which, in turn, were a precondition for marriage. These prestige goods — cattle — were obtained from the neighbouring Malinke by means of trade. About the turn of the century, when this trade came to an end, the supply of prestige goods was endangered. The main factor in the re-establishment of the supply was the fact that the dominant group within the Diola mode of production — the elders — sent the young men off to sell their labour power outside the Diola region in the places where cash-crops were grown. The money they earned this way was spent on the traditional prestige goods, and when they returned to their villages these goods were handed over to the elders. This appears to have been the essence of the initial articulation between the old Diola mode of production and the capitalist one.

The development of internal African trade plays an important role in this chapter. It accounts for the very first incorporation of the Diola into the capitalist market economy. In the nineteenth century, the expansion of capitalism outside the Diola region appeared to have very clear repercussions for the Diola, although so far they had been only indirectly affected by the market economy through their traditional trade partners (who had been incorporated into it already). Meillassoux, especially, does not seem to appreciate this form of indirect expansion of capitalism in Africa: he views the African domestic communities and their modes of production as being more or less isolated socio-economic systems and would seem to underestimate the significance of the trade relations involving these systems.

Notes

1 This chapter is based, in part, upon field-work that I conducted in Lower Casamance in 1974 and 1975 as a member of a multi-disciplinary research team from the African Studies Centre, Leiden.

2 The Diola consist of a number of sub-groups which, though they all have certain features in common, also have their own characteristic features (Thomas, 1958, 1959, 1963, 1965). In this chapter, the Diola referred to are those living in the central part of Lower Casamance, the 'Boulouf'. Reference is primarily to the situation prevailing in the village of Diatock; structural variation in the Boulouf is not explicitly taken into account.

3 The ethnographic present in this section of the chapter clearly refers to about 1900. My historical reconstruction is based, in part, on Mark (1976) and Roche (1976). Additional oral data, and the methodological difficulties attending such reconstruction, will be discussed in my forthcoming doctoral dissertation.

4 Archives Nationales du Sénégal (Dakar), 13 G 498 5.

5 Park refers to the Diola as 'Feloops' and to the Malinke as 'Mandingo'.

6 For a long time, groundnuts were referred to in Europe as 'slave food' (Johnson 1964: 41).

7 Up until the 1870s, slaves were still shipped illegally to South and Central America. It was not until Brazil abolished slavery in 1880 that the trans-Atlantic slave trade came to an end.

8 An earlier attempt in Carabane in 1836 did not prove successful.
9 Archives Nationales du Sénégal (Dakar), 13 G 498 5.
10 Hecquard, a Frenchman who travelled through the Diola region in 1863, noted that 'Laws are laid down only by physical violence and wealth'.

References

Amin, S. (1974a), Introduction, in Amin (1974b): 3–124.

Amin, S. (ed.) (1974b), *Les Migrations contemporaines en Afrique de l'Ouest*, Oxford University Press.

Bohannan, P. & Dalton, G. (eds) (1962), *Markets in Africa*, Northwestern University Press.

Curtin, P. D. (1975), *Economic Change in Precolonial Africa*, University of Wisconsin Press.

Johnson, F. R. (1964), *The Peanut Story*, North Carolina: Mufreesboro.

Leprince, J. (1905), 'Notes sur deux tribus de la Basse-Casamance', *Revue Coloniale*, no. 33: 513–37.

Mark, P. (1976), 'Economic and Religious Change among the Diola of Boulouf (Casamance), 1890–1940', Ph.D. dissertation, University Micro Films, Yale University.

Meillassoux, C. (1962), 'Social and economic factors affecting markets in Guroland', in Bohannan & Dalton (1962): 279–98.

Meillassoux, C. (1975), *Femmes, greniers et capitaux*, Paris: Maspero.

Meillassoux, C. (1977a), 'L'évolution du commerce africain depuis le XIXe siècle en Afrique de l'Ouest', in Meillassoux 1977b: 215–74.

Meillassoux, C. (ed.) (1977b), *Terrains et théories*, Paris: Anthropos.

Park, M. (1969), *Mungo Park's Travels in Africa* (ed. R. Miller), London/New York: Dent/Dutton, reprinted (originally published in 1799).

Pélissier, P. (1966), *Les Paysans du Sénégal*, Saint-Yrieux: Imprimerie Fabrèque.

Rey, P. -P. (1971), *Colonialisme, néo-colonialisme et transition au capitalisme*, Paris: Maspero.

Rey, P. -P. (ed.) (1976), *Capitalisme négrier*, Paris: Maspero.

Roche, C. (1975), 'Conquète et résistance des peuples de Casamance 1850–1920', Lille: Université de Lille, Service de réproduction des thèses.

Roche, D. (1976), *Conquète et résistance des peuples de Casamance: 1850–1920*, Dakar/Abidjan: Nouvelles Editions Africaines.

Suret-Canale, J. (1964), *Afrique noire occidentale et centrale II: L'Ère coloniale 1900–1945*, Paris: Editions Sociales.

Thomas, L. V. (1958), *Les Diola*, vol. I, Dakar: Institut Français de l'Afrique Noire (IFAN).

Thomas, L. V. (1959), *Les Diola*, vol. II, Dakar: Institut Français de l'Afrique Noire (IFAN).

Thomas, L. V. (1963), 'Economie et ostentation chez les Diola', *Notes africaines*, no. 98: 32–42.
Thomas, L. V. (1965), 'Bukut chez les Diola Niomoun', *Notes africaines*, no. 108: 97–118.
Villard, A. (1943), *Histoire du Sénégal*, Dakar: Editions Maurice Viale.

Chapter 4

Imposing capitalist dominance through the state: The multifarious role of the colonial state in Africa

Peter Geschiere

Introduction[1]

The role of the colonial state has always been problematic as a topic in anthropology. To anthropologists of the old school, who worked in Africa under colonial rule, the colonial state did not constitute a properly anthropological subject. In their opinion, the anthropologist's main task was to analyse the functioning of 'traditional' African societies before these were disrupted by western influences. After the spate of recent publications on 'Anthropology and Colonialism', there is hardly a need to go into the shortcomings of this perspective.[2] To mention just one point: when decolonization became unavoidable in Africa, anthropologists had very little to say about the large-scale processes of change on the African continent, and were thus in danger of losing their leading position in the study of African societies to development economists, political scientists and sociologists.

After decolonization, anthropologists did devote more attention to current events and the problems they entailed: the changes at the local level, interventions by the post-colonial state, and relations between villagers and the new state authorities. In the 1960s, the colonial antecedents of the new states still received little attention: there was a clear tendency to perceive the colonial period as an interlude that was over and done with.[3] But in the 1970s it became apparent that this view also had clear limitations, and more attention was devoted to the continuity between the colonial and the post-colonial periods. After decolonization, a new African élite might have taken control of the state apparatus, but the system itself had been built up during colonial times in

94

accordance with the aims of the various colonial governments. And it was during that period that the foundations had been laid for the present position of the African political-administrative élite and for this élite's problematic relationship with the rest of the population.

Even though anthropologists and African historians now devote more attention to the colonial state, the topic remains difficult and complicated. In Africa, the role of the colonial state seems to have been extremely varied, not to say capricious. Vast regions of the African interior had been exposed to little western influence until the military conquest around the turn of the century. Particularly in those new territories, colonial exploitation confronted the European administrators with tremendous problems. The maintenance of law and order, the development of trade and the promotion of surplus production for the market made it necessary for these civil servants to engage in all kinds of experiments. Sometimes they were able to come to terms with pre-existing African authorities, but more often they had to devise new means of exerting direct pressure on the African producers. In the African setting, the conduct of the European civil servants could thus become very unexpected, sometimes grotesque and often shocking.

I came across a striking example of this in one of the first series of reports I consulted in the colonial archives of Yaoundé, the capital of Cameroon, while preparing for my field-work among the Maka (southeast Cameroon). According to the reports (dated 1938), French officials tried to carry out a number of drastic measures that year. Their aim was nothing short of a complete reorganization of village life. Villagers were to be subjected to a strict timetable. Between seven in the morning and four in the afternoon, no one was allowed to be in the village; everyone had to be out at work. Dancing, drinking and hunting were allowed only after four o'clock. The women as well as the men had to be divided into *équipes* which each had its own leader and its own job to do. The villagers were warned that there were to be regular close checks to make sure everyone was working satisfactorily. The officials were apparently aware that these measures were indeed very comprehensive, and some degree of doubt was discernible in the reports. But the tone still remained resolute. The officials were obviously not willing to let things go on as they were: in one way or another, the Maka peasants had to be forced to

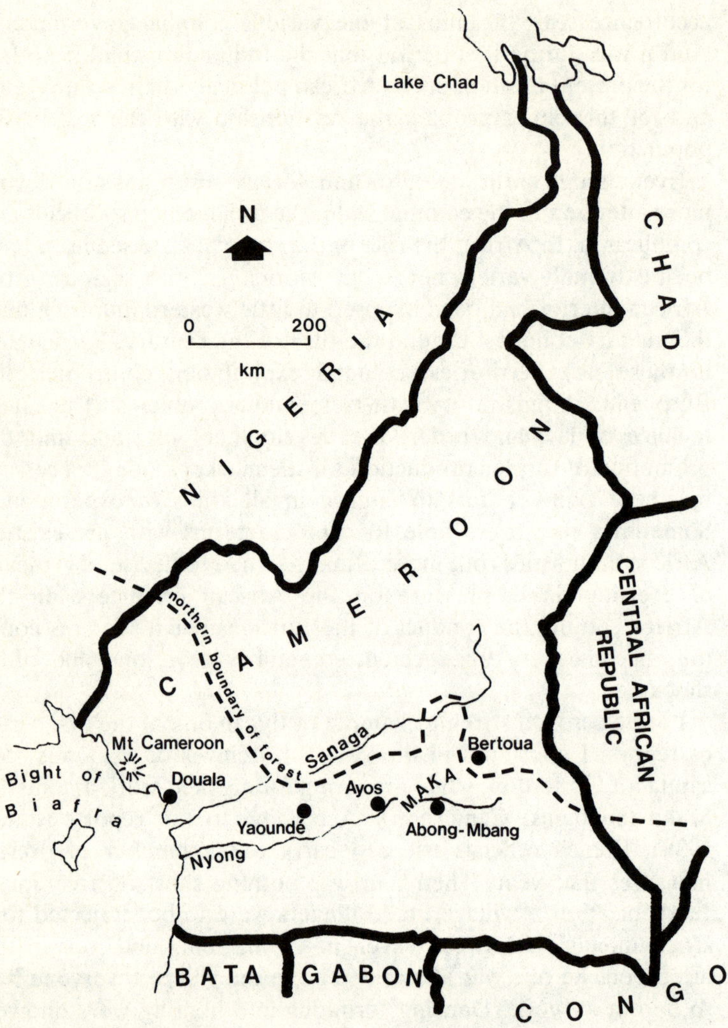

Figure 4.1 The Maka in their environment

produce more. Of course the question arises of how to account for this drastic interference by French officials in village life. Why did they consider it quite normal that, as civil servants, they should have such total control over life in the villages? This pretension was certainly not in keeping with prevalent views in the metropole on the role of the state.

96

There are only a few general discussions of the role of the colonial state in Africa which might help us to answer questions such as these. Regarding colonial administrative policy in general, there is the well-known discussion on the differences between British and French rule, i.e. between indirect rule (the British respect for the pre-existing organizational patterns) on the one hand, and assimilation (the French efforts to raise Africans to be real Frenchmen) on the other. Obviously the juxtaposition of indirect rule and assimilation can hardly clarify the example cited above of French colonial policy in Makaland. The concept of assimilation is totally incapable of explaining why French officials attempted such a drastic reorganization of Maka village life in 1938. The reasons given by the officials themselves had much more to do with the *mise en valeur* (exploitation) of the areas and the necessity to increase the productivity of the Maka. Concepts such as indirect rule or assimilation were part of the official ideology of the colonial powers, and therefore quite unsuited to serve as the basis for a truly analytical model of the colonial state and of the various effects of government intervention on the local level.[4]

A more analytical view of the role of the colonial state can, however, be deduced from the theories of the French anthropologists introduced earlier in this book, who try to apply Marxist concepts to anthropological data.[5] In particular, their idea of an articulation of different modes of production seems to be highly relevant to our topic. In their view, the changes on the African continent in the twentieth century can be characterized as a process in which the old pre-capitalist communities became increasingly subservient to the functioning of the dominant capitalist mode of production. To a certain extent, the old production communities did retain their coherence, but at the same time they had to supply surplus labour for the further development of trade and of the new capitalist sectors. This articulation of old and new relations of production could be achieved in a wide range of ways, depending on the specific form of the capitalist penetration and, even more, on the specific 'footholds' offered by the pre-capitalist patterns of organization. An important question, for instance, is the degree to which capitalist expansion could fit in with existing forms of paying tribute or of production for the market. It is in the context of the laborious establishment of capitalist dominance over the old production communities that the colonial state had to play its role.

And it is against this background of various articulation patterns and possibilities that variations in the impact of the colonial state can be accounted for.

Until now, the French Marxist anthropologists usually only touched in passing upon the role of the state. The purpose of this chapter is to investigate further at close range how their model of an articulation of modes of production can help to analyse the specific features and variations in the role of the colonial state in Africa. Our explorations will be based notably on some empirical examples from Cameroon and French Equatorial Africa. In the last sections, the relevance of the discussion to present-day conditions will be assessed. To what extent can this type of analysis of the colonial state provide an insight into the role of the post-colonial state — frequently characterized as 'capricious' or 'unpredictable' — and of the ruling groups in modern Africa?

An example: Colonial officials trying to reorganize Maka peasant production

The events in Makaland (southeast Cameroon) briefly referred to above can serve as the starting-point for our discussion.[6] What exactly were the French colonial officials trying to achieve at the time? In the first place, it must be noted that such interventions by the French were nothing new to the Maka. Previous colonial officials had also decided that drastic measures were necessary in order to make the Maka produce surpluses for the market, with an eye to the development of colonial trade. For decades, officials had complained about the area's utter stagnation. It looked as though every effort to promote the exploitation and the economic development of the region was to be in vain. Makaland had always been a problem area of the colony. The Germans, the first colonial rulers of Cameroon, had met with great difficulties in their attempts to subjugate the tiny Maka group. After 1904, several military expeditions were necessary in order to gain control over the area, and it was not until 1910 that it was 'pacified'. The military problems of the Germans can partly be explained by the lay of the land. The Maka live in a dense and swampy forest, traversed by numerous brooks and creeks. This gave them ample opportunity to evade the German expeditions or to make surprise attacks themselves. But the main obstacle to the German attempts to pacify the region was the social organization of the Maka, reflecting their love of liberty and their aversion to any outside authority.

The old Maka organization was strongly segmentary. In principle, each patrilineage (the largest exogamous kinship group) constituted an independent village, usually with little more than 100 inhabitants, and there was no co-ordinating authority of any kind between the villages. Nor were authority relations within the villages very strict. As heads of families the elders did have a certain degree of control, but there were strong levelling counterforces. As soon as the authority of an elder came to be experienced as oppressive, the group would split up. Then dissatisfied persons would leave, making their way into the forest in order to found a village of their own. So it was no easy matter for the Maka to adjust to the new colonial subjugation. The very idea that adult men could simply be ordered by strangers to do all kinds of jobs (for instance as porters, or to work on the roads) completely bewildered them. Precisely because, under the old system of relations, there had been no levying of tribute and no central authority, nor any self-evident form of hierarchy between the kingroups, draconian measures proved to be necessary in order to establish the new colonial relations of authority.

Nevertheless, the area initially seemed to have great economic potential. About 1900, German merchants estimated that this region was one of the richest rubber areas of Africa. The German conquest was accelerated by rumours that Dutch and Belgian traders had already gained access to these resources by way of the water network of the Congo rivers. Under German rule, however, the rubber trade soon grew so chaotic that it became sheer plunder. Trade caravans in search of the 'black gold of the jungle' set out to pillage the widely dispersed villages in this inhospitable region, not only to acquire food but also to force the men to work as porters. The rubber trees were often simply chopped down instead of being tapped, so that production soon began to decrease. Moreover, after 1910, rubber from the plantations of southeast Asia, which was of considerably better quality, began to present serious competition on the world market. Thus the trade in wild rubber from the Maka area was soon to collapse for good.

Shortly after the outbreak of World War II, the French conquered this part of the German colony. But as far as politico-economic problems were concerned, this did not change matters very much. The French officials also complained vociferously about how difficult it was to get the Maka to work harder; colonial trade would never flourish if things went on like that. Just as in the German period, there was a great shortage of labour. The Maka region was (and is) extremely thinly populated. Moreover, it was infested with sleeping-sickness, so that draught-animals could not survive there. All the trade goods had to be carried by porters. So it is obvious why traders as well as officials were constantly searching for new porters. Moreover, a large number of men were needed for the construction and maintenance of the long roads to the coast. And, most important, labour had to be mobilized in one way or another to supply products for the market. Before the colonial conquest, there were no regular markets in the area, nor were the Maka accustomed to regularly producing surplus goods to trade with.[7] If colonial trade was to develop in the region, the Maka would have to be spurred on to greater efforts.

French colonial officials tried to solve this 'labour problem' with the usual coercive measures: the levying of taxes in money so that the peasants had to sell some products on the market in order to acquire money, the constant requisitioning of labour for the government and for the French *colons* (traders and planters), and furthermore, the forced cultivation of market crops. In order to carry out these measures the French, like the Germans before them, imposed a complete resettlement of the Maka communities. The patrilineages, until then scattered throughout the forest, each in their own small village, were forced to settle alongside the new roads. This was to make it easier to keep a check on them. Moreover, larger villages were formed in which several patrilineages were forced to live together. Each village was placed under the command of one village chief, a completely new type of leader, appointed by the colonial authorities. The chief was expected to exercise authority over the other patrilineages in his village as well. He was also held responsible for carrying out government orders, particularly with respect to the requisitioning of labour and the levying of taxes.

In the Maka region, the chaos due to the constant requisitioning of labour was made even worse by severe epidemics (especially of sleeping-sickness). After the colonial conquest, the relative isolation of the villages was broken. Moreover, in the trade caravans and in the road construction gangs, workers were crowded together under the most miserable living conditions.

100

Under these circumstances, old and new diseases could spread like wildfire. Many Maka reacted to all these unsettling events by migrating. Some moved deeper into the forest to get away from the pressure exercised by the new authorities. Others sought refuge in the nearby Centre-Sud province which had been opened up earlier and where politico-economic relations had already become more stable. Consequently in the 1920s and 1930s, French officials repeatedly expressed the fear that, in this region, because of epidemics and migration, not enough labour would be left to keep the administration going — i.e. to see to the maintenance of the roads and the food-supply for the administrative centres. One official concluded in an offhand manner that the Djem, the Maka's neighbours, were 'apparently doomed to disappear from the face of the earth — which has also been the fate of other peoples who didn't know how to profit from the potential of their natural surroundings.'[8]

As was also the case in other parts of the French colonial empire, the increasing under-population threatened to make colonial exploitation impossible. The French authorities reacted by organizing an extensive campaign in the region against the sleeping-sickness; in the course of the 1930s this campaign was quite effective. Moreover, in order to make sure that a sufficient number of workers remained, the officials also instituted strict police-checks along the borders with other provinces in the hope of again stabilizing the population. Only if the villagers stayed in their own villages would it be possible to keep a check on them and to force them to make greater productive efforts. Only then could taxes be levied, and only then could traders buy and sell their merchandise, and the exploitation of this 'refractory' forest region be effective.[9]

It is in the context of this policy that our first example, the large-scale actions of 1938, is to be seen.[10] The reports by Pernet, one of the officials involved, give a detailed account of his experiences. He was driven by truck from Abong Mbang, the administrative centre of Makaland, to the ferry at Ayos, a distance of fifty miles. From there he travelled back, carried in a litter — a fourteen-day trip from one village to the next — to announce the official orders. The essence of these orders has already been briefly indicated. From then on, the villagers had to work every day from seven in the morning to four in the afternoon. Only after four o'clock were they free to do as they pleased — to dance, hunt, go to sleep or visit the mission church. The women were divided into *équipes*,

101

each with its own *capita-femme* or 'woman captain', a kind of leader that was completely new to the Maka. Each team had to work two days a month on the upkeep of the village in accordance with detailed instructions; thus, weeds had to be cleared away in an area of fifteen yards around the houses and thirty yards at the entrance to the village. On the other days of the month, they had their farming work to do. Each woman had to cultivate a field of sixty yards for food crops (cassava, bananas, maize etc.) and a second field of the same size for groundnuts to be sold on the market. In addition, they had to grow a certain amount of rice, also for the market, and take care of the already existing fields, because 'that is not much trouble'. The men were likewise divided into teams, each with its own specific task. One team had to see to the maintenance of the roads. Another was in charge of keeping the houses and the fences round the village in good repair and of cultivating coffee and cocoa. A third team had to go into the forest to pick palm-nuts and to tap rubber. Each man had to take at least fifty-five pounds of rubber to the market every month. Only the men who had managed to get themselves employed as wage-labourers (for the *colons* — the French traders and planters — or for the government) were exempt from all these duties.

No one was allowed to leave the village without the permission of the village chief. 'Vagrants' were to be arrested by the authorities and severely punished. In addition, within a fortnight everyone was to have bought a blanket and a bar of soap from the European traders. Dirty people would no longer be admitted to the government offices. Pernet also announced that in the future the government would keep a constant check to make sure that all these orders were being carried out. The village chief would have to report to the proper authorities anyone who was 'lazy'. Within a month, Pernet was to make another tour of all the villages with his gendarmes to 'discipline' anyone who had been 'disobedient'. But that was not all: in the meantime, the European traders were to keep an eye on things and let the authorities know if there were any villages where the new orders were not being observed strictly enough.

To anyone who knows anything about life in the Maka villages, it must be clear that Pernet and the other officials were playing a Don Quixote role. The carrying out of these types of totalitarian measures would be problematic anywhere, but within Maka society it was (and is) totally unfeasible. Even today, the men in the villages rarely work according to any fixed schedule. Every man works as he sees fit. Some of them stay on the coffee and cocoa plantations for a couple of days in a row, spending the night in temporary shelters. Then they spend the next few days in the village, where there are always issues calling for immediate — and extensive— discussion. Moreover, it is an absolute necessity that certain festivities and ceremonies be attended elsewhere in the region (marriages and, even more important, funerals) in order to maintain the vast network of familial relations outside the village. Hunting also was and still is an extremely irregular form of production.

To the Maka, it is still inconceivable that anyone could command a man to work on his own land. After the colonial conquest, they may have learned that in the towns a new kind of obedience is called for towards the new authorities, but in the villages the right of every able-bodied man to run his own life as he sees fit is still virtually unaffected. In principle, the same holds true for the women: they also largely schedule their work in the fields as they see fit. But it must be noted that their farming tasks, which are much more extensive than those of the men, and their domestic duties do require a greater degree of regularity.

In view of the rather irregular working habits of the Maka and the traditional autonomy of each producer (man or woman) in organizing his or her own work, it is no wonder that Pernet's next trip in 1938 was a great disappointment. The traders had already told him that most of the women started to clear the new fields only after they heard that he had left Abong Mbang on his way to them. When Pernet arrived in a village, people often told him that they certainly had started new clearings, but that the fields were too far away in the forest for Pernet to come and see them. The maintenance of the roads had not improved much, either. Most of the men did not start working until they heard the sound of an automobile in the distance, and as soon as the vehicle had disappeared from sight they would stop again. Pernet blamed all these problems on the lack of any real authority in the villages. The *capita-femmes* whom he had appointed did do their best, but their own husbands were the first to ridicule them. Of course, this was hardly surprising since the Maka had never heard of women playing a leadership role outside the specific framework of kin relations. But Pernet's greatest dissatisfaction was occasioned by the village chiefs, because they did not even dare to command the villagers to work for fear of them running away into the forest or to the town. This again is hardly surprising, in retrospect. As has been noted above, the idea that these village chiefs could exercise authority over the various patrilineages in their village was also completely new to the Maka. In former times, all an elder could expect was obedience from his direct descendants. Of course, as representatives of the new government, the village chiefs had new types of sanctions: gendarmes with their handcuffs and their whips, the threat of the prison in the new administrative centre. But apparently the coercive methods of the new authorities — no matter how impressive they may have been in the eyes of the Maka — were not sufficient to enforce a complete reorganization of village life.

What led these French colonial officials to such totalitarian ambitions? In Europe, it certainly was not common practice for the state to try and regulate the lives of citizens in such great detail. Organizing work-brigades of peasants or obliging producers to stick to fixed working-hours were never tasks of the state (such developments were rather effected by the market mechanism and by interventions of private entrepreneurs). Nor was it common practice for state officials to force people to buy particular commodities (as was the case with the blankets and the soap in the example cited above). Why did the French officials in Makaland apparently take it for granted that matters like these were prerogatives of the colonial state? French administrative reports from this period usually justify this line of conduct in racist terms. According to these officials, the 'native' was afflicted with 'a gentle inertia' which 'kept him from expending energy and engaging in productive activity'. They referred to

> the indolence and laziness of people whose evolution has not
> yet reached a stage enabling them to accept the principles of our
> economy[. . .] The law of supply and demand may stimulate
> civilized people to engage in productive activities, but this does
> not hold true for these carefree primitive people, whose needs
> are few, who depend on nature and are wary of exertion, which
> is the only thing that leads to material and moral progress
> [. . .] The only remedy is to force them to work.[11]

Obviously, only the state could administer this remedy.

Later developments among the Maka by no means confirmed this kind of racist stereotype. After 1945, when there was a considerable rise in the prices of coffee and cocoa on the world market and these new market products did offer obvious benefits to the villagers, there was little evidence of any 'inertia' or 'indolence' on the part of the Maka. Without government coercion of any kind, the villagers were quite willing to expand their coffee and cocoa plantations rapidly, turning the Maka region into the richest part of the eastern province. Social scientists today are less inclined to explain the problems of state officials organizing the exploitation of the newly colonized territories in terms of racial differences; instead, they devote their attention to specific features of the colonial economy. In the above-mentioned perspective of an articulation of modes of production, the developments in Makaland are a typical example of the difficult imposition of a capitalist market economy on a 'domestic' mode of production in which, up to then, market trade had played only a minor role. The basic problem facing the French conquerors was how to utilize the old production communities for the development of the colonial (capitalist) economy. From the example above, it is evident that the French authorities in Makaland soon realized that the rapid depopulation and the destruction of the village communities would make any further form of *mise en valeur* impossible in the region. Therefore government policy became more oriented towards stabilising the old production communities. It was *within* these communities that producers had to be compelled to supply new surplus goods and it was these communities that had to provide cheap labour so that the capitalist sector (in Makaland, mainly colonial trade) could develop. In the words of Rey (1976: 50), 'Capitalism subjugates the older modes of production, it feeds on the labour, the foodstuffs and the raw materials taken from the older modes.'

The colonial state and the imposition of capitalist dominance

In this perspective of an arduous articulation of the old pre-colonial patterns and the new capitalist relations, it is evident that the difficulties encountered by the colonial state in Makaland were not exceptional. Of course, the conquest of the Maka region was part of a much larger process, the notorious 'scramble for Africa' at the close of the nineteenth century. Until 1880, the European presence in most parts of the African continent was still restricted to a few settlements — trade factories — along the coast. However, there was growing competition between the various European powers for access to the interior of Africa, and after 1880 the conquest of the continent took place at a rapid pace. In 1884 and 1885, the Congress of Berlin drew borders all across Africa, and in the ensuing decades the various European governments were busy establishing their authority in the spheres of influence granted to them. Thus capitalist relations were introduced in vast areas which had hitherto experienced hardly any capitalist influence. In large parts of the interior, European trade had not yet penetrated, and the invasion of the colonial armies was the first confrontation with white man. In these regions, the establishment of colonial rule brought a completely new way of life. The exploitation of these areas often proved to be virtually impracticable because of the absence of roads to the coast, the low population density and the unfavourable climate. Nevertheless, the colonial authorities were determined to get some kind of profit out of these regions as well. In each part of the colony, the *mise en valeur* had to be realized in one way or another. No matter how, the vast newly-conquered regions were also to be incorporated into the economic system dominated by the mother country.

The French anthropologists quoted above emphasize that the establishment of capitalist dominance in such peripheral regions was a far from automatic process. In Rey's view, old production communities can effectively resist capitalism by defending their autarky. With every new expansion in a non-capitalist environment, the first problem for capitalism is how to 'make a breach' in that autarky (Rey 1976: 55). As is sometimes the case with Rey's formulations, the objection can be raised that modes of production seem to be presented here as if they were acting persons; consequently any possible discrepancies between the conscious motives of the human actors and the structural implications of modes of production may be overlooked.[12] Nevertheless, Rey notes a very real problem: as long as a peasant community lives off its own products and makes its own means of production, it is difficult to involve it in the development of capitalism. Capitalist expansion presumes that labour is recruited and new markets are opened up within the pre-capitalist communities or that capital can be invested there. As long as a peasant community is not dependent on the market and not really incorporated into the money economy, the possibility of autarky continues to exist.

106

Then neither the sale of capitalist products, nor the supply of raw materials or labour, nor the investment of capital are an 'automatic' process (i.e. ensured by the market mechanism).

During the first decades after the colonial conquest, this problem manifested itself all over Africa in various forms. But nearly everywhere the general solution was to be the same. The direct representatives of capitalist interests, the European firms, turned to the colonial state for help. There may have been considerable differences within colonial Africa in the exact form of government intervention, in part due to the different relationships which the colonizers encountered locally. But the principle remained the same: the colonial state had to play a crucial role in the establishment of capitalist dominance; it had to dismantle the autarky of the old production communities so as to facilitate further capitalist expansion.

This general pattern is clearly illustrated by the events involving the very first establishment of colonial rule in Cameroon: the German occupation of the port of Duala in 1884. In that year, the German explorer and scientist Nachtigal, commissioned by Bismarck, sailed the cruiser *Die Möwe* to the Bight of Biafra. Nachtigal landed in Duala, signed treaties with several local 'kings' and hoisted the German flag. The news hit Europe like a bombshell. It was one more of Bismarck's many surprise moves in the complicated game of European diplomacy. At that time there were many British, German and French trading-posts all along the Bight of Biafra. The British in particular were indignant at Bismarck's manoeuvre. Up till then, the British merchants had occupied a privileged position in Duala. Moreover, Bismarck was said to have deliberately misled the British Foreign Office about the real aims of Nachtigal's expedition. The British consuls on the coasts of Africa had even had orders from London to help Nachtigal with his 'exploration'. Five days after the hoisting of the German flag in Duala, the British consul Hewett, later often referred to as 'Too Late Hewett', arrived on the spot with similar orders to sign treaties with the Duala chiefs. It was not until he got there that he heard about the Germans landing and occupying Duala. His attempts to get the Duala chiefs to reconsider and accept British sovereignty were in vain.

So it does seem somewhat fortuitous that Cameroon became a German colony rather than a British one (and that afterwards, during World War I, it was to be largely conquered by the

French). Nevertheless, the establishment of colonial rule as such did have a clear structural background. Bismarck's surprising move did not simply come out of the blue. The German chancellor had received numerous requests, mostly from Hamburg trading firms, to subject this part of the African coast to German rule. Nachtigal arrived in Duala with official instructions from Bismarck, but the appendix included a more extensive and more specific instructions from two firms in Hamburg. Consequently Rudin (1938: 38) draws the following conclusion: 'Thus, Nachtigal, an imperial commissioner, became in a very real sense the personal emissary of two German commercial houses, Woerman and Jantzen & Thormählen.'

Why did these firms turn to the German state for help? A memorandum sent to Bismarck by the Hamburg Chamber of Commerce a year earlier makes the answer quite clear. It gave the following reasons for a German state intervention in Africa:

> The interior of Central Africa, its dense population [*sic*] of potential consumers and its large markets, mentioned by all the explorers, offers a very favourable outlet for the products of European industry [. . .] Therefore it is of great importance to open up this outlet for the German industry, which needs export possibilities; but this is hindered both by *other foreign colonies* and by the *independent Negro tribes* living along the coast.

Direct contact with the interior:

> can be realized only . . . if the coast *is brought under direct control of a European power*; and it is the power that occupies the coast that will have the lion's share of the commerce.

(quoted from Stoecker 1960: 57; emphasis added).

The reasons touched upon in this quotation for bringing the Duala coast under German rule were explained in greater detail in the rest of the memorandum. In the first place, there was the need to protect German traders from the British and French competition (the 'other foreign colonies'). Here state intervention manifested itself as a logical consequence of the internal contradictions within European capitalism — the increasing competition between England on the one hand, and the countries that became industrialized at a later date, such as France and Germany, on the other.

In addition, the Hamburg traders considered the establishment

108

of colonial rule to be necessary to open up the hitherto almost inaccessible market potential of the inland regions, of which they evidently had such high expectations (see Wirz 1972: 21). Apparently trade could not expand rapidly enough by way of the economic mechanism of supply and demand. Government intervention had to break down the relative autarky of the old production communities in the interior.

The German colonial state and the 'labour problem' in Cameroon

The same general problem manifested itself in a somewhat different form in the course of the second decade of German colonial rule in Cameroon. At the turn of the century, the colonial economy became more complex. Exploitation of the colony turned out to be feasible not only by means of trade, but by means of a plantation system as well. In the course of the 1890s, the Germans discovered that, just beyond the Duala coast, conditions were quite favourable for setting up European plantations. On the slopes of Mount Cameroon, the climate was less detrimental to the Europeans' health than on the coast. Moreover, the soil there proved to be very suitable for growing cocoa. As time went on, however, the development of the plantations did not turn out to be an unmitigated blessing for the colony. The German planters came to have an insatiable need for new labourers. This was to be a heavy burden on the shoulders of the colonial authorities, and it was to poison relations within the German colonial community.

Initially, the German planters recruited many of their African labourers from outside Cameroon (from Senegal, Sierra Leone, Fernando Po and other parts of the African coast where wage-labour had already been developed). However, this recruitment became more and more difficult because France, England and Spain objected to the drain of labour from their colonies. In 1887 the German government itself had unconditionally forbidden the shipping of labourers from Cameroon to other parts of Africa, evidently with the intention of reserving the much needed labourers for employment within the colony.

At first the population in the immediate vicinity of the plantations could satisfy the German demands for labour. Due to the confiscation of land for the expansion of the European plantations, the African peasants who had formerly worked this land had little choice now but to engage in wage-labour. But the planters needed more and more labour, and they did not succeed in attracting labourers from further away. In their opinion, the solution was obvious: new labour reservoirs had to be tapped in the inland regions. This was why the planters exerted pressure on the government to hasten the conquest of the inland regions, for that was where new and much larger supplies of labour were to be found. And it did indeed become common practice for the German colonial authorities to requisition *Strafarbeiter* (convicts) from the defeated population after the conquest or after the quelling of a rebellion. These *Strafarbeiter*, serving a term of two years or longer, could be used for government projects such as the construction of railways. Quite often the men were also transported to the coastal region, to the German plantations near Mount Cameroon. Even after the final 'pacification', the recruitment of plantation labourers in the inland regions continued to be enforced by all sorts of official coercion (Rudin 1938: 320; Hausen 1970: 163).

Under these circumstances, the 'labour problem' became the subject of heated political conflicts in German colonial circles. The traders in particular felt that their interests were endangered by the deportation of labourers from the inland regions, whether by force or on the basis of 'voluntary' contracts. Especially in the more remote areas, the traders were in great need of porters. Furthermore, their trade would collapse if too many labourers were removed from the villages and no surplus goods were to be produced there any longer. Consequently, after 1900, the colonial authorities had constantly to juggle the conflicting demands of the traders and the planters. But on certain occasions, these two factions joined to form a united front against the authorities, if in their opinion the government was recruiting too many labourers for its own projects. For example, the advisory council of the colony (which consisted of representatives of the various white interest groups) threatened to veto a government proposal for extending a railway if the authorities did not promise to put more labourers at the disposal of private enterprise.[13]

In the end, the planters as well as the traders turned out to be completely dependent on the government for the solution to their 'labour problem'. Up to the end of German rule all their attempts to recruit labourers themselves — by promising them money, liquor or arms — had met with very little success. This was not at all surprising, since to the population of the interior, employment

110

on the plantations near the coast must have been roughly equivalent to a death sentence (Mandeng 1973: 93). According to official figures, the annual death-rates among the labourers on some of the plantations were 20% or higher. At one plantation, a mortality rate of 'only' 7½% was referred to as an 'excellent' record. According to officials in the interior, usually fewer than half of a contingent of forced labourers were still alive when their period of work (two or three years) was over. Mortality among the workers was appallingly high, not only becuse of the poor living and working conditions, but also because along the coast, the prevailing diseases and the food habits were very different from those in the interior. Labourers working for the traders encountered conditions that were hardly any more favourable. As porters in the trade caravans, they were often chained together to prevent them from escaping. They also had to march long distances through unfamiliar regions where the living conditions were completely new to them (Rudin 1938: 328; Hausen 1970: 164; Rüger 1960: 221).

So it is no wonder the villagers often fled into the forest as soon as rumours started that labour recruiters had been spotted in the area. There were recurrent complaints from German recruiting agents employed by private enterprise that their task was impossible. Only the granting of official status would enable them to inspire the villagers' respect enough to make recruiting possible. In 1913 the government drew its conclusions: it prohibited all recruitment by private persons. From then on, only government officials were allowed to recruit labourers or draw up labour contracts. For every labourer they were provided with, the planters and traders were to pay the government a fixed amount. Just as in the first example — the attempt of the French authorities to reorganize life in the Maka villages — it is again striking how directly the colonial state interfered with economic developments. In the end, the German government assumed complete responsibility for solving the labour problem of the German traders and planters in the colony.

Variations in the role of the colonial state: Differing 'footholds' offered by the pre-existing relations of production

Of course, in Europe as well, during the development of

capitalism, the state did intervene to help to solve the labour problem. In the seventeenth, eighteenth and nineteenth centuries, 'poor laws' against idleness and vagrancy were proclaimed in practically all the countries of Europe. So here the state also helped to discipline and organize the working class. In Europe as well, this kind of state intervention was clearly in keeping with the demand for wage-labour in the developing capitalist sector. Nevertheless, there were important differences from the African examples cited above. In Europe, the governments did not use direct coercion to extract labourers from the old production communities. Indeed, that was hardly necessary. Ever since the fifteenth century, changes had been taking place in feudal agriculture which had 'automatically' freed labour from the rural production processes. In the Europe of the late middle ages, particularly in England, the development of trade could fit in with the basic contradiction in feudal society between landlords and serfs. The feudal lords developed an increasing need for money — for new kinds of arms, and for luxury commodities required for representative purposes at the royal court. The serfs' feudal obligations (land-rent) were transformed more and more into money, and this process was of crucial importance to the further development of wage-labour and of capitalist labour relations. In Europe, it was the intensification of the contradictions within the old feudal society itself which provided the foundation for the growth of capitalism. In many regions a 'class alliance' was possible: the interests of the feudal landlords and the capitalist entrepreneurs were largely parallel. The development of urban industry created new markets for agricultural products, which stimulated the landlords to rationalize their farming systems. Of course a well-known example was the 'enclosure movement' starting in the sixteenth century in England, where the feudal lords switched to sheep-breeding for the wool industry, so that they needed less labour and earned more money. The result of all these developments was that an increasing number of people were driven off the land and became available as 'free' workers for wage-labour within capitalist forms of production.

The above is a very brief and certainly too simplified version of the analysis by Rey (and Marx) of the articulation of feudal and capitalist relations of production in Europe. Still, it can provide some insight into our subject, the role of the colonial state.[14] Apparently, in large parts of Africa, capitalist expansion required different methods because there pre-capitalist relations offered fewer 'footholds' than in Europe. In the examples from Cameroon cited above, the colonial state clearly had to play such a large role in solving labour problems because there were hardly any possibilities for capitalist entrepreneurs to enter into 'class alliances' with dominant groups from the old modes of production. To put it in more general terms: wherever sharp contradictions have developed within the old production relations, as was the case in feudal western Europe, capitalist entrepreneurs can find 'footholds' within the old production communities themselves to aid them in their efforts to develop surplus production, trade and wage-labour. If such possibilities are extremely restricted, as was the case in the forest of southern Cameroon, entrepreneurs become more dependent on intervention by the state, employing its coercive means to 'break open' the old production communities and adapt them to the demands of the capitalist system (see Geschiere 1981, in press, a).

Of course, in this respect there is no sharp contrast between Europe, as a continent, on the one hand, and Africa on the other. It is rather a question of gradual differences. In Africa, examples can also be found of 'class alliances': pre-capitalist power groups who served as 'footholds' for the activities of European entrepreneurs. Apparently, in Africa, this role could be played by very different groups: in Buganda, for instance, by an élite of pre-colonial chiefs, and in central Senegal by the marabouts of the Murids, an Islamic brotherhood (see Mamdani 1976; Cruise O'Brien 1971). None the less, the possibilities for 'class alliances' in these regions of Africa were clearly not so great as to make the capitalist development a virtually 'automatic' process (in other words a process mainly propelled by the market mechanism, as was the case in some parts of Europe). In these parts of Africa as well, state intervention remained necessary in order to stimulate production for the capitalist market. In Buganda, for example, the state abruptly introduced a completely new form of landed property, suddenly turning the old Ganda chiefs into large landowners with their own tenants. In the first years after the colonial conquest, this was to lead to a surprisingly rapid development of cotton production in this area. In central Senegal, the colonial state helped to drive the original inhabitants (Fulani cattle-nomads) from the *Terres Neuves*, so that these 'new lands' could be cultivated. This stimulated the equally rapid development of groundnut farming under the supervision of the Murid marabouts. Here again, the colonial state saw to the construction of the roads and railways needed to transport the cash-crops (see Suret-Canale 1964:339; Cruise O'Brien 1971).

Thus, even in these African examples, the state had to intervene more directly in the imposition of capitalist relationships than in Europe. But this state intervention was still less direct than in the Cameroonian examples referred to above. In Buganda or among the Murids of Senegal, existing forms of surplus labour and tribute could be used to help to solve the labour problem of capitalist entrepreneurs, and for the production of new surplus goods for colonial trade.

Sharply contrasting examples of how capitalist dominance could be established, and of the role of the colonial state, are to be found in French Equatorial Africa. Here the colonial authorities found it necessary to institute the same kinds of drastic measures as in Makaland in order forcibly to bring about a rise in the production of new surpluses. In most parts of French Equatorial Africa, the old relations of production exhibited much the same characteristics as in Makaland. In this area, prior to the establishment of colonial rule, there had also scarcely been any development of tributes or *corvées*. Nor was there any regular surplus production for trade. Except in the coastal area and along the Congo rivers, regular markets were still unknown. Thus the pre-capitalist organization here again provided very few 'footholds' for capitalist entrepreneurs. Indeed, in these regions, after the colonial conquest the 'labour problem' manifested itself as sharply as in southern Cameroon. Here it was again the colonial state that had to step in: until after 1930, the French authorities considered the same kinds of raiding-parties for labourers to be as necessary as did the Germans in Cameroon. And here also it was mainly the involvement of the colonial state in the labour problem that threatened to lead to a general disruption in some regions.[15]

Suret-Canale (1964: 56) cites official figures showing that in the second decade of the nineteenth century the total population of this part of the French empire (Congo-Brazzaville, Gabon, Oubangi-Chari) decreased by more than 40%.[16] He imputes this to the same forms of forced surplus production and requisitioning of labour as were described in our Cameroonian examples above. However, in these regions, the French transported labourers over even greater distances. The French military operations extended all the way from the Congo coast to Lake Chad, so that the supply caravans for the military expeditions had to cover distances of thousands of miles. After the pacifications, the rush for rubber and ivory began here as well.

In this sparsely populated area, there was soon the same shortage of labour and food as in southern Cameroon. The trade caravans and military expeditions plundered the villages' food supplies and too few producers remained in the villages to keep food production going. Large-scale famines and epidemics broke out. In 1921, construction began on the railway from Brazzaville to the coast. It was to lead to a massacre unparalleled in the colonial history of Africa. In 1929, five years before the completion of the railway, the total mortality among the railway workers was already estimated at 17,000. For 1927, official statistics showed an annual death-rate of 45.20%, for 1928 39.18% and for 1929 17.34%. In these years, government authorities even went so far as to import labourers from Oubangi (over a distance of about 600 miles). In some cases, fewer than 25% of the men transported in this way actually arrived at the work-site (Suret-Canale 1964: 262; Cohen 1971: 63).

However, after 1925, the authorities in these regions became increasingly concerned about such a drastic reduction of the labour potential of the colony. As in so many parts of French Africa, they came to view under-population as the greatest obstacle to the exploitation of the area. Just as in the Maka region, the stabilization of the population became a primary aim of government policy. The surplus production of the African producers was to be organized *within* the village communities. But the government did continue to play a crucial role. The only difference was that now new forms of official coercion were tried; in order to increase surplus production within the villages, the civil servants still considered official coercion to be an absolute necessity. For this purpose, the notorious system of *cultures forcées* (compulsory cultivation) was applied, particularly in French Equatorial Africa.[17]

In the course of the 1920s, this system was first introduced on a large scale by Governor Eboué, one of the first blacks (he hailed from French Guyana in South America) to have a successful career in the French colonial service. Eboué signed contracts with a number of private cotton companies, which were to supply the seeds and see to the processing of the cotton. In exchange, they were granted a monopoly for buying up all the cotton in their district, whereas the government assumed responsibility for organizing the production. For this purpose, an entire staff of agricultural consultants and overseers was appointed. The production of the villagers was to be strictly controlled by the gendarmes, who could punish the slightest disobedience with whipping or, even worse, with prison sentences. The local population soon came to refer to the cotton-fields as 'the fields of the *Commandant*' (the local French colonial official). Once a year they all had to go to the administrative centre in order to hand over their harvest to the cotton company. For most of the peasants, it was a day of tension and fear. They had to wait in a long line for their turn at the scale, where the company clerk supervised the weighing. Each peasant would put his harvest on the scale. If it did not meet the minimum weight requirement, the gendarmes would push him into the line of the *mauvaises têtes* (villains), who would spend the night in jail and run the risk of being shipped off the next day to work as 'volunteers' on the dreaded Congo railway. If the amount was sufficient, then the man would be paid the (low) price fixed by the government in collusion with the cotton company. Any objections to the price or to faulty weighing would be immediately penalized by the gendarmes. The cotton company often paid the peasants with tax receipts from the government. Thus the government officials no longer had to take the trouble of collecting taxes.

Indeed, this example shows very clearly how the colonial state could play a dominant role in the articulation of capitalist and 'domestic' relations of production. Evidently, state coercion became the only effective way to attune the peasants' production to the capitalist market economy in areas where old forms of tribute or trade networks did not present any 'footholds' and where the peasants were not accustomed to producing a regular surplus for the market. In other words, the less support offered by class alliances with pre-capitalist interest groups, the more essential the role of the colonial state was to be, as a bridgehead for capitalist expansion into pre-capitalist society.[18]

Further developments in the role of the colonial state: The articulation of modes of production as a process

In the previous section, the model of an articulation of modes of production was used mainly to analyse regional variations in the role of the colonial state: in various parts of Africa, the old relations of production offered differing 'footholds' for the establishment of capitalist dominance, and this had indeed differing implications for the intervention by the colonial governments. Another question is how far this model of an articulation of modes of production can also provide an insight into further changes in the role of the colonial state. Rey and Meillassoux both stress that this kind of articulation of old and new relations is always unstable. The dominance of the capitalist mode invariably leads to the weakening of the old production communities. Within this perspective of an inherently unstable articulation, what can be said about the development of the colonial state, culminating in its transition to the post-colonial state?

Our first example (the efforts of French officials to reorganize life in the Maka villages) already indicated a distinct re-orientation in the policies of the colonial government. After an initial stage of short-term exploitation, sometimes involving little less than the plundering of the old production communities and their labour resources, at the end of the 1920s government policies came to be increasingly directed towards the stabilization of the village communities: the surplus production by the Maka peasants for the market was to be organized *within* the old production units. In the example of French Equatorial Africa, also briefly referred to above, a similar kind of re-orientation could be noted — first the removal of labour from the villages, and later a policy of compulsory cultivation of cash-crops *within* the old village communities.

In order to understand the logic of this transition, Meillassoux's analysis of the 'domestic community' may be enlightening. Indeed, the aim of Meillassoux's analysis is notably to explore the possibilities presented by the 'domestic' forms of organization for capitalist exploitation. In this respect, the following quotation gives the crux of his line of reasoning (1975: 166):

> The exploitation of the domestic community is supported by two of its properties. On the one hand it is a collective organization of production and it can be exploited more profitably as a collective than on an individual basis. On the other hand it produces surplus labour.

To start with the second 'property' referred to in this quotation:

in Meillassoux's view, the exploitation of the domestic community is possible by way of the extraction of *labour* rather than of *products*. In general, in communities of this kind, there is hardly any regular surplus production. In so far as a surplus of, for example, food is produced, it is indispensable for the continuation of the village economy (as seeds for sowing, or as protection against crop failure). On the other hand, the domestic economy does produce a certain surplus of labour. Not all the labourers of the community are needed permanently for the maintenance of the village economy. Some of the villagers can temporarily be employed elsewhere without this immediately endangering the reproduction of the old relations of production. But the extraction of labour is possible only if the old community retains its coherence (see Meillassoux's emphasis in the above quotation on the exploitation of the domestic community as a collective). Or, to put it more concretely, only if domestic food production continues to function can the domestic community serve as a reservoir of cheap labour for the new capitalist sector. This idea of Meillassoux has been discussed earlier in this book (see chapter 1, p. 5). He argues that in large parts of present-day Africa, wages can remain relatively low because the old production communities still bear many of the costs which, in 'real' capitalist relations, have to be included in the wages: in Africa, the wives and children of urban workers still spend much of their lives in the villages; even the workers themselves return to the villages during their unproductive periods — illness, old age — and there they do not live off their wages but off the yield of domestic food production. In other words, in Africa wages usually have to cover only the living expenses of a single man during his productive period. The reproduction of labour, i.e. the maintenance of women and children, is borne by the old relations of production. This is why the establishment of capitalist dominance does not require the immediate dismantling of the old relations of production; on the contrary, in its expansion, capitalism benefits from the partial conservation of the old domestic communities.

Viewed from this perspective, it is clear why German and French economic policy during the first decades after the colonial conquest had such disastrous effects in areas like Makaland or French Equatorial Africa. Colonial policy at the time was based on a complete misunderstanding of the essential properties of the domestic community, as analysed by Meillassoux. Trade caravans often plundered the villages in these sparsely populated regions, in order to get some food. Officials, traders and planters all engaged in a veritable hunt for labourers, who were often withdrawn from the village economy for lengthy periods. Food production in the villages stagnated, and thus the real basis of the domestic community, the reproduction of the labour potential, was affected. So it is no wonder that French officials started to worry about their colonies becoming depopulated. Or, as Governor General Carde of West Africa put it at the time: a primary aim of colonial policy had to be 'faire du nègre' ('to produce negroes', quoted from Deschamps 1953: 166).

It was against the background of this general disruption that, in Meillassoux's view, 'throughout Africa a colonial policy took shape that tried to use and to organize the productive capacities of the domestic economy' (1975: 166). Only at this stage was a true articulation of new capitalist and old African relations of production to be effected. The aim of the colonial government was now to graft, in one way or another, new forms of surplus production and surplus labour on to the old relations of production. It is this wider background of the European intervention which may account for the attempts of French officials such as Pernet to reorganize life in the Maka villages during the 1930s. Their aim was to stabilize the old village communities and to force the villagers to produce new cash-crops within the framework of the old relationships. Thus the reproduction of labour within the old domestic system would be guaranteed.[19]

As indicated above, after World War II, major changes again took place in the relations in Makaland and the role of the colonial state. Up to the beginning of the 1940s, the state continued to use force in order to make the Maka peasants produce surpluses for the market. At the time, the system of *cultures forcées* was still very much in effect in Makaland. Gendarmes would check that everyone had planted the required number of coffee shrubs, and peasants who did not produce enough were subject to severe punishment. After 1945, there was suddenly no longer any need for this type of control. On their own initiative, the Maka started to expand their coffee and cocoa plantations (see p. 105 above). Nowadays, the Maka themselves look upon a grown man who has not planted any coffee or cocoa as a lazy good-for-nothing or a weakling. This change has previously been attributed mainly to the increase in coffee and cocoa prices (related to the general boom on the world market after World War II). This factor certainly did play a role, as did the fact that the infrastructure in Makaland underwent considerable improvements at the time (new bridges), so that market products could be transported more easily. Nevertheless, it seems probable that more hidden causes played a role as well: changes within the village communities themselves which might explain why the Maka suddenly abandoned their passive resistance to production for the market. In this respect, Rey's general analyses can shed some light (see, e.g. Rey 1971: 121, 350, 416f.; 1973: 161; 1976: 62f.).

In Rey's view, the colonial state played a crucial role in the articulation of capitalist and domestic relations of production only during a short transitional stage. State coercion was needed in order to 'break open' the old production communities for the circulation of money. As soon as this had been achieved, capitalism could 'take root' in the old organizational patterns. Even in systems with relatively undeveloped hierarchies, traditional obligations would soon be transformed into payments in money. Then the autarky of the old production communities was shattered and state coercion was no longer necessary: the peasant would automatically be forced to enter the market to sell his products or his labour. If he did not earn any money, his position would become impossible, even in his own community.

An example of this process is to be found in Rey's analysis of the developments in the Mossendjo region (Congo-Brazzaville), where he himself did field-work. Here French officials also launched a veritable hunt for labourers. The peak was reached around 1930, when the French needed more and more labourers for the notorious Congo–Ocean railway, not far to the south of Mossendjo (see p. 115 above, on the high mortality rate among the African labourers on this railway). About 1932, however, quite a sudden change took place in this area. It became less and less necessary for government authorities to exert coercion to recruit labourers, since young villagers were increasingly willing to engage in wage-labour on their own initiative. Rey attributes this change to the fact that money had not really penetrated the village economy until then. According to him, the real function of the large-scale labour levies by the government was not so much to complete certain projects (such as the railway), but rather to 'break open' the village communities to the market economy. Until 1930, money played hardly any role within the villages. What

120

little money the villagers earned was almost immediately extracted from the villages by the collection of taxes. But that changed in the 1930s. No matter how negligible the amounts that were paid for labour or food, the enlistment of an increasing number of labourers for the railway and the compulsory sale of food (for the railway workers) did bring a certain amount of money into circulation in the villages. This almost immediately led to the monetarization of traditional obligations and exchanges.

Rey particularly emphasizes the role of bridewealth, which he sees as the crucial relationship in the lineage mode of production. To him, bridewealth is a relationship of exploitation between elders and juniors. Not only was the bridewealth transformed into money payments during the 1930s but these 'bride-prices' also increased very rapidly during the ensuing decades (a general phenomenon throughout West and Central Africa). As a result of these transformations and the continuing significance of pre-capitalist relations, young men had no choice but to earn money somehow. Coercion by the state was no longer necessary to enforce surplus production or to enlist labourers.

In his analysis, Rey's emphasis is clearly different from Meillassoux's (see Geschiere 1978b). But his analysis is certainly pertinent to the developments in Makaland as well, notably to the changes that took place after World War II: the rapid develop-ment of coffee and cocoa farming, and the concurrent changes in the relation between state officials and the Maka villagers. In Makaland as well, the old institution of bridewealth lost nothing of its former significance. On the contrary, ever since the early 1930s, the rapid rise in 'bride-prices' has been a matter of constant concern to government officials, missionaries, development workers and other 'agents of change', apparently without their being able to do anything about it. Today the question of how to get enough money to pay for a bride is one of the main preoccupations of every young Maka man. According to data from my older Maka informants, money did not penetrate the circuit of bride-goods until the 1930s. At that time, 'bride-prices' were usually no more than a few hundred French francs. Shortly after World War II, 'bride-prices' of a few thousand French francs were paid. The rapid rise in 'bride-prices' took place mainly in the 1950s. Nowadays, an amount of 80,000 francs C.F.A. (about £160) is normal. In addition, the gifts expected include all kinds of western products which also have to be bought for money.[20]

Moreover, villagers now also need money for a wide range of other items if they are to play their role within their own community. The women demand more European gifts from their husbands as well as from their lovers. Money now plays a central role in the funeral rituals (for example, the agnatic relatives have to 'buy' the body from the deceased person's mother's brothers — for £50 or more — before they can bury it). In addition, money is also needed for expenses of a more modern nature. In hunting, traditionally one of the ways for a man to prove his worth, rifles are increasingly being used, and consequently they have now become one of the most important status symbols. About 1950, the advantages of western education became clear to the villagers. In those years the few Maka boys who had a school certificate were able to rise rapidly in the ranks of the civil service. Ever since then, an increasing number of parents have been sending their children to school, and that also costs money.

Against this background, it is easy to understand why, after 1945, the Maka villagers reacted so enthusiastically to the rise in coffee and cocoa prices. Due to the penetration of money into the village economy — in all kinds of traditional institutions such as bridewealth, which continued to retain their force — capitalism had 'taken root' in the old relations, to use Rey's (and Marx's) term. Direct government coercion was no longer needed to make the villagers produce for the market, and the system of *cultures forcées* was no longer enforced after 1945. Since then the villagers have been more than willing, of their own accord, to expand their coffee and cocoa plantations.

The emergence of the post-colonial state: A new phase in the articulation of capitalist and domestic relations?

What is the relevance of these colonial developments for analysing the emergence of the post-colonial state and its present role in Africa? Rey's analysis has certain implications which may be less applicable to the further development of the role of the state in a region like Makaland after 1945. The main question is: to what extent is the role of the present-day African governments to be viewed as continuing the role played by the colonial state, and to what extent have true changes taken place?

Rey tends to interpret the forcible intervention of the colonial state in the villagers' production as a kind of transitional stage, necessary in order to force a breach in the autarky of the village economy. He seems to suggest that later, once capitalism has taken root in the old production communities, direct intervention by the state in the villagers' production would no longer be necessary.[21] However, this was not at all what happened in Makaland. On the contrary, it is striking how directly the state has continued to be involved in the cultivation of market crops in all kinds of ways, up to this very day. The state intervenes not only by way of all kinds of propaganda or indirect coercion: whoever does not plant coffee or cocoa can count on a very cool reception at the government agencies, or he will not get a licence for a rifle; whereas successful planters receive medals of distinction, etc. Furthermore, in particular the marketing of cash-crops is still under the complete control of the state.

In the 1950s, the government established 'marketing boards' (*caisses de stabilisation*) to protect the peasants from price fluctuations in their products on the world market (and also to level out price differences within Cameroon because of differences in transport costs). Consequently, the boards were granted the right to fix buying prices for each market crop which were to be uniform throughout Cameroon and which could remain stable for several years in spite of fluctuations on the world market (when world prices were high, the marketing boards were to build up reserves which would protect the peasants from price falls in the following years).

However, the boards nearly always fixed prices in such a way that they were left with a gigantic surplus. To give just one example: according to some estimates, until recently 70% of the export price of cocoa went to the state via the marketing board, whereas the peasants themselves received only 30% of the export price. Similar estimates have been made for other cocoa-producing countries (Nigeria, Ghana, Ivory Coast).[22] In many regions, cocoa-growers were not unaware of the differences between the export price and the price they received. Thus, according to some experts, the stagnation of Cameroon's cocoa production after 1974 was a result of the peasants' discontent about these price differences. They chose to neglect the cultivation of market crops because prices remained so low, and to confine themselves to food crops. In Cameroon, the government reacted by drastically raising cocoa prices (in 1977 alone, from 150 to 220 francs C.F.A., viz.

from £0.30 to $0.44 a kilo, and in 1978 again to 270 francs C.F.A.). But even after this price rise, more than 50% of the export price still went to the state, according to several estimates. For other export products as well, the direct control of the marketing boards over the peasants' production provided the Cameroonian state — and practically all the African states — with enormous sums of money every year.

An even more direct form of control has been the co-operatives. Under French rule, the state had instituted various types of co-operative organizations for a variety of purposes. But especially in the 1960s, the Cameroonian government concentrated on expanding the co-operative institutions. In Makaland, ZAPIs (*Zones d'Action Prioritaire Intégrée*) were set up. Within each zone, the state would grant the ZAPI organization a complete monopoly to buy up the market products from the peasants. After 1970, the number of ZAPIs was further increased, particularly in the eastern province of Cameroon. Officially, the main aim of these co-operatives was to put an end to the exploitation of the peasants by private traders (mostly Greeks, Frenchmen and Bamiléké from western Cameroon). In the course of time, the peasants themselves were to take over the management of the ZAPIs and the sale of their own products. In practice, a more immediate effect was that, through these same organizations, the market and, indirectly, the peasants' production came completely under government control.

In this connection, the growing influence of the government in the ZAPIs may be noted. About 1970, the ZAPIs were still dominated by French 'technical assistants', who saw to it that the ZAPIs were not simply incorporated into the state bureaucracy. At the time, the more democratic behaviour of ZAPI officials was in clear contrast to the authoritarian and bureaucratic style of party functionaries and government officials. The ZAPI officials always explained to the peasants that they had not come to order them around but to listen to them, and that the peasants themselves should make proposals which the ZAPI would then try to help them to carry out, and so forth. The established regional élite of politicians and bureaucrats then clearly felt threatened by the ZAPI leaders, whom they thought of as subversive elements doing nothing but stirring up trouble in the villages.

In the 1970s, however, in accordance with the original aim of these co-operatives, the ZAPI boards were rapidly 'Cameroonized' and the French experts were relegated to subordinate technical positions. Apparently, without such external leadership, the co-operatives have had a hard time maintaining their autonomy against the state bureaucracy. Government officials now have very much influence within the co-operatives at all organizational levels. When they visit the villages, the ZAPI leaders are now often accompanied by bureaucrats, party functionaries and even police officials, making it difficult for the villagers to see the difference between these visits and the tours of inspection by administrative officials.

A speech made by a *sous-préfet* (District Commissioner) at the end of 1979 in one of the Maka villages made it clear how rapidly the bureaucratization of the co-operatives had taken place. At elections for the ZAPI committee in the village in question, the peasants had not voted in accordance with the wishes of the *sous-préfet*, even though he had expressed these wishes in no uncertain terms. He therefore interrupted the election procedures with the following threatening words:

> I think I had better put an end to these sterile discussions. The purpose of this meeting was to hold elections in accordance with the instructions of Monsieur le Gouverneur, whom I shall present with a report on your reactions [. . .] It must be clear to you that your stubborn attitude is endangering the representative function of your committee. Once again, I beg you to reconsider your behaviour and its possible repercussions . . .

The fact alone that a government official presided at elections for the ZAPI was completely contrary to the initial aims of this co-operative. The speech quoted above makes it clear that, within the co-operative organization, the peasants were now being approached in the same manner as in their relations with other state officials — as somewhat childish and rather troublesome persons who have to be kept under control by stern admonitions. In spite of the idealistic intentions, within a matter of years the ZAPI has indeed been assimilated into the state apparatus: the co-operative tends to function ever more as an extra form of political control over the village economy by the politico-administrative élite.

This political control may become all the more important because there are clear signs that, in the future, these co-operatives want to occupy themselves not only with the sale of market crops, but also with the organization of production. There are plans to form *équipes de travail* (work-groups) of peasants under direct supervision of the ZAPI *moniteurs* (lower staff). These *équipes* are to serve as a starting-point for a reorganization of the peasants under close ZAPI supervision. In this way, the state would eventually get a direct hold on the production of the peasants — on the organization of their labour and the management of their land. The terms *équipes* and *moniteurs* in themselves are sufficient to call to mind the French attempts at reorganizing the production of the Maka peasants in colonial times (our first example).

In this sense, then, there is a clear continuity between the activities of colonial state officials and the post-colonial efforts of co-operatives and development workers. After all, the latter type of intervention is equally unable to guarantee that the peasants have much of a say in their own co-operatives — especially not since the political régime in Cameroon is still very strongly centralized. Indeed, the centralist tendencies within the political structure in Cameroon certainly did not decrease after decolonization. On the contrary, a small élite at the national political top has succeeded in attaining almost a complete say over all the decisions made at a regional and even at a local level. Under such a régime, it seems nearly inevitable that the institution of co-operatives, regardless of their idealistic inspirations, will present the government with new opportunities to reorganize the production of the peasants according to its own views, and to restrict the autonomy of the producers.

The further erosion of the domestic relations and the role of the post-colonial state

In present-day Africa, state intervention of the type described above in the peasants' market production is the rule rather than the exception. Although it has long since ceased to be necessary to force peasants to sell their products on the market, as was the case in colonial times, the government still insists on gaining complete control over the economy. This does not fit in all too well with Rey's model, as it was summarized above. According to Rey, direct state coercion was needed to 'break open' the peasant community and allow capitalism 'to take root' there. But once this had succeeded, the market mechanism could be expected to be strong enough to ensure the further penetration of capitalist relations; by way of such processes as capital investments, the increase of scale and the rationalization of production, an increasing amount of labour would be 'freed' (in other words would be driven off the land) and the old relations would be broken down even more.

In this context, Rey refers to rural developments in France in the nineteenth and twentieth centuries (1976: 54). This comparison may serve to highlight the specific features of present-day developments in Africa and the specific role of the post-colonial state. In France, the abolition of feudal landownership during the Revolution had created a rural mode of production of small independent peasants. But according to Rey this independence was to become more and more of a fiction in the course of the nineteenth century; the peasants became increasingly dependent on capitalist interest groups. This process was largely stimulated by the fact that land had become a commodity (in other words, could be bought and sold).[23]

According to Rey, the money-value land had acquired represented an important foothold for further capitalist penetration of the peasants' mode of production (*mode de production de la paysannerie parcellaire*). Owing to increasing competition on the market, the peasants were forced to rationalize and mechanize their production. This led to a growing need for money: the peasant could no longer manufacture his own tools and he had to buy more of his means of production on the market. Often, the only way he could get the money he needed was either by selling part of his land or by mortgaging all of it. The mortgages 'strangled' the independence of the petty farmer: if prices fell he could no longer afford the interest and would be forced to sell all his property. In this way, the land of the peasants became incorporated into larger farms, so that further mechanization and capital investment was possible, whereas the peasants themselves were turned into wage-labourers. These changes were achieved mainly by economic mechanisms; all the state had to do was to regulate these processes (at any rate in the nineteenth century and at the beginning of the twentieth century). In France, as in most European countries, no state coercion was needed to break down the last remains of the autarky of the peasant households. In Europe, it has long since become quite impossible for the peasants to withdraw into an economy of self-subsistence. The market mechanism, supported by the necessity for mechanization and the money-value of land, has already penetrated too deeply into the peasants' production system.

Of course the present situation in Makaland is quite different. Land still does not have any money-value there. This has to do with the fact that there is as yet no land scarcity in this sparsely populated region, but also with the unimpaired force of the old communal control over land. In the Maka villages, the rights to the land are still vested in the patrilineal communities. At most, individual members of a patrilineage can acquire the rights to the usufruct of the fields which they cultivate within the lineage domain. Occasional rumours that a man plans to lease or even sell 'his' land always meet with firm opposition on the part of the other members of the lineage. On the other hand, coffee and cocoa cultivation in Makaland still offers very limited possibilities for mechanization. Even on the large-scale European plantations, of which there are a few in this region, much of the work (e.g. harvesting) is still done by hand. The introduction of tractors on the African plantations (for instance to clear the forest and to prepare the fields for cultivation) seems to be hardly feasible for the time being, because it would require such a fundamental reorganization — a considerable increase of scale of the unit of production, and an extremely costly expansion of the infrastructure.

In a situation like this, the autarky of the peasants is far from having been completely destroyed.[24] The peasant households still produce most of their own food. Unfavourable market conditions do face the peasants with certain problems — they need money for taxes, for bridewealth, for medical care and so forth — but at any rate they have enough to eat. The production processes themselves hardly offer any basis for further capitalist expansion: there is little room for the economic mechanisms which 'automatically' ensured the further increase of scale and the penetration of capital into the farming sector in Europe.

Against this background, it becomes quite understandable why the post-colonial state continues to interfere so directly with the peasants' production. Just as in colonial times, the state is still the main agency for enforcing the further growth of production for the market and the further increase of scale in commercial agriculture. Economic developments alone (the market mechanism, opportunities for capital investment) are not sufficient to bring about the further breaking down of the peasants' autonomy; various forms of political control remain necessary as well. For example, it is striking that the government co-operatives in Makaland, as in other parts of Africa, are very keen on creating credit facilities for the peasants. Often credit has first to be more or less forced upon the peasants by extensive government propaganda in the village. Another common feature in the policies of the co-operatives is the reorganization of the peasants into larger production units. These are precisely the processes which, in Europe, during the capitalist transformation of agriculture, were brought about 'automatically' — i.e. by the market mechanism and without direct intervention by the state.[25]

In Rey's view, French peasants were gradually brought into a position of *economic* dependence during the nineteenth and twentieth centuries. Because of the need for mechanization and intensification of production they had little choice but to get into debt. The practice of mortgaging land inevitably brought rural production under the control of capitalist entrepreneurs, banks or large companies. In Makaland, developments seem to lead to completely different forms of dependence. For the time being, the Maka peasants seem to be little threatened by this kind of economic dependence. Instead their autonomy is threatened by an increasing amount of government intervention and an increasing *bureaucratic* dependence.

In Makaland, it was also certainly possible for the peasants to fall into debt. Private traders were very generous about giving them advance payments and gifts. Their intention was clear: the peasant was then under the obligation to sell his harvest to his 'benefactor' in the following years as well. It is striking, however, that in a situation such as that in Makaland, unlike in Europe, there are very clear limits to this practice of gaining control over the peasants by granting them credit. For example, it would hardly be possible for traders to bring a peasant so deeply into debt that he would be obliged to give up control over his means of production. Land, the most important means of production, is not scarce, and under the still prevailing system of communal land rights, it cannot be transformed into money. Under these circumstances, private capitalist entrepreneurs are hardly in a position to enforce a transformation of the peasants' production by putting them into debt. The recent intervention by the state co-operatives, however, created a completely different situation, since they can count on government support. They do not have to be so cautious about granting credit to make the peasants dependent, because in the final instance they can always count on the government to force the peasants to pay them back. The power of the state may enable the co-operatives to bring about a real transformation of the relations of production — to enforce an increase of scale of the production units — so as to make mechanization and the further investment of capital possible in the future (cf. however, Rey, 1971: 520 for a differing interpretation).

The granting of monopolies to government co-operatives put the peasants in a new and direct dependence relationship. This is not only the case in Makaland, but in many other parts of Africa as well. Nearly all the post-colonial governments are trying to gain more control over the peasants' production by means of measures like these. In Senegal, for instance, ever since the beginning of the 1970s, the government has been involved in imposing a fundamental reform of the system of land tenure. There, control over the land is being transferred from the old communities to a complicated hierarchy of new peasant committees under the direct supervision of government officials. The immediate result of this government intervention will also be that a small élite at the head of the state will have a more direct hold on the peasants' production (see van der Klei 1978).

None the less, in this connection as well, considerable differences can be noted on the African continent. In some countries, during the colonial period government, measures had already led to the development of private land ownership and of a land market. That was the case in settlers' colonies such as Kenya and Zimbabwe; furthermore, in some parts of Uganda, the colonial authorities originally followed a policy of development by white colonization, and for that reason introduced private land ownership, but later decided not to encourage the further expansion of a white settler community (see Mamdani 1976: 40f.). In all these regions the rise of a land market proved to facilitate the development of larger farms, further mechanization and the further penetration of capital into the peasants' production, just as in Europe. Under these circumstances, a class of African entrepreneurs and richer farmers was able to build up an independent power-base in the relations of production, and this could act as a counter-force to the attempts by the bureaucratic authorities to acquire more direct control over rural production.

For the time being, however, these regions seem to be the exception to the rule. In most parts of Africa, land still does not have a market value and the mechanization of agriculture is taking place slowly. Under these conditions, the effect of the market mechanism on the peasants' production remains limited and the post-colonial state continues to be the most important support for further capitalist expansion. In this sense there is a clear continuity in these regions with the role of the colonial state. As one of my Maka informants told me, with some degree of resignation: 'The French have taught us that we are like women; if someone comes from the town to tell us what to do, all we can do is say Yes; that's the way it was under the French and that is still the way it is.'

In a region such as Makaland, the articulation of the old relations of production with the capitalist world market is still completely dominated by the state, just as in colonial times. Further developments on the production level will be largely determined by the relations of the Maka peasants with the administrative-political élite.

Conclusion: The relevance of the model of an articulation of modes of production

Of course the above discussion of several African examples is no more than a preliminary exploration of how the role of the colonial and the post-colonial state may be analysed with the aid of the model of an articulation of modes of production. The scope of this kind of study could be expanded, for instance by including examples from the former English and Portuguese territories. None the less, it may have become clear that this model does indeed suggest some useful research propositions. It could be interesting, for example, to analyse further the connection between variations in the role of the colonial state and the 'footholds' the old relations of production provided for the imposition of capitalist dominance. In this sense, the model may serve, indeed, to shed some light on the background of present-day power relations in Africa and the specific features of the post-colonial state.

A striking feature of modern African societies is a phenomenon that can be described as 'the dominance of the political'. A recurrent complaint in the modern African context is: 'Everything is politics here.' In a country like Cameroon, time after time it turns out that any conflict, no matter how trivial — within a university faculty or among hospital staff — can easily have national-political ramifications. Even conflicts that seem to be purely private can immediately link up with the intricate competition between factions and lobbies in the arena of national politics. One consequence is that, for example, university politics in Africa is of an intensity which make European universities seem quite peaceful. Members of the new African élite often complain that, for any job whatever, one needs an extremely highly developed political instinct. The background of this phenomenon may be clear after the preceding discussions. In colonial times, the state in Africa had a crucial role to play as a capitalist 'bridgehead', precisely because the grafting of capitalist relations on to the old organizational patterns proved to be so difficult. Even today, there are still a great many obstacles to the further penetration of the market mechanism in the old relations of production; consequently, the state still has to play an essential role in the further expansion of capitalism. In view of this colonial and post-colonial background, it is hardly surprising that in the modern societies of Africa, the state (or 'politics') dominates so many aspects of life.[26]

On the other hand, the continuity from the colonial to the post-colonial state should not be over-estimated. It is certainly true that, in many respects, the post-colonial state did follow in the footsteps of the colonial state. But there is at least one important difference. In colonial times, the role of the state in promoting further capitalist expansion in the colony was directly controlled by interest groups in the metropole. After decolonization, however, the state apparatus was taken over by an African élite of bureaucrats and politicians, and the role played by this group thus became a new complicating factor in the analysis of the role of the post-colonial state (see Saul 1974). This new élite group may not yet be very clearly defined, but it does have its own group interests. The historical role of this new African élite is often characterized as that of an intermediary group within the world capitalist system. But on numerous occasions in the recent past it has become evident that these élite groups have enough leeway to utilize their intermediary role for the furtherance of their own position. In practice it is apparently even possible for them to act against capitalist interests. Although western support had helped them to come to power, the régimes of Amin and Bokassa instigated a kind of havoc and destruction that was certainly not in keeping with capitalist aims. The confident international politics of the Nigerian leaders, which often run counter to established western interests, is a more positive example. So, in Africa, there is every reason to stress the inherent momentum of the process of state formation. The problems involved in establishing capitalist dominance over the old African relations of production explain why the state had to play such an important role in the colonial period. But afterwards, the state developed its own dynamics and, as far as the new African élites were concerned, it was precisely their control over the machinery of the state that enabled them to expand their own power and to augment their privileged position with respect to the rest of the population.[27]

The theories of Rey and Meillassoux, and their stress on the unstable articulation patterns of old pre-capitalist and new capitalist relations, can be viewed as a further elaboration upon Marx's famous statement that capitalism emerges 'dripping from head to foot, from every pore, with blood and dirt' (Marx 1886: 786). Marx was referring to the rise of capitalism in Europe, but his comment is clearly just as applicable to the later capitalist expansion in Africa. On this continent as well, the expansion of capitalism was anything but an automatic process. On the contrary, breaking open the old production systems and subjugating them to the further development of capitalism required all kinds of experiments and coercive measures. In order to analyse these chaotic developments, the model of an articulation of differing modes of production may serve to clarify the numerous variations in the articulation patterns and their implications with respects to contemporary power relations. Our argument suggests two possible lines for further developments. In some parts of Africa, capitalist dominance soon led to a drastic transformation of the old relations of production. This was due to various factors, for example the fact that capitalist penetration could be based upon 'class alliances' with African power groups, or the fact that the colonial state introduced drastic alterations in the systems of land tenure. In these areas, the new African élite now has every opportunity to build up its own economic power basis. In Kenya, for example, quite a few members of the new élite have invested the earnings from their administrative-political careers in land. There the state increasingly came under the control of an independent economic class (Leys 1978). But, more often, capitalist expansion in Africa was primarily dependent on the role of the capitalist state, without this leading to drastic alterations in the control over the old means of production (land). In these regions, opportunities for members of the élite to invest their earnings productively within the country are still limited, and it is difficult for the élite to develop into a real economic class with its own hold on the means of production. Thus, the state — the political 'instance' — continues to dominate economic life. There, the often changeable patterns of competition between the various factions in national politics still determine the power positions of the élite figures and the development of internal class relations.[28]

In this sense, the laborious implantation of capitalism in the old African relations of production, the various forms of capitalist dominance and the range of articulation patterns with the old relations form the structural background of the multifarious role of the colonial state and of the variations in the development of classes within modern Africa.

Notes

1 I would like to thank the other contributors to this collection — notably Wim van Binsbergen and Klaas de Jonge — and the students participating in my Marxist anthropology seminar (Free University, Amsterdam) for their comments on earlier versions of this text. I collected the material on the Maka, used in this study, during my field-work in the Maka area in 1971, 1973 and 1980, initially under the supervision of H. G. Schulte Nordholt (Free University, Amsterdam). This field-work was made possible by a grant from the Netherlands Foundation for the Advancement of Tropical Research (WOTRO, The Hague), by the kind co-operation of the Cameroonian authorities and, most important of all, by the impetuous cordiality of the Maka themselves. The final version of this text was written during my stay as a fellow at the Netherlands Institute for Advanced Studies (NIAS) at Wassenaar, in 1980–1.
2 Cf. e.g. Asad (1973) and Leclerc (1972). Both authors emphasize that it was precisely because so little attention was devoted to colonial relations that the structural-functionalist paradigm, with its emphasis on stability and integration, could play a dominating role in the field of anthropology. Colonial 'pacification' artificially stabilized the societies studied by anthropologists; cf. also Copans (1975); Diamond (1974).
3 The tendency to overlook colonial history was particularly prevalent among modernization sociologists and political scientists of the 1960s; cf. Apter (1965). Traces of this tendency can also be discerned among anthropologists; for instance, in Dutch anthropology, in Thoden van Velzen's studies of political relations on the village level in southern

134

Tanzania (cf. van Hekken & Thoden van Velzen 1972). Thoden van Velzen devoted a great deal of attention to the influence of the national political centre on the village level. In this respect, he arrived at really elucidating conclusions; but he hardly referred to colonial history and to the evolvement of specific relations between officials and peasants during that period.

4 Cf. Suret-Canale (1964): 99; Crowder (1968). The discussion between Deschamps (1963) and Crowder (1964) may be viewed as conclusive for the long debate on assimilation and indirect rule. Crowder concluded that, in practice, French policies were hardly influenced by the ideal of assimilation and that the French applied the principle of indirect rule as well: like the British they did make use of African chiefs. One essential difference, however, was that the French, due to their highly centralist tradition of government, had the tendency to use the African chiefs purely and simply for the execution of their administrative decisions.

5 The argument in this chapter refers in particular to Meillassoux (1975) and Rey (1971, 1973, 1976). Cf. also Amin (1973, 1974); see also chapter 1 (the Introduction to this book); furthermore Gerold-Scheepers & van Binsbergen (1978) and Geschiere (1978b, 1982b).

6 The Maka live in the dense forests of southeastern Cameroon on the head-waters of the Nyong and the Doumé Rivers, just to the south of the border between the forest and the savannah. They speak a Bantu language (Guthrie classified the Maka in the A80 group along with the Djem, their neighbours to the south, and the Ngoumba, who live further away near the Atlantic coast). The Maka refer to themselves as Məká; the French administrators and the Catholic missionaries often called them Makya or Makaa. See for further information on the Maka: Geschiere (1978a, 1982a); and specifically on the colonial period; Geschiere (in press, b).

7 Before the colonial conquest, there was at most a very irregular exchange of food products and utensils between the Maka villages (for instance, if a village's crops had failed, the women could exchange earthenware for tubers with other villages). In addition, the Maka groups regularly exchanged prestige goods (notably iron objects) on special occasions (funerals, bridal payments). In the entire forest region of southern Cameroon, there were no regular markets until the German conquest ($\pm$ 1900); cf. also Laburthe-Tolra (1977), Henn (1978), Wirz (1972).

8 Archives nationales, Yaoundé, APA 10784/C, rapports et lettres 1931–2: rapport semestriel, 12 August 1931, Abong Mbang (under the heading 'Démographie').

9 In the 1930s and the 1940s government policy in the Maka area was clearly dominated by the concern to consolidate the village communities and to enforce surplus production for the market *within* these communities. But this should not suggest that government policies were completely consistent during these two decades: government officials were also confronted with alternative ways of organizing the 'mise en valeur' of the region. In particular, the rapid development of

a few European plantations in the 1930s seemed to present alternative possibilities for exploiting the region: through large-scale production by European planters and Maka wage-labourers, rather than by small-scale cash-crop production by peasants in the villages. Cf. Geschiere (in press, b) for an analysis of how government policies in Makaland were influenced by these various possibilities in the 1930s. Around 1940 the French officials decided in favour of a 'mise en valeur' by Maka peasants and against the further expansion of European plantations and wage labour, largely because the former strategy provided the best safeguard for the government's own interests (the need for sufficient labour on the government projects and for the strengthening of the authority of the 'chefs coutumiers').

10 The reports on the activities of French officials in 1938 can be found in *Archives Institut des Sciences Humaines* (formerly *Archives IRCAM*), Yaoundé, dossier H, Haut Nyong: report by Barbarin, *chef de région*, March 1938, and reports by Pernet, *chef de subdivision*, July 1938 and September 1938.

11 Archives nationales, Yaoundé, dossier APA 11643, rapports et lettres 1920: Plan de campagne pour l'année 1921 and letter from Briaud, *chef de région* to Monsieur le Commissaire de la République in Douala, Abong Mbang, 14 December 1920. See also Geschiere (1978a): 132f. and (1982a) ch. IV B.

12 Cf. Geschiere (in press, b) for a concrete example of what is meant here by possible discrepancies between the structural implications of modes of production and the political level of human actors. In Makaland, the development of the 'mise en valeur' was strongly influenced by specific interests of the administration: in order to ensure a sufficient number of labourers for government projects, the French officials were even willing to restrict the development of wage-labour in the region, which was definitely not in the interest of the French entrepreneurs there (cf. also note 9).

13 Cf. Rudin (1938): 317 and Wirz (1972): 25. The substantial role played by a faction of planters seems to have been a normal phenomenon in the German colonies. In Southwest Africa and in Tanganyika, active communities of planters also developed soon after 1900 (the influx of colonists was probably relatively large in the German colonies, due to the small size of the German colonial empire). And in these colonies the settlement of German planters also led to heated conflicts between them and the German colonial administration. Cf. Wallerstein (1976): 43; Bley (1967): 261; Iliffe (1969): 13. See, for a very lively sketch of the practice of the German labour-levies, Brain (1977) — a tense and melancholic novel on the vicissitudes of a German labour agent.

14 Macfarlane (1978) recently criticized *inter alia* Marx's analysis of the 'freeing' of labour in England at the end of the Middle Ages. His 'refutation' of Marx seems to imply that the feudal economy in England had already produced 'free' labourers at a much earlier date than Marx assumed. This aspect, no matter how interesting it might be, is not directly relevant to Rey's attempt at applying the Marxian

analyses in Africa — to the capitalist expansion and to the solution of the labour problem on that continent.

15 The French first tried to exploit French Equatorial Africa by means of a system of concessions. The colonial government granted private companies a trade monopoly for a certain region, including all kinds of official powers there. Usually these companies had hardly any capital at their disposal; therefore the only way they could exploit 'their' area was by forcing the African population to produce new surpluses. In most of these areas the concession system soon led to either the total disruption of the African communities or the utter neglect of the concession (if a company was incapable of exploiting its area). Especially after 1920, the government intervened, trying to restrict the concessions and to make the companies rationalize their system of exploitation; cf., e.g., Coquery-Vidrovitch (1972).

16 According to Coquery-Vidrovitch, Suret-Canale's figures were based on erroneous estimates, but she agreed that there must have been a considerable demographic decline. Her own conclusion was that between 1910 and 1930 the population of French Equatorial Africa must have been reduced by one third and that there had been a marked fall in the population especially after 1918; cf. Coquery-Vidrovitch (1972): 72, 219, 494.

17 Cf., e.g., Suret-Canale (1964): 291; Homet (1934); Stürzinger (1980).

18 Rey is even prepared to speak of a class alliance between capitalists pre-capitalist relations of production; the 'colonial mode of production' was facilitated by an alliance with the old dominant classes, even in the case of 'domestic', uncentralized societies; see Rey (1971): 121, 454, 518; (1976): 63. However, one may wonder whether the term 'class alliance' is really applicable here, especially if this term is taken to imply some sort of conscious collaboration. Rey's argument is that both capitalists and elders profited from the monetarization and the inflation of the bridewealth, the old 'relation of exploitation' in these societies. But the question remains whether both parties were really aware of such coincidence of interests. In practice, colonial administrators strongly opposed the inflation of the bridewealth which they viewed as an obstacle to development; see Geschiere (1978b, 1982c, in press, c, and ch. 7 below). In any case, the authority of the elders only rarely seemed to have offered an immediate 'foothold' to capitalist penetration. In all regions where — besides the authority of the elders — no other forms of hierarchy, tribute, or regular surplus production for the market had developed, the colonial state had an important role to play (notably direct coercive extraction of labour and products from the villages) in guaranteeing capitalist dominance over the pre-existing forms of production.

19 In Meillassoux's opinion, this pattern of an articulation of old and new relations of production can easily lead to a disaster. The increase of migrant labour and the expansion of cash-crop cultivation drains the resources of the domestic community; food production stagnates so that normal set-backs (such as droughts) can no longer be dealt with. This was the real reason for the severe famines in the Sahel in the early

1970s; cf. Comité d'Information Sahel (1975). Fortunately, this final calamitous stage has not been reached yet in the Maka region, notably because here land is not yet a scarce resource, and because cash-crop production and food cultivation are still not clearly competitive branches of production. See also Geschiere (1978a): ch. 6; (1982a): ch. 5.

20 See also Geschiere (in press, c).

21 Cf., e.g., Rey (1971): 435, 445ff., 519. Rey referred here to a 'colonial mode of production' (characterized by direct state coercion towards the imposition of a regime of forced labour) as a kind of transitional phase, necessary in order to really subject the lineage mode of production to capitalism. His formulations seem to imply that after such a (brief) transitional phase during the colonial period, the state no longer had to play a direct role in the articulation of capitalist and pre-capitalist relations of production; the 'colonial mode of production' rapidly lost its *raison d'être* and the state was to be re-integrated into the old lineage system. In a later publication, Rey did devote more attention to the continual involvement of the post-colonial state in the development of capitalism in Africa (see 1976: 57). In any case a term like 'phase de transition' seems less opportune here: there is after all a clear continuity between the coercive interventions by the colonial state and the attempts of the post-colonial state élites at getting direct control over the peasants' production.

22 Cf. *Africa Research Bulletin*, 31 October 1978 and *Jeune Afrique*, 23 September 1977: 29f (with thanks to Egbert Jacobs of the Foundation of Dutch Volunteers, The Hague, for these references and relating data). More conservative estimates assess that the peasants only receive from 40% to 60% of the world market prices their crops fetch; cf. Van der Laan (1978).

23 In Rey's view, the fact that land came to have a price in France is not only related to its growing scarcity. He rather considers the land price to be a transformation of the old land rent. Against the background of the old feudal relations — the landowner's right to receive land rent from his serfs, and the later transformation of this land rent into money — it can be understood how, in Europe, land came to have a price. This is a stage that in some parts of the world has not been reached yet. Cf., e.g., Rey (1976): 55.

24 In the 1970s, in other parts of rural Africa there were instances of peasants — for example groundnut-growers in Senegal or cotton-growers in northern Cameroon — tending to withdraw into food cultivation for their own consumption because they gained too little on the market crops. This new tendency to return to autarky shows that the subjection of the peasants' production to the capitalist market had still not become a self-reproducing relationship.

25 Within the scope of this chapter it is impossible to analyse the role of co-operatives in this context. At any rate it seems necessary to distinguish various types of co-operatives. In Europe, for example, co-operatives played an important role in creating credit facilities for farmers and in the further penetration of capitalism into the agrarian

sector. However, usually these European co-operatives were not directly dominated by the state. This type of co-operative also played a role in Africa, particularly in those regions where a class of richer farmers had emerged, who then strengthened their own position by founding co-operatives (for instance, among the Bamiléké in western Cameroon). In this article, however, I am referring to a different kind of co-operative, which is more prevalent in Africa: co-operatives founded on the initiative of the government and functioning under the direct supervision of government officials: cf. also Achterstraat (1977).

26 Bayart in his recent book about the state in Cameroon sketched a configuration which clearly illustrates what forms this 'dominance of the political' can take in modern Africa; cf. Bayart (1979): 260. He described how, in Cameroon, all kinds of deviant behaviour — theft, prostitution, but also the predilection of some youngsters for eye-catching clothes — are all attributed with direct political significance. The ideology of the government views this type of behaviour not only as anti-social, but also as an example of political 'subversion'. Thus the government relates 'vagabondage' to former guerrilla activities by the communist opposition movement. From this Bayart concluded 'vaga-bondage' to be a form of political protest on the part of the subordinate class (the 'cadets sociaux'). The question remains as to whether this latter interpretation — particularly the reference to the subordinate class as 'cadets sociaux' — is really convincing. But at any rate, Bayart did show how all sorts of relations are directly interpreted in terms of national politics. Precisely because the state is such an omnipotent agent, phenomena like prostitution or vagabondage are not only perceived as social problems (as in western Europe) but are taken to be political acts as well.

27 Of course this emphasis on the internal dynamics of the state formation process is related to the widely-used notion of 'the relative autonomy of the state'. In the discussions on the (post-)colonial state in Africa, this concept was often used in order to explain the central role of the state in the (post-)colonial developments. However, the analytical value of this concept is not always apparent (it may be used as a kind of blanket-concept impeding further analysis); cf., e.g., Saul (1974) and Geschiere (in press, a). Recently Jewsiewicki (1982) gave a new and interesting elaboration upon this concept. In his opinion, the autonomy of the colonial state in the Belgian Congo was based on the creation of a 'customary indigenous society'. Under the specific form of primitive accumulation in the Belgian Congo, it became the main task of the state to 'form and maintain an indigenous social order, administrated by a customary apparatus'. Jewsiewicki stresses, however, that all this was a 'customary fiction'. In reality, the primitive accumulation necessitated a drastic re-organization of the indigenous sector, and exactly this necessity was the basis of the autonomy of the colonial state. In many ways, Jewsiewicki's interpret-ation is in keeping with the analysis given above. In the perspective of an articulation of modes of production, the dominant role of the (post-) colonial state is also based on its task of re-organizing the old

production communities and incorporating them into the development of a capitalist economy. An important difference, however, is that Jewsiewicki takes it for granted that the old organizational patterns were completely broken down and replaced by 'pseudo-customary' relations. The question remains as to whether this conclusion can be put in such general terms, even for the Belgian Congo. In the perspective of an articulation of modes of production, one would expect marked regional variations to develop in the course of capitalist penetration. On the one hand, capitalist dominance must always lead to drastic transformations of the old organizational patterns; but, on the other, old institutions — like communal forms of land tenure, bridewealth etc. — may continue to play an important and very variable role. It is a matter of research to analyse how the old principles of organization were intertwined with the new relations and how this led to variable patterns of contradictions within the present social formations.

28 Cf. Mamdani (1976): 315 and Buijtenhuijs & Geschiere (1978b): 15. Of course the differences involved here are only gradual. Nevertheless there does seem to be a clear contrast between relations in, for instance, Kenya and Tanzania. In Kenya the élite can invest its earnings in land and industry, and thus develop into an independent economic class with direct control over the means of production. In Tanzania, the élite has remained much more of a 'political' class, whose main opportunity to gain control over production is by way of the expansion of the economic role of the state, so that its power basis remains completely dependent on its control over the machinery of the state.

References

Achterstraat, A. N. (1977), '"Animation rurale": een strategie voor de ontwikkeling van het Afrikaanse platteland — een drietal praktijk situaties uit Senegal en Kameroen', doctoraal scriptie, Free University, Amsterdam.

Amin, S. (1973), *Le Développement inégal: essai sur les formations sociales du capitalisme périphérique*, Paris: Minuit.

Amin, S. (1974), 'Le capitalisme et la rente foncière', in Amin & Vergopoulos (1974): 8–62.

Amin, S. & Vergopoulos, K. (eds) (1974), *La Question paysanne et le capitalisme*, Paris: Anthropos.

Apter, D. (1965), *The Politics of Modernization*, Chicago University Press.

Asad, T. (ed.) (1973), *Anthropology and the Colonial Encounter*, London: Ithaca Press.

Bayart, J.-F. (1979), *L'Etat au Cameroun*, Paris: Presse de la fondation nationale des sciences politiques.

van Binsbergen, W. M. J. & Hesseling, G. (eds) (in press), *Aspecten van staat en maatschappij in Afrika: Recent Nederlands en Belgisch onderzoek*, Leiden: African Studies Centre.

van Binsbergen, W. M. J. & Meilink, H. A. (eds) (1978), *Migration and the Transformation of Modern African Society, African Perspectives 1978/1*, Leiden: African Studies Centre.

Bley, H. (1967), *South West Africa under German Rule 1894–1914*, Evanston: Northwestern University Press.

Brain, R. (1977), *Colonial Agent*, London: Faber.

Buijtenhuijs, R. & Geschiere, P. (1978a), Introduction, in Buijtenhuijs and Geschiere (1978b): 7–19.

Buijtenhuijs, R. & Geschiere, P. (eds) (1978b), *Stratification and Class Formation, African Perspectives 1978/2*, Leiden: African Studies Centre.

Cohen, W. B. (1971), *Rulers of Empire: The French Colonial Service in Africa*, Stanford University Press.

Comité d'Information Sahel (1975), *Qui se nourrit de la famine en Afrique noire? Le dossier politique de la faim au Sahel*, Paris: Maspero (2nd rev. edition).

Copans, J. (ed.) (1975), *Anthropologie et impérialisme*, Paris: Maspero.

Coquery-Vidrovitch, C. (1972), *Le Congo au temps des grandes compagnies concessionaires 1898–1930*, Paris/The Hague: Mouton.

Crowder, M. (1964), 'Indirect rule: French and British style', *Africa*, 34: 197–206.

Crowder, M. (1968), *West Africa under Colonial Rule*, London: Hutchinson.

Cruise O'Brien, D. B. (1971), *The Mourides of Senegal: The Political and Economic Organization of an Islamic Brotherhood*, Oxford: Clarendon Press.

Deschamps, H. (1953), *Les Méthodes et doctrines coloniales de la France*, Paris: Colin.

Deschamps, H. (1963), 'Et maintenant Lord Lugard?' *Africa*, 33: 293–305.

Diamond, S. (1974), *In Search of the Primitive*, New Brunswick: Transaction Books.

Gerold-Scheepers, T. J. F. A. & van Binsbergen, W. M. J. (1978), 'Marxist and non-Marxist approaches to migration in Africa', in van Binsbergen & Meilink (1978): 21–35.

Geschiere, P. (1978a), 'Stamgemeenschappen onder staatsgezag, veranderende verhoudingen binnen de Maka dorpen sinds 1900', doctoral dissertation, Free University, Amsterdam.

Geschiere, P. (1978b), 'The articulation of different modes of production: old and new inequalities in Maka villages in southeast Cameroon', in Buijtenhuijs & Geschiere (1978b): 45–69.

Geschiere, P. (1981), 'De post-koloniale staat in Afrika: inzichten en vragen vanuit een marxistische visie', *Mens en Maatschappij*, 56 (boekaflevering): 26–47.

Geschiere, P. (1982a), *Village Communities and the State*, London: Kegan Paul International.

Geschiere, P. (1982b), 'Produktiewijzen en verandering: enkele themas uit het werk van Franse marxistische antropologen', *Antropologische Verkenningen*, 1: 45–75.

Geschiere, P. (1982c), 'Politiek-economische patronen in de geschiedenis van Afrika', in Wiard Beckmanstichting (1982): 11–87.

Geschiere, P. (1982d), L'Agriculture de subsistance, l'autonomie de la femme et l'autorité des aînés chez les Maka (Cameroun)', *Journal d'Agriculture traditionelle et de botanique appliquée*, 29, 3–4: 307–21.

Geschiere, P. (in press, a), 'Marxistische visies op de post-koloniale staat in Afrika — de discussie in RAPE en de historische benadering van Rey', in van Binsbergen & Hesseling (in press).

Geschiere, P. (in press, b), 'European planters, African peasants and the colonial state, alternatives in the "mise en valeur" of Makaland during the interbellum', *African Economic History*, 1983 (papers SOAS workshop 'Business Empires in West Central Africa', London, May 1982).

Geschiere, P. (in press, c), 'Bruidsprijzen en kapitalistische expansie bij de Maka: Marxistische theorieën en de praktijk van antropologisch veldwerk', *Te Elfder Ure*, 33.

Gutkind, P. C. W. and Wallerstein, I. (eds) (1976), *The Political Economy of Contemporary Africa*, Beverly Hills: Sage.

Hausen, K. (1970), *Deutsche Kolonialherrschaft in Afrika: Wirtschafts-interessen und Kolonialverwaltung in Kamerun vor 1914*, Zürich: Atlantis.

van Hekken, P. M. & Thoden van Velzen, H. U. E. (1972), *Land Scarcity and Rural Inequality in Tanzania*, The Hague: Mouton.

Henn, J. K. (1978), 'Peasants, workers, and capital', Ph.D. thesis, Harvard University.

Homet, M. (1934), *Congo, terre de souffrances*, Paris: Montaigne.

Iliffe, J. (1969), *Tanganyika under German Rule 1905–1912*, Cambridge University Press.

Jewsiewicki, B. (1982), 'La raison d'État ou la raison du capital: accumulation primitive au Congo belge', paper, workshop on 'Business Empires in West Central Africa', London, SOAS, May 1982.

van der Klei, J. (1978), 'Customary land tenure and land reform: the rise of new inequalities among the Diola of Senegal', in Buijtenhuijs and Geschiere (1978b): 35–45.

van der Laan, L. (1978), 'De Afrikaanse Marketing Boards', *Intermediair*, 14 (41): 23–8.

Laburthe-Tolra, P. (1977), *Mínlaaba, histoire et société traditionelle chez les Bëti du Sud-Cameroun*, Paris: Champion.

Leclerc, G. (1972), *Anthropologie et colonialisme*, Paris: Fayard.

Leys, C. (1978), 'Capital accumulation, class formation and dependency', *Socialist Register 1978*: 241–66.

Macfarlane, A. (1978), *The Origins of English Individualism: The Family, Property and Social Transition*, Oxford: Blackwell.

Mamdani, M. (1976), *Politics and Class Formation in Uganda*, New York: Monthly Review Press.

Mandeng, P. (1973), *Auswirkungen des Deutschen Kolonialherrschaft in Kamerun*, Hamburg: Buske.

Marx, K. (1886), *Capital* (I), translated into English by S. Moore, E. Aveling and F. Engels, London: Glaisher.

Meillassoux, C. (1975), *Femmes, greniers et capitaux*, Paris: Maspero.

Rey, P. -P. (1971), *Colonialisme, néo-colonialisme et transition au capitalisme*, Paris: Maspero.

Rey, P. -P. (1973), *Les Alliances de classes*, Paris: Maspero.

Rey, P. -P. (1976), *Capitalisme négrier: la marche des paysans vers le prolétariat*, Paris: Maspero (together with E. le Bris and M. Samuel).

Rudin, H. R. (1938), *Germans in the Cameroons 1884–1914*, Yale University Press (here quoted from the 2nd edition, Archon Books, 1978).

Rüger, A. (1960), 'Die Entstehung und Lage der Arbeiterklasse unter dem deutschen Kolonialregime in Kamerun 1895–1905', in Stoecker (1960): 149–242.

Saul, J. S. (1974), 'The state in post-colonial societies: Tanzania', *Socialist Register*, 1974: 349–72.

Stoecker, H. (ed.) (1960), *Kamerun under deutscher Kolonialherrschaft*, I, Berlin: Rütten & Loening.

Stürzinger, U. (1980), *Der Baumwollanbau im Tschad: Zur Problematik landwirtschaftlicher Exportproduktion*, Zürich: Atlantis.

Suret-Canale, J. (1964), *Afrique noire occidentale et centrale, II, l'ère coloniale 1900–1945*, Paris: Editions sociales.

Wallerstein, I. (1976), 'The three stages of African involvement in the world economy', in Gutkind & Wallerstein (1976): 30–58.

Wiardi Beckmanstichting (ed.) (1982), *De Smalle Marge van de Onafhankelijkheid, Opstellen over Afrika*, Amsterdam: Bert Bakker.

Wirz, A. (1972), *Vom Sklavenhandel zum kolonialen Handel: Wirtschaftsräume und Wirtschaftsformen in Kamerun vor 1914*, Zürich: Atlantis.

Chapter 5

African literature between nostalgia and utopia: African novels since 1953 in the light of the modes-of-production approach

Simon Simonse[1]

A theoretical perspective

Until a large number of French and British colonies in Africa attained independence, around 1960, the concept 'African litera-ture' was unknown. Today this concept has been widely accepted. It refers, as any initiate knows, to an ever-increasing collection of novels, poetry, and drama written by African authors in, usually, the languages of the former colonial powers. If Africa's right to political sovereignty came to be recognized in a fairly spasmodic way, the recognition of African literature or, as some prefer to call it, 'neo-African literature', has come about no less suddenly. Today there are scores of African literary periodicals. Chairs in African literature have been created or, at least, courses in the subject are being offered, not only at African universities, but also at universities in Europe and particularly in North America. The African writer has attained international esteem and attracts general attention not only because of the literary work, but also, and particularly, because of the writer's role in the public affairs of African countries. In some countries the writer has been the head of state, like Leopold Senghor and the late Agostinho Neto. In other countries the writer may from time to time be in prison, on the ground of having expressed opinions unacceptable to the regime; Ngugi wa Thiong'o in Kenya and Wole Soyinka in Nigeria are well-known examples. More often even the writer lives in exile, like Ayi Kwei Armah, Bessie Head, and the late Camara Laye. The Nigerian writer, Chinua Achebe, finally, was one of the major advocates of the Biafran secessionist movement at the time. In the wake of this sudden international recognition a

144

number of controversies arose as to the specific nature of African literature. As a result of these efforts to determine the African essence of African literature, it happened more than once that authors were disqualified for being insufficiently African.

In this chapter, I hope to demonstrate that it is more fruitful to approach the African novel from the Marxist perspective of the modes of production and their articulation than from an approach that focuses on its specific African content. Selecting those novels on which literary criticism and debate have particularly focused so far, I shall argue that the relation between capitalist and pre-capitalist modes of production constitutes the central preoccupation, be it implicit or explicit, of all these novels. Second, I intend to demonstrate that this concern with the relation between the new and the old modes of production offers us a key for analysing these novels in a systematic way. Finally, I suggest that this approach enables us to classify the novels in a coherent way and to relate them to the main political ideologies on the African scene since independence.[2]

The specific nature of African literature: The present state of the debate

As a first step in my argument, I shall assess how two prominent African authors define the specific nature of African literature. As someone who does not mind being called 'the Nestor of African literature' and as the series editor of the principal English-language series within which African writers publish their works, Achebe has, more than anyone else, tried to define the boundaries of African literature. This definition does not appear to be too easy a task. For, while it would be convenient to use such a criterion as language or language area to delineate Dutch or German literature, this criterion does not apply in the case of African literature. Achebe tries to strengthen his case by stressing the emerging language differences within the anglophone world: besides American and Australian English, also Nigerian, Kenyan, and other Third World Englishes have come into being (Achebe 1975: 58). This tactic, however, does not lead him very far, for nearly all African authors use standard English or, as the case may be, French. Could the literary form then provide a criterion? We know that Senghor uses an African metre in his poetry. Achebe stresses the fact that his own narrative style is characterized by the use of proverbs and African expressions (1975: 61). Other writers again enliven their narratives with samples of English as spoken locally or of some African language; but this is not a general characteristic. Then the solution must lie in the content of African literature: Achebe passionately claims that African literature should be of a particularistic, African nature. It should resist the temptation to deal with universal problems (1975: 19). From this point of view Achebe regrets that Laye chose a white man to be the main character for his *Le Regard du roi* — a book that Achebe admires for other reasons, though (1975: 54). Similarly Achebe takes Armah to task for discussing, in *The Beautyful Ones are Not Yet Born*, a universal existentialist problematic — thus ignoring the fact that (as in Achebe's contention) the African nature of Ghanaian society is incompatible with the emergence of such miscreants as Armah's anonymous main character in that novel.[3] In other words, the criterion of content immediately puts two of the most significant African novels in an outsider's position. Achebe himself realizes that content as such cannot be decisive; especially not, one is tempted to suggest, since he would not like to see his own work anthologized along with Joseph Conrad's and Joyce Cary's (1975: 55). Thus what remains of the points suggested by Achebe is the social commitment of African literature. Achebe draws a comparison with the effigies that the Owerri Igbo made in order to embellish the temple of the Earth Goddess for the occasion of the *mbari* ceremony. Certain villagers were released from all other work for periods sometimes exceeding one year to enable them to work on the effigies. These depicted village life and were shown to the community during a large festival. The effigies held a mirror to society: the good were praised, the bad criticized. If in fact the essence of African literature lies in this mirror function, we should go and look at what image confronts us from that mirror.

This function is precisely the one Achebe's fellow-countryman, Soyinka, sets out to perform in one of his collections of essays (Soyinka 1976). Soyinka starts with the assertion that in the case of African authors there is no 'literary ideology', no literary movement that determines the form and the problem of the literary work. This situation is different from the one prevailing in Europe. In Africa there is no psychological novel, no naturalism or expressionism, let alone something like the *nouveau roman*.

146

The social commitment of the African author rules out that kind of specifically literary orientation. The identity of the African writer is determined by the vision of society underlying his work. On the basis of these visions of society Soyinka offers a tentative, intuitive classification of African novels. First, he distinguishes between the religious and the nonreligious writers. In the former category we find the Christian William F. Conton, the Muslim Hamidou Kane, and also the ambivalent traditionalist Achebe as the author of *Arrow of God*. The latter category is divided in three subgroups: the critics of religion, with Mongo Beti as the critic *par excellence* of Christian missions and Yambo Ouologuem as the critic of Islam: *Le devoir de violence* is claimed to be some kind of 'anti-Kane', and some passages seem to confirm this view. In the second subgroup we encounter a varied company: Sembène Ousmane of *Les Bouts de bois de dieu*, Armah of *Two Thousand Seasons*, and Laye of *Le Regard du roi*. The factor that unites them is their common search for something that Soyinka calls 'racial retrieval': an attempt to regain the authenticity that has been lost as a result of European and Islamic influence. Such an approach obviously does not do justice to the fact that Sembène claims to be a communist.

What evidence does Soyinka cite in support of his view that the strike around which *Les Bouts de bois de dieu* revolves is in fact a truly indigenous 'movement'? (Soyinka 1976: 118.) Only one short passage in the book when Tiemoko, one of the strikers, pleads that his father's brother, a scab, should be summoned to appear before a tribunal of the strike committee, rather than being given a sound flogging. Armah belongs to Soyinka's second subgroup mainly on the basis of a superficial reading of the title of Armah's first book and of the contents of what at the time of Soyinka's writing was Armah's latest book, *Two Thousand Seasons*.

Finally, Soyinka discusses the negritude writers as a third subgroup. His approach is reminiscent of the embarrassment one may show with regard to an illegitimate child. Why should this group of writers be dealt with in a category of their own, if the second group is also characterized by 'racial retrieval'? Soyinka elaborates on this point. He reproaches the negritude authors for their Manichean attitude: because they want to be the opposite of the European conquest culture, they imprison themselves in a negation of things western, thus remaining victims of the latter and being caught within the magical circle of Manicheism. Manicheism is a mode of thought involving mutually exclusive opposites; to Soyinka this mode of thought is unacceptable since it is un-African. Africa has a culture which is most radically anti-Manichean (1976: 127). Does not Soyinka here fall into the very pit he claims the negritude writers have fallen into? Does not he himself base his entire argument on a radical opposition?

The only way to escape from this vicious circle is to drop the opposition western–African, a truly Manichean pair of concepts. We ought to relate the concepts *western* and *African* to a more fundamental reality and to explore the material content that underlies these cultural concepts. Neither the African 'anti-Manicheism' nor what Soyinka calls the 'western cast of mind' exists without relation to more fundamental conditions, but these are not directly related to race — whatever Soyinka's racial retrieval and negritude may suggest (1976: 37). From a materialist point of view, the 'casts of mind' of groups of people (Manichean or anti-Manichean as the case may be) are part of a larger whole in which the production process plays a role along with ideational or cultural processes. This larger whole is ignored both by negritude and by Soyinka's critique of negritude. Both viewpoints are variants of a perspectival distortion that could be called 'idealist' or 'culturalist'. For this reason Soyinka's classification cannot distinguish between such writers as Sembène and Laye, who are worlds apart, and at the same time this classification imposes artificial distinctions like those between Laye and the negritude writers — distinctions that are meaningless in reality.

Method

It is my contention that the confrontation between the capitalist and the pre-capitalist modes of production constitutes the rock bottom that the African writer's creative imagination cannot help but touch when giving a literary shape to his vision of society. It is immaterial whether or not the writer is aware of this confrontation. The novel is seen as a literary form in which fundamental social contradictions are reflected. This point of view derives from the school of Georg Lukács and Lucien Goldmann.[4] Lukács, for instance, associates the novel with a form of society in which the central values of the culture are no longer self-evident, in which humanity has become uprooted and has to find its way without the aid of a pre-established orientation. In this social situation the novel is characterized by the problematic hero, in contrast to the epic hero who is nonproblematic. Goldmann tries to go one step further, suggesting that the conflict between authentic and non-authentic values, between which the hero is torn, constitutes a literary transposition of the contradiction between exchange value and use value in the capitalist mode of production. Thus he explains the fact that the novel and capitalism emerged in Europe simultaneously.[5] I wish to retain both ideas: a number of African novels can best be interpreted as elaborations of the contradiction between 'culture', or 'symbolic order', on the one hand, and, on the other hand, capitalism defined as an autonomous system propelled by the complementary and contradictory coupling of exchange value and use value, tendentiously excluding any determination by symbolic value or symbolic ambivalence. Other African novels can to a large extent be analysed in accordance with Goldmann's suggestion, as revolving around the value contradiction within capitalism.

In theoretical preparation of the specific analyses that I shall offer in the course of this article, it is necessary to discuss briefly at this juncture my use of the concept of mode of production. In line with the French Marxist approach in anthropology, I define a mode of production not exclusively by reference to the nature of the economic sphere (as in vulgar Marxist approaches), but also, and primarily, by reference to the way in which the economic, the political, and the ideological aspects of society (as distinct levels or 'instances', as in the French usage) are linked to each other.[6] The social process of production is the absolute condition for the politico-juridical and the ideologial spheres. The latter, however, are not mere epiphenomena of the former. The production process in itself already presupposes a certain combination and a certain hierarchy of the economic, the politico-juridical, and the ideological levels. This so-called internal articulation (or segmentation) of the mode of production is its most pertinent distinctive feature. One usually speaks of the dominance of a level if, within the hierarchically segmented mode of production, one of the levels prevails over the others. Thus, dominance can refer to the relative prevalence of one level within the segmented mode of production, but it may also refer to the prevalence of any one mode within the linkage of more than one mode of production, e.g. such as may result from the penetration of capitalism.

A simplifying combinatory game now leads to the construction of three modes of production, each with economic, political and ideological dominance. The first mode coincides with capitalism: the economy has become an autonomous process and politics and ideology are geared to the unhampered functioning of the economy, at least in classical capitalism. As has been repeatedly argued, colonial and post-colonial capitalism in Africa offers a different picture: colonial political control has for a long time been an absolute condition for the expansion of the capitalist mode of production.[7]

If the political level is dominant, we find ourselves in a tributary, feudal, or slavery mode of production. The monopoly of physical force determines who is master and who servant. States with a tributary mode of production once stretched over the whole of Africa, from the Islamic kingdoms of the Sahel to the Bantu kingdoms in South Africa. The decisive role of violence, however, is more than most societies can bear; it is usually concealed under all sorts of ideological forms. How do we imagine a mode of production in which the ideological is dominant? In the negative sense, the answer is a situation in which all permanent relations of power and exploitation are impossible. In the positive sense, such a society would obtain where the fundamental social rule of reciprocity, first formulated by Marcel Mauss, would have free play in both enmity and friendship, without being subject to relations of power and exploitation (Mauss 1924). The rule imposing the obligation to give, to receive, and to give back, cannot be derived from the logic of the other levels. It is the heart of what I should like to call the 'symbolic order', in line with the structuralist approach in anthropology. The term *ideology* I should like, then, to reserve for a situation in which this symbolic order fulfils only a secondary, supporting function in regard to other levels. To avoid misunderstanding it should be clear that the dominance of the 'symbolic order' does not mean universal harmony and peace. Ethnographers working in that type of society have observed plenty of self-interest and power games. These forms of manipulation, however, follow a logic that is quite different from that that we find in a capitalist mode of production. Before the colonial era Africa still possessed a large number of societies in which the symbolic order was dominant within the mode of production. Even in villages that had been incorporated into a tributary system the symbolic order continued to play an

150

important part at the local level. This dominance of the symbolic order, however, nowhere occurred in a 'pure' form. In what is called the 'domestic mode of production', this dominance was always accompanied by established positions of power that old men held at the expense of youths and women, but this power was based on the elders' role in the exchange of gifts and not on their monopoly of violence or of the means of production.

When capitalism is imposed upon these other modes of production, as happened for instance during the colonial era in Africa, two types of tension are generated: tensions between the basic principles of the respective logics of the two conflicting modes of production and tensions between the classes as defined by each of the two modes of production. Normally the capitalist and the pre-capitalist modes of production do not continue neatly to confront each other according to all the rules of the gentle art of fencing, until such time that one will have slain the other. On the contrary, all sorts of cross-connections emerge between both modes of production. The basic principles of the two systems intertwine to such a degree that social intercourse is increasingly governed by a logic that is internally contradictory. In addition to this, the classes as defined by both modes of production may enter into complex relations, one of the most common of these being an alliance between the dominant classes of both modes.

This brief discussion may serve to indicate that, within the African social reality, the tensions are much more numerous, many faceted — and also much more confusing — than could be represented by the simple schemas on which, in Lukács's and Goldmann's views, the European novel is based. The range of contradictions that the African novelist has at his disposal is altogether broader than that of his European colleague. In most cases the African writer uses only a limited selection out of this total range, and in doing so the writer simplifies the image of society that is offered. 'The Great African Novel', to which continuous reference is made in current literary criticism, for instance by Achebe (1975: 54), still remains to be written!

The works of some prominent African writers as seen from the perspective of the articulation of modes of production

We shall now consider the work of six African writers and assess to what extent the vision of society that underlies their works is a reflection of one or several of the contradictions discussed above. The selection of these authors is partly determined by the fact that their books are well known, partly by the controversial nature of these works (Armah, Laye), and partly by their being available in English. All books to be discussed here, with the exception of Bessie Head's, are also commented upon in the collections of essays by Achebe and Soyinka quoted above. For a detailed assessment of my argument I must refer the reader to the texts of the various novels themselves. For within the scope of this article I could not even begin to offer anything like a complete summary and analysis of the contents of the works in question.

In my discussion of these works I shall arrange them more or less chronologically. First I shall deal with Laye (Guinea) and Achebe (Nigeria). Laye's *L'Enfant noir* was the first major French novel to be written by an African; similarly *Things Fall Apart* was the first major African novel in English. For both authors, the symbolic order is the essence of things African. The next author, Ouologuem (Mali), radically opposes this view with his *Le Devoir de violence*. According to him, violence and power struggles are characteristic of Africa. In the works of Bessie Head (South Africa, Botswana) and Sembène Ousmane (Senegal) all attention focuses on economic life, and dynamics of the production process are a source of hope — albeit in a different sense for these two writers. Finally Armah's work draws, in reversed order, the balance sheet of the problematic of these five authors: in *The Beautyful Ones Are Not Yet Born* the economy takes the central position, in *Why Are We So Blest?* it is the political order, and in *Two Thousand Seasons* Armah investigates the vicissitudes of symbolic exchange in Africa.

Achebe's nostalgic farewell to symbolic riches

The world that disintegrates in *Things Fall Apart* is, as I have already indicated, the symbolic order, that used to give integration and meaning to life in Umuofia and that Achebe portrays through various drum rhythms, the auspicious flight patterns of birds, the taboos surrounding birth and death, the status hierarchy of adult men, the duels, the festivals. The dominance of the symbolic order, however, is not reduced to something idyllic and nothing more. Such dominance demands sacrifice. Ikemefuna, a child that was once given to Umuofia in compensation for murder and that has grown up as a playmate of the son of the main character, Okonkwo, is sacrificed by order of the oracle. In Umuofia power is in the hands of the council of Elders, and of the *egwugwu*. The *egwugwu* is the assembly of masked ancestral spirits. It constitutes the highest juridical authority and is impersonated by the elders, those who have acquired the highest fame. The narrative makes clear that the power of the elders is entirely based on their symbolic position as concretized by their masks. When the mask is torn away, at the aptly chosen dramatic climax of the story, the power of the *egwugwu* is broken for ever.

Likewise, economic activities are dominated by the symbolic order. By working hard a man is able to sponsor festivals and thus to acquire titles. The accumulation process does not take on a life of its own. This fact is also clear from the way the community deals with the debts that Okonkwo's father has incurred. He is not forced to work in order to pay off the debts; rather, he is relegated to the lowest rung of the status ladder and, thus, becomes one of the *efulefu*, the meek ones, those whom one can insult and call 'woman'. His self-chosen role of dreamer, storyteller, and musician is not infringed upon.

The world Achebe presents to us thrives solely on symbolic exchange. The radical student of economic anthropology would have a whole series of questions to ask in this context: 'Do the titled men and the *efulefu* have equal opportunities?' 'Is difference in status merely a function of prowess and industriousness?' 'Do the *osu* merely form a group that is symbolically inferior and unclean or do they also perform certain services for the "free men" of Umuofia?'

It is significant that Achebe hides these, and other, questions under the cloak of symbolism, as if to emphasize the contradiction between the social order within which he himself writes and the social order that he is describing. Achebe, however, applies his culturalist vision consistently. Political violence and economic influence stay in the background even when he describes the victory of the Church and the colonial administration in Umuofia. The colonial presence does not seem to amount to more than a catalyst that enables the ancient order to destroy itself. For this ancient order turns out to contain its own antagonistic contradictions. The way Achebe conceives these contradictions is again totally symbolic: between those who are, symbolically, insiders and those who are outsiders. Insiders are the free men, particularly the titled men, and of the latter especially the elders, who are members of the *egwugwu* assembly, and priests, officiants. Outsiders are, foremost, the unclean slaves; moreover, the men who have no titles, the so-called *efulefu*; the young men in general, who themselves have no ritual office yet; and, finally, the women, among the latter it is particularly the mothers of twins (who have to be left exposed in the wilds) who turn out to bear a grudge against the system. The symbolic outsider *par excellence* is the boy Ikemefuna who has been given as a compensation for murder by a neighbouring village and who is eventually sacrificed to appease the gods. For that system to fall apart, all that is needed is that the missionary (who brings a new way of being insider) mounts his 'iron horse' and, lo and behold, his new converts fill the ranks (Achebe 1958: 102). First the slaves accept Christianity; then the mothers who want to retain their twins. The one-time playmate of Ikemefuna becomes the first catechist, and finally the *efulefu* realize that the Church forms a means to compete with the titled men.

Sociologically speaking, the dramatic climax of the narrative is flawless. All contradictions within the narrative appear here in concentrated form. The festival of Mother Earth is to be held on a Sunday. Because the *egwugwu* are expected to arrive in the village any moment, the *women* are not allowed to leave the church and go home. If they did, it would be a terrible insult. A delegation of church members manages to persuade the *egwugwu* to retire a little while, so as to enable the women of the congregation to pass. One of the members of the delegation, however, is Enoch, a son of the priest of the snake cult who has become totally committed to the new faith. Enoch boasts that the *egwugwu* would not dare to touch a Christian anyway. Then one of the *egwugwu* hits Enoch with his cane, and Enoch retaliates by tearing off the *egwugwu*'s mask, an unprecedented act of sacrilege. This tearing-off of the mask settles the case once and for all. The skirmishes that follow only reinforce the demise of the ancient order.

In *Things Fall Apart* Achebe has managed to subdue Umuofia to colonial rule and to incorporate it into the capitalist economy without firing a single shot and without the faintest tinkling of money. The cash crops that the villagers have begun to cultivate, and the store with its colonial commodities, are only mentioned in order to indicate, in a 'realistic' way, that the times have changed. They are not conceived as the forces that have contributed to the destruction of the ancient order. In the narrative, the District Commissioner's prison only features as a place where the process of unmasking the elders, in their own eyes and those of the community, is carried to its ultimate conclusion.

If Achebe had been a social scientist, one could have classified him in one category with theoreticians of culture contact, such as Malinowski (see Malinowski 1945). Achebe's vision, however, is more advanced in at least two ways: it takes into account such contradictions as exist within the non-European culture and as provide a foothold for western penetration; moreover, he disposes of the idea of gradual 'acculturation'. *Things Fall Apart* is a study in culture conflict.

Laye's way back

Just like *Things Fall Apart*, Laye's *L'Enfant noir* is the description of a process of deculturation. It is the autobiographical narrative of Laye's expulsion from his parents' culture. The more he progresses in school, the more he loses contact with his own world. From the way that world is described, it is clear that it has not yet 'fallen apart'.

The road taken by Laye with his second book is far more interesting than this exodus from the parental culture. For in *Le Regard du roi* Laye attempts to find the way back towards that culture. Here his road parts from that of Achebe. For in the latter's second novel, *No Longer at Ease*, we follow the inhabitants of Umuofia into the world that has fallen apart and contemplate the ambiguous world of African capitalism. Laye, by contrast, goes back, in search of the ancient coherent order.

To express this project clearly, Laye has to create the greatest possible contrast between the journey's point of departure and the regained order. For this reason his main character is not an African, or a European interested in Africa, but a European who is totally alien and estranged: Clarence, a white gambler. Because of gambling debts Laye has him thrown out of the company of his whisky-drinking white friends. Thus Clarence has to depend entirely on his African environment. He goes and looks for a job, trying his luck with the person Clarence considers to be the main employer in the indigenous labour market: the king. Once he has come near to the king it becomes clear that the principles of the labour market scarcely apply here. In order to qualify for a certain profession — for instance a simple job as drummer — one has to belong to a certain lineage.

> 'That is not a simple occupation,' said the beggar. 'The drummers are drawn from a noble caste and their employment is hereditary. Even if you had been allowed to beat a drum, your drumming would have had no meaning. You have to know how. . . . You see, you're a white man!' (Laye, 1976: 39)

This remark sums up the program of the novel. We could paraphrase the beggar's lesson as follows: 'Here labour is not sold, it does not have any exchange value, and the use value (the production of drum beats) is not very important either. What does count is the symbolic value, but to that you are an outsider.'

Clarence has to hear this message time and again without understanding it. Thus the beggar (whom Clarence takes at first for a dirty lumpenproletarian) turns out to be a character with a considerable amount of professional pride. For who equals him in the gentle art of asking, and accepting favours? The only thing that really counts is expertise in giving and receiving, in symbolic exchange. The exchange of commodities forms the model that Clarence constantly takes for granted, but that does not apply here. As the beggar teaches him, 'chance' does not exist (i.e., opportunities within an unpersonal, autonomously functioning system); 'the only thing that exists is favours' (i.e., opportunities within a personalized and meaningful order) (1976: 13). Thus we are in a better position to understand why Laye had to portray Clarence as a gambler.

All habitual notions of capitalism are undermined in *Le Regard du roi*. Thus Diallo, the axe-smith, demonstrates that there is no separation between producer, product and means of production (Laye 1976: 21):

> But what will the king want with an axe? . . . He will accept it; at least I hope he will accept it, and perhaps he will even deign to admire it: but he will accept it and admire it only in order to give me pleasure. After all, what sort of pleasure could he take

in it? There will always be axes that are finer and more deadly, more murderously sharp than any I can fashion. . . . Yet I go on forging it. . . . Perhaps I am like a tree which can bear only one kind of fruit. Yes, I am like that tree.[8]

This passage again stresses that it is the value as a gift that matters, while the exchange value and the use value of the axe are immaterial. The labour relationship into which Clarence finally enters, and the sort of labour he performs mocks all laws of labour under capitalism. In exchange for a woman and an ass the beggar transfers Clarence to one of the king's vassals, for whom Clarence will discharge 'certain light assignments'. The real nature of these assignments is obscure to him until the day that he happens to enter the women's quarters and notices that the children present there have a remarkably light skin colour. He realizes that he is nothing but a 'rooster' or a 'stallion', a role commonly ridiculed in his environment. Each night he is drugged in order to perform. Just like the axe-smith, Clarence in his work is 'a tree which can bear only one type of fruit'.

Clarence's capitalist attitude disintegrates more and more in the course of the narrative. At the vassal's court he is constantly watched by two guardians, and, in fact, he is a slave, within a mode of production of the tributary type as defined above. More and more, however, the story acquires overtones of an initiation. Retrospectively, Clarence's moments of despair turn out to have been stages towards his complete partaking of the symbolic order. At the moment that his despair reaches a climax, the king appears in the palace of his vassal and, with a high-priestly gesture, offers to Clarence a place underneath his cloak, close to the source of the true life and the heart of the community.

With *Le Regard du roi* Laye has written the perfect 'anti-Kafkaesque' novel. Between Kafka's characters and their environment lies a chasm similar to that between Clarence and his environment. At one side of this chasm exists the symbolic order with its personalized logic of giving and receiving; at the other side is the world of capital based on impersonal probability. Kafka's characters are in search of redemption but, instead, find destruction in a world of impersonal calculation. Laye's hero, whose expectations are cut to the measure of this impersonal world, finds a redemption of a sort that runs counter to his own calculations. Therefore, it does not make sense to reproach Laye (as Soyinka

(1976: 125) does) for his un-African, Kafka-like approach. In Laye's work, the Kafka-like chasm is only there in order to be bridged.

This desire to bridge, by means of the old African symbolic material, the chasm that in the west capitalism has created between person and world and between humans, is the essence of negritude. If one is to judge the negritude movement, one has to base one's judgment upon its finest expressions and not on the reflections of one author who happened to be in a position to raise negritude to a state ideology or on the reflections of a western philosopher who has praised negritude by means of a toast whose effect was 'to drink it under the table' (Soyinka 1976: 134). Soyinka, however, does base his judgment on such reflections and, as a consequence, he does not quite know what to make, within the framework of negritude, of impressive poetry like Birago Diop's *Souffles*. In order to understand what negritude is one should read Senghor's poetry rather than his public speeches; *Le Regard du roi* rather than Sartre's *L'Orphée noir*.[9]

Ouologuem's demystification offensive

For Achebe and Laye, but also for many other authors such as Kane and Conton, the essence of the African social reality lies in its symbolic nature. In an unexpectedly fierce way, Ouologuem opened a frontal attack on this vision with his *Le Devoir de violence* in 1968. His reconstruction of African history makes short work of the culturalist position, whether of the Islamist, the negritude, or the cultural anthropological variant.[10]

Since 1202 Nakem, the fictive kingdom around which this reconstruction is built, has been recklessly ruled by the dynasty of the Saifs. It is a state of the tributary type, with all the typical elements, such as an aristocracy and a priestly class, tribute-paying peoples, and slavery on a large scale. The slave trade plays an important part in international relations. The power of the Saif is based on a class of feudal lords and slave owners: after the colonization, which in Nakem was quite 'indirect', this set-up displays what we would call, with Pierre-Phillipe Rey, a 'class alliance' of the colonizer and the indigenous aristocracy (1973). Power is exercised through violence and ideological deception.

The Saifs are cunningly expert in both. Thus the Saif has at his disposal an intelligence and liquidation service that (by means of snakes that have been specially trained for this purpose) can dispose of people without leaving a trace.

The Saif's inventiveness and flexibility in ideological matters are even more far-reaching. He manages to enlist the support of nearly all great African ideological systems. First, there is the Saif's identity as a Jew. Just as it does for the Ethiopian *negus*, the Saif's Jewish descent endows him with an unrivalled dignity; it also gives him the right to reproach the Christian missions in his country in a fatherly fashion, especially when he finds that the latter are too successful: 'Israel is here to admonish the church to vigilance' (Ouologuem 1971: 72). Islam is the state religion of Nakem. When, towards the end of the nineteenth century, the Europeans enter Africa, the Saif realizes that he has to fabricate some progressive image and to be one step ahead of the intruders as far as the abolition of slavery is concerned. The Saif poses as some sort of *mahdi*. Under the banner of his new variety of Islam, 'a deliberately confused mumbling about human dignity, a learned mystification', he manages to bring about a number of reforms and to create a new unit in his empire (1971: 23). In his relation with the colonial powers he uses another ideology again: the *Shrobeni-usology*. Shrobeniusology was thrown into his lap by the ethnologist Shrobenius, who visited Nakem in 1910 and became convinced that 'African life . . . was pure art, intense religious symbolism, and a civilization once grandiose — but alas a victim of the white man's vicissitudes' (1971: 87). The Saif can well use such an ideology, which ignores relations of power and exploitation within Africa and openly blames Europeans. The Saif does not mind at all trying his hand at this kind of ideology:

> 'Ever so often,' Saif improvised, 'the tools used to carve a mask were blessed seventy-seven times by a priest, who all the while flagellating himself, gave blessings until the third day of the seventh year after the tree to be felled was chosen' (1971: 94).

Saif turns out to be a negritude philosopher *avant-la-lettre*. Ouologuem shows how this ideology serves several interests at the same time: In the first place a smoke screen of inconceivably profound symbolism will hide the political manipulations of the Saif from the eyes of both the European colonists and the African masses, although, the latter are 'Only too pleased to hear from the mouth of a white man that Africa was "the womb of the world and the cradle of civilization" ' (1971: 94). The European colonizer, moreover, has thus found a rhetorical means for the definition of his relation with the African potentates; African art objects flow towards European museums. Lastly, ethnologists acquire permanent positions at European universities.

Ouologuem lays extra stress on the deceptive nature of religion and ideology through the pious exclamations with which he punctuates his narrative of violence: 'God keep his soul' or 'A prayer for him' after another vicious murder (1971: 8 and 9). When Shrobenius departs for Europe, laden with art treasures: 'O Lord, a tear for the childlike good nature of the nigger-trash! Have pity, O Lord!' (1971: 95).

Le Devoir de violence not only criticizes the way in which religion and ideology have been dabbled with in Africa, but also expresses a vision of the relation between the colonizer and the colonized, and this vision transcends the rigid schema of 'the western oppressor' versus 'the oppressed African'. Among the novelists to be discussed in this article, Ouologuem comes closest to the viewpoint of the 'articulation of modes of production'. The European colonizer does not start his oppression from scratch (1971: 24):

> But to Nakem the colonial powers came too late, for with the help of the local notables a colonial overlord has established himself long since, and that colonial overlord was none other than Saif. All unsuspecting, the European conquerors played into his hands. Call it technical assistance. At that early date! So be it! Thy work be santified, O Lord. And Exalted.

After a while a veritable class alliance, in Rey's sense, emerged but only when France needed the Saif's military support against the Germans. Before that time the governor had made several attempts to free the people from their bonds of tribute and slavery, but to no avail. What was meant to be universal, compulsory education remained limited, through the intervention of the Saif, to just one easily intimidated category of the population. The slave trade continued to exist: the Saif's henchmen liquidated the governor, Vandame, 'Humanist, governor, friend of black freedom, civilizer of Nakem, family man, and republican' at the moment when this worthy is about to expose a slave trade network (1971: 114). The Saif rules that marriage between slaves is henceforth permitted. This ruling, however, is introduced in combination with a second one subjecting the women in the empire to clitoridectomy and infibulation. In this way Saif ingratiates himself with the men and nothing is changed in the overall balance of social violence in his empire. In the end the interests of colonizer and aristocrat turn out to coincide, for example, in the matter of labour recruitment. The forced labourers who construct the roads and railways are the aristocrats' slaves, who have been temporarily released for this work. This class alliance is finally sealed when the son of one of the Saif's domestic slaves is elected a member of the French Parliament. Even though Kassoumi obtained a brilliant Ph.D. degree — hence his epithet 'Black Pearl of French civilization'[11] — he cannot disentangle himself from the power network of the Saif, and he remains at the ruler's mercy. For this reason he is the most appropriate candidate for Parliament (1971: 165):

> Under these circumstances, the election of Raymond-Spartacus Kassoumi would satisfy people's hunger for miraculous destinies and at the same time flatter the white man, who would squeal with glee, that he had civilized his underdeveloped charge: *Ouhoum! gollè wari!*

While Achebe presented us with the vision of a culture conflict ending in the destruction of pre-colonial African society, here we see a power conflict from which the indigenous prince emerges as the major victor. With Kassoumi's appointment to Parliament, Saif ben Isaac al-Heit's task of subjecting the educated nigger-trash was completed' (1971: 167). In Ouologuem's perspective, Laye's king would only be a phantasm of an estranged intellect, which no longer knows the facts of African despotism, and Clarence could at best have been a puppet in a power game. White men who imagine themselves finding some kind of redemption in Africa are the African despot's chosen victims.

Ouologuem's message is unequivocal: no hope can be derived from the African past. He leaves us disillusioned, without offering us an alternative. Likewise, the next two authors do not expect anything from the past; but they differ from Ouologuem in that they do have hopes for the future.

Bessie Head's green revolution

We might as well be frank about it from the start: Bessie Head does believe in the emancipatory potential of capitalist development. It is her contention that small-scale capitalism on a co-operative basis offers a realistic opportunity for revolutionizing the stagnated relations of production in the countryside. *When Rain Clouds Gather* describes such a revolution.

In Botswana, a British development worker and a South African political refugee jointly try to get an agrarian development project for women off the ground. The project is thwarted by at least two factors: the local society is male dominated, and local — tributary — authorities consider the project a threat. These authorities, however, are subsequently defeated, in the course of what is a veritable class struggle at the village level. The two groups confronting each other are, on the one hand, the development workers as supported by the women and, on the other, the village headman and a politician who propounds African socialism. These, of course, are the very same enemies of the people as depicted in *Le Devoir de violence*: tributary potentates and a mystifying ideology.

The struggle centres on the use of communal land. According to ancient custom the village headman is to authorize such use, particularly if one is going to fence off plots and to construct permanent installations, such as irrigation tanks. When finally the men, too, side with the development project, the headman finds himself left without any support and commits suicide.

It is most remarkable that Bessie Head does not bat an eyelid when it comes to abolishing communal land tenure — a breach of custom that Achebe or Laye would have approached very differently. Head is particularly explicit about the sort of relations of production she envisages for Golema Mmidi (the village featuring in *When Rain Clouds Gather*): 'Makhaya [the South African] liked the idea that the whole of Golema Mmidi would be full of future millionaries' (1968: 156). In a developed Golema Mmidi, wealth has the shape of money: it is capital. Therefore we encounter our development worker expounding the elementary principles of capitalism. The relation between Golema Mmidi's subsistence economy and the market is, in the development worker's view, characterized by the cycle 'commodity–money–commodity' that he wants to change into a cycle 'money–commodity–

money', in other words, to initiate a process of capital accumulation (1968: 142):

> 'How many cattle do you have?' he asked.
> 'Eight,' she said.
> He was silent a moment making a swift mental calculation.
> 'You must sell the damned beasts,' he said '. . . You will have nine hundred pounds in the bank.'

The use values of the subsistence system or the prestige values of the cultural system, as embodied in the cattle, have to be converted into exchange values. Once this conversion has succeeded, the rest will follow in due course. Economic relations will have become dominant, and politics and ideology will follow suit. Bessie Head's God, who materializes towards the end of the narrative and then turns out to have played an important role, is independent from political and economic processes, which can be perfectly understood without recourse to that God. This God does not — as does the deity in Achebe's work — directly interfere through his oracles; nor is this God a king who takes part in social life, as in Laye's work. Bessie Head demonstrates the classical Calvinist separation between belief and action, which, as Max Weber (1958) has taught us, is one of the preconditions for capitalist development.

Head's optimism is largely based on the growth of productive forces, which are to bring about capitalist development. Therefore she shows great interest in technical details: 'If you have fifty-two fowls, you must build a coop, fifteen feet by twenty-five feet' (1968: 27 and again 71). 'The plan was to keep no more than two hundred cattle at a time on a ranch of seven thousand acres. If fewer beasts were kept. . . .' (1968: 39). The novel is a dithyramb on productive forces as liberated by science. For Bessie Head there is neither a way back, as in Laye's work, nor nostalgia, as in Achebe's work. The sooner things fall apart, the sooner we tear loose from the radiance of the king, the better!

Sembène's proletarian revolution

Like Head, Sembène Ousmane does not shed a tear for the disappearance of pre-capitalist Africa, even though he has an open eye for the destructive effect of the capitalist mode of production.

In his novelette *Le Mandat* he shows this destructive effect through the example of the proletarianization process in which the pious Senegalese Dieng is involved. Everyone in Dieng's environment tries to profit by the small amount of money that Dieng has temporarily entrusted to him. In the narrative this exploitation goes on under such pretexts as fraternal assistance, kin solidarity, assistance between neighbours. These pre-capitalist categories turn out to have lost all positive content. They have been reduced to a respectable façade, which conceals a capitalist process of accumulation, i.e., expropriation. This lesson is taught to Dieng, who is too preoccupied with piety and with his bigamous marital arrangements to understand the wider social processes in which he is involved. This lesson is driven home most painfully when Dieng's own nephew finally manoeuvres him into a position where he has no choice but surrendering his last possession, his house, to that nephew. Despite all this misery Sembène detects a glimpse of light in this proletarianization process: 'You think everyone is corrupt? No. Not even those who work are happy. Things will change' (1972: 136).

These discontented workers are depicted by Sembène in *Les Bouts de bois de Dieu* — the dramatized account of the railway strike on the Dakar–Niger railway in 1947. The people described by Sembène are full-fledged labourers. Their identity is determined by capitalism and by the productive forces created by capitalism (1970: 132):

> Their fellowship with the machine was deep and strong;
> stronger than the barriers which separated them from their
> employers, even stronger than the obstacle which until now had
> been insurmountable — the colour of their skin.

The railway management, however, tries to represent the labour dispute as a race conflict and, in fact, does experience it as such (1970: 270):

> It was probably Dejean, however, for whom the crisis was not
> only the most unexpected but the most totally incomprehen-
> sible. A discussion between employer and employees presup-
> poses the fact that there are employees and there is an
> employer. But he, Dejean, was not an employer; he was simply
> exercising a function which rested on the most natural of all
> bases — the right to an absolute authority over beings whose

colour made of them not subordinates with whom one could discuss anything, but men of another, inferior condition, fit only for unqualified obedience.

Whites who question this ideological postulate can no longer be maintained within the colonialist community and are fired like the failed negrophile ethnographer Leblanc, who had become a railway official. The ranks of the colonized are divided too. The well-to-do Islamic spiritual leaders are in collusion with the colonial administration; they condemn the strike as an ungodly act and even adopt the racist ideology wholesale (1970: 195). The strikers, however, can stand on their own against this class alliance. All the time the development of the strike demonstrates how, in the wake of the labour struggle, the pre-capitalist power relations crumble. The spiritual leaders are challenged, family ties give way to class solidarity, and witchcraft accusations are revoked. This disintegration of pre-capitalist power relations is particularly manifest in male–female relations. Both the petty bourgeoisie, as headed by the spiritual leaders, and the colonial authorities attempt to exploit traditional male–female relations in order to break the strike. The shopkeepers refuse credit to the strikers' wives and the city council cuts off water supplies in the hope that the wives will persuade their husbands to give up the strike. These measures, however, have a contrary effect. In Dakar they lead to a confrontation between women and the police, and the women of Thiès, which is the seat of the railway management, organize a protest march on foot to Dakar. The strike brings men and women closer to each other and forces a breakthrough in the ancient role patterns (1970: 75):

> When a man came back from a meeting, with bowed head and empty pockets, the first thing he saw were always the unfired stove, the useless cooking vessels, the bowls and gourds ranged in a corner, empty. Then he would seek the arms of his wife, without thinking, or caring, whether she was the first or the third. And seeing the burdened shoulders, the listless walk, the women became conscious that a change was coming for them as well.

Men will take on themselves chores that until then were women's work, such as fetching firewood and water; and the women see their opportunity to assume tasks that until then were reserved to men. The culmination of this process is the protest march to Dakar, when men obey the directives issued by Penda, the female leader of the march; behind the women, the men trundle bicycles loaded with water and food.

Sembène's book is a eulogy of hope. He shows how the struggle of the working class creates a new form of solidarity between humans, which also implies the end of such pre-capitalist forms of oppression (male and female, old and young, sorcery, religion) as may still exist among those fighting the proletarian class struggle.

Armah: vulnerability in a demystified world

The odour of capital: Armah's The Beautyful Ones Are Not Yet Born

It is hardly possible to conceive of a stronger contrast than that between the hopeful militants of Sembène and the subdued, anonymous railway worker who is the main character of *The Beautyful Ones*. The latter's relation with the railway world is not one of pride, as among the men of the Dakar–Niger railway. He wonders, 'Why, between here and there, was it necessary that there should be a connection?' (Armah 1969: 27). He does his work in order to earn wages: 'A job was a job. It did not matter at all that nothing was done on most jobs' (1969: 183), but also in order to escape for a while from his wife, who complains that there is not enough money in the house to buy bare necessities and who wants him to make a career, just as his cousin Koomson has done. She admires Koomson, who has risen to the position of government minister and, believes that, if her husband cannot attain a higher position, he might at least accept bribes, just as everyone else does.

The workers at the goods station where he is employed, exhibit not the slightest form of revolutionary spirit, but merely cynical admiration for money and power (1969: 129):

> 'He is only a small boy . . .'
> 'Yes, it's the CPP that has been so profitable for him . . .'[12]
> 'Two cars now . . .'
> 'No, you're way behind. Three. The latest is a white
> Mercedes, 220 Super.'
> 'You will think I am lying, but he was my classmate, and now
> look at me.'

'Ah, life is like that.'
'Ei, and girls!'
'Running to fill his cars. Trips to the Star for weekends in
Accra. Booze. Swinging niggers, man.'[13]
'Girls, girls. Fresh little ones still going to Achimota and Holy
Child . . .'[14]
'These Holy Child girls!'
'Achimota too!'
'He is cracking them like tiger nuts.'
'Contrey, you would do the same . . .'
'True . . . money swine.'
'Money swine.'

Ghana is in the grip of some form of state capitalism. Despite the
'socialist' anticorruption legislation, party bosses and civil servants
amass private fortunes within the State Furniture Corporation, the
State Marble Corporation and the Ghana National Trading
Corporation:

> The G.N.T.C., of course, was regarded as a new thing, but only
> the name had really changed with Independence. The shop had
> always been there, and in the old days it had belonged to a rich
> Greek and was known by his name, A. G. Leventis. So in a way
> the thing was new. Yet the stories that were sometimes heard
> about it were not stories of something young and vigorous, but
> the same old stories of money changing hands and throats
> getting moistened and palms getting greased. Only this time if
> the old stories aroused any anger, there was nowhere for it to
> go. The sons of the nation were now in charge, after all. How
> completely the new thing took after the old (1969: 11, compare
> also pp. 172, 174).

The embodiment of these sons of the nation is Koomson: the
cousin of 'the man', now a Plenipotentiary Minister and a Hero of
Socialist Labour, and a one-time docker (1969: 66). He lives in a
super house and has a wife who, when she shakes hands with 'the
man' from within the car, withdraws her hand 'as quickly as if
contact were a well-known calamity, and the woman inside seems
plainly to have forgotten about the man outside' (1969: 45). In
fact, Koomson's hands have undergone a transformation since the
time when he worked in the harbour, but the transformation was
not in the direction one would expect (1969: 153):

Ideological hands, the hands of revolutionaries leading their people into bold sacrifices, should these hands not have become even tougher than they were when their owner was hauling loads along the wharf?

Koomson is Armah's portrait of the ruling class in Ghana. It is a class that derives its position from a combination of political and economic power typical for a situation in which the state constitutes the principal capitalist. This class is complemented by an apathetic working class, as personified by 'the man'. Armah does not depict third parties in the class struggle — elements that might derive from other modes of production. The contradiction in Ghanaian society is exhaustively described by the struggle — which, however, has reached an all-time low — between the two classes of capitalism.

The Accra of *The Beautyful Ones* is in the grip of money. Money puts a hazy shine over the city, but if you look closer the shine is merely a veil that covers the process of decay. If you happen to belong to the happy few who partake in the glamorous shine you have to be constantly alert lest you be polluted, as described above for Koomson's wife. The refuse-bins whose reassuring inscriptions, 'Keep Your Country Clean By Keeping Your City Clean' (1969: 8), are still wet with paint, hardly rise above the garbage that has piled up at their feet. Shine and freshness form a varnish that hardly conceals the decay underneath; also in the case of Koomson's wife, with her wig, the deodorant in her armpits, and her perfume 'trapped in creases of prematurely tired skin' (1969: 42).

Significantly Koomson's real nature is revealed at the moment of Nkrumah's fall. From a distinguished gentleman he is changed into, literally, a bag of shit (1969: 191f.):

His mouth had the rich stench of rotten menstrual blood. The man held his breath until the new smell had gone down in the mixture with the liquid atmosphere of the Party man's farts filling the room. At the same time Koomson's insides gave a growl longer than usual, an inner fart of personal, corrupt thunder.

The same Koomson who declined making use of the man's latrine is now forced to use its sewer as an escape route.

What is the meaning of this shine and this decay? Nothing but the deceptive effects of money. Money (i.e., exchange value) carries the suggestion of adding some special value to people and things but, in fact, devalues and corrupts those people and things — as in the case of the gleam of the floodlights of the Atlantic Caprice Hotel (1969: 12):

> It was getting harder to tell whether the gleam repelled more than it attracted, attracted more than it repelled, or just did both at once in one disgustingly confused feeling all the time these heavy days.

That all this refers to the false shine of money is further brought out in the following passage (1969: 3f.):

> In the weak light inside the bus he peered closely at the markings on the note. Then a vague but persistent odor forced itself on him and he rolled the cedi up and deliberately, deeply smelled it. He had to smell it again, this time standing up and away from the public leather of the bus seat. But the smell was not his mistake. Fascinated, he breathed it slowly into his lungs. It was a most unexpected smell for something so new to have: it was a very old smell, very strong, and so very rotten that the stench itself of it came with a curious satisfying pleasure.

'The man' seeks an escape from this sham world. The only person with whom he can discuss a problem that hinges on the symbolic is the Teacher; this is a man who has totally dissociated himself from society but that does not make him less cynical (1969: 65):

> 'But, you see; it is not a choice between life and death, but what kind of death we can bear, in the end. Have you not seen there is no salvation anywhere?'
> 'My wife thinks there is.'
> 'There is salvation of some kind, of course,' said the naked man, 'but only with the cycle of our damnation itself.'

This cycle is the cycle of capital; the military coup is not going to change it. In the final scene of the book 'the man' walks back home and watches soldiers at a road block exacting bribes from the driver of a minibus; this bus carries the inscription 'The beautyful ones are not yet born'.

Armah deprives us of whatever hope Sembène and Head had inspired us with. In his second and, to my mind, best novel, which centers on a political problem, his pessimism equals that of Ouologuem.

A political castration

Why Are We So Blest? argues the absolute impotence of the African revolutionary intelligentsia. Modin Dofu, one of the three autobiographical narrators in the novel, decides to give up his dissertation on the Maji-Maji rising,[15] which he has been preparing at some American university, and instead to offer his services to the liberation movement in Congheria. He arrives at this decision as he realizes that the more he studies the anticolonial resistance movement the more he gets out of touch with the *maji*, the binding force of the movements (Armah 1974: 222):

> But those of us who get into a position to find out the composition of the European poison absorb so much of it ourselves, we become completely incapable of creating a real, workable maji. We are addicted to the poison that kills us.

He departs with the intention of finding the answer to the question 'how to end the oppression of the African, to kill the European beasts of prey, to remake ourselves' (1974: 230).

Aimée, his white girl friend and the second narrator of the book, accompanies him. There is, however, no place for their ideals within the liberation movement, which boasts the slogan 'Le silence de chacun assure le repos de tous' ['When everyone remains silent, all will enjoy a restful peace'] (1974: 262).

The movement's leader, Jorge Manuel, can only understand people who are after power. He cannot see why Modin has given up his study and finds his desire to participate with the people, foolish, 'You forget this. Our people down there, they are, how can I say it, they are rough people, uncultivated' (1974: 252).

It turns out that for Modin there is no way out of the white empire. The *maji* is outside his reach, if it exists at all. Solo, the third narrator of *Why Are We So Blest?* and a translator at the party bureau, takes it that the revolution has betrayed this *maji*. Along with the other one-time militants of the movement, he feels cheated. These militants constitute, in the words of a veteran, 'l'essence de la révolution' in the double sense of the French word *essence*: they are the fuel of the revolution, which is spent in the course of the process, and they are its essence. Thus little is left of the revolution: 'The arrangements made for fighting privilege were themselves structures of privilege' (1974: 114). Within this setup there is 'space for the beggar and the newly rich, for cannon fodder and the briefcase-carrying traveller' (1974: 115). Instead Solo had expected to find some new form of social solidarity. When he saw that little of the sort was in fact brought about, he resigned from the movement. The reaction of his one-time comrades was scornful, 'Ah, yes. That one. His nerves failed him' (1974: 13), or reproachful (1974: 12):

> Why he chooses to spend his time making such a mysterious
> thing of love when all around us there is so much to be done,
> when the revolution in its making demands so much time, so
> much energy, so much of everything that can be given.

The paralysing grip of the imperialist power structure extends right into Modin's love life. Except in his affair with the Afro-American girl Naita, he remains lonely in all his other relationships, which all involve 'the daughters of our white death' (1974: 123, 230). In the case of Mrs Jefferson it is Modin who retains the attitude of an observer (1974: 130), in the cause of Aimée it is she who, at the moment she undresses, 'seemed to situate herself somewhere outside what was happening' (1974: 178). In fact Modin is being used by her (1974: 167):

> I was another rare creature, an African vehicle to helm them to
> reach the strange destinations of their souls. It did not matter
> that I learned so well to stay detached. They did not need
> closeness to another human being.

'Exploitation' has to be an element in this imperialist eroticism. When Modin wonders why he does not seek sexual contact with his own people, he has to admit to himself that those people confront him much more with the painful nature of his own existence (1974: 208):

> Easier to let white females absorb the loving impulse, use the
> accumulated energy within our black selves to do work of
> importance to their white selves. Of what other use have
> Africa's tremendous energies been these many centuries but to
> serve the lusts of whites?

The castration scene with which this story ends is the apotheosis of this eroticism. At the same time it manages to concentrate Modin's political impotence in one image, which we can analyse in tabulated form.

Four soldiers of the colonial army seize Aimée and force her to copulate with Modin who is tied to the ground.	The European is on top and the African lies underneath and is powerless; the European who 'really' takes an interest in the African is yet a puppet of the European power game. The African intellectual is linked to his oppressor by means of his very desire.
By pulling a thin iron wire they cut off the tip of Modin's penis in erection.	The mutilation physically completes the process by which European imperialism cuts the African intellectual loose from his fellows, a process which started at the first school day. Even now the cutting depends on the intellectual's desire.
Aimée sucks the blood that flows from the wound.	The European empire can always use and absorb the African's *maji*, even the last drop.
She asks Modin: 'Do you love me?'	The European oppressor just takes it for granted that he receives recognition for his exploitative work which he sees as an act of love.
When Modin does not answer, Aimée accepts the soldiers' offer of a lift in their vehicle, leaving Modin behind in the desert.	The European revolutionary can ultimately fall back upon his fellow-Europeans.

What happened between Aimée and Modin is only one phase in her strategy for survival. Or, as Solo puts it (1974: 232):

> She played at love; her aim was survival, not union: to survive, a possessor of the experience, not its victim. And if the

experience was the death of her companion? The intenser the experience, the blinder fool the dead.

While Ouologuem showed us how the interests of the indigenous aristocracy coincided with those of colonialism, Armah here claims that there is no essential difference between the political structures of the capitalist world system and that of a revolutionary African state. Both are inimical to the form of togetherness which Modin and Solo — and Armah himself — are after. It is this form of togetherness that is explicitly treated in Armah's next book, *Two Thousand Seasons*.

Armah's utopia

Two Thousand Seasons is a reconstruction of a thousand years of African history, organized around the question 'What happened to the Way?' The Way is the rule of reciprocity: of giving, receiving, and returning the gift. The Way precludes power and internal personality splits. The Way has originated as the result of a long struggle between men and women in prehistory. This Way ruled in Africa for thirty thousand seasons, until Anoa's prophecy of doom foretold two thousand seasons of destruction and death, as a penalty for excessive generosity: 'Turn from this generosity of fools. The giving that is split from receiving is no generosity but hatred of the giving self, a preparation for the self's destruction. Turn' (Armah 1973: 25). Her counsel is ignored and the time of disaster begins. In the first one thousand dry seasons the people of the Way are pestered by the Predators from the desert. At first the latter settle as guests among the people of the Way. As soon as the Predators see the opportunity, however, they seize power. When after a long struggle the intruders have spent their energy, the autochthonous princes follow their example and create states. Armah is even more dismissive than Ouologuem of the golden age of the tributary mode of production in Africa: 'The quietest king, the gentlest leader of the mystified, is criminal beyond the exercise of any comparison' (1973: 100). During the reign of Koranche, who had stretched the prerogatives of kingship to a point where princes of the blood no longer needed to participate in initiation, the 'destroyers' from across the sea set foot on African soil. With their advent the next thousand wet seasons of disaster began.

King Koranche made a treaty with the whites. The royal

councillor, Isanusi, warns the king and the people that this will mean the end of the Way. Desirous of trade commodities, the king drives Isanusi into exile. From his undetectable hiding place in the forest Isanusi keeps on preaching the Way and observing the custom of initiation. Then a group of initiates is sold to the whites as slaves. They manage to escape while on their way to the coast and return to Isanusi to form, under his spiritual leadership, a core of resistance against the mounting destructive influence of the whites.

A new phase of white domination is reached when this group of conspirators, in collusion with Prince Kamuzu, who is likewise opposed to Koranche, manage to conquer the whites' fortress and to free the prisoners there.[16] Kamuzu does not stick to his promise to destroy the fortress but settles in it himself; for (1973: 268):

> Power, he informed us, was a thing always to be taken as it was found, just whichever way it was found, not as the taker would wish it to be. We now had power in our grasp. If we were interested in finally moving away forever from victim situations, we should not be hesitant to step into the white people's shoes.

Kamuzu continues to trade with the whites, and soon he has himself called 'Osagyefo' — indeed.[17] The whites consider the small group of adherents of the Way as troublemakers and promise to asist Kamuzu if he can silence them. Again the adherents retreat to the forest. There they defend their domain, which can only be found by initiates. Isanusi dies. The only consolation he leaves his followers is that at the end of the two thousand seasons the trial will be over; then the Way will be restored in all its splendour and disconnectedness and estrangement will come to an end.

The unity of Armah's work

We have come full circle. After a number of visions in which the emancipatory possibilities and impossibilities of the political and economic relations were dominant, Armah has brought us back to a society based on the order of giving, receiving, and returning gifts. Armah, thus, seems to provide rear cover for Laye and Achebe. Does this mean that we have returned to our point of departure, or is the circle in fact a spiral?

At any rate Armah's vision is wider. Contrary to Laye and

174

Achebe, he explicitly recognizes the paralysing grip of tributary and capitalist relations of production. Armah has no illusions about the workers' struggle in Africa or about the struggle against imperialism. He certainly lacks all affinity with the petty capitalist perspective as presented by Bessie Head. On the other hand, his faith in an 'African Way' is unshakable.

What to think of this faith?

It certainly is rather dogmatic. It has not been woven into the fabric of a reality with which we can still feel empathy, as Laye and Achebe did in their evocations of their African background. Armah's vision has a much more theoretical ring. One sometimes has the impression of reading a stylized paraphrase of Mauss's *Essai sur le don*.

Armah's African Way is not a life form that he has known from experience and wishes to retain, but one in which we want to believe despite and against the existing reality. The postulative tone that characterizes Armah's evocation of the Way and of a possible return to that Way is the tone of Utopia, of a land that is not to be found in the existing world but nevertheless serves as a frame of reference to condemn and overcome that world. For where can we find Isanusi's forest so that the anonymous main character of *The Beautyful Ones Are Not Yet Born* and Modin might find some shelter in it? Where are the historical bearers of the recollections of the Way and of its future restoration? The Teacher in Armah's first novel and Solo in his second are both heroes of the inward eye, isolated characters without any audience.

Armah is not capable of bridging the chasm between, on the one hand, his African Way and, on the other, the Congherian pseudorevolution and the sham world in which his anonymous 'man' has to live. Even with the Way writ large on his banner, the 'man' will remain lonely, and Modin's political aspirations will retain their suicidal nature. Was it not precisely their search for the Way that estranged them from their environments?

Armah's three novels constitute one coherent whole. *Two Thousand Seasons* expresses whatever remained implicit in the earlier works. Therefore, Soyinka is wrong when he interprets the fine flower painted on the back of a minibus (which, as we have seen, lent its name to Armah's first novel), as the harbinger of a more hopeful vision that was only to mature in *Two Thousand Seasons* (Soyinka 1976: 116). Armah's point of view has not changed. All three novels express one utopian vision. The search for a way out of the sham excremental world of *The Beautyful Ones Are Not Yet Born* and Modin's quest for the authentic *maji* are mirrored by the deadly disconnecting effect of the tributary Predators and the capitalist destroyers in the living way of reciprocity. In all three novels destruction and alienation belong to the present world injected as it is by the deadly poison of the West, whereas life and fulfillment belong to a past African utopia.

Armah's last book to date, *The Healers* (1979), does not fundamentally change this orientation. Again we are presented with a group of people of the Way who from their sacred groves try to unite their following to make a last stand against western intrusion. Betrayed by their kings and militarily defeated by technological superiority, they become witnesses of the onset of the western Apocalypse. The remark of one of the healer-prophets that ends the book — 'Does it not amuse you that in their wish to drive us apart the whites are actually bringing us work [the unification of the people in accordance with the Way] for the future' (1979: 309) hardly seems to reach the ears of the other healers in their distress.

Conclusion: Towards a periodization of the African novel

Between the publication of Laye's *L'Enfant noir* in 1953 and Armah's *Two Thousand Seasons* in 1973 a change has taken place: a movement from a nostalgic vision of the African symbolic order to a utopian vision. Both Laye and Achebe write on the basis of a painful awareness that some reality they were once part of, or might have been part of, has been lost. They have no clear conception of the adverse forces. In their vision these forces are external to the African world they are trying to describe. Armah writes on the basis of an — even more painful — awareness that these adverse forces have been victorious. In his novels it is the African tradition itself that has become external to the world he describes. We can now understand why Achebe had to disqualify Armah as an 'un-African' writer. Achebe's allegation exactly measures the distance separating his own nostalgia from Armah's utopia.

On the basis of the above analyses it is now possible to group the authors discussed according to three fundamental orientations in the way they conceive the relation between the pre-capitalist modes of production and capitalism.

A. In a nostalgic orientation attention is focused on culture and on the lost coherence of a world ordered according to the principles of symbolic exchange. This is where negritude belongs, along with the religiously committed authors insofar as their religion is conceived of as a total order encompassing social life, as in the case of Hamidou Kane. In this vision the contradiction western–African overrules any contradiction that may be derived from the tributary or capitalist modes of production.

B. The authors sharing the second orientation — Head, Sembène, and Ouologuem — turn their backs on the African past and look for alternatives in the African society as they find it. They have a clear eye for the cross-links between the various modes of production and the complex class relations deriving from these linkages. Where Head bets on the peasant with small-holdings, Sembène draws his hope from the struggle of the working class. Ouologuem's sociological analysis of the Empire of Nakem brings him to the conclusion that there are no classes that can bring any fundamental change. For the purpose of this classification one could call this orientation 'realistic'. Achebe's later novels also belong to this orientation.

C. In a utopian orientation the capitalist mode of production and the power system connected with it, have taken complete possession of social life. African culture is formulated as counter-culture.

These orientations can be seen as literary equivalents to some of the political ideologies that have played a role on the African scene in the past twenty years.

Nostalgia with its emphasis on the communal and symbolic nature of African society, and with its implicit denial that capitalism and its class relations have come to stay, would correspond to the ideologies of African Socialism. African Socialism pretends to have found a shortcut from traditional communalism to a form of modern socialism in which the old brotherhood, freed from the distorting effects of colonial domination, would be maintained.

The second 'realist' group of authors, who turn their backs on the temptation of the past, finds its political equivalent in movements that are based on contradictions inside the existing African social formations: Sembène in the struggle of workers and peasants against capitalism and its allied classes; Bessie Head in the political visions that animate the hopeful works of rural development schemes, cooperatives and aid agencies.

Ouologuem's cynicism and Armah's utopianism are not easily translated into an official political practice. On the personal level this orientation results in either resignation or exile, positions that are not uncommon among African intellectuals.

It is tempting to see these three orientations as a historical sequence. At its starting point the African novel tries to connect with the pre-capitalist past that is still considered sufficiently alive to form the basis for a new authentically African society. In a second movement the novel looks away from the pre-capitalist modes of production that it sees as corrupted by and subordinated to capitalism and points to hopeful tendencies in the present situation. In a third and (for the purpose of this periodization) last phase, we find Armah evoking an African utopia that is far removed from actual historical reality. This reality is seen as completely absorbed by the forces of capitalism and imperialism.

Viewed within the framework of this periodization the African novels here analysed form mile signs indicating the desolate expansion of the capitalist mode of production in Africa.

Notes

1 This chapter has been published as a separate article in *Research in African Literature*, vol. 13, no. 4, 1982: 451–88. I thank the editors of *RAL* for their kind permission to include the article in the present volume. Moreover, I am indebted to the other contributors to this book for their stimulating criticism of my argument while I was preparing the original Dutch version of this text. The English translation was made by Wim van Binsbergen, to whom I am also grateful for his editorial contributions. Finally I wish to acknowledge the excellent work of M. Brouwer and W. Freeke, who typed successive versions of this paper.

2 In this article it is not my intention to deal with the specific literary means used by the authors. Neither is this the place to add to the lengthy theoretical discussions on the nature of the relationship between the novel and social reality.

3 Achebe (1975: 25). One may wonder how an existentialist problem could be universal if, at the same time, it would be inapplicable to Africa. Does Achebe share here in the common underestimation of Africa — which at other times he fights with such determination?

4 Lukács (1920) and Goldmann (1964).

5 An obvious question in this connection is whether the rise of the African novel is an indication of the final dominance of capitalism over the preceding modes of production.

6 See Meillassoux (1964) and (1975); Rey (1971), (1973) and (1976); Godelier (1973) and (1975); Terray (1969) and (1975).

7 For example in the works cited in note 6.

8 This is a theme that permeates the entire narrative.

9 For a more detailed reading of Laye as a negritude author, see Simonse (1976).

10 From what follows it will be clear that (contrary to Soyinka's contention) Ouologuem by no means limits himself to an attack on Islam in particular. Neither does he leave room for an authentic African heritage, one uncontained by violence. See Soyinka (1976: 104f.). Here I do not wish to discuss the plagiarism (notably from Graham Greene) that Ouologuem has been accused of. Our point is not so much the literary merit of the work — on that count more could be said against it — but its ideological merits; and the latter are not tainted by plagiarism. The ideological originality of the work amply compensates for any infringement of copyright.

11 Léopold Senghor was called by this epithet. He was Senegal's president for twenty years and made an important contribution to French civilization through his poetry and his francophile political attitudes. After World War II he was for some time a member of the French Assembly.

12 CPP: Convention People's Party, Nkrumah's one party.

13 Star Hotel: the favourite haunt of Accra's upper ten.

14 Achimota and Holy Child: prestigious secondary schools.

15 Revolt against German colonial rule in East Africa, 1905–7.

16 President *Kamuzu* Banda of Malawi is well known for his good relationship with South Africa.

17 Nkrumah's honorific title; it means 'Liberator', 'Redeemer'.

References

Achebe, Chinua (1958), *Things Fall Apart*, London: Heinemann.

Achebe, Chinua (1975), *Morning Yet on Creation Day*, London: Heinemann.

Armah, Ayi Kwei (1969), *The Beautyful Ones Are Not Yet Born*, London: Heinemann.

Armah, Ayi Kwei (1973), *Two Thousand Seasons*, Nairobi: East African Publishing House.

Armah, Ayi Kwei (1974), *Why Are We So Blest?* London: Heinemann (first published in 1972 by Doubleday).

Armah, Ayi Kwei (1979), *The Healers*, London and Ibadan: Heinemann.

Bloch, Maurice (ed.) (1975), *Marxist Analyses and Social Anthropology*, London: Malaby Press.

Godelier, Maurice (1973), *Horizon, trajets marxistes en anthropolgie*, Paris: Maspero.

Godelier, Maurice (1975), 'Modes of production, kinship, and demographic structures', in Bloch (1975): 3–27.

Goldmann, Lucien (1964), *Pour une Sociologie du roman*, Paris: Gallimard.

Head, Bessie (1968), *When Rain Clouds Gather*, New York: Simon & Schuster.

Laye, Camera (1976), *The Radiance of the King*, trans. J. Kirkup, Glasgow: Fontana/Collins. First published in 1954 as *Le Regard du Roi*, Paris: Plon.

Lukács, Georg (1920), *Die Theorie des Romans*, Berlin: Paul Cassirer.

Malinowski, Bronislaw (1945), *The Dynamics of Culture Change*, ed. P. M. Kaberry, Yale University Press.

Mauss, Marcel (1924), *Essai sur le don, forme archaïque de l'échange*, Paris: Année sociologique.

Meillassoux, Claude (1964), *Anthropologie économique des Gouro de Côte d'Ivoire*, Paris: Mouton.

Meillassoux, Claude (1964), *Femmes, greniers et capitaux*, Paris: Maspero.

Ouologuem, Yambo (1968), *Le Devoir de violence*, Paris: Seuil (here quoted from the English translation by R. Manheim, *Bound to Violence*, London: Heinemann, 1971).

Rey, P.-P. (1971), *Colonialisme, néo-colonialism et transition au capitalisme*, Paris: Maspero.

Rey, P.-P. (1973), *Les Alliances de classes*, Paris: Maspero.

Rey, P.-P. (1976), *Capitalisme négrier*, Paris: Maspero.

Sembène, Ousmane (1960), *Les Bouts de bois de Dieu*, Paris: Le Livre contemporain (here quoted from the English translation by F. Price, *God's Bits of Wood*, Garden City: Anchor Books, 1970).

Sembène, Ousmane (1966), *Le Mandat*, Paris: Présence africaine (here quoted from the English translation by C. Wake, *The Money Order*, London: Heinemann, 1972).

Simonse, Simon (1976), 'A White Hero for Negritude: a Materialist Reading of Camara Laye', paper presented at the International Seminar on Text and Context in Africa, Leiden, African Studies Centre.

Soyinka, Wole (1976), *Myth, Literature and the African World*, Cambridge University Press.

Terray, Emmanuel (1969), *Le Marxisme devant les sociétés 'primitives'*, Paris: Maspero.

Terray, Emmanuel (1975), 'Class and class consciousness in the Abron kingdom of Gyaman', in Bloch (1975): 85–135.

Weber, Max (1958), *The Protestant ethic and the Spirit of Capitalism*, New York: Free Press.

Chapter 6

From tribe to ethnicity in western Zambia: The unit of study as an ideological problem

Wim van Binsbergen[1]

> To get inside just one African tribe with as able and lucid a guide as Dr van Velsen is both a salutary and a pleasurable experience and one which can be confidently recommended.
>
> *Times Educational Supplement*[2]

Introduction

Not only on the ground, in the political and economic aspects of the lives of the people we study in Africa, has the 1970s been a decade of discontinuity. Academically this discontinuity has meant the discarding of so much of established anthropology. A different type of anthropology is emerging: one blending with history and political economy, and one in which structural-functionalist one-tribe approaches hinging on culture or custom have given way, by and large, to more comprehensive regional approaches. Historical process and dialectics are about to take the place of function. Alleged firm and rigid cultural and ethnic boundaries turn out to be breached by economic, political and ideological processes of much wider scope than, e.g., 'the Tallensi', 'the Kikuyu', or 'the Zulu'.

Turning to new paradigms, anthropology in Africa has shed the tribe or ethnic group as its basic unit of study. In this chapter I shall argue that Zambian rural anthropology is on the decline, and that this decline is related to the reliance, among anthropologists, on this unit of study in the past. The problem of the tribe as a unit of study is, however, complicated by the fact that members of Central African society themselves structure their social experience partly in terms of tribes; it is hard for a researcher to tear himself away from such a folk categorization. I shall discuss this problem with reference to my own research among the Nkoya of western Zambia. I shall then argue that one way to escape from the tribal model on the analytical plane, without sacrificing the subjects' own organization of their experience, is to try to explain this experience as a form of consciousness emerging out of the dialectics of political incorporation and, even more fundamentally, the penetration of capitalism, in other words, the articulation of capitalism and non-capitalist modes of production. This leads to a picture of complex relationships, of much greater scope and abstraction than, and extending in time and place beyond, anything that could be meaningfully defined as a unit of study. The alternative proposed here for the tribal model as a unit of study is *not* another, better unit of study (e.g. mode of production, social formation, or a well-defined spatio-temporal portion of reality), but a growing awareness of possible problems and interrelations, informed by insights from history and political economy. Thus this paper, much like my other recent work (cf. van Binsbergen 1981b and in press), will be an exercise in the interaction of anthropology and history in the analysis of a specific set of data. Such a form of anthropology could try and make its come-back on the scene of rural studies of Central and Southern Africa.

My analysis is set within the framework of the articulation of modes of production — the guiding idea of the present book. However, the inconclusive nature of my argument reflects the fact that recent Marxist studies have not yet made much progress towards a proper understanding of the ideological aspects of modes of production and their articulation.[3] As will be argued by Raatgever in her contribution to this book (chapter 8), Godelier's attempts in this respect, dwelling on the applicability of the infrastructure/superstructure metaphor, have not managed to produce much clarity; moreover, his work seldom specifically deals with the process of articulation of modes of production. Yet, among the modern French Marxist authors, Godelier appears to have been the only one to consider explicitly the problem of ethnicity (Godelier 1973: ch. 1.3, pp. 93–131, 'le concept de tribu'). His Marxist inspiration is, however, largely used to arrive at a formal and epistemological critique of the concept of tribe in classic anthropology. Godelier does not yet attempt (as is my intention in the present chapter) to identify the political economic conditions, and the intersubjective dynamics of participant observation, under which a group of people and a researcher studying them, would adopt or reject the notion of tribe. With regard to other members of the French School, it is only fair to admit that the notion of bounded ethnic groups as more or less self-evident units of analysis was at first uncritically adopted by them; it is the work of Meillassoux and Terray which has made such groups as the Guro and the Dida famous.[4]

More recently, a Marxist perspective on ethnicity is beginning to be formulated by writers in the Anglo-Saxon tradition, and largely by reference to East African data. Thus John Saul, in a study of the dialectics of class and tribe in that part of Africa (1979: ch. 14), offers three allegedly complementary approaches along which ethnicity could be drawn within the orbit of a Marxist analysis. Ethnicity, he argues, could be viewed, first as a response to imperialism, at the sub-national level; second, as an ideological aspect of the articulation of modes of production; and third, as a form of ideological class struggle. Surprisingly, Saul fails to indicate the obvious connections between these three interpretations, which in fact appear to be very closely related. Behind political and military domination, imperialism very obviously served the imposition of the capitalist mode of production. It was thus a major factor in the articulation between that mode of production and such modes of production as were already in existence locally. In so far as it is inherent in the articulation process that these pre-capitalist modes of production retain their own distinct existence — if only in an encapsulated and subservient form — a neo-traditionalist expression of this distinct 'identity' (the very word refers to a problematic which is typical of capitalist encroachment) would readily assume the form of ethnicity. In so far as capitalist encroachment involves local people in new, capitalist relations of production, it amounts to class formation and thus to manifest or latent class struggle.[5] If the ideological expression of such articulation is predominantly in ethnic terms, the creation and assertion of ethnic identity vis-à-vis other emerging ethnic identities that form part of the ideological lay-out of the social formation, might certainly take on militant overtones, but yet such ethnicity would serve to *conceal* the underlying class nature of the process that is thus being expressed. Therefore it would be more appropriate to view ethnicity as an ideological diversion of class struggle, rather than as ideological class struggle in itself. The point has already been made in

Mafeje's (1971) earlier analysis of 'tribalism', which draws on a more general Marxist inspiration without using the idea of an articulation of modes of production: such ethnicity could essentially be called 'false consciousness'.

In his review article on possible explanations of ethnicity as found in the recent work by Mamdani (1976), Leys (1975) and others, Joel Kahn is less sure of the appropriateness of the term 'false consciousness' in connection with ethnicity (1981: 48–9). Kahn offers a number of stimulating ideas. He dwells on the problematic of the relative autonomy of the ideological instance, the specific forms of domination found in the world-wide or national peripheries (cf. Meillassoux 1975; articulation of modes of production is however not explicitly mentioned), the significance of class analysis in this context, and the relevance of colonial forms of domination. Somewhat superfluously, Kahn stresses that in the ten pages of his article he is not 'attempting to develop a universal theory of primordialism' (1981: 51). And while many of his pointers have parallels in the analysis of ethnicity in western Zambia as set out in the present chapter, my attempt would even be more modest in that I will largely focus on the concrete ethnographic and historiographic forms in which this ethnicity manifests itself to the researcher — shunning the explicit, abstract, Marxist theorizing in which Kahn hopes to find the key for the explanation we both seek.

Finally, there is — precisely at the ethnographic level — a dimension of ethnicity which is surprisingly absent in scholarly analyses of the phenomenon: ethnicity may be an ideological process at the level of participants in any society under study, but our attempt to come to terms with this process in the course of our own intellectual production also has clear ideological implications.

In this chapter I shall argue a view of ethnicity as a response, among African participants, to the articulation of the pre-existing modes of production with capitalism. Alternatively, it is now fairly widely accepted to look at early anthropology as an ideological expression, among North Atlantic participants, of an imperialism seeking to create conditions for the world-wide penetration of the capitalist mode of production (Leclerc 1972; Asad 1973; Copans 1975). This imperialist heritage is likely to have some continued, if hidden, impact on whatever study of whatever topic modern anthropology undertakes in that part of the world where conditions of peripheral capitalism prevail. Considering how long it took anthropology to take up the study of incorporation processes, capitalist penetration, etc. (a very small trickle up to the 1960s, such studies became a major topic only in the 1970s), one begins to suspect that anthropology is genetically conditioned to turn a blind eye to the very processes of articulation of modes of production to which it owes its own existence. Indulging in a Freudian analogy, one might say that there is here a Primal Scene which anthropology could not, until quite recently, afford to face, for the sake of its own sanity. Since anthropology is primarily a matter of intellectual, i.e. ideological, production, this problematic might have a less devastating effect on anthropological studies of economic or political aspects of the articulation process — studies that do not concentrate on ideology. But when anthropologists turn to the ideological dimensions of the articulation of modes of production, and begin to study for instance religious or ethnic responses under conditions of capitalist encroachment, then the ideological complexity of this research undertaking is raised.

For two ideological processes oddly converge in the anthropological study of ethnicity: first, among anthropologists, the modern transformation of an anthropology which started out as an ideological transformation of imperialism; and second, the emergence, as an ideological response to capitalist encroachment in the Third World, of new 'ethnic' group identities which seek historical legitimation by posing as reminiscences or re-enactments of pre-capitalist African social forms allegedly unaffected by capitalism. Could such a convergence ever produce meaningful and reliable results at all?

The answer to this question cannot be given before we have fully analysed the extent to which the modern social sciences reflect, in their theorizing as well as in the concrete organization of their intellectual production processes, the contradictions inherent in present-day capitalism — in other words, before we have assessed to what extent modern anthropology succeeds in escaping from its imperialist heritage. The good intentions of today's anthropologists, the inclusion of Third World colleagues among their number, the emergence of a self-reflexive, even revolutionary, anthropology, the radical political stances a minority of anthropologists take in public life — all this may be encouraging, but it is not sufficient proof that the fundamental orientation of anthropology has completely altered since its inception a century ago. The complexities of the situation are further revealed when we look at the relations of intellectual production that prevail in modern anthropology. These largely follow the pattern of modern capitalism: intellectual wage-labour, separation between intellectual workers and their means of production (libraries, computers, office space, motor vehicles used in the field), the bureaucratic organization of production, the reliance on underpaid local assistants in the field, the commoditization of such intellectual products as books, articles, degrees, academic honours, the ensuing academic market pressures, competition, etc. And this confusing complexity manifests itself not just at the impersonal level of structures of academic production, but also in the very personal intimacy of individual thought-processes, motivation in research, the sort of 'rapport' a field-worker concentrating on ideological themes manages to establish with his or her informants, and the force with which that research is drawn towards these informants' own viewpoints.

Once an ideological representative of capitalist encroachment, the anthropologist today may be tempted to identify with, if not to join, the forces fighting this encroachment, e.g. through such ideological forms as ethnic identity, authenticity, negritude, the African personality, Christian independence, prophetic religious movements. These forms appear to express aspirations which as yet — under conditions of intercontinental dependence in the military, monetary and cultural field — are still largely deprived of economic and political reality. In this chapter I shall describe an instance of such identification, on the part of the anthropologist, as a temporary by-product of research into ethnicity. The example does not stand on its own: several researchers of modern religious expressions in Africa yielded to similar pressures by temporarily joining the religious organizations they were studying (Jules-Rosette 1975; Martin 1975). Are these responses, among researchers, positive forms of solidarity with the ideological struggles of their informants, or do they amount to intellectual betrayal in so far as they further the production of 'false consciousness' — stressing ethnic or religious, over economic, analyses of reality?

These are immense questions, which bear on our intellectual integrity, our class position in the world system and the viability of a Marxist anthropology. My present argument will not offer adequate answers. Suffice it to say that anthropological analysis of the ideological dimensions of the articulation of modes of production contains a double bind, an ideological puzzle, which more than justifies a closer look at the anthropological researcher

186

involved in such an exercise. This is why, in the course of this chapter, I shall have to pay some attention to my own role as a researcher blundering through 'Nkoya' ethnicity. At the same time it may be the fundamental reason why, as yet, any analysis of the ideological dimensions of the articulation of modes of production will remain unsatisfactory. However, it is to such an analysis that I shall now proceed.

The end of rural anthropology in Zambia?

Any analysis of ethnicity in Zambia today has to reckon with the exceptionally rich tradition of colonial anthropology in that country, as created by the Rhodes-Livingstone Institute. In order to understand the reliance on the tribal model among the Rhodes-Livingstone Institute researchers of rural Zambia, we should not overlook the fact that they were adopting, into their analytical frameworks, emic categories employed at the time by Zambian villagers, townsmen, and colonial administrators alike.

In addition, their academic discipline provided these researchers with at least two other resons for upholding the tribal model. First, the concept of culture at the theoretical level reinforced the notion of tribe (as the most obvious carrier of a distinct, internalized, many-faceted culture); it provided a perspective on allegedly deeply-rooted, 'primordial attachments', which Shils and Geertz have stressed with regard to ethnicity (see Doornbos (1972) and references cited there). And second, the adoption of prolonged and intensive participatory field-work as the main method of data collection did much to strengthen, among anthropologists, the concept of tribe at a personal level. The intimate communion with the one culture that one studies as an anthropologist can be seen both as an irritating cliché of the professional sub-culture of classic anthropology, and at the same time as a genuine existential dimension of doing fieldwork in that tradition. It suggests the adoption of one particular unit of study: that those boundaries are defined by the limits of the cognitive and language field in which the anthropologist, after long and painful study, acquires a certain (always hopelessly defective) mastery: *'my people'*, *'my tribe'*.

The Rhodes-Livingstone Institute researchers working in rural Zambia have seldom explicitly considered the analytical status of the ethnic labels they used for their main units of study. The titles

187

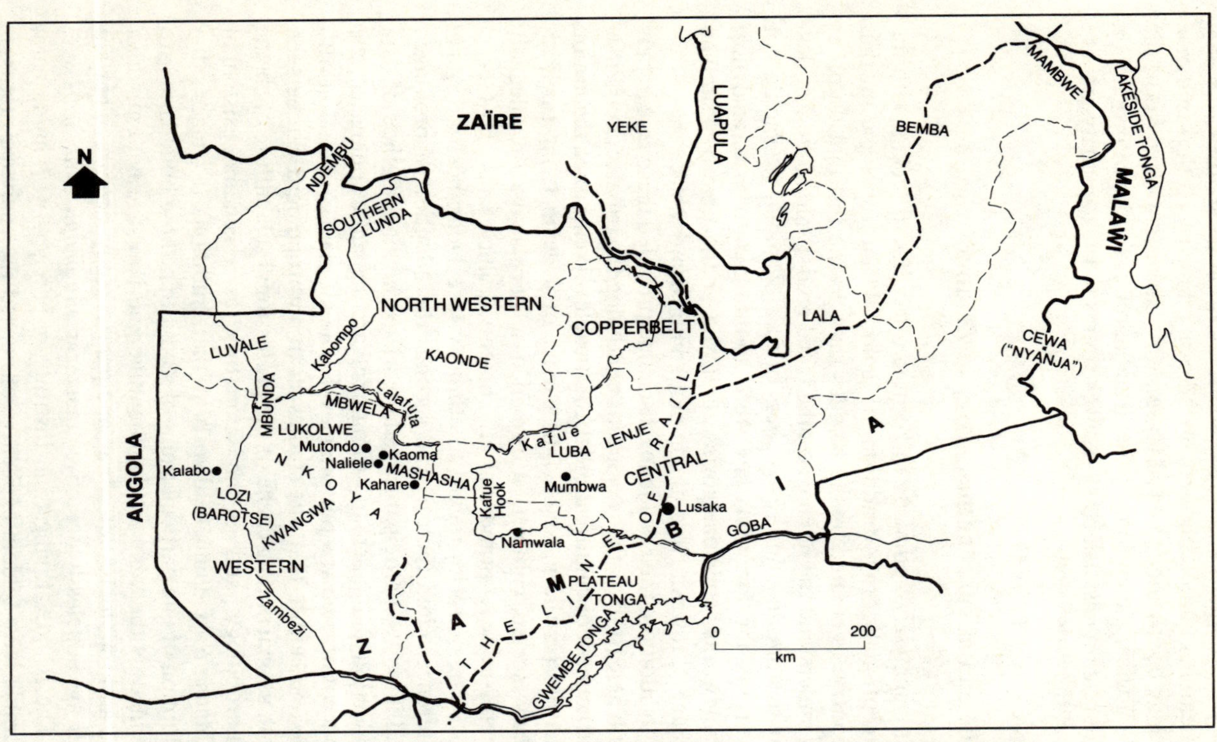

Figure 6.1 Localities and approximate local concentrations of ethnic groups, Zambia

of their main publications demonstrate that they defined their units of study loosely in terms of tribes or ethnic groups.[6] Much sophistication, admittedly, went into the assessment of the transformation these rural ethnic labels underwent when they were introduced into the urban areas.[7] Within what was called the 'industrial-colonial complex of urban Northern Rhodesia', these labels were claimed to acquire categorial and situational overtones quite different from the 'total way of life' they were assumed to represent out in the rural areas. Not that the rural researchers claimed to analyse this way of life exhaustively. In fact, most of the Rhodes-Livingstone Institute studies emphatically concentrated on only one major aspect of 'tribal life': kinship, marriage, the judicial process, formal and particularly informal political organization, community crises, ritual.

The concept of culture so conducive to the classic tribal model, was rarely used explicitly; instead Gluckman and associates preferred the term *custom*, with its Malinowskian bird-of-paradise feathers. In contrast with American idealist culturology, the Manchester researchers were little inclined to view 'custom' as autonomously determining the course of the social process. If blame them we must, it could be for under-analysing, rather than for exaggerating, the cultural dimension of social life. Van Velsen and Turner[8] presented dynamic and situational approaches to village life in southern Central Africa that were far richer and more convincing than anything the classic structural-functionalist paradigm had ever managed. Yet, even if one had to limit one's detailed study to selected aspects of 'tribal' life, even if one studied these aspects in a masterly way, the tribe remained the basic unit of study. African village life was essentially depicted as closed in itself and following a logic of its own. 'Outside contacts' with European administrators, missions, the modern market economy, migrancy, nationalism, were tackled in introductory or concluding chapters or in scattered articles, but not in the main books.

The anthropological discipline had at the time no theoretical solution to offer to the formidable problems posed by the persistence of encapsulated neo-traditional communities in a situation of articulation of modes of production. Individual researchers could hardly be blamed for the historical limitations of their discipline, especially not when they themselves were aware of these limitations. Like Jaap van Velsen who, finally realizing that the most fundamental questions concerning labour migration could not be anwered from within Tongaland, in the last minute withdrew his chapters on this topic from the very galley-proofs of *Politics of Kinship*.[9]

Two exceptions to the general pattern are Gluckman's study of *The Economy of the Central Barotse Plain* and Cunnison's *Luapula Peoples* (1959). Both take as their main unit of study not a single 'tribe', but geographical areas which they see as filled with a variety of tribes. While Gluckman takes tribes for granted, leaving the concept unanalysed,[10] Cunnison (1959: ch. 2) engages in a painstaking assessment of the local and analytical meaning of the concept of tribe in the Luapula context. It was the particular poly-ethnic structure of their respective rural research areas that forced Gluckman and Cunnison to discuss, with different degrees of sophistication, the interactions *between* 'tribes'. The other researchers were little concerned with internal organization at the tribal level, but used the tribe rather as a comprehensive setting within which the microscopic face-to-face social process, in which they were really interested, took place and which they studied with excellent results. This approach is particularly clear in Turner's *Schism and Continuity* (1957: xvii): 'I focus the investigation upon the village, a significant local unit, and analyse it successively as an independent social system and as a unit within several wider sects of social relations included in the total field of Ndembu society.'

Paradoxically, the study that, among the Rhodes-Livingstone Institute work, was the most concerned with the relations between a local rural Zambian society and the wider world as dominated by the capitalist mode of production (Watson's *Tribal Cohesion in a Money Economy*, 1958), was at the same time the study that tried to make the most of the tribe, conceived in terms that were essentially those of structural-functionalist anthropology. Mambwe tribal society, far from being a loosely-descriptive (and hence pardonable) category, is for Watson a living, and surviving, integrated entity (1958: 228), tending 'to adjust to new conditions through its existing social institutions. These institutions will survive, but with new values, in a changed social system.'

Regrettably, Long's (1968) impressive attempt to break away from all this, in *Social Change and the Individual*, was at the same time virtually the swan-song of Zambian rural anthropology. Long studied what might have been called 'Lala village life' not as the enacting of changing tribal institutions or of some manipulative internal social process, but rather as the 'social and religious

190

responses to innovation in a Zambian community'.[11] As a unit of study he used, at the descriptive level, a geographically defined 'Kapepa Parish'. Here he sought access, analytically, not to representative glimpses of 'Lala society' but to a structurally complex social field, accommodating both local cultural and structural elements, and economic and social-structural pressures, as well as occupational and religious experiences pertaining to distant urban areas (Long 1968: 6f). In the extended-case studies of van Velsen and Turner, custom, elsewhere considered king, had been dethroned, giving way to a complex social process that was determined by the internal dynamics of local rural society; in Long's analysis, the wider world was finally allowed to step in, and it offered altered patterns of agriculture and farm management, dynamics of power and prestige, and religious experience, that drove home the fact that the single tribe is not a feasible unit of study at all.[12]

It is difficult to believe that Long's book, published in 1968 and dealing with the situation in 1963–4, is in fact one of the most recent full-length anthropological studies to be devoted to rural Zambia. In addition to Turner's *Drums of Affliction* (1968b) (where occasional references to social and political conditions surrounding Ndembu village society cannot hide the fact that Ndembu society remains the crucial unit of study, just as in Turner's earlier studies), the only other examples to come to mind are Elizabeth Colson's *Social Consequences of Resettlement* (1971), Stuart Marks's *Large Mammals and a Brave People* (1976); and George Bond's *Politics of Change in a Zambian Community* (1976), based on field-work in the same priod as Long's. Whatever anthropology Robert Bates's (1976) *Rural Responses to Industrialization* contains is best left undiscussed here (see van Binsbergen 1977). There must be some interesting rural studies lying buried in unpublished PhD theses. Lancaster's and Poewe's articles foreshadowed full-length books to be published in 1981.[13] But, on the whole, workers on Zambian rural anthropology have been eloquently silent during the 1970s. There has been only a faint trickle of publications, based mainly on field-work conducted before the mid-1970s: this includes articles by Bond, Colson, Scudder, Anita Spring Hansen, Marks, Robin Fielder, Lancaster, Hansen, Holy, and myself. Today, the growing-points for the study of Zambian society are history and political economy — and not anthropology. The anthropological study of Zambia's rural areas has hardly been a field in which the University of Zambia has excelled, and little rural anthropology has been published in the Lusaka-based journal *African Social Research*. One of the most significant studies of rural southern Central and Southern Africa, including Zambia, to be published in the 1970s was *The Roots of Rural Poverty* (Palmer and Parsons 1977); this book was inspired, to a limited extent, by radical anthropology (including the recent French Marxist school) as developed with reference to other parts of the Third World, but towards its argument Zambian rural anthropology did not make much of a contribution.[14] Similarly, the Centre of African Studies in Edinburgh could organize a full-length conference on 'The Evolving Structure of Zambian Society' (1980) without a single anthropologist among the contributors, and virtually without so much as a passing reference to Zambian rural anthropology in the footnotes to the papers.

This characterization of the present state of the art in Zambian rural anthropology relies of course on a particular conception of anthropology, which may well be debatable. I have considered this question at somewhat greater length elsewhere (see van Binsbergen 1981a). Here let it suffice that by anthropology I mean that body of social-scientific work that directly (i.e. in a neo-classical, often implicitly structural-functionalist form) or preferably indirectly (i.e. in a form inspired by regional, historical and political-economic considerations) derives from the methods and problematics of the classic anthropology of the 1940s and 1950s.

It would seem as though anthropology, with its prolonged participatory field-work and its profound insights into family and kinship, the micro-dynamics of the political and economic processes, and the participants' construction of social and ritual meaning in terms of a local particularistic symbolic idiom, is unable to make a meaningful contribution, either to the understanding of rural stagnation today, or in general to current research by historians, economists and political scientists. This is in fact an opinion found, expressly or tacitly, among many colleagues from other disciplines currently engaged in the analysis of rural southern Central Africa. Rural anthropology in this part of the world may have been too slow, or too entrenched in its classic problematics, to address itself to the academic and societal problems of today. Given its reliance, in the past, on the tribe or ethnic group as a standard unit of study, a reassessment of the unit of study may help to find a way out of this dead end. For I am convinced that the predicament is largely a theoretical one, and cannot be explained away by such practical problems as the availability of research funds, permits, and the hardships of rural field-work.

At the same time I would claim that the perspective developed in the present book (that of modes of production and their articulation) does provide a means for coupling traditional, and meaningful, anthropological concerns to the economic and political realities beyond the local rural community. Without denying the specificity and the internal logic of the domestic or tributary mode of production, the analysis does not stop short there, but instead the conditions are identified for the continued existence (in other words, the reproduction) of this mode of production; and these conditions are sought, not in internalized culture or similar primordial attachments, but in the material and ideological processes through which surpluses generated in modes of production such as identified locally, are appropriated by other modes (particularly the capitalist one) in such a way that the domestic community is accorded a measure of distinct, but encapsulated and neo-traditional, identity.

The unit of study

For an outsider to the social sciences, and perhaps particularly for a natural scientist, it would be difficult to appreciate a situation where libraries have been filled with studies about southern Central and Southern Africa, and specialists hold conference after conference, conversing happily without more than the usual terminological confusion, whereas no real consensus has been reached as to the solution of the problem of the unit of study in this field of enquiry.

What makes our present situation less dramatic than it might seem to outsiders is the fact that considerations of the unit of study tend to refer to a much higher plane of abstraction and analysis than that on which our raw data are usually collected. On the level of the life experiences of the people inhabiting the part of the world we are studying, the concrete data are fairly straightforward. Our research notes consist of interviews, documents, observations, local words and their meanings, and sometimes (for those of us who are engaged in participatory research) the subjective experience of sharing to some extent in an initially unfamiliar variety of human social life. These elementary particles of social and historical research in Africa may form, in a strict methodological sense, our real units of study, but they are not the ones that concern us here. We have, I suppose, a sufficient amount of trust in each other's professional skill and integrity to accept the descriptive evidence each of us digs up from his particular academic gold-mine. The problem of the unit of study as I understand it arises only when it comes to *collating* these minute facts into meaningful patterns, into more comprehensive complexes that have a systematic extension in space and that go through an identifiable process in time. The question boils down to: What scope of vision should the blinkers allow through which we peer at reality? For, ultimately, everything social is related to everything else; so only the whole world constitutes an adequate unit of study. But such a unit is impossible to handle, and is as little interesting to read about as the tiny particles of information that constitute our raw data. An adequate unit of study should enable us to select as well as to synthesize. We might define such a unit of study, tentatively, as an analytic construct which, in a manner acceptable to a specialist academic audience, allows for the meaningful and systematic integration of disconnected research data around a common focus, in such a way that the analytic construct thus arrived at is relevant for the pursuit of a specific scientific and/or societal problematic.

This sums up a couple of crucial points. First, the distinctions we impose upon the phenomena we study are essentially arbitrary man-made constructs, and do not in themselves emanate from the nature of these phenomena. Second, the choice of a particular construct as a meaningful unit of study is subject to a process of negotiation between colleagues.[15] Third, a unit of study is not on the same level as our concrete research data, or on the most abstract level of grand theory, but on some intermediate level: that on which our disconnected raw data are processed so as to bring out patterns capable of being generalized and explained in fairly general terms that are yet somewhat proper to the geographical area and the historical period we are concentrating on. And, finally, the choice for one unit of study rather than another may be fairly arbitrary from the point of the True Structure of Reality (which we see only in a Glass Darkly, anyway); but this choice is far from arbitrary when considered within the process of academic production, where such units of study should be selected as have the greatest potential of enlightening the problematic which informs the research that is undertaken. Such problematics, moreover, are not exclusively defined by academics, holding conferences, sitting on boards that distribute research funds between them, or deciding on the publication of each other's papers and books. The study of kinship terminology and the symbolic lay-out of homesteads would be even more of a booming field of research[16] if research problematics were exclusively defined by so-called disinterested intellectual concerns alone. Fortunately, however, scholars are free, to a considerable extent, to turn to problematics that seem to be of particular social relevance, and that may help to explain, if not to alter, the vital predicaments that beset the people they are studying. In this respect, to study the 'roots of rural poverty' (Palmer and Parsons 1977) may be more relevant, as a problematic, than the kinship terminology and symbolic structures obtaining in the same part of the world. And whereas the latter problematic may lead one to distinguish between a host of different tribes or ethnic groups, each with its own total culture including kinship terminology and spatial symbolism, the former problematic would lead one to look for broad, comprehensive, regional patterns that would explain the remarkable similarities in the present-day predicament of the people of Southern Africa. Here, of course, anthropology is merging with history and political economy, and the present non-anthropological work on rural Zambia (e.g. by Muntemba, Klepper, Palmer, Vail) takes on a new significance.

Nor is it only the conscience of more or less committed scholars, and the whims of funding agencies usually located in the North Atlantic region, that suggest the adoption of one problematic rather than another. The official institutions in the areas our research concentrates on, and the very villagers and petty administrators that provide us with our data on the ground, coax us towards the adoption of particular problematics, and thus towards the adoption of particular units of study. Needless to say, their prodding is not always in a direction that coincides with the choices academics would wish to make. The crisis at the University of Zambia early in 1976, or the state of the social and historical sciences within the Republic of South Africa, are only two examples that suggest that the adoption of a radical problematic may not make us, as researchers, more attractive in the eyes of the (élite) members of the society we study. Below I shall reflect on my personal experience with this problem at a local level, in the course of my participatory and oral-historical research in Kaoma district (western Zambia), and among people from that area now living in Lusaka, 400 km east of Kaoma.[17]

That definitional and methodological rigidity is necessary in the handling of one's unit of study has particularly been emphasized by scholars trying to compare the phenomena pertaining to different geographical areas or different periods. The problem of the definition of the units of cross-cultural comparison has haunted comparative studies in the social sciences ever since the end of the last century. Although there have been several attempts at cross-cultural comparison in the Southern African region,[18] the problem of the unit of study was infrequently explicitly considered in the course of these attempts, and probably some of the data used derived from loosely-defined units ('tribes', 'ethnic groups', 'cultures', 'societies') that were essentially incomparable. The assumption was that, e.g., 'the Bemba', 'the Lozi', 'the Tonga', etc. not only really existed as collective representations of participants in Zambian society, but that they also formed viable units of analysis.

The example of urban ethnicity may illustrate that adopting a particular unit of study enlightens a certain problematic, but at the same time forces, like all classification, an essential volatile and dynamic reality into a strait-jacket. In their Copperbelt studies Mitchell, Epstein and Harries-Jones have treated ethnic identity primarily as a logical device to classify individuals. These researchers stressed the *situational* aspects of urban ethnicity. Reliance on a particular ethnic identity is only one of many options a town-dweller has for his personal organization of urban relationships. He may temporarily drop this identity and emphasize, in different urban situations involving the same or a different set of people, a different ethnic identity. Among themselves, and vis-à-vis 'Lozi', the Lusaka migrants from Kaoma district would identify themselves as 'Nkoya', but in many urban situations they would pose as 'Lozi', and sometimes they would try to pass for 'Bemba' or even 'Nyanja'. Alternatively, the town-dweller may, situationally, stress a social identity derived from class, occupation, educational level, political or religious affiliation. The ways in which ethnicity is alternately dominant or played down can be

196

understood only against the background of the total social process in which the participants are specifically involved.

Description implies fossilization, no matter how dynamic a reality we try to capture. The inevitable result is lack of precision. It is tedious to have to indicate all the time that the unit of study one imposes covers only a certain aspect of the social reality, only in certain situations, and subject to the participants' own conscious and unconscious manipulation. One has to adopt short-hand formulae, and these tend to acquire a life of their own in the course of one's argument. This accounts, for instance, for the following paradox. In his work of the 1950s and early 1960s Mitchell is on the one hand clearly aware of the situational and manipulative aspects of ethnicity, yet does not shrink from detailed studies of, e.g., intertribal prestige scores and differential fertility, where these tribes are neatly boxed and appear as entries in sophisticated, computerized tables — as though they formed both emic and etic categories at the same time (see Mitchell 1956, 1965).

This methodological problem, by the way, is not limited to the main unit of study that we adopt in our analyses. Ever since the extended-case method has made us aware of the shifting, inchoate, situational, competitive elements in the social process, persuading us to consider these elements as the real basic data out of which we have to build a picture of a 'social structure' and a 'culture', we run into the epistemological difficulty that, in order to discuss the data, and the emerging interpretation, at all, we have to lend them far greater invariability and stability than our analysis would yet show them to possess.[19]

Studying the Nkoya

I have already indicated how the choice of a particular unit of study can be suggested to the researcher on the basis of other than strictly academic concerns, for instance by his commitment to a problematic that is of wider social relevance, or under the pressure of members of the society he is trying to study. In so far as participants are often ideologically determined to ignore the true make-up of their own situation, there may be considerable tension between these two possible influences on one's choice of a unit of study. In the remainder of this paper, I shall bring out both the lure of the tribal model as a unit of study for rural western Zambia, and its spuriousness in the light of a more profound analysis. In my conclusion I shall indicate the implications of this experience for the problem of the unit of study in general.

My first research contact with people from western Zambia was in Matero, a fairly respectable residential area in the northwestern part of Zambia's capital. Early in 1972 a friend took me and my family to a nocturnal healing session, staged by one of the senior leaders of a cult of affliction that had been founded by the prophet Simbinga in Kaoma district in the 1930s and that had been introduced into Lusaka in the 1950s. The languages spoken at the session were Nkoya, Nyanja, Lenje, Luvale, and English, in that order of frequency. Most of the cultic personnel, and most of the patients and onlookers, would when among themselves identify as belonging to the 'Nkoya tribe' (*mushobo wa shinkoya*), although, as already indicated above, for many social purposes within the capital they would claim to be 'Lozi', and would use, with varying success, the Lusaka *lingua franca*, Nyanja.

Hoping to penetrate the cultic and social idiom acted out in that nocturnal urban session and in many others I was to witness, deeply impressed by the dramatic and aesthetic aspects of the cult, and in general comfortably unable to resist the very great attraction that the remarkably close-knit, encapsulated group of 'Nkoya' immigrants in Lusaka was exerting on us (an uprooted nuclear family of Dutch expatriate academics), I allowed the Nkoya-ness of this set of ritual and social relations to dominate all other aspects of my urban research (which had started out as a sociological survey of religious organizations in Lusaka . . .). I learned the Nkoya language (and no other) and got deeply involved in Nkoya urban network contacts and collective ceremonies, which even in town were of an amazing scope: while the number of Nkoya in Lusaka, including children, was only about 1,000 out of a total urban population of about 350,000 (early 1970s), for girls' puberty ceremonies, healing sessions and funerary wakes, scores, even hundreds, of participants were mobilized from all over the capital. We were introduced to urban members of one Nkoya royal family, and would be visited by the Chief himself in our urban home whenever his membership of the House of Chiefs took him to Lusaka. As we acquired a working knowledge of those aspects of Nkoya culture that were still prominent in the urban relationships of our Nkoya friends and informants, my research began to concentrate on urban–rural relations between what I then labelled, provisionally, Nkoya village society, and Lusaka recent immigrants from that society. After initial exploratory visits we settled in Chief Kahare's capital, Kaoma district, for participatory, quantitative and oral-historical research into the rural ends of the urban–rural networks whose urban ends we had previously come to know fairly well. And while my main published academic output during those years remained focused on more general, regional concerns,[20] my main Zambian field-work experience, and my main emotional identification as a researcher in Zambia, came to lie with the Nkoya: a small ethnic minority whose homeland was structurally peripheral to the Zambian nation-state, and whose political and economic history over the past century and a half had been determined by their being peripheral even within Barotseland (where they had been labelled a 'Lozi subject tribe' along with so many other groups).

Developing out of a context of urban ritual among migrants, I had certainly not selected my initial set of informants on the basis that they might form a tribe. It was they who told me that they were a tribe, very different from the scores of other tribes which (according to a folk classification system they shared with virtually all Zambians, urban and rural) make up the population of the country. My earlier research in rural North Africa, far from preparing me for a countryside apparently parcelled up into neat tribal units, had instead preconditioned me to look at a cultural region or subcontinent as displaying essential cultural, structural and historical continuity, and to play down local idiosyncrasies in this regional pattern (see Gellner and Micaud 1972); urban–rural differences might be far more significant than intra-rural variation. I also knew that the anthropology of sub-Saharan Africa since the late 1960s had been moving away from the tribal model; such tribes as anthropologists, administrators and Africans had distinguished were beginning to be looked at as more or less recent emic constructs, responses to increase of political scale, as the creation of new political arenas (late pre-colonial, colonial, and post-colonial) called for new symbolic definitions of group opposition.[21]

And yet I could not resist the very strong illusion implanted by day-to-day close interaction with people who, in their dealings with me at least, emphatically identified themselves as Nkoya.

Their Nkoya-ness very soon became their main, even only, characteristic in my eyes; and I myself became more or less Nkoya-ized in the process.

Rich and rewarding though the experience was, I had some reservations, and felt uneasy about them. As an anthropologist I knew that my friends, modern peasants and proletarians, were not just Nkoya and nothing more; but agreement on their Nkoya-ness had become the *raison d'être* of our frequent interactions. Although I circulated my early papers on the Nkoya widely among my Nkoya friends, I did not dare to show them a conference paper I wrote shortly after my main field-work (van Binsbergen 1975). There I tried to demonstrate that, when all was said and done, Nkoya ethnic identity was only a dependent variable, to be explained by reference to the economic and political dynamics of relatively recent incorporation in a market economy and wider state structure, both pre-colonial and colonial; and I could trace the process of this response in some detail. A few years later, when I gave a seminar at the University of Zambia, Robert Serpell pointed out the extent to which my research had a Nkoya bias, and wondered how very different my analysis might have turned out had I not learned the Nkoya language but conducted my urban research in Nyanja. I pretended not to understand what he was aiming at: the fact that most of the social life of my Nkoya friends was determined by principles other than their claim to be Nkoya. Yet, only a few weeks earlier, during a field-trip to Kaoma district, I had conducted collective interviews with chiefs' councils, and had consciously felt how the notables present (representing both traditional and modern rural élites) were manipulating me as a likely ally in the expression of a new, proud Nkoya identity that would provide them with a political base in a district and a province that were dominated by people adhering to ethnic labels other than Nkoya (notably Lozi, Luvale and Mbunda). But then again had I not in the course of the same field-trip (which had brought me back to the area after three years' absence), at a collective celebration for which Chief Kahare had spontaneously made available his royal (though 100% state-subsidized) orchestra, been formally declared a Nkoya (*'baji kankoya! baji kankoya!'*), by the same Chief's prime minister; and had not the headman of the segment of the Chief's capital, where we had lived during most of the main spell of rural field-work, on that occasion publicly called me his sister's son (*'baji ba mwipa wami!'*), offering me the most intimate relationship that can exist between men in this local society . . . ?

Already the situational use of Nkoya-ness in the urban situation, and particularly the 'passing' to more prestigious ethnic identities of certain middle-class people born as Nkoya, made me realize that primordial attachments based on a unique, total tribal heritage did not apply at all to the Nkoya situation. But there was much more. For reasons of space I must refrain, in this chapter, from a discussion of inter-ethnic relations at the level of interpersonal, face-to-face relationships, both in town and in the rural areas, as reflected in residence, sexual and marital relations, friendship, political and economic support, ritual and medical interaction. My monograph on the 'Nkoya' research will be more explicit on this point. Concentrating here on more or less static attributes of 'Nkoya-ness', the data I had collected mainly by virtue of the generosity of the Nkoya made it very clear that the Nkoya were not a 'tribe' characterized by a unique combination of language, culture, political and social organization, and economy, dating back to the pre-colonial era.

Most people who identify themselves as Nkoya are effective members of the Nkoya speech community and in this respect language could be said to underpin Nkoya identity. But most are also fluent in one or more other western Zambian languages or urban *linguae francae*; and due to the massive amount of rural–rural and rural–urban migration, a considerable number (perhaps 15%) of the people who today in their homes use Nkoya as their main language were born in a different speech community or will spend their later life in yet other speech communities.

Moreover, there never was a 'traditional' Nkoya culture, with unique distinctive features or with a unique combination of more widely distributed features. Asked to define Nkoya-ness in cultural terms, my respondents invariably came up with features which were far from peculiar to the Nkoya: their system of name-inheritance (*ushwana*); their collective nocturnal celebrations in which a singing and joking crowd dances round an orchestra composed of xylophones and drums (*ruhñwa*); girls' puberty ceremonies (*kutembwisha kankanga*); absence of male puberty ceremonies (*mukanda*); their skills as elephant-hunters and musicians. Yet apart from their language, which, however, closely resembles Luyana,[22] Kwangwa, and southern Lunda, there are no features of so-called Nkoya culture that are not also found with lesser or greater prominence in other parts of western and even central Zambia. From girls' puberty ceremonies to the Lunda-type ceremonial culture surrounding chieftainship, from patterns of hunting and cultivation to ancestral ritual and name-inheritance: whoever knows the ethnographic literature of Zambia, or, better still, has intensively participated in any rural village in western or central Zambia, will have strong illusions of *déjà-vu* in a Nkoya village today. Admittedly, there are specific details. Nkoya music has unmistakable qualities which have allowed it to become the court music *par excellence* throughout western Zambia. There are specific variations in style patterns as manifested in cultivation or hunting, in food habits, girls' initiation, dancing, etc. Also it is possible that the amazing cultural and structural homogeneity that characterizes present-day western Zambia is partly a result of processes of political and economic incorporation over the past hundred years; these may have obliterated much that was uniquely local, and may have replaced it by a neo-traditional hotch-potch of peripheral-capitalist rural culture as prevailing throughout the region. There are indications in the field of chieftainship and religion that such a converging transformation was one among several intertwined processes of cultural change affecting western Zambia. Present-day similarities should not automatically be taken as proof of past identities.[23] Yet it is difficult to conceive of so-called Nkoya culture as something other than a slightly idiosyncratic combination and permutation of productive, social-organizational and symbolic patterns that are widely and abundantly available throughout the region.

Some of the potentially distinguishing cultural features of Nkoya-ness underwent considerable change over the last few centuries. A case in point is male circumcision (*mukanda*), which, introduced around the middle of the nineteenth century by a Nkoya ruler with close Lunda connections, became a fairly widespread practice among Nkoya-speaking groups until about the 1920s,[24] but which over the past fifty years has entirely vanished. The fact that today Nkoya ridicule *mukanda* as a distinctive feature of Luvale and Mbunda ethnic groups, with whom they have been in heavy political and ecological competition since the 1920s (when these immigrants from Angola started to arrive in Kaoma district in large numbers), suggests that the absence of male circumcision became a distinctive feature of Nkoya-ness only recently and in response to Luvale/Mbunda encroachment.

This does not mean that in the pre-colonial past there never was a group of people designated as Nkoya. Although the ethnic distinctions operating today in Central African society have been greatly influenced by intergroup processes within political arenas defined by the colonial and post-colonial state, and therefore must be seen as essentially recent phenomena (see Colson 1968; Ranger 1982), there can be no doubt that many of the ethnic labels and cultural symbols employed in that modern context have *nominally* a pre-colonial origin, whatever fundamental changes in form and function they have since undergone.

As anywhere else in the world, people in pre-colonial Zambia saw themselves and each other as belonging to various named groups defined by any one of the following criteria, or perhaps a loose combination: by language, place of residence, culture, political organization, economic speciality, etc. Named social groups of wider or lesser scope are too prominently and too consistently present in oral traditions to be explained away as mere projections of colonial or post-colonial realities into a pre-colonial past. Moreover, the same names appear in written documents generated in the nineteenth and early twentieth century before the imposition of a colonial administration could have made a deep impact on the way people structured and named their social environment. However, it is more than likely that, like almost anywhere in the world, the various generic and proper names for groups thus distinguished by Zambians in the pre-colonial period operated at various levels of inclusiveness; that their various dimensions did not coincide (e.g. named political units did not coincide with linguistic or economic ones); that these groups were situational and often had blurred boundaries; and that they were constantly manipulated in the course of intergroup interaction. Only in this way did 'tribes' exist in pre-colonial Zambia;[25] and, even so, clans were more prominent forms of social organization. Distinctions and identifications at the level of 'tribe' (the word exists in every Zambian language) may have occasionally provided a framework for political and military mobilization, but are not likely to have automatically determined actual group processes; rather they were the shifting results of such processes. A tribal model, such as that propounded by classic structural-functionalist anthropology, could have explained pre-colonial societies in Zambia no more than it throws light on contemporary social realities in that part of the world.

The name 'Nkoya' stems without any doubt from before the imposition of colonial rule.[26] According to particularly convincing oral traditions, it is claimed to derive from a toponym denoting a forest area near the confluence of the Kabompo and the Zambezi Rivers, where one of the royal clans (the one owning the Mutondo chieftainship) of the Nkoya is said to have lived about 1800.[27] As the names of a social group, 'Nkoya' appears in several royal praise-names with which Nkoya rulers acceded to their respective thrones in the course of the nineteenth century; I am certain that these boastful mottoes are not recent fabrications projected into the past. But there never was, in the pre-colonial era, an autonomous Nkoya polity encompassing the many thousands of people who today are claimed to be Nkoya. Instead, the area has, since the end of the eighteenth century, been the scene of a number of mutually independent chiefdoms, typically with short-lived dynasties, which hived off or replaced each other following a complicated fissionary pattern, and without much of a recognized hierarchy among them. The group named 'Nkoya' obviously had a political dimension, but it was a very small group, and, moreover, its boundaries certainly did not coincide with the (much more extensive) areas of distribution of the linguistic, cultural and economic features displayed by, among others, the members of that group. In reports dating from the nineteenth and twentieth centuries, the 'Mashasha' group centring on the Kahare dynasty is at least equally prominent. Both the mutual definition of 'Nkoya' and 'Mashasha' as major constituents (along with Mbwela, Lukolwe, the Nkoya offshoots in the Zambezi plain, etc.) of today's Nkoya, and the contiguous geographical areas imputed to them on tribal maps, have gone through a number of different versions since David Livingstone first marked the Bamasa (= Mashasha) on the 'Detailed Map' in *Missionary Travels and Researches*.[28] An analysis of these versions[29] would take us too far in the present context; but it would certainly corroborate the point I am trying to make: that as an ethnic category, 'Nkoya' is fluid, and expanding.

The extension of the name Nkoya to an entire cluster encompassing several mutually independent chiefdoms throughout western Zambia dates only from the second half of the last century, and was due, largely, to the incorporation, with different degrees of effectiveness, of these several shifting and unstable chiefdoms into the Kololo/Luyana state, and its heir, the Barotseland

Protectorate. This ethnic labelling in the context of Lozi tributary relations was further formalized when in the first decade of the twentieth century a *boma* was established, and Mankoya[30] (sub-)district was named after what was then considered to be the main 'tribe' inhabiting the district. Thus contained within a well-defined administrative and territorial unit, Nkoya identity could further develop within the arenas created by the colonial state, and the Lozi neo-traditional government depending upon that state.

Ethnicity, history and the Nkoya experience

How did the Nkoya, against so many odds, manage to convince me that they were 'a tribe'? Why was I lured into adopting this unit of study? My tentative answer is that, although the Nkoya had never been a tribe in the sense of classic anthropology, I became involved with them at a point in their history when they were trying very hard to believe that they constituted such a tribe; when this attempt was finally beginning to pay off; when I was in a position to help the attempt to succeed, because of my access to venues for publication; and particularly when, on my part, underneath their mistaken idiom of ethnic expression I detected a sense of deprivation, protest, struggle, with which I could identify — and identification grew as I learned their language and culture, and exposed myself and my family to appalling conditions of rural life which, although commonplace to the Nkoya, seemed to epitomize their deprivation.

For there was a serious, real-life dimension which my earlier, hidden, conference paper had not managed to capture. The Nkoya experience may be understandable as a product of historical circumstance; may even (as I shall argue below) contain elements of one-sidedness and exaggeration — but this does not make it less real. The Nkoya ethnic pathos swept me off my feet not so much because it provided a temporary shelter for my own uncertain identity, but particularly because it was so clearly and timely an active reaction to a collective historical experience. And I was not the first anthropologist to struggle with the experiential side of ethnicity. Whereas Mitchell's later work on urban ethnicity (1970, 1974) was primarily a (successful) attempt to remedy the analytical confusion of emic and etic aspects in urban ethnic categorization, Epstein went much further in his revision. In *Ethos and Identity*

(1978), he elaborated on aspects which the Copperbelt studies initially had left untouched: the emotive aspects of identity as deriving from a sense of collective history, and from identification between (alternate) generations. Perhaps the emotional struggle to do justice to this experiential side has tempted so many students of ethnicity to adopt such terms as identity and primordial attachments, as ultimate explanations.

Let me summarize how contemporary Nkoya look upon their history since the emergence of their own major chieftainships in the early nineteenth century. They migrated to their present territory, in the course of the last centuries, under the impact of Kaonde and Yeke pressure.[31] Their royal capitals were pillaged by the Lozi — who earlier, in Mulambwa's time (the early nineteenth century), are believed to have come to beg for chiefly medicine and chiefly instruments from the Nkoya! Since the first decade of this century they were supervised and humiliated by Lozi representative *indunas*, and, since 1937, relegated to an inferior position altogether with the creation of the Mankoya Native Treasury and the Lozi court at Naliele (near the Kaoma district centre), occupied by a senior member of the Lozi royal family. Their lands, since the 1920s, had been encroached upon by Lozi and especially by thousands of Angolan (Mbunda, Luvale, Luchazi) immigrants into the district. They were evicted from much of their agricultural and hunting territory at the creation of Kafue National Park in the 1930s. They were left without adequate mission-provided educational and medical facilities, which (in the Nkoya view) were concentrated near the centres of Lozi power in the district and in Barotseland as a whole.

Neither did the first ten years of Zambia's independence do much to restore Nkoya pride. In the district's primary schools, the use of Nkoya textbooks was abolished, and Lozi ones substituted, in the late 1960s the predominantly non-Nkoya teachers were blamed for the very poor educational success of their Nkoya pupils, most of whom received their education in a language (Lozi) they did not speak at home. Secondary school entrance was very low, and access to higher educational institutions negligible. Radio broadcasting in the Nkoya language, never more than a few minutes per week anyway, was discontinued. At the provincial level, Lozi, and at the district level especially Mbunda and Luvale, dominated the national party, UNIP, as well as the various elected bodies of local government; and the Nkoya mainly supported

ANC until this party was integrated into UNIP at the creation of the one-party state (1972). Like the whole of western Zambia, the Nkoya saw their major access to capitalist labour markets cut off when labour recruitment for the South African mines was stopped shortly after UDI. But, somewhat unlike the Lozi, the Nkoya, because of their different educational and mission history, and because of their lack of previously established urban footholds, could find little compensation in migratory opportunities along the Zambian 'line of rail' (the central belt of the country, with developed infrastructure and predominantly capitalist relations of production). Cash-cropping opportunities were slowly increasing in the district, including agricultural extension work, the erection of National Agricultural Marketing Board depots, and a massive tobacco and maize scheme of the Tobacco Board of Zambia. But again very few Nkoya benefited by these, except as low-paid agricultural workers. And people in the outlying villages negotiated in vain for tractors to come to their villages and plough their maize-fields. Among the villagers, cash-crop production still tends to be limited to a few bags of maize a year; seed maize and fertilizer are difficult to get, and after marketing their crops and peasants have to wait for months until they get paid. In 1969 the name of the district was changed from Mankoya to Kaoma, wiping out the last traces of official recognition that originally the distict was Nkoya land. The two main Nkoya Chiefs, Kahare and Mutondo, continued to maintain a state-subsidized royal establishment, as guaranteed under the 1964 Barotse Agreement (the 1969 alterations did not affect this point). But they were denied the status of senior chiefs, and their subsidies were substantially lower than those received at Naliele.

The Nkoya keenly resent their lack of success in wider society, which they blame on their history of deprivation. By the mid-1970s, the Nkoya could boast only one university graduate (junior partner in a law firm). In addition, a few dozen had, through their good fortune, political credit and education, managed to occupy middle-range positions in government institutions and private enterprise in the urban areas. A similar small number were established as modern farmers in Kaoma, Mumbwa and Namwala districts. Among these people, the pressure from poor relatives and the stigma of belonging to a despised ethnic group is severely felt, and some go through periods when they deny being Nkoya, and no longer honour claims to kinship support.

The majority of the Nkoya, meanwhile, are still dependent on labour migration for their family income, and have only unskilled labour to offer. They maintain to some extent a pattern of circulatory migration and family separation which for others in Zambia is increasingly a thing of the past. The Nkoya presence in the urban areas along the line of rail is limited and has a rapid turnover: it even seems to be declining under the effects of a shrinking market for unskilled labour, and the increasing competition from people from areas that have more established urban footholds (easterners in Lusaka, northerners on the Copperbelt).

Above I have rendered this stereotyped experience as a collective representation among a set of people[32] — recent history as most Nkoya today would see it, and not history as a detached historian with free access to all relevant sources would write it.[33] For instance, the extent and variation of nineteenth-century Lozi and Kololo control over the eastern part of what is now Western Province remains a problem which crops up again and again in Nkoya oral sources: some admit established tributary relations, others stress the common origin between Nkoya and Lozi, and still others deny any Lozi domination over the Nkoya prior to colonial rule. How, and where, to distinguish between history as self-expression, and history as a detached outsider's undertaking? The point is crucial, since the Nkoya today are a people united not so much by the distinguishing features of a common language, culture, or rural production system, but by a particular conception of their recent past. They define themselves mainly as the bearers of a common history, and (as came out very clearly in the course of my work sessions with the chiefs' councils at the two main Nkoya royal establishments in the district) they expect from the explicit formulation, and circulation, of this version of history an internal mobilization and an outside recognition which, when translated into political and economic benefits, will remedy their predicament through government appointments and development projects coming their way.

In this emic version of their history, their misery is set off against delusions of past grandeur and of immense geographical extension, comprising all speakers of Nkoya, Mashasha, Mbwela and related dialects, and their descendants, throughout Zambia's Western, Northwestern, Central and Southern Provinces. It is not so much the redefinition of history in the hands of an ethnic group,

208

but rather the creation of history as an aspect of the contemporary emergence of an ethnic group.

The Nkoya today would thus appear to be a case of what Abner Cohen (1969: 2) has so aptly termed *retribalization*:

> a process by which a group from one ethnic category, whose members are involved in a struggle for power and privilege with the members of a group from another ethnic category, within the framework of a *formal* political system, manipulate some customs, values, myths, symbols and ceremonials from their cultural tradition in order to articulate an *informal* political organization which is used as a weapon in that struggle.

During the colonial period various attempts to confront Lozi domination led to utter defeat. Chief Kahare Timuna was temporarily demoted in 1923 (Gluckman 1968b: 95). When in the 1930s Watchtower agitation in Mankoya district was challenging the Lozi administration, the latter banned the preachers and threatened with demotion the Nkoya chiefs siding with them (see van Binsbergen 1981b: 344f., nn. 73, 77, and references cited there). Soon after the creation of the Naliele court, the incumbent of the Mutondo chieftainship died under what the Nkoya consider to be suspicious circumstances; ten years later his successor Muchaila was dethroned and exiled to Kalabo for ten years (Shimunika, in press; anonymous, n.d.). Witchcraft cases in Mankoya district in the late 1950s, directed in part against the local Lozi establishment, were vigorously quelled (Reynolds 1963). In 1960 a Nkoya-based ANC[34] branch was refused registration, as 'it was felt that any political organization in the Nkoya area would stir up long-standing secessionist agitation among a subject tribe against the Barotse government' (Mulford 1967: 223). Attempts to organize a Nkoya tribal association along the line of rail, and a political party largely on a Nkoya ethnic basis, were also undertaken about 1960, but failed, partly due to difficulties arising from the recently enacted Societies Ordinance.

It was probably no coincidence that my research among the Nkoya took place in a period when the tide seemed to turn for the Nkoya, due to a number of developments at the national level in Zambia. The same move that led to the alteration of the district name from Mankoya to Kaoma, implied far-reaching measures that all but dismantled the remnants of the Lozi state within the Republic of Zambia, and that marked the defeat of the strong Lozi faction within the Zambian government (Caplan 1970: 223). This diminished the extent to which non-Lozi west Zambians would be dependent on Lozi patronage for a political career; in fact, the former became likely allies of the state against the Lozi establishment. The integration of ANC into UNIP in 1972 relieved former ANC candidates from the stigma of disloyalty, and the one Nkoya candidate, defeated on an ANC ticket in 1968, was victorious for UNIP in the 1973 and 1977 general elections. He became the first Nkoya MP (representing, though, only part of the area inhabited by Nkoya). Yet he might just as well have identified as Lozi (and in fact often does): his father was Lozi, but he spent part of his childhood at one of the Nkoya chief's capitals, from where his mother originated. In addition, a few Nkoya became appointed, non-elected members of the Kaoma Rural Council, partly on the strength of their traditional offices. No Nkoya played leading roles in UNIP at the district level (Regional Office) or above.

Modern Nkoya politicians rely not only on their roots in the Nkoya royal families, but also try to instil a sense of new possibilities existing at the national and district level, now that Lozi power is so clearly on the decline. They stir up a new ethnic pride. Thus they create a local following; their action manages to pull local people, distrustful of the independent Zambian state and of UNIP, back into national political participation. One of their proudest achievements is that in the newly-established party branches, for the first time in Zambian history, well-known UNIP songs (such as *Tiyende pamodzi*) are now sung in Nkoya translations. Besides their political activities, they also further the interests of traditional leadership, instigating discussions about the rate of subsidies for Nkoya chiefs, the revival of chieftainships that were abolished in the colonial era, and the creation of senior chieftainships among the Nkoya. A sign of the changing tide is the reinstallation in office (1980) of Chief Muchaila Mutondo, decades after his demotion and exile. Besides these political activities the new leaders availed themselves of the new economic opportunities, particularly those the Tobacco Board of Zambia is creating in the district. In this context they act as employers of agricultural wage-labour and as entrepreneurs in the retail trade.

In addition to active Nkoya politicians in recent times, a major builder of Nkoya ethnicity has been the Rev. J. M. Shimunika. Born about 1910 as a member of the Mutondo royal family, he is rumoured to have been a *nganga* (diviner-priest) before his conversion to Christianity, which came to the district in 1923 (after A. W. Bailey's abortive attempt in 1913–14). Shimunika was a teacher, an evangelist and finally a pastor with the South Africa General Mission (now the Africa Evangelical Fellowship; its missionary activities have led to the creation of the Evangelical Church of Zambia). Shimunika's translation of the New Testament and the Psalms was published in 1952;[35] his Old Testament translation was completed in the 1970s. In the 1950s he published a short pamphlet in the Nkoya language, *Muhumpu wa Byambo bya Mwaka* (anonymous n.d.), which is a selection taken from his larger work, *Likota lya Bankoya* (*The History of the Nkoya*), which is now in press (Shimunika). Instead of boosting Nkoya morale, *Muhumpu* created internal animosity, because of the allegations it contained about the weak stand of a particular Nkoya royal family *vis-à-vis* the Lozi. Educated Nkoya of a younger generation than the Rev. Shimunika's have invested a great deal of time and energy in order to enable me to publish *Likota* in a form that is to avoid similar animosity in future.

My research was firmly supported by both traditional office-holders, and their kinsmen, the Nkoya modern politicians. Without the introductions extended by the latter, a substantial part of my data could never have been collected. But in the first year of my Nkoya research this element was still absent. The eager support the Nkoya townsmen in the compounds offered me at that stage derived from a less sophisticated perception of my possible role, but was likewise cast in ethnic terms. The following episode brings this out clearly:

By May 1973 I had decided to add some systematic, quantifiable census data to my observational and participatory urban data as acquired so far. I prepared a mimeographed one-page questionnaire, and administered it to scores of Nkoya assembled for a girl's puberty ceremony in a Lusaka compound. One elderly man showed a healthy suspicion, and wanted to know why I needed the basic information I had asked him. But before I could explain my intentions at length, he was scolded by his fellows: 'You better answer him, you stupid fool. Otherwise we are never going to have a book about ourselves, like the Lozi have and all those other tribes!'

This eagerness to tell their tale, to have themselves put on the ethnographic and historical map, was even the main force behind my initial concentration on the Nkoya, during my urban research. Confronted with the very strong force with which this emerging ethnic group positively attracted me, I had no reason to resist.

Nkoya ethnicity, the articulation of modes of production, and the dialectics of consciousness

With the preceding two sections of this chapter, we may have gained tentative insights into the nature of Nkoya ethnicity which could not have been arrived at through consistent application of the classic tribal model. The contemporary Nkoya situation turns out to have many of the ingredients stressed by current interpretations of ethnicity in the Central African context. Underneath a strongly situational and manipulatory surface which is particularly apparent in urban and middle-class contexts, there is a genuine Nkoya identity, but it is based not so much on primordial attachment to a way of life, culture and language, but on a collective sense of deprivation in the course of a shared recent history. Expecting to extract, from the state and the party, goods and services which until recently have been denied them (see Bates 1973), peasants identifying as Nkoya on the basis of this historical consciousness give voting support to politicians from their midst; the latter, linked to Nkoya royal families, but likewise, through their education and careers, involved in modern economic life, explore the possibilities of ethnic identification, and actively further the building of Nkoya ethnicity in an attempt to safeguard their own positions (see Molteno 1974), as well as to serve their people's interests at the same time. Their efforts at retribalization converge, and sometimes coincide, with those of local intellectuals. Just like everything social, Nkoya ethnicity turns out to be man-made, and even amazingly recent; but to realize that the Nkoya are not a 'natural', primordial unit bestows a social and historical meaning on Nkoya-ness, instead of — as I thought in my first disappointment — depriving it of meaning.

However, showing how one particular unit of study, the tribe — already subjected to so much criticism — is inadequate in the Nkoya case as well, goes only half-way towards solving the problem of the unit of study. I shall now carry the argument further, sketching the wider sociological implications of the picture of Nkoya ethnicity presented above, and arguing that the structure of the social field, which thus becomes visible, solves the problem of the unit of study for us.

I have discussed Nkoya ethnicity as a form of consciousness which may lead on, situationally, to social and political mobilization, but which primarily is a process of self-definition among a set of people perceiving themselves as sharing a common history of deprivation. One of the major tasks confronting the social sciences today is the development of a sophisticated theory of the conditions under which particular forms of consciousness relate to particular social, political and particularly economic processes. As has been argued by Kahn in the article referred to above (1981), an idealist, culturological position, such as that taken by those looking for primordial attachments, is just as untenable as a vulgar-materialist position which, against all evidence, posits a simple one-to-one relationship between economic conditions and the attending forms of consciousness. The task is fundamental, on the one hand because the social sciences in themselves are a form of consciousness; on the other because it is precisely by the phantasms of consciousness that conditions of deprivation, injustice, exploitation persist — just as they are actively challenged, and altered, as a result of an emerging, truer consciousness.

What further insights into Nkoya ethnicity can we gather if we subject this form of consciousness to a Marxist-inspired contextual analysis?

In order to answer this question, let us briefly review the history of the social formation of the Kaoma district, in terms of the articulation between successively emerging modes of production (see van Binsbergen 1981b: 258–63).

In the nineteenth century dramatic changes took place in that social formation. By the end of the eighteenth century, the social formation was already a highly complex one, in which, as a result of the emergence and articulation of various modes of production in previous centuries, various mutually dependent branches or forms of production[36] co-existed: highly developed hunting and gathering; rather crude fishing and farming; a limited form of domestic slavery;[37] and petty commodity production (particularly ironware) for local trade circuits. Clan chieftainship was largely concerned with ritual functions concerning the land, and with exclusive claims to certain proceeds from hunting, which were locally consumed or hoarded but were not yet circulated in long-distance trade and tribute.

Oral tradition, and written documents relating to the late nineteenth and early twentieth centuries,[38] as well as the converging evidence from scholarly studies of neighbouring areas,[39] suggest the following trends for the period starting *c.* 1800. Small militant groups coming in from the north brought a new, more exalted style of chieftainship, as well as some of the economic prerequisites (better crops, cattle, and cattle-raiding) with which to generate a surplus on which such chieftainship could thrive. Domestic slavery was greatly increased, and lost the earlier kinship connotations of pawnship. Between local communities and the emerging chiefly courts, and between courts of different importance, tributary networks were developed, along which travelled not only the products of local branches of production, but also slaves in increasing numbers. This process was further intensified by the advent, around 1850, of long-distance trade in the hands of Mambari and Swahili caravan traders, and the marked ascendance, some 200 kilometres to the west, of the Luyana/Kololo state. In the last quarter of the nineteenth century the economy of that state became largely dependent upon slave labour; hence large raiding expeditions for slaves and cattle were organized, and they extended well to the east of the Nkoya lands. Whereas in the social formation before 1800 a domestic mode of production could be said to be dominant, the later period saw the gradual subordination of this mode to tributary and, via long-distance trade, mercantile-capitalist modes of production. The new modes of production emerging in the nineteenth century were closely linked to each other. Most if not all slaves were controlled by chiefs and their office-bearers; this gave these nobles unique opportunities to have a local surplus generated, available for long-distance trade. It appears that domestic slavery rapidly declined to a trade in humans from which even close kinsmen (notably sisters' sons) were not excluded.

The precise inter-relations between the tributary and the mercantile-capitalist mode of production await further research. Both were still groping to establish themselves, and both never attained the full realization of their respective models. But what is important here, and fairly well documented, is the subordination of the domestic mode of production to these two other modes.

As the penetration of the capitalist mode of production in the social formation of Kaoma district proceeded (and as this social formation itself became integrated in a much wider formation:

Northern Rhodesia, the capitalist world), the tributary and mercantile-capitalist modes of production (having gained dominance in the nineteenth century) were encapsulated and largely destroyed. That colonial rule was committed to the spread of capitalist relations of production no longer requires a lengthy discussion. Very soon after its imposition (1900) the flow of commodities into the area would be channelled through the rather ill-equipped rural trading stores, but particularly through the purchases by labour migrants at their distant places of work. Long-distance trade was forced to an end. The tributary mode of production was destroyed by colonial legislation abolishing slavery and tributary labour. Government subsidies allowed some of the chiefs and aristocrats to keep up the remnants of a political and ideological pre-capitalist structure, after the relations of production underlying that structure had been radically altered.[40] These subsidies were paid out of the revenues from hut tax, a direct form of surplus extraction imposed by the colonial administration, and one that soon forced people to sell their labour for money, after the rapid breakdown of local participation in the agricultural market (van Horn 1977: 154f.). The circulation of traders, commodities and slaves (the local manifestations of extraction by an as yet invisible mercantile capitalism) had given way to the circulation of money and of labour migrants, and many people had become directly (though seldom permanently) involved in capitalist relations of production.

The contemporary Nkoya situation provides a good illustration of the articulation of a domestic mode of production, stripped, to a considerable extent, of the remains of the tributary mode, and articulated to the dominant industrial capitalist mode. The old branches of production organized by kinship are more or less surviving, although they have been encroached upon by state control (alienation of land for game reserves and (para-)statal agricultural enterprise; and prohibitions on hunting). Likewise they have been eroded by the exodus of male labour; the penetration of capitalist consumer markets (all clothing, most implements and some food, are now bought from outside); and the introduction, on a limited scale, of cash-cropping and agricultural wage-labour.

Adult males participate as migrants in the urban capitalist economy, and a minority of them manage to set up and maintain urban nuclear families which, if continuously successful in town,

215

are going to contribute directly to the reproduction of the capitalist sector. However, the footing of these urban migrants is particularly insecure; and many of the members of their households may ultimately end up in the rural sector. While remaining in town, these migrants can find greater security in the domestic domain by participation in dyadic networks as well as collective ceremonies and rituals, which encompass both urban wage-earners, recent arrivals, urban drop-outs about to return home and people without any participation in the urban relations of production: women and villagers. The domestic sector extends well into the urban areas, and into the households of the urban wage-earners. Religious and ethnic ceremonies, mobilizing a large proportion of the 'Nkoya' population of a particular town, provide a setting for this interpenetration, as well as a means to recirculate money earned in the urban capitalist sector to those debarred from it. They are an instrument of articulation, and notably one which syphons resources back into the domestic sector, contributing to the latter's reproduction rather than to its exploitation.

Armed with this cursory analytical view of the articulation of modes of production as determining the Nkoya situation today, let us now return to their collective view of Nkoya history. Seen as a possible response to the articulation of modes of production, it is a crucial feature of the Nkoya view of their history that no distinction is made between those aspects of local decline that were due to national or global processes of the penetration of capitalism as mediated by the colonial state (and that, therefore, affected the people of the district in a way unrelated to them being, or not being, Nkoya); and those that more directly reflected intrusion by other Africans (Lozi, Angolans). Analytically, only the latter — if still only superficially — could be dealt with in ethnic terms. The colonial state served the creation of capitalist conditions, and the attuning of pre-existing non-capitalist modes of production to these conditions. However, the colonial state realized its aims partly by furthering a neo-traditional indigenous Lozi administration, sanctioning the latter's hold upon the peripheral groups in Barotseland, as well as allowing the settlement of large numbers of Angolan immigrants — not, of course, near the centres of Lozi presence, but in the same outlying areas. The Nkoya clearly perceived the Lozi and the Angolan immigrants, but failed to detect the forces of the colonial state and of capitalism behind them. Therefore, the colonial state remained fairly neutral in the conscious historical perception of the Nkoya. The frequent expressions of Nkoya protest in the colonial period, if they did take on any political overtones and were not entirely clad in religious forms (see van Binsbergen 1981b: 58f. ch. 4, and for sources pp. 344–6) were directed against Lozi domination, and not against the state. One of the most shocking aspects of my field-work in a newly-independent country was to hear peasants, as a standard turn in their everyday conversation and certainly not prompted by interviewing, praise colonial conditions and the economic and political security they had implied, in contrast with the situation after independence. The penetration of capitalism had numerous structural effects on the local society (wage-labour, migrancy, monetarization of bridewealth, fragmentation of pro-ductive units and of settlement, partial dismantling of traditional authority by divorcing it from its exploitative economic base). But in so far as these effects were not welcomed (they often were), they were blamed on the Lozi. The negative aspects in the Nkoya collective experience came to be almost entirely perceived in terms of ethnic conflict. Even the modern national state is for the Nkoya primarily veiled under ethnic perceptions. For the Nkoya today the modern state of Zambia is largely considered a remote affair of the Bemba, Tonga, Lozi and Chewa, in various shifting alliances; Nkoya peasants even frequently use the word 'Zambia' when from the context it is clear that they exclusively refer to the 'line of rail': the area extending from Livingstone, through Lusaka and Kabwe, to the Copperbelt — and the part of Zambia where the capitalist mode of production is the most manifest and dominant. As recently as 1973, when the district authorities staged meetings in the villages in preparation for the general elections, these meetings were boycotted or challenged because they were in the hated Lozi language; and the two opponents of the one Nkoya candidate were primarily unattractive since they were known to be Mbunda or Luvale.

This ethnic fixation, however, enables Nkoya politicians to look to the post-colonial state with new expectations, now that the main perceived enemy, the Lozi ethnic group, is no longer so closely allied with the state as it used to be in the colonial era and in the first years after independence.

It would be foolish to accept the Nkoya's one-sided view of history, and to attribute their predicament entirely to the effects of Lozi domination. As a 'Lozi subject tribe', the Nkoya were exposed to both Lozi and European imperialism. Historically these followed each other in quick succession, and the two could be argued to be indirectly related also in the pre-colonial period,[41] for both were specific forms through which the penetration of the capitalist mode of production was ultimately effected. After 1900, the class alliance between the Lozi aristocracy and the colonial powers led to fundamental changes in the type of economic exploitation to which the people in the eastern periphery of Barotseland were subjected. The taking of slaves, and the payment of tribute, within two decades after the imposition of colonial rule had completely given way to forms of taxation which virtually reduced the Lozi to an administrative presence, whereas the economic exploitation was achieved through the mechanisms of labour migration as furthered by the colonial state. In that period, the deprivation on the surface (in the field of chieftainship, educational and medical facilities, etc.), for which the Lozi were blamed, ultimately sprang from the logic of imperialism. From this angle, Nkoya ethnicity, even in the powerless form in which it expressed itself during the colonial period, had the effect of obscuring such class-consciousness as might have emerged among the villagers in the first decades of their incorporation into capitalism. Indirectly, such ethnicity appears as an ideological effect of imperialism.

Interestingly, among the non-Nkoya inhabitants of western Zambia, the prevailing stereotype about the Nkoya is not that of people deprived under the impact of Lozi domination, but that of hunters drinking honey-beer, expertly playing their xylophones, hiding in the forest from the responsibilities and vicissitudes of modern life, uninterested in commercial farming, and actively furthering truancy in their children. In other words, people who can afford to shun participation in modern life because their old ways are still fairly intact — rather than people who have been denied access to modern life as a result of Lozi machinations. This would suggest, as a possibility, that it is precisely the relative viability of their non-capitalist modes of production which prevented them from successfully manipulating capitalism to their own lasting benefit. But of course, stereotypes are not enough to go by.

The French School of Marxist anthropology (see Meillassoux 1975; Rey 1971, 1973; and the extensive discussions elsewhere in the present book) has two illuminating insights to offer for an understanding of the Nkoya situation. First, capitalism penetrating

218

the Third World has a well-defined interest in the partial survival of encapsulated, non-capitalist modes of production: for these are the niches where a new labour force is reproduced and where a discarded labour force is taken care of, at virtually no cost to the capitalist sector. And second, capitalism makes inroads into these non-capitalist modes of production by means of class alliances between capital, on the one hand, and the exploiting class-like groups in the non-capitalist modes of production, on the other.

What the Nkoya resent in their situation today, from this perspective would appear as common features of a labour reserve in a context of peripheral capitalism: lack of capitalist amenities that serve the reproduction of the labour force (schools, hospitals); and the limited size of local capitalist markets for labour and petty commodities (cash crops). But the other side of the coin is that, in their area, non-capitalist modes of production have persisted throughout the colonial era and, even if made subservient to the reproduction of labour for capitalist markets, still proved to be viable. Hunting, fishing, collecting and subsistence agriculture, organized on a kinship basis, even today are still economically vital undertakings, especially in the eastern part of the district. Of course, these forms of non-capitalist production cannot in themselves supply the cash needed today for clothing, tools, transport, etc. Moreover, none of these forms persists unaffected by capitalism. For instance, the Nkoya hunter today is often a youth who does not own the gun and ammunition he uses, but offers his skills to the owner of the gun in exchange for a portion of the bag he brings home; and this owner is usually at the same time a senior kinsman of the hunter, a village headman, and a retired labour migrant who has purchased a gun out of the proceeds of his sale of labour in the capitalist sector, and who sells most of the meat thus procured. Relations of production in hunting combine capitalist aspects (separation between worker and means of production, and between worker and product, and sale of this product as a commodity) with forms of authority and reciprocity proper to domestic and tributary modes of production outside capitalism.

These historical relations of production can survive, more or less, only if they continue to be embedded in the social, judicial and ritual forms in which they used to be enshrined in the past; or, more accurately, in forms mimicking these historical ones. Although these forms do not derive from a capitalist logic, it is not in the interest of capital to destroy them. And in some cases, particularly those where capital can strike a class relationship with exploitative elements in the older modes of production, it actively supports them. For a different part of Africa, Rey (1971) has argued how the monetarization of bridewealth was one way to synchronize the interests of capital and village elders: thus the latter could continue to exploit male youths through their control over marriageable women, but now in a form which forced these youths to go and sell their labour as migrants. This process took place also among the Nkoya. But an even more striking form of class alliance formed the subsidies which the state paid to chiefs. Due to historical circumstances which we need not enter into, in Barotseland these subsidies were higher than anywhere else in Northern Rhodesia, and the Nkoya chiefs shared in them. At independence, this state of affairs was reinforced, and in recent years the subsidies have even been substantially increased. Paid out of state revenue, and in the early years consisting of a fixed percentage of the revenue from hut tax, these subsidies amount to a sharing out of the fruits of capitalist exploitation to the remnants of a tributary mode of production. Capitalism, while reproducing still a substantial part of its labour-force via an encapsulated *domestic* mode of production, such as found among the Nkoya today, in its turn reproduces an encapsulated *tributary* mode, at least in its symbolic and ceremonial form of councillors, retainers, *kapasus*, royal musicians, a palace of sorts. In passing we note that Nkoya chiefs benefit from an updated form of a treaty between the colonial state and the Lozi aristocracy; so surely the Lozis' effect on the Nkoya experience was not entirely negative.

Much more important is that we now find, in the political economy of that area, a reason for the Nkoya's insistence on the existence and persistence of their 'tribe'. As a distinct culture and society, in other words as a tribe, the Nkoya have never existed. However, to the extent to which the persistence of historical forms in an encapsulated, neo-traditional version is part and parcel of the mechanisms of the reproduction of cheap labour, and to the extent to which the articulation of modes of production in the expanding social formation to which the Nkoya area belongs, crystallizes around a state-subsidized neo-traditional chieftainship,[42] Nkoya ethnicity can be considered a product of this situation of articulation.

In this perspective, the view of ethnicity as a primordial attachment to a tribal model dating back to pre-colonial times becomes more than bad social science: it becomes part of the ideology of capitalism itself — but I am sure that advocates of that view would have equally nasty things to say about the conception of ethnicity advanced here.

In the juxtaposition between non-capitalist aspects of Nkoya rural society and capitalism, the specific features of the former take on a new function: they are to be the legitimation of kin-based claims of assistance, and the resulting security through which people peripherally participating in a capitalist order seek shelter in non-capitalist relations of production which exist in the shadow of, and in servitude to, that capitalist order. Nkoya ethnicity is the expression of this problem at the level of consciousness: by stressing the viability, splendour and antiquity of the non-capitalist modes of production, it struggles to keep them intact, so that the individual worker in the process of peasantization and proletarianization can effectively benefit from what remnants of these non-capitalist modes still exist. Their survival has become both problematic and vital — hence they need ethnicity to endow them with rather more reality and resilience than they in fact possess.

Also the role of modern politicians is thrown into relief. At the level of the state's organizational and ideological apparatus (government and the party), these leaders represent a new phase in the class alliances by means of which capitalism imposes itself on pre-existing modes of production. Combining traditional élite connotations, ethnicity-building and their own capitalist enterprises, they represent solutions for the contradictions inherent in articulation. Through their activities in the retail trade, agricultural development schemes (for which they hire wage-labour), and their supervisory capacity as members of party and local government bodies, they further capitalism at the same time as helping to buttress non-capitalist modes of production against capitalism by the emphatic support they give to traditional authorities and the Nkoya ethnic identity in general. They further incorporation in the national state, but in a form that conceals the exploitative and manipulative elements of the political process, and of their own role; and thus, as political and ideological brokers, they legitimate the state in the eyes of the Nkoya, and at the same time further Nkoya interests within national and subnational political areas.

Under these conditions it would be ludicrous to expect, with John Saul (1979), the Nkoya to display explicit surface manifestations of class struggle, albeit in the ideological idiom of ethnicity. Both the incorporation in the Lozi state in the course of the nineteenth century, and the peripheral integration in capitalism, objectively can be taken as forms of class formation: the imposition of new form of exploitation. It would not be altogether unjustified ultimately to attribute the depth of emotion and the vehemence of expression attending Nkoya ethnicity today to a form of class struggle seeking in vain to break through. This, I realized much later, is probably an important reason behind my own emotional identification with the Nkoya.

The analysis of Nkoya ethnicity in terms of the articulation of modes of production brings out both the limitations of ethnicity and its power. In their ideology of ethnicity the Nkoya express a partial interpretation of historical developments: they identify the Lozi as their suppressors, but fail to recognize the forces of capitalism and colonialism that lie behind Lozi domination. In this respect there would be some reason to consider ethnicity, with Mafeje (1971), as 'false consciousness'. Yet such a characterization would be less adequate in so far as it underestimates the very real power of ethnicity — its emotional appeal. In the perspective of an articulation of modes of production we have the beginning of an explanation of why ethnicity can take such a powerful hold on people: ethnicity is revealed as an ideological reaction not to phantasms of the imagination but to very real conditions — the uprootedness resulting from capitalist penetration.[43]

However, the trappings of ethnicity, under conditions of articulation and class alliances, prevent the Nkoya from adopting anything remotely resembling a revolutionary consciousness. Considering the remarkable choice of revolutionary and counter-revolutionary ideological positions available in the district in the 1970s — from Maoist Chinese building the Lusaka–Kaoma highway, through MPLA and SWAPO guerrilla camps, to the South African sponsored adventurer Mushala — the Nkoya have not exactly shown an inclination towards left-wing radicalism, to say the least.

Conclusion

Seeking to project himself against the surging flood of data, the researcher tentatively cuts out a field of study for his personal

222

attention; and since he is studying people who themselves are constantly constructing and reconstructing their reality, he may be tempted to let his analytical distinctions coincide with folk distinctions. What the would-be Nkoya expected from me, in this context, was that I would lend my own intellectual resources, access to national and international media of publication and scholarship, not for the production of a more penetrating and thus liberating form of knowledge and consciousness, but for the buttressing of their own emerging ethnic illusion. It was up to me to describe 'the Nkoya' in all the historical glory of their nineteenth-century chieftainships, and to enlist, among the present-day population of Zambia, a maximum number of inhabitants of western and central Zambia as *de facto* or potential members of the 'Nkoya tribe'. I have described how I was at first caught in this trap, and how I scrambled out of it by the adoption of the analytical framework of modes of production and their articulation, which not only belong to a different realm of discourse from that in which the Nkoya consider themselves a tribe, but that also explodes the whole notion of the Nkoya, or some such groups, as a unit of study. What remains is a complicated picture of relationships, informed by Marxist anthropology, history and political economy, and far removed from the Nkoya experience and from the unit of study it seemed to suggest. There is no obvious, let alone a natural, unit of study that is more likely than others to give insight into the sorts of relationships which I have tried to disentangle in this argument. A simple spatio-temporal delineation would not do either: the picture of a field of specific relationships which emerges as the major result of my Nkoya research is neither geographically contiguous (for it extends far beyond the Nkoya chief's areas of Kaoma district, into urban Zambia, North Atlantic metropoles, and my own department), nor historically defined — extending as it does from the twentieth century into the eighteenth.[44]

Instead of a clear-cut unit of study as a source of security for the field-worker and as a handy artefact to be manipulated by the cross-cultural comparativist, we thus end up with an awareness of interesting questions and possible sources of inspiration; an interdisciplinary outlook; and the intention to analyse the dialectics of consciousness not only among the people selected for study, but also within the realm of scholarship, and ultimately, in one's private reactions as a researcher.

The emerging picture, while explaining to some extent the nature of Nkoya-ness, helps, I hope, to eradicate the stereotype of bounded ethnic groups which happily lend themselves to cross-cultural analysis. As the Kaoma district governor exclaimed during a heated political meeting, in preparation of the 1973 general elections:

> This nonsense has to stop! Chief, you must control your people! There are no Nkoya! 'Nkoya' does not exist!

Neither do the Lozi, Bemba, Tonga or Ndembu, unless as phenomena at the level of consciousness, whose dialectics we — as the producers of a different, and possibly more liberating, sort of consciousness — should trace and explain, instead of adopt. Our results may at first puzzle, disappoint or infuriate the people we are writing about; but ultimately we may manage to show them their own situation in a form less veiled by the phantasms produced by their political-economic conditions.

Notes

1 Earlier drafts of this chapter were presented at the *Journal of Southern African Studies*/Social Science Research Council Conference on the Interactions of History and Anthropology in Southern Africa, Manchester, September 1980; and at the African Studies Centre's Africa Colloquium, Leiden, February 1981. An earlier version was published in *Journal of Southern African Studies*, 8, 1: 51–81; it is here reprinted in a revised version, by the kind permission of the journal's editors and of the Oxford University Press. I am indebted to R. Buijtenhuijs, C. Bundy, R. Frankenberg, P. Konings, A. Mafeje, C. Mitchell, C. Murray, T. Ranger, P. Worsley and especially P. Geschiere for comments and criticism; for full acknowledgments concerning my research into 'Nkoya' ethnicity, see van Binsbergen (1981b): 5f. The approach as developed in this chapter was greatly influenced by the discussions of the Amsterdam Work-group on Marxist Anthropology; however, for reasons set out in the Preface to the present book, this chapter could not benefit from specific discussions within the work-group.

2 Quoted on the jacket of Colson (1970); this quotation is meant to illustrate the uncritical use of the tribal model in anthropology as manifested by the *Times Educational Supplement* review, not as an adequate description of van Velsen (1964).

3 Some progress, however, has been made with regard to the religious aspect of modes of production, see Houtart (1980), Houtart & Lemercinier (1977), and with special emphasis on articulation, van

Binsbergen (1981b).

4 Cf. Meillassoux (1964); Terray 1969; similar criticism also in Kahn & Llobera (1980): 88: 'these writers appear to share the view that "societies" as conceived by traditional anthropology are relevant units of analysis.' Rey, however is a different case: without explicitly discussing the problem of ethnicity, in his monograph (1971) on the Mossendjo area (Congo-Brazzaville) he takes not a 'tribe', but the region as his unit of analysis.

5 This point is argued at great length in van Binsbergen (1981b): chs 1, 7, 8.

6 This is already clear from the book titles of Colson (1958, 1968, 1970), Watson (1958), Turner (1968a, 1968b), Colson & Gluckman (1951), Gluckman (1957, 1965), Cunnison (1959), Marwick (1965), Scudder (1962). This selection does not include articles and papers; studies by Rhodes-Livingstone researchers outside rural Zambia; or studies (like Richards 1939) not published under the aegis of the Rhodes-Livingstone Institute.

7 Mitchell (1956, 1969), Epstein (1958), Gluckman (1960), Harries-Jones (1969).

8 Van Velsen (1964, 1967), Turner (1968a). Strictly speaking, of course, van Velsen's work was not a direct contribution to Zambian rural anthropology, based as it was on field-work in Malawi. its impact on both rural and urban studies in Zambia was, however, immense.

9 J. van Velsen, personal communication, September 1980.

10 Gluckman (1968a); cf. Gluckman (1945), where the concept of tribe is used in the same fashion. One would have expected a lengthy discussion of the problem of tribe in Gluckman's *Closed Systems and Open Minds: The Limits of Naïvety in Social Anthropology* (1964); but apart from a cursory remark relating to Bailey's research in India, little of relevance can be found here. The book is about the uses and limitations of anthropologist's naïvety vis-à-vis other disciplines, not vis-à-vis their own. Hence, I suppose, the statement by Gluckman (p. 199, n. 44) that he considers himself to possess an 'expertise on tribes' . . .

11 The sub-title of Long (1968).

12 Perhaps the last time that, on the basis of his own field-work, a researcher discussed contemporary social situations in rural Zambia in terms of a 'tribal community' was Johnson & Bond (1974). However, in his monograph, Bond (1976) did much better than that. Meanwhile the Zambian material remains available for non-field-workers to take their pick. Thus Sharp (1981) discusses an Afrikaans South African M.A. thesis, on ethnicity in Zambia, by J. H. Booyens, PUCHO, 1978. Based on library research, Booyens's argument is built on the notion of nineteenth-century tribes (*ethniee*) founded in primordial attachments and insurmountable mutual hostilities. Sharp points at the close links between such a view of ethnicity, and the ideology of Apartheid.

13 Lancaster (1966, 1971, 1974, 1977). The title of Lancaster's book (1981) follows the Rhodes-Livingstone pattern in its loosely-descriptive

use of the tribal label. Poewe's work is remarkably free from tribal illusions (1978, 1979, 1981), in which she continues the pattern set by Cunnison.

14 Extensive reference, however, is made to Gluckman's work on Barotseland. Gwyn Prins's (1979) dismissive review of *Roots* (as the book is affectionately called among Southern Africanists, who have already accorded it the status of a modern classic) seems to imply that the book could have done with rather more anthropological inspiration.

15 On the crucial significance of the specialist audience in the process of methodological and theoretical innovation, see de Groot (1966): 27f.

16 Cf. Kuper (1977b, 1980). Quoted in this context, these references do not do full justice to the type of regional comparative analysis Kuper is engaged in.

17 My field-work was conducted alternately in Kaoma district, western Zambia, and Lusaka, from February 1972 to April 1974; September–November 1977; and August 1978.

18 Douglas (1964), Richards (1950), Turner (1967), van Binsbergen (1981b); the latter study, however, does reflect on the problem of the unit of study, cf. (1981b): 13f., 66f., 136f., 216f.

19 See van Binsbergen (1979): 31f. for a discussion of this problem with regard to the definition of kin-groups among the 'Nkoya'; the significance of situational aspects in the description and analysis of religious phenomena is stressed in van Binsbergen (1981b): 37f., 84, and in the Introduction of van Binsbergen & Schoffeleers (in press).

20 Notably, an exploration of regional patterns of religious change throughout southern Central Africa; see van Binsbergen (1981b).

21 See Helm (1968); Gutkind (1970); Godelier (1973). While the concept of 'tribe' is under heavy attack in modern anthropology, we should not ignore the fact that outside this discipline, and particularly in political science, there is a considerable amount of literature that still attaches primary, or at least independent, significance to ethnic factors (such authors as Bienen, Rotchild, LeVine).

22 Luyana (see Givon 1971) is the old court language among the Lozi. It has managed to preserve itself despite the rapid and universal adoption of the southern Bantu Kololo language in the first half of the nineteenth century. Luyana and Kololo (= Lozi) are not mutually intelligible, but Luyana and Nkoya (or Mashasha) are.

23 See van Binsbergen (1981b): 21, where this point is argued at greater length.

24 It was reported, as such, by G. H. Nicholls, 'Notes on the natives inhabiting the Baluba sub-district', 1906, enclosure in KTJ 2/1, Zambia National Archives, Lusaka; Stirke (1922): 63; Smith & Dale (1920): vol. 1, p. 94; Clay (1946): 4; Shimunika (in press). For a daring, but historically untenable approach to male puberty ceremonies in this part of Zambia, see de Heusch (1978).

25 Cf. Colson (1964, 1968). In her 1964 chapter she critically assesses the tribal model as applied to pre-colonial Africa. However, the greater sophistication vis-à-vis tribes in Colson's later work does not seem to affect the validity of my observations concerning the implicit, loosely

descriptive use of the tribal model in much of the Rhodes-Livingstone Institute work, including her own. Further see Lancaster (1974), Roberts (1976): 63f.

26 See Tabler (1963a); Nicholls (see note 24); reports on the Gielgud-Anderson expedition to the Kafue Hook, BSI/93 and KTJ 1/1, Zambia National Archives, Lusaka; Shimunika (in press), Bailey (1913, 1914), Smith & Dale (1920), Holy (1975).

27 Shimunika (in press); interview, Naliele Royal Establishment, Kaoma district, 28 October 1977.

28 Livingstone (1858). In addition to the sources mentioned in note 26, and the official tribal and linguistic maps published over the years by the Surveyor General, sources on this point include: Merle *et al.* (1933): 'tribal map'; Fortune (1959, 1963); and Mankoya District Notebook, KSX 4, Zambia National Archives, Lusaka.

29 Adopting Lancaster's (1974) approach.

30 The Lozi prefix *Ma-* instead of the Nkoya form *Ba-* points to the fact that the administrators' perception of the Nkoya as an ethnic group reflected Lozi views, rather than the local people's self-perception. The word *boma* means district centre in tropical English.

31 The probably more substantial pressure from the side of Chinyama chiefs coming in from the north is not reflected in collective Nkoya memory as documented in my data — probably as a result of two factors: extensive assimilation of Chinyama and Mbwela/Nkoya elements over the past centuries, and the considerable geographical distance between the main sites where I conducted oral historical research and the area where the Chinyama impact was primarily felt. See, however, Derricourt & Papstein (1977), Papstein (1978).

32 A very similar case are the Luvale as studied by Papstein (1978, 1980). My discussions with Robert Papstein since 1974 have greatly contributed to my understanding of Nkoya history and its crucial role in Nkoya ethnicity.

33 For the history of western Zambia, see Mainga (1972). Dr Mainga's work is particularly resented by modern and traditional Nkoya leaders today because of the way she handled the oral materials presented to her at the Nkoya chiefly capitals; however, this is not the place to assess whether such resentment is justified. Further see Caplan (1970); Stokes (1966); Mulford (1967): ch. vi; Prins (1980); Ranger (1968). For approaches from a Marxist point of view, see Clarence-Smith (1979); Frankenberg (1978). On the Nkoya specifically: Clay (1946); Shimunika (in press), anonymous (n.d.); van Binsbergen (1981b): chs 4, 5, 7.

34 ANC = African National Congress, the political party from which UNIP (= United National Independence Party) branched off in 1959; in 1972 ANC was incorporated in UNIP as part of the creation of 'one-party participatory democracy' in Zambia.

35 *Testamenta ya Yipya/Nyimbo*, (1952).

36 The term 'branch of production', for a complex of productive activities that can be meaningfully distinguished within a mode of production, derives from Terray (1969). Beach applied this term successfully to the

pre-colonial Shona economy (1977), although his argument is essentially non-Marxist. A related concept is that of 'form of production', defined by Le Brun & Gerry (1975: 20) as existing for instance, 'at the margins of the capitalist mode of production, but . . . nevertheless integrated into and subordinate to it'. For a preliminary desription of branches of production in the social formation at Kaoma district, see van Binsbergen (1978): however, that analysis is theoretically still very defective. A much revised version is forthcoming in *Africa*.

37 Oral evidence on this institution and its historical development is scanty, but we may surmise that what was involved was actually a local version of the institution of pawnship, postulated by Douglas (1964) to form a general feature of clan structures in the Central African matrilineal belt.

38 In addition to oral traditions I myself collected, there are four collections systematized by their collectors/authors: Clay (1946); Ikacana (1971); Shimunika (in press); anonymous (n.d.). Extensive treatment of this material and relevant archival data is in my forthcoming monograph on the Nkoya.

39 Mainga (1973); Papstein (1978); van Horn (1977); Clarence-Smith (1979).

40 Stokes (1966); Caplan (1970); van Horn (1977): 155f.

41 Materials for such an interpretation could be gleaned from: Mainga (1972); Prins (1980); Roberts (1976): 115f.; Flint (1970).

42 This is an important point. Allegiance to a particular chief tends to form a focus for a Zambian's perception of his or her rural home and ethnic affiliation. This is reflected, and reinforced, in Zambia's administrative procedures. Since independence in 1964, ethnic affiliation has never been asked by census enumerators — in '*One Zambia One Nation*' (one of UNIP's main slogans) ethnic affiliation officially does not exist; but a person's chief appears on a citizen's National Registration Card.

43 This interpretation of ethnicity as an ideological response to the articulation of modes of production comes close to my analysis of religious, as distinct from ethnic, mobilization in the case of the Lumpa church in northern Zambia; see van Binsbergen (1981b): 48–65, 266–316.

44 If one were to define the concept of social formation as the particular interrelationship between various articulated modes of production at a given time and place (Terray), rather than as a specific interrelationship between infrastructure and superstructure at a given time and place (Godelier), such a concept of social formation might in fact begin to provide the sort of unit of study under which to subsume the present analysis of ethnicity in terms of, among others, a response to the articulation of modes of production. However, such a social formation would have to be considered, Wallerstein-fashion, in the context of the total world system, since the dialectics of Nkoya ethnicity refer at the same time to the provincial, the national and the intercontinental level; the analytical gains of adopting such an expanding, and theoretically contentious, unit of study would then be very limited.

References

Anonymous [J. M. Shimunika] (n.d.), *Muhumpu was Byambo bya Mwaka-Nkoya*, n.p.

Asad, T. (ed.) (1973), *Anthropology and the Colonial Encounter*, London: Ithaca Press.

Bailey, A. W. (1913), 'A year on the Lalafuta river', *SAGM* [South Africa General Mission] *-Pioneer*, 36: 185–6.

Bailey, A. W. (1914), 'Northern Rhodesia: A letter from Mr Bailey', *SAGM* [South Africa General Mission] *-Pioneer*, 37: 151–2.

Bates, R. (1973), *Ethnicity in Contemporary Africa*, New York: Syracuse University, East African Studies, no. xiv.

Bates, R. (1976), *Rural Responses to Industrialization*, Yale University Press.

Beach, D. (1977), 'The Shona economy: branches of production', in Palmer and Parsons (1977): 37–65.

van Binsbergen, W. M. J. (1975), 'Ethnicity as a dependent variable: The "Nkoya" ethnic identity and inter-ethnic relations in Zambia', paper read at 34th Annual Meeting, Society for Applied Anthropology, Amsterdam.

van Binsbergen, W. M. J. (1977), 'Occam, Francis Bacon, and the transformation of Zambian society', *Cultures et développement*, 9: 489–520.

van Binsbergen, W. M. J. (1978), 'Class formation and the penetration of capitalism in a Zambian rural district', paper read at a seminar on Social Stratification and Class Formation in Africa, Leiden: African Studies Centre.

van Binsbergen, W. M. J. (1979), 'The infancy of Edward Shelonga: An extended case from the Zambian Nkoya', in van der Geest & van der Veen (1979): 19–86.

van Binsbergen, W. M. J. (1981a), 'Dutch anthropology of sub-Saharan Africa in the 1970s', in Kloos & Claessen (1981): 41–81.

van Binsbergen, W. M. J. (1981b), *Religious Change in Zambia*, London: Kegan Paul International.

van Binsbergen, W. M. J. (in press), 'The interpretation of myth in the context of popular Islam: Oral history in the highlands of north-western Tunisia', in van Binsbergen & Schoffeleers (in press).

van Binsbergen, W. M. J. & Schoffeleers, J. M. (eds) (in press), *Theoretical Explorations in African Religion*, London: Kegan Paul International.

Bond, G. C. (1976), *The Politics of Change in a Zambian Community*, University of Chicago Press.

Le Brun, O and Gerry, C.(1975), 'Petty commodity producers and capitalism', *Review of African Political Economy*, 3: 20–32.

Caplan, G. L. (1970), *The Elites of Barotseland, 1878–1969*, London: Hurst.

Clammer, J. (ed.) (1978), *The New Economic Anthropology*, London Macmillan.

Clarence-Smith, G. (1979), 'Slaves, commoners and landlords in *Bulozi*, c. 1875 to 1906', *Journal of African History*, 20: 219–34.

Clay, G. C. (1946), *History of the Mankoya District*, Rhodes-Livingstone Institute Communications no. 4, Lusaka: Rhodes-Livingstone Institute.

Cohen, A. (1969), *Custom and Politics in Urban Africa*, London: Routledge & Kegan Paul.

Cohen, A. (ed.) (1974), *Urban Ethnicity*, London: Tavistock.

Colson, E. (1958), *Marriage and the Family among the Plateau Tonga*, Manchester University Press.

Colson, E. (1960), *Social Organization of the Gwembe Tonga*, Manchester University Press.

Colson, E. (1964), 'African society at the time of the scramble', in Gann & Duignan (1964): 27–65.

Colson, E. (1968), 'Contemporary tribes and the development of nationalism', in Helm (1968): 201–6.

Colson, E. (1970), *The Plateau Tonga*, Manchester University Press; repr. of 1962 ed.

Colson, E. (1971), *Social Consequences of Resettlement*, Manchester University Press.

Colson, E. & Gluckman, M. (eds) (1959), *Seven Tribes of British Central Africa*, Manchester University Press.

Copans, J. (1974), *Critiques et politiques de l'anthropologie*, Paris: Maspero.

Copans, J. (ed.) (1975), *Anthropologie et impérialisme*, Paris: Maspero.

Cunnison, I. (1959), *The Luapula Peoples*, Manchester University Press.

Derricourt, R. M. & Papstein, R. J. (1977), 'Lukolwe and the Mbwela of North-Western Zambia', *Azania*, 11: 169–75.

Doornbos, M. R. (1972), 'Some conceptual problems concerning ethnicity in integration analysis', *Civilisations*, 22: 263–84.

Douglas, M. (1964), 'Matriliny and pawnship in Central Africa', *Africa*, 34: 301–13.

Epstein, A. L. (1958), *Politics in an Urban African Community*, Manchester University Press.

Epstein, A. L. (ed.) (1967), *The Craft of Social Anthropology*, Manchester University Press.

Epstein, A. L. (1978), *Ethos and Identity*, London/Chicago: Tavistock/Aldine.

Flint, E. (1970), 'Trade and politics in Barotseland during the Kololo period', *Journal of African History*, 11, 1: 71–86.

Fortune, G. (1959), *A Preliminary Survey of the Bantu Languages of the Federation*, Rhodes-Livingstone Institute Communications, no. 14, Lusaka: Rhodes-Livingstone Institute.

Fortune, G. (1963), 'A note on the languages of Barotseland', in *The History of Central African Peoples*, Rhodes-Livingstone Conference Proceedings, Lusaka: Rhodes-Livingstone Institute.

Frankenberg, R. (1978), 'Anthropology or political economy: The Barotse social formation', in Clammer (1978): 31–60.

Gann, L. H. & Duignan, P. (eds) (1964), *Colonialism in Africa*, vol. I: *The History and Politics of Colonialism, 1870–1914*, Cambridge University Press.

van der Geest, J. D. M. & van der Veen, K. W. (eds) (1979), *In Search of*

Health: Essays in Medical Anthropology, Amsterdam: Anthropological Sociological Centre, University of Amsterdam.

Gellner, E. & Micaud, C. (eds) (1972), *Arabs and Berbers*, London: Duckworth.

Givon, T. (1971), *The Si-Luyana Language*, Lusaka: Institute for African Studies, Communication no. 6.

Gluckman, M. (1945), 'Seven-year research plan of the Rhodes-Livingstone Institute of Social Studies in British Central Africa', *Rhodes-Livingstone Journal (Human Problems in British Central Africa)*, 4: 1–32.

Gluckman, M. (1957), *The Judicial Process among the Barotse*, Manchester University Press.

Gluckman, M. (1960), 'Tribalism in modern British Central Africa', *Cahiers d'études africaines*, 1, 1: 55–70.

Gluckman, M. (ed.) (1964), *Closed Systems and Open Minds: The Limits of Naïvity in Social Anthropology*, Edinburgh/London: Oliver & Boyd.

Gluckman, M. (1965), *The Ideas in Barotse Jurisprudence*, Manchester University Press.

Gluckman, M. (1968a), *Economy of the Central Barotse Plain*, Rhodes-Livingstone Institute Papers no. 7, Manchester University Press, repr. of 1941 ed.

Gluckman, M. (1968b), *Essays on Lozi Land and Royal Property*, Rhodes-Livingstone Papers no. 10, Manchester University Press, repr. of 1953 ed.

Godelier, M. (1973), *Horizon, trajets marxistes en anthropologie*, Paris: Maspero.

de Groot, A. D. (1966), *Methodologie*, The Hague/Paris: Mouton.

Gutkind, P. C. W. (ed.) (1970), *The Passing of Tribal Man in Africa*, Leiden: Brill.

Harries-Jones, P. (1969), ' "Home-boy" ties and political organization in a Copperbelt township', in Mitchell (1969): 297–347.

Helm, J. (ed.) (1968), *Essays on the Problem of Tribe: Proceedings of the 1967 Spring Meeting of the American Ethnological Society*, Seattle/London: University of Washington Press.

de Heusch, L. (1978), 'Les camps de circoncision en Afrique noire', paper presented at Conference on Iron-working Bantu-speaking peoples of Southern Africa before 1800, Leiden.

Holy, L. (ed.) (1975), *Emil Holub's Travels North of the Zambezi, 1885–6*, trans. C. Johns, Manchester University Press.

van Horn, L. (1977), 'The agricultural history of Barotseland 1840–1964', in Palmer & Parsons (1977): 144–69.

Houtart, F. (1980), *Religion et modes de production précapitalistes*, Brussels: Editions de l'Université de Bruxelles.

Houtart, F. & Lemercinier, G. (eds) (1977), *Religion and Tributary Modes of Production, Social Compass*, 24, 2–3, Louvain: Centre de Recherches Socio-Religieuses.

Ikacana, N. S. (1971), *Litaba za Makwanga*, Lusaka: Neczam (repr. of 1952 ed.).

Johnson, A. & Bond, G. C. (1974), 'Friendship and exchange in two communities', *Journal of Anthropological Research*, 30: 55–68.

Jules-Rosette, B. (1975), *African Apostles*, Cornell University Press.

Kahn, J. (1981), 'Explaining ethnicity: A review article', *Critique of Anthropology*, 4, 16: 43–52.

Kahn, J. S. & Llobera, J. R. (1980), 'French Marxist anthropology', *Journal of Peasant Studies*, 8, 1: 81–100.

Kloos, P. & Claessen, H. J. M. (eds) (1981), *Current Issues in Anthropology: The Netherlands*, Rotterdam: Netherlands Sociological and Anthropological Association.

Kuper, A. (ed.) (1977a), *Leiden in Africa*, Leiden: Institute for Cultural Anthropology, University of Leiden.

Kuper, A. (1977b), 'Structure and variation in seven Tswana kinship terminologies', in Kuper (1977a): 29–54.

Kuper, A. (1980), 'Symbolic dimensions of the southern Bantu homestead', *Africa*, 50: 8–23.

Lancaster, C. S. (1966), 'Reciprocity, redistribution and the male life cycle', *African Social Research*, 2: 139–57.

Lancaster, C, S, (1971), 'The economics of social organization in an ethnic border zone', *Ethnology*, 10, 4: 445–65.

Lancaster, C. S. (1974), 'Ethnic identity, history, and "tribe" in the Middle Zambezi Valley', *American Ethnologist*, 1: 707–30.

Lancaster, C. S. (1977), 'The Zambezi Goba ancestral cult', *Africa*, 47: 229–41.

Lancaster, C. S. (1981), *The Goba of the Zambezi*, Norman: University of Oklahoma press.

Leclerc, G. (1972), *Anthropologie et colonialisme*, Paris: Fayard.

Leys, C. (1975), *Underdevelopment in Kenya*, London: Heinemann.

Livingstone, D. (1858), *Missionary Travels and Researches in South Africa*, New York: Harper; 1971 repr., Johnson Reprint Corporation.

Long, N. (1968), *Social Change and the Individual*, Manchester University Press.

Mafeje, A. (1971), The ideology of tribalism', *Journal of Modern African Studies*, 9: 253–61.

Mainga, M. (1973), *Bulozi under the Luyana Kings*, London: Longman.

Mamdani, M. (1976), *Politics and Class Formation in Uganda*, New York: Monthly Review Press.

Marks, S. (1976), *Large Mammals and a brave People*, University of Washington Press.

Martin, M.-L. (1975), *Kimbangu: an African Prophet and his Church*, Grand Rapids, Mich.: Eerdmans.

Marwick, M. G. (1965), *Sorcery in its Social Setting: A Study of the Northern Rhodesian Ceŵa*, Manchester University Press.

Meillassoux, C. (1964), *L'Anthropologie économique des Gouro*, Paris: Mouton.

Meillassoux, C. (1975), *Femmes, greniers et capitaux*, Paris: Maspero.

Merle, J. *et al.* (1933), *Modern Industry and the African*, London: Macmillan.

Mitchell, J. C. (1956), *The Kalela Dance*, Manchester University Press.

Mitchell, J. C. (1965), 'Differential fertility amongst urban Africans in Zambia', *Rhodes-Livingstone Journal (Human Problems in Central Africa)*, 37: 1–25.

Mitchell, J. C. (ed.) (1969), *Social Networks in Urban Situations*, Manchester University Press.

Mitchell, J. C. (1970), 'Tribe and social change in South Central Africa', in Gutkind (1970): 83–101.

Mitchell, J. C. (1974), 'Perception of ethnicity and ethnic behaviour', in Cohen (1974): 1–35.

Molteno, R. (1974), 'Cleavage and conflict in Zambian politics', in Tordoff (1974): 62–106.

Mulford, D. C. (1967), *Zambia: The Politics of Independence, 1957–1964*, Oxford University Press.

Palmer, R. & Parsons, Q. N. (eds) (1977), *The Roots of Rural Poverty*, London: Heinemann.

Papstein, R. J. (1978), 'The Upper Zambezi: A history of the Luvale people, 1000–1900', PhD thesis, University of California, Los Angeles.

Papstein, R. J. (1980), 'The transformation of oral history under the colonial state', in Papers Presented to the International Oral History Conference, 24–26 October 1980, Amsterdam: University of Amsterdam, 1980, vol. ii, pp. 548–69.

Poewe, K. O. (1978), 'Matriliny in the throes of change', *Africa*, 48: 205–19 and 353–67.

Poewe, K. O. (1979), 'Regional and village economic activities', *African Studies Review*, 22: 77–93.

Poewe, K. O. (1981), *Matrilineal Ideology: Male–Female Dynamics in Luapula, Zambia*, London: Academic Press.

Prins, G. (1979), 'The end of the beginning of African history', *Social History*, 4, 3: 495–508.

Prins, G. (1980), *The Hidden Hippopotamus*, Cambridge University Press.

Radcliffe-Brown, A. R. & Forde, D. (eds) (1950), *African Systems of Kinship and Marriage*, London: International African Institute.

Ranger, T. O. (1968), 'Nationality and nationalism: The case of Barotseland', *Journal of the Historical Society of Nigeria*, 4, 2: 227–46.

Ranger, T. O. (1982), 'Race and tribe in Southern Africa: European ideas and African acceptance', in Ross (1982): 121–42.

Rey, P.-P. (1971), *Colonialisme, néo-colonialisme et transition au capitalisme*, Paris: Maspero.

Rey, P.-P. (ed.) (1973), *Les Alliances de classes*, Paris: Maspero.

Reynolds, B. (1963), *Magic, Divination and Witchcraft among the Barotse of Northern Rhodesia*, London: Chatto & Windus.

Richards, A. I. (1939), *Land, Labour and Diet*, Oxford University Press.

Richards, A. I. (1950), 'Some types of family structure among the Central Bantu', in Radcliffe-Brown & Forde (1950): 207–51.

Roberts, A. D. (1976), *A History of Zambia*, London: Heinemann.

Ross, R. (ed.) (1982), *Race and Colonialism*, The Hague: Martinus Nijhoff

Saul, J. S. (1979), *The State and Revolution in Eastern Africa*, New York: Monthly Review Press.

Scudder, T. (1962), *The Ecology of the Gwembe Tonga*, Manchester University Press.

Sharp, J. S. (1981), 'The roots and development of *volkekunde* in South

Africa', *Journal of Southern African Studies*, 8, 1: 16–36.
Shimunika, J. M. (in press), *Likota lya Bankoya/The History of the Nkoya*, trans. M. M. Malapa, ed. W. M. J. van Binsbergen, Leiden: African Studies Centre.
Smith, E. W. & Dale, A. M. (1920), *The Ila-Speaking Peoples of Northern Rhodesia*, London: Macmillan.
Stirke, D. W. (1922), *Barotseland: Eight Years among the Barotse*, London: J. Bale Sons & Danielsson; 1969 repr., Negro Universities Press.
Stokes, E. (1966), 'Barotseland: The survival of an African state', in Stokes & Brown (1966): 261–301.
Stokes, E. & Brown, R. (eds) (1966), *The Zambesian Past*, Manchester University Press.
Tabler, E. C. (ed) (1963a), 'The diaries of G. Westbeech 1885–1888', in Tabler (1963b): 23–101.
Tabler, E. C. (1963b), *Trade and Travel in Early Barotseland*, London: Chatto & Windus.
Terray, E. (1969), *L'Organisation sociale des Dida de Côte-d'Ivoire*, Annales de l'Université d'Abidjan, série F. tome i, fascicule 2; doctoral dissertation, Paris, 1966.
Testamenta ya Yipya/Nyimbo (1952), London: British and Foreign Bible Society (Nkoya new Testament and Psalms).
Tordoff, W. (ed.) (1974), *Politics in Zambia*, Manchester University Press.
Turner, V. W. (1967), *The Forest of Symbols*, Cornell University Press.
Turner, V. W. (1968a), *Schism and Continuity in an African Society: A Study of Ndembu Village Life*, University of Manchester; repr. of 1957 ed.
Turner, V. W. (1968b), *The Drums of Affliction: a Study of Religious Processes among the Ndembu of Zambia*, Oxford University Press.
van Velsen, J. (1964), *The Politics of Kinship*, Manchester University Press.
van Velsen, J. (1967), 'The extended case method and situational analysis', in Epstein (1967): 129–49.
Watson, W. (1958), *Tribal Cohesion in a Money Economy: A Study of the Mambwe People*, Manchester University Press.

Chapter 7

Marxist theory and anthropological practice: the application of French Marxist anthropology in field-work

Wim van Binsbergen and Peter Geschiere

Introduction[1]

Is there a case for a Marxist approach in anthropological field-work?

The present collection of papers explores the relevance of the theories of French Marxist anthropologists for empirical anthropological analysis. Our work-group's interest in these theories sprang mainly from the fact that here, we hoped, new perspectives were to be found for the analysis of our own field-work data. The preceding chapters may have indicated in what ways these Marxist theories can be used for interpreting specific sets of anthropological data. However, our project equally raises questions as to the relevance of these theories for the actual practice of anthropological field-work — for data collection itself. As has been emphasized in chapter 1 by Geschiere and Raatgever, our own field-work, in its design and execution, was still little influenced by Marxist theories. Moreover, in general it is as yet far from clear to what extent these theories have specific implications for the practice of anthropological field-work. Therefore in the present chapter we shall embark on a discussion of these practical implications, leaving the more theoretical evaluation of the French school to Reini Raatgever (ch. 8 below).

The main issue in this chapter is in what way these theories are to be used in the earlier phases of the anthropological empirical cycle: to what extent do they suggest new starting-points and new leading questions for the anthropologist in the field? Of course this question is related to the wider problem of whether a Marxist anthropology can remain within the framework of the anthropological discipline or demands a completely new approach — a topic of lively discussion within our work-group. Clearly, in the practice of field-work a Marxist anthropologist cannot but apply the time-honoured techniques of anthropological research, developed under the inspiration of other theories. In this sense a Marxist-inspired practice of field-work will always be coloured by a certain eclecticism.[2] But it is equally clear that a Marxist field-worker will have to renew and complement the usual anthropological research-techniques by focusing on specific issues. In this sense there is a case for a Marxist approach to anthropological field-work. Moreover, it is our contention that more attention to this pratice of field-work is essential for stimulating further theoretical discussion in Marxist anthropology.

The French Marxist anthropologists themselves have written surprisingly little on their practice of field-work.[3] Clearly, in the course of their own field-work, they followed standard anthropological methods and interests: drawing up genealogies, studying kinship relations and territorial divisions, analysing the circulation of prestige goods. But apparently they also followed original conceptions while they were in the field. Meillassoux, for instance, during his research among the Guro, must have paid special attention to the interplay of the relations of production and the relations of (biological) reproduction (1964). And to Rey the contradictions within the 'lineage' societies and their modern transformations under capitalist dominance must have been topics of special interest right from the start of his research in Congo-Brazzaville (1971); the influence of Marxist viewpoints on his field-work may also be apparent from Rey's consistent refusal — as early as 1967 — to accept the 'tribe' as a meaningful unit of study (see chapter 6). However, so far a general evaluation of the specific possibilities and problems for a Marxist-inspired practice of anthropological field-work has been lacking.[4]

This relative neglect of the practice of field-work may be related to the French anthropological tradition in which the Malinowskian ideal of a complete and prolonged submersion in the culture to be studied was never really popular. To many French anthropologists field-work still seems to be a matter of shorter expeditions 'sur le terrain', after which the data collected may be analysed in more 'civilized' surroundings. None the less, for Marxist anthropology in particular, reflection on the implications of the theory for the practice of field-work seems to be vital. The recent popularity of the theory may lead to problems in several respects. The models and concepts run the risk of being generalized and simplified into clichés, cut and dried formulas that are deceptively easy to apply to data — however collected, by whatever methods, and under the initial inspiration of whatever theoretical perspectives. Indeed, if Marxist models are simplified and dogmatized to a point where they begin to lose their meaning (and this is often the case in the bowdlerized versions of French Marxism now circulating in Anglo-Saxon literature — see Geschiere and Raatgever, chapter 1 above — one might be tempted to limit field-research to short surveys — already yielding enough data to allow for the classification of a particular group or field situation into the neat boxes of a textbook caricature posing as Marxism. Moreover, the flow of reactions and polemics can easily stagnate in formalistic discussions, which remain restricted to the theoretical level (see chapters 1 and 8). Meillassoux, who has considerable field-work experience, has lately shown some disappointment over the one-sided theoretical tenor of the reactions to his theoretical explorations.[5] Indeed, further theoretical progress in Marxist anthropology seems to depend particularly on new stimuli from such empirical research as is explicitly linked to the theory. But this requires a sharper insight into the specific consequences of Marxist theory for anthropological field-work. It was especially this issue, of the relation between field-work and theory, which our work-group discussed with Meillassoux and Terray when they visited the Netherlands. In this chapter our questions and suggestions, but also their reactions during these discussions, will be reflected.

The structure of our argument

After the preceding chapters of this book it may be clear that the theories of the French School have implications for anthropological field-work at least on one crucial point — namely, as to how anthropologists are to relate their research on a local level to developments of a much wider geographical and historical scope. Thus, the central theme in the work of Rey and Meillassoux in particular can be briefly summarized as the subjugation and the continuing attrition of 'domestic' communities by capitalism; and this does suggest valuable propositions for anthropological research: how is surplus labour extracted from the old production communities? what is the varying role of 'footholds' for capitalist penetration in the old relations of production, notably in the pre-existing forms of surplus labour? how are old and new contradictions intertwined? and so on.

In this chapter we shall focus on a more general problem: how should the emphasis, in Marxist theory, on the level of production be reflected in the practice of field-work? Connected with this is the question of how the inter-relatedness of production and other societal spheres, such as politics and ideology, should be dealt with while doing field-work. Our first topic, the role of the level of production, will be discussed in relation to the application, in field-work, of the concept of mode of production; we shall concentrate on some practical problems attending the use of the model of a 'lineage mode of production' as first formulated by Rey and Terray. Our next issues concern the inter-relatedness of the sphere of production — or 'the economic' — with other aspects of social organization. Of course, on this topic there is no lack of theoretical fireworks in the literature. But rather than allowing ourselves to be blinded by those, our concern here will be with some practical questions related to the reality of the anthropological field-work situation. One such problem concerns the relation between the economic and politics. Our discussion on this point is prompted by the fact that, in the research of some Marxist anthropologists, surprising functionalist-teleological tendencies have appeared, betraying a somewhat naïve view of the analytical relation between on the one hand the level of the structural logic of modes of production, and the political level of decision-making, strategies and social actors on the other. In relation to this point we can return to another problem in the application of the mode of production concepts: namely the ethnographic identification of boundaries between a number of modes of production as articulated within one contemporary social formation where our field-work is located. Of course this problem is directly connected to the central issue in the preceding chapters of this book — the application of the concept of articulation of modes of production. Our discussion of this 'boundary problem' in studying articulated modes of production during field-work will focus on one particular political setting — that of a contemporary chief's court in Zambia.

Another vital issue, particularly apparent in anthropological analysis, is the relation between the economic and ideology. Whereas the economic instance may be dominant under capital-

238

ism, the French School (and Godelier in particular) have argued that in the societies where anthropologists habitually work, instances from what under capitalism would have been the superstructure tend to be dominant. Indeed a vital challenge to a Marxist anthropology seems to be the question of how to study the particular relations between production and ideology in these societies. Rather than embarking on a theoretical critique of this premise, we intend to assess again its implication for the practice of anthropological research by concentrating on the ethnographic context of religious plurality in a contemporary African social formation.

A Marxist discussion of the anthropological practice of field research would hardly be complete without reference to the current political contexts in which anthropologists have to carry out their work. The case for a committed, leftist research practice has already been stated with such vigour as to allow us, in the present paper, to concentrate on more narrowly methodological issues which have received far less attention (see note 40 below).

The level of production as a problem in anthropological field-work

Data on production

Of course, one of the most obvious implications of the Marxist theories for anthropological research is that primary importance is attributed to the level of production. French Marxist anthropologists have always criticized current anthropological approaches for the fact that whenever they happened to pay attention to the economic, this meant (in accordance with the liberalist inspiration of bourgeois anthropology) stressing not production, but circulation: i.e. relations of exchange and the role of the market (see Dupré and Rey 1973; Godelier 1973: 23f.). By contrast, Marxist analyses should depart from the premise that in the last instance production, and relations of production in particular, are of determining consequence.

Yet it is not automatically clear what this premise amounts to in the practice of anthropological field-work. One might easily suppose that from such a perspective every anthropological research undertaking should begin with the collection of detailed, ideally quantitative, data on production. But in practice this will lead to all sorts of problems. The first difficulty is that anthropologists today almost always work in communities that have been touched by the capitalist system. Therefore, a reconstruction of the old modes of production has always to abstract from modern economic changes. This alone would drastically reduce the possibility of collecting valid and reliable quantitative data on relevant aspects of the old relations of production. Another difficulty is that too much emphasis on the collection of production data will almost inevitably lead to a certain one-sidedness in field-work. Especially in communities with a simple hunting or agricultural economy, research into the more practical aspects of production is extremely time-consuming. For instance, in slash-and-burn cultivation, enormous variations exist in the use of land and labour, in harvest yields, etc. In order to collect systematic data on the level of production — measuring labour investment, average yields, the amount of surplus labour appropriated from the direct producers, etc. — one often has to surmount so many practical difficulties that even a whole team of anthropologists in the field could barely cope. If in a Marxist practice of field-work each research was required to begin with a thorough analysis of production, we run the risk that hardly any time would remain for research into other aspects of society. And this would then run counter to the emphasis which French Marxist anthropologists have laid on the autonomous role — on the 'dominance' — of such super-structural aspects as kinship, politics or religion in the types of society habitually studied by anthropologists.

Significantly, the monographs of the French School limit themselves to fairly global analyses of the technical and quantitative aspects of the production process. Here one finds few attempts to analyse the reality of production by way of painstaking calculations — e.g. of the labour time expended, the relation between invested labour and product, the consumptive needs of the producers. Such calculations are more typical of American anthropologists of the 'ecological' or 'cultural-materialist' school.[6] However, precisely these anthropologists have often been accused by their French colleagues of 'vulgar materialism' because of their one-sided attention to the technical aspects of production.[7] Rey even stresses that the analysis of the immediate processes of production is by definition inadequate if one wishes to identify the characteristic relation of production within a mode of production.

240

In his view, each mode of production is characterized by a specific relation of exploitation, which forms the basis for a specific class contradiction. According to Rey, Marx demonstrated that, under capitalism, the reproduction of the relation of exploitation takes place primarily by means of the buying and selling of labour-power, i.e. *outside* the sphere of immediate production. The same holds true, Rey claims, for all other modes of production: the specific forms of exploitation, and their reproduction, cannot be reconstructed from the technical sides of the production process; rather, the reality of production can be analysed only on the basis of the class contradiction (Rey 1971: 40, 160; see also Rey 1979).

The concept of 'mode of production'

We shall come back to Rey's rather complex views in this matter. However, it will be clear at this stage that from the viewpoint of the French Marxist School extensive collections of data on production are in themselves of limited value. In anthropological field-work the determining role of production should be acknowledged in a less positivist way, notably by taking the concept of *mode of production* as one's point of departure. It is here in particular that French Marxist anthropology does offer practical pointers for field-work design. One of the merits of these anthropologists — especially Meillassoux, Terray and Rey — is that they have taken the concept of mode of production seriously. They do not content themselves with such cure-all concepts as 'peasant mode of production' (for a critique of this concept, see Ranger 1978); rather, they attempt to derive a number of specific modes of production from anthropological data, *each mode with its own logic and its own dynamics*, which are retained even after subordination to capitalist dominance. The practical significance of such attempts will be clear: if field-workers could just draw on an elaborate typology of modes of production, a brief survey of production would be sufficient to classify properly the social formation under study — to explain its specific peculiarities on the level of production by reference to a certain type of mode of production. Elsewhere in this book it is made abundantly clear that Marxist anthropology has not reached this advanced stage yet (see chapters 1 and 8): French Marxist anthropologists themselves are still in the midst of a debate on the operationalization of the concept of mode of production, and the implications of this debate for the design of anthropological field-work are still far from clear. In view of this state of affairs, the collection of more elaborate and quantitative data on production itself might be opportune. However, more than anything else, a further elaboration and operational definition of the concept of mode of production is a prerequisite for progressive cross-fertilization between theory and practice in Marxist anthropology.

The clearest formula for the operationalization of the concept of mode of production is to be found in Rey's and Terray's works. Both stress that the relation of exploitation should be the point of departure in the analysis of any mode of production (see Rey 1971, 1973; Terray 1975, 1979a). However, this formula turns out to raise difficulties also in application. This may become clear from a brief discussion of how anthropologists can utilize the model of the 'lineage mode of production', which occupies such a central place in Rey's and Terray's work. For both, the crucial relationship in that mode of production is the exploitation of the youth by their elders (taking these terms as social and not as biological categories). Often this exploitation finds expression in the elders' control over certain prestige goods, which may circulate in the form of bridewealth. The elders' authority over the young men is then confirmed by the former's monopoly on the prestige goods and their tight control of the exchange of women between groups.[8] Above, it became clear that this model has indeed considerable explanatory power in the analysis of African societies organized on a kinship basis, especially because it brings out the implications, for the elders' authority, of the circulation of bridewealth and prestige goods (see chapters 2, 3 and 4 above).

All the same, further elaboration is required if this model is to be really useful for field-work design: for how can one, within the confines of this model, do justice to all kinds of variations in the authority basis of the elders, and in the reproduction of the subordination of the youth? And how to capture the culture-specific, often extremely subtle, forms of interaction, transfer of goods and services, communication and sanctioning, that form the constituent elements in the authority and power relations between elders and the youth?

Variations in the 'lineage mode of production' in Black Africa

The preceding chapters of this book have indicated that even between the 'lineage' societies of Black Africa, variation can be very considerable.[9] Our own field-work experiences may illustrate the problems which can rise when applying the concept of the 'lineage mode of production'. When one of us made a study of the Maka, a highly segmented group in the tropical rain-forest of southeast Cameroon, the link between bridewealth and the elders' authority proved to be extremely relevant (Geschiere 1981, 1982, in press, b). The coherence of Maka kin-groups under the authority of one elder is still primarily expressed through that kin-group's co-operation in the matter of bridewealth; by the same token, imminent fissions within the group first begin to manifest themselves in the way of conflicts concerning the elders' role in the payment and distribution of bridewealth. And it still is the payment of bridewealth which gives an elder *ijuga* (paternal authority) over a youth; this even leads quite regularly to a social redefinition of the relations of genealogical descent. However, among the Maka, control over marital payments is not linked with a clear authority of the elders over food production — which today means primarily the cultivation of bananas, cassava and ground-nuts, while in the old days hunting was also important.

The Maka ethnography is all the more remarkable since Terray (1969) and Meillassoux (1975) attach some significance to the elders' 'functional authority' in agriculture. Among the Maka there is hardly any trace of this. At best, the Maka elders have a formal control over the distribution of plots between the individual producers, but they are not directly involved in the organization of production or in the regulation of labour relations. Neither is there any pooling of produce to be administered by the elders. Maka women, who do the lion's share of the agricultural work, in all sorts of ways act as independent producers, and each woman administers her own harvest. Yet the Maka may still be considered to fit in more or less with the model of the 'lineage mode of production': in Rey's terms, they would then be an example of a situation where the relation of exploitation between youth and elders is confirmed by the circulation of prestige goods, but has not yet penetrated the sphere of direct production.[10]

However, when we compare the Maka with other 'lineage' societies in Black Africa as described in this book, more important irregularities catch the eye. Both among the Nyakyusa of southern Tanzania (see chapter 2) and among the Diola of southern Senegal (see chapter 3), certain types of plots have permanent value, enabling elders to exercise direct control over production. Moreover, bridewealth is of only secondary importance among the Diola: there, the elders' control over prestige goods (notably cattle) is located rather in the organization of initiation rites, which, as some sort of functional equivalent of bridewealth, ensured the reproduction of the Diola youths' subordination. Even when we limit our analysis to the material aspects of the various prestige goods that feature in this context, it becomes manifest that there may be many more variations between the 'lineage' societies of Black Africa. Rey, Meillassoux and Terray write on societies where 'inanimate' prestige goods circulate (iron objects, jewellery, etc.). However, in numerous African societies cattle constitute the most important prestige good (for a Marxist approach, see Bonte 1977). This cannot remain without effect on intergenerational relations: by contrast with inanimate prestige goods, cattle play an important role in production and consumption. Their upkeep demands a continuous investment of labour. Moreover, cattle lend themselves to biological reproduction: they tend to multiply. On the other hand they are much more vulnerable to natural disasters than are most inanimate prestige goods. It is therefore very likely that under such circumstances different relations of production and different forms of exploitation will develop from those found in societies for which the model of the 'lineage mode of production' was formulated in the first place.[11]

Material conditions, however, are not the only factors resulting in significant variation between 'lineage' societies. The case of the Nkoya of Zambia, among whom one of us did research, brings out the significance of other means of production besides land as a source of control for the elders, but particularly highlights the importance of ideological means in this context. Our discussion of the Nkoya case, moreover, touches on their involvement in the urban capitalist sector — an aspect which, of course, is also implied in the other examples.

Among the Nkoya, the situation somewhat resembles that among the Maka, but the overall picture is different. Although there has in recent years been some slight but mounting pressure on a particular type of riverside gardens (*matapa*) that are extremely suitable for the main cash-crop (maize), land among the Nkoya is in fact still so plentiful that the elders' control, waning as it is, rests not on the allocation of land but on a combination of other factors.

Some of these lie in the sphere of production, notably hunting. The elders own the guns that procure the game-meat on which depend almost all locally-consumed animal protein and (since much of the meat is sold) a large proportion of the regional cash flow. The elders have acquired the guns through inheritance or on the basis of town-earned money; usually they let them be handled by young expert hunters, whose own share of the proceeds is limited.

Moreover, the elders exercise considerable (but by no means absolute) control over nubile women, and thus over the younger men's opportunities to have female labour-power at their disposal — as well as legitimate offspring which they can count upon for political and economic support in later years. The situation is somewhat complicated by the fact (not uncommon in southern Central Africa) that divorce is easy and frequent — in other words, control over women by elders and husbands is limited; and that a young man often ends up offering his residential and labour support to a (classificatory) mother's brother, rather than to a (classificatory) father — in other words, even if a man submits (by paying bridewealth) to the control some elder exercises over a nubile woman, he is by no means certain of subsequent control over his legitimate offspring. In this context of uncertainty, however, additional checks are found in the ideological sphere. The extensive ritual powers that are attributed to the elders enable them not only to control, to a considerable extent, the marital and residential choices of their younger followers (through curses, threats of sorcery, or alternatively by ritual protection and healing), but also to influence the flow of cash earned by the young men in the urban capitalist labour market: some of this cash is appropriated by the elders as a fee for their healing services. Likewise, through these powers (in particular their dominance of village shrines and the ancestral cult) the elders control young men's access to prestigious names and titles which are indispensable for establishing oneself as an elder, i.e. a village headman (van Binsbergen 1977b, 1981: chs 6, 7; n.d., a).

The 'lineage mode of production' in North Africa

The need for refinement and closer delimitation of the concept of a 'lineage mode of production' may be even more cogently demonstrated by an example from somewhat further afield.

Certain members of our work-group have also done field-work in the rural areas of northwestern Tunisia.[12] In the course of our work-group discussions, it was therefore a recurrent topic to assess to what extent the model as derived by Rey, Terray and Meillassoux from research in Black Africa would also be applicable to North Africa. On the surface, the North African peasant societies would appear to display many traits characteristic of Rey's and Terray's 'lineage mode of production', or Meillassoux's 'domestic community'. Also in North Africa many anthropologists would consider the 'lineage' to form the core of social organization; kinship has long formed the dominant organizational principle, and the family elders exercised a firm authority over the youth, manifested among other things in the elders' control over marital payments. Of course, on closer inspection all kinds of differences became apparent. For instance, on the level of production the peasant society of northwestern Tunisia is in many ways characteristic of the Mediterranean as a whole (see Davis 1977), but contrasts sharply with the types of slash-and-burn cultivation prevailing in Black Africa. In North Africa agriculture has traditionally used the plough. There has been a close connection between agriculture and animal husbandry; access to draught animals for ploughing was indispensable for the agricultural cycle. The main crop was wheat, and this could regularly be cultivated on the same piece of land, provided one observed short fallow periods. As a result, kin-organized communities had a close, more or less permanent, link with the land. Another result was fragmentation of land-holdings: the holdings of the various kin-groups were often interspersed. In many regions the increasing pressure on the land had turned the purchase or hire of land into common practice long before the colonial conquest.

It will be obvious that this form of production offered quite different footholds for the family elders' authority. By contrast with most slash-and-burn economies in Black Africa, in North Africa land had by definition a lasting value and it therefore constituted an essential part of the inheritance. Moreover the agricultural cycle required the use of complex means of production — plough, draught animals — which, contrary to the hoes and slashers of Black Africa, were by no means available to each producer. Therefore control over essential means of production did offer the North African elders a direct grip on the production process and on the young men's labour. On the other hand, because of the limited access to the means of production, in the rural areas of North Africa various additional forms of surplus labour and exploitation could develop. Landless peasants could as share-croppers (*khammas*) get access to land, while the institution of the dependent herdsman (often marrying into his employer's family) was also well developed. In the process of articulation of these old relations of production with capitalism it was precisely such forms of surplus labour which came to play an important role: since there was already a considerable amount of labour which had been 'freed' from the means of production, in the first phases of capitalist penetration the 'labour problem' did not assume such acute forms as in large parts of Black Africa (see chapter 4).

Of course, these specific traits on the level of production go hand in hand with all sorts of differences in other spheres of life. The emerging overall picture raises serious doubt as to whether North African 'lineage' societies do fit into the 'lineage mode of production'.[13] For instance, for these societies also one might very well speak of the 'dominance' of kinship as an organizational principle. But this shows, at the same time, how easy it is to abuse kinship as some sort of mystifying concept (see Meillassoux 1975: 37; Rey 1971: 207). In fact the North African systems of kinship and marriage display a number of traits which deviate widely from the 'lineage' societies of Rey, Terray and Meillassoux. Thus it is remarkable that in North African societies women circulate on a much smaller scale: there is a strong tendency towards endogamy, both within the kin-group (there even is the explicit ideal of patrilineal endogamy, although few marriages are in fact so contracted), and within the local village community, which in many respects could be regarded as a localized bilateral kindred (van Binsbergen 1970, 1971, n.d., b). This is linked to the fact that the circulation of goods at the time of marriage clearly differs from the system of bridewealth in large parts of Black Africa. In the Tunisian rural areas the bride adds (at least in principle) her own inheritance (notably land) to the conjugal estate; and an important portion of the money paid by the bridegroom has to be put at the disposal of the bride herself. Also on the ideological level — e.g. in the organization and functioning of regional cults — relations have developed which are peculiar to North Africa in comparison with 'lineage' societies elsewhere on the African continent.[14]

Discussion

The important question is not so much whether the Tunisian peasant communities fit into the model of a 'lineage mode of production'. The point is rather to demonstrate that this model will need to be further refined before it can be used as a starting-point in anthropological field-work. In view of the great variation between kin-organized societies, even within Black Africa, one might well ask if in fact a number of different modes of production are involved. If we are to follow Rey's and Terray's emphasis on the relation of exploitation as the determining and distinctive feature of a mode of production, the question would be how, and on the basis of which criteria, such a relation of exploitation is to be considered as being sufficiently different to allow us to speak of a different mode of production when comparing African 'lineage societies'.

Terray appears to be of the opinion that with the current state of anthropological and historical research we should lay great emphasis on the differences in exploitation and in the modes of production they entail. Only if we start from these differences may further research enable us to develop an elaborate typology of modes of production.[15] In the Introduction to this book (see chapter 1), reference has already been made to Godelier's criticism of this point (1979: 17): he takes it to imply that each field-worker may return from his or her research with a private freshly-discovered mode of production; this would be the surest way of depriving the concept of mode of production of all analytical power. On the other hand, the dangers of working with all too general models of modes of production will be equally clear: such models can easily function as 'blanket' concepts underneath which the multiple variations in exploitative and authority relations are obscured, and the contemporary dynamics of these relations under conditions of capital dominance smothered. Therefore, if we are to retain concepts such as, for instance, 'lineage mode of production', it would be necessary to try and demarcate, within such a type, important variations, each with its own underlying logic. It is especially on this point that further empirical and comparative research could stimulate the theoretical discussion.[16]

A useful point of departure for such comparative research would be Rey's emphasis — which has somehow gone unnoticed,

248

so far — upon 'the regrouping of the producers in relation to the production' (1971: 158); for Rey, this seems to constitute the main criterion to distinguish between modes of production. As sketched above, in Rey's view the 'determining relation of production' in each mode of production is the relation of exploitation and the class contradictions it entails. Rey adds (1971: 154):[17]

> the essential moment in the reproduction [of this determining relation — WvB & PG] is the process by which the members of the dominated class, i.e. the direct producers, are regrouped in order to produce. In the capitalist case this moment is the buying and selling of labour power. In the feudal case it is the contract of man to man, between the serf and his landlord [. . .] In the lineage mode of production, it is the double process of the circulation of men and women [. . .] to the profit of the dominating class [. . .] This process by which the producers are re-grouped can take place only outside immediate production.

In his monograph on the Mossendjo region, Rey (1971) uses this criterion in order to analyse the shift in dominance which attends the articulation between the 'lineage mode of production' and capitalism.[18] However, it stands to reason that this criterion of the 're-grouping of the producers' can also be utilized for an analysis of the differences between various pre-capitalist modes of production, or in order to identify the essential variations within the 'lineage mode of production'. At any rate, for comparative research, this criterion has the advantage that it focuses our research not just on the sphere of production but also on variations in the functioning of various political and ideological institutions.

It would be worthwhile to try to translate Rey's general insights into more concrete proposals for further research. As we said above, it is notably in their explorations involving the concept of mode of production that the French Marxist anthropologists offer the opportunity for meaningful cross-fertilization between the theory and the practice of field-work. But this would require further creative exploration of how the concept of mode of production can be operationalized towards concrete ethnographic and historiographic settings.[19]

Production and politics

The danger of functionalist teleology

Further refinement in the operationalization of the mode-of-production concept seems to be equally required, in the course of our field research, to deal with the thorny problem of the inter-relatedness between the level of production and other spheres of life. By using shortened, stereotyped formulas to indicate the structural coherence of a mode of production, or the internal logic of the articulation of various modes, anthropological enquiry may get bogged down in shallow, functionalist arguments. This danger is apparent, for instance, when we deal with the relation between production and politics. In anthropological field-work as much as in any other practice, we are facing the well-known Marxist dilemma of how to connect the determining role of production with the inherent dynamics of political processes and, by implication, with the autonomy of political actors. If in our explanation of a particular process we immediately invoke the logic of the mode of production or the logic of the articulation of various modes involved, there is just the risk that we overlook the political level of consciously acting actors and the groups to which they belong. Our research may then stagnate in the demonstration of the functional requirements of modes of production or of their articulation, without paying due attention to the power processes from which the extant relationships derive in a more direct sense — often resulting in a rather unstable and precarious outcome.

Meillassoux and the politics of kin-group composition among the Guro (Ivory Coast)

Numerous examples from the monographs produced by the French School could show that this danger is far from imaginary. Thus Meillassoux, in one of the most interesting and best documented chapters of his Guro monograph (1964: ch. 5), expounds how biological reproduction adapts to the requirements of the relations of production. Chance fluctuations in procreation are levelled out by the circulation of producers between the units of production. To put it more concretely: on the one hand, natural and inevitable differences in demographic reproduction exist between the small kinship units, each under the authority of one elder; but on the other hand these familial production units turn out, in practice, to be constituted in such a way as to result to a large extent in the same overall internal balance between '*actifs*' and '*inactifs*' (i.e. between productive and non-productive group members). Various mechanisms — among them fission and adoption — correct the demographic inequalities and result in viable production units.[20]

Meillassoux touches here on a theme that is of particular importance in anthropology: the relation between production and kinship. But the more important the topic, the more essential it is to stress that Meillassoux's analysis contains major gaps. Thus it remains fairly unclear how in actual social practice the Guro achieve such a well-balanced distribution of productive and non-productive persons within the various familial production units. Yet in itself the fact of such a balanced distribution is rather surprising. Every Africanist is familiar with the adage that, in Black Africa, wealth and power are primarily based on control over people. Therefore, one would expect that among the Guro, too, the various family heads would do everything in their power to expand their own group to the utmost. The ethnographic literature on Black Africa teems with examples of family elders involved in heated rivalry over a following of junior kinsmen.[21] Are the Guro an exception? Among this people there are obviously powerful levelling mechanisms at work which limit the extent of inequality in group composition. The problem is, however, that Meillassoux nowhere indicates how in this society the allocation of producers — i.e. young men — over the various production units is achieved in practice. He gives only one case of an adult man and his elder involved in a conflict that threatened to escalate into group fission. However, that case is treated so cursorily — in a footnote (Meillassoux 1964: 171) — that we scarcely get an impression of how the elders bind the young men to their own group, and of how the young men can try to disassociate themselves from this group. It is hardly sufficient to claim that the reproduction of viable production units is brought about because 'the link of consanguinity is transformed into social filiation' (1964: 168).[22] In order to gain a true understanding of this process, more attention ought to be paid to political relationships: the means the elders have at their disposal so as to exercise control; the young men's process of decision-making; and in general the participants' strategies which determine the actual composition of the production units in the most direct sense.[23]

Rey and determinism

As we have seen, the problem of the relation between determination as stemming from the level of production, and the autonomy of political actors, is as old as Marxism itself; it lies, e.g., at the root of Marx's treatment of class consciousness. Little wonder that this problem looms large in the work of Rey, who is most insistent on the crucial importance of the notion of class in the analysis of any mode of production. Right at the beginning of his monograph (1971), Rey quotes a saying of Engels: 'Men make their own history but within a given milieu which conditions them' (1971: 18; cf. Engels 1967: 4f.). In a polemic with Sartre, Rey comes back to this point and lays full stress on the second half of Engels's dictum:[24]

> Individual strategies, however autonomous they may seem, are nearly completely determined by the position of the individuals in the process of reproduction [viz. the reproduction of the mode of exploitation which, according to Rey, determines the 'given milieu' in Engels's dictum — WvB & PG]

> There is no political subject nor an economic subject. The classes 'who make history' are themselves determined by the process of reproduction (Rey 1971: 22).[25]

In itself it is difficult enough to bring such deterministic formulas into line with Rey's stance at the end of his monograph, where he invokes the class struggle as the factor which will ultimately determine the future of the societies he studied in the Mossendjo area, Congo-Brazzaville (see Rey 1971: 520). The relative neglect of the political level, of social actors and class actions, in Rey's study may give the reader the impression that, towards the end, class struggle is produced only as some sort of *deus ex machina*.[26] However this may be, our point here is of a more general nature. The views expressed in the above quotations from Rey can lead to considerable problems in anthropological field-work. One possible criticism of Rey's monograph would be that the book, while containing extremely interesting analyses of the structural mechanisms behind the articulation of the 'lineage mode of production'

252

with capitalism, does not offer the reader a convincing insight into how these mechanisms find expression and realization in the conscious actions of the people and groups involved. This is particularly manifest in Rey's handling of the notion of class alliance (1971: 121, 434, 518; see also Rey (1973) and (1976): 62–3).

In his analysis of capitalist expansion in the Mossendjo region, Rey is directly inspired by the well-known Marxian analysis of a class alliance between feudal landlords and capitalists which facilitated the birth of capitalism in Western Europe. In Rey's opinion, capitalist expansion in his research area came about as a result of a somewhat similar class alliance between capitalists, on the one hand, and elders, the dominant class in the 'lineage mode of production', on the other. In Europe the monetarization of land rent benefited not only the feudal landlords but also the capitalists, by solving their labour problem: large numbers of peasants were driven from the land and became available as 'free' wage-labourers. By the same token, in the Mossendjo area the monetarization of bridewealth, which formed the crucial relation of exploitation in the old 'lineage mode of production', benefited not only the elders but also the capitalists: when bridewealth was first expressed in money, and then underwent inflation, youths were driven to the labour market in order to earn more and more cash.

In itself Rey's interpretation is of considerable value. He succeeds in bringing to the fore a more or less hidden mechanism which in all likelihood played an important role in many parts of Africa (see Geschiere 1978). However, in the context of our present argument, it is relevant to stress that Rey's conclusions are primarily his own deductions as extrapolated from archival materials. Rey confines himself to a rather global analysis of the transformations of bridewealth in terms of monetarization and inflation (1971: 116f., 317). He does not seem to have felt the need to check the stages in this process with his informants in the field, or to trace in enough detail the ways in which colonial civil servants perceived this process (1971: 368, 416, 435). Generally speaking, the reader hears little about the parties involved, their views of the changes, their strategies. Thus one cannot help wondering whether the 'class alliance' between 'lineage' elders and capitalist interest groups (here the civil servants, in particular) did spring at all from the conscious strategies of either party.

Class alliance between elders and capitalists: The Maka case (S.E. Cameroon)

Observations on the basis of the field-work of one of us among the Maka of southeast Cameroon, already referred to, may indicate that an analysis in the manner of Rey does give rise to complex problems in the field. The Maka inhabit a region in the tropical rain-forest of Equatorial Africa not too far from Rey's research area. Capitalist penetration in the Maka area was attended by difficulties similar to those described by Rey. Also among the Maka, the task of involving the old village communities in the capitalist economy proved to be an arduous one (see chapter 4). Until as late as the 1930s the colonial economy remained based on the most stringent forms of state coercion: through the 'customary chiefs' (who, in this strongly segmented society, were in fact entirely new creations of the colonial state itself), the colonial civil servants organized regular labour raids in the villages. Moreover, the administration tried to force the villagers, in all possible ways, to produce surpluses for the market. At first the Maka responded by attempts to withdraw from administrative control and from the authority of the new 'customary chiefs'. The civil servants would complain that time and again the Maka disappeared into the forest, and that the newly-formed villages constantly split into smaller units which could barely be controlled. However, by 1935 a radical change occurred. Less and less direct state coercion became necessary, since obviously the villagers were increasingly keen to earn money: the Maka began to enter into wage-labour or to establish cash-cropping farms on their own initiative. It is clear that, also in this part of Africa, the villagers' increasing involvement in the money economy was connected with transformations in the pre-existing forms of 'exploitation'. Extensive data on the composition of marital payments, derived from informants and from archival materials demonstrate that, about 1930, money first entered the bridewealth circuit, and that the money component of bridewealth began to rise gradually, especially after 1935 (Geschiere in press, a, b).

Rey's analysis of the mechanisms that play a role in the articulation of the 'lineage mode of production' and capitalism, thus turns out to be extremely relevant to understand developments in the Maka area. However, in the Maka case it certainly seems far-fetched to speak of a class alliance, e.g. one between

Maka elders and the colonial civil servants. It is almost certain that the mechanisms as postulated by Rey were rarely reflected at the political level of conscious strategies and decision-making. Administrative reports indicate that, from the very beginning, the colonial authorities viewed the monetarization and the inflation of bridewealth as a big problem. They made every possible effort to contain a further rise of bridewealth: to them this meant that more and more money was withdrawn from circulation for what, in their eyes, appeared as unproductive goals. State intervention, intended to deflect a further increase of bridewealth, turned out to be in vain, and it still is. It is, however, very clear that the civil servants did not look at the transformation of bridewealth as a possible solution for the pressing demand for labour.[27]

On their part, the Maka elders were, to all appearances, equally unaware of their 'alliance' with the colonial state. Instead, one gets the impression that they felt constantly threatened by the measures the colonial masters took. Geschiere's informants emphasized, for instance, how the fixed preference, among colonial civil servants, for installing young 'dynamic' chiefs (who then would be proclaimed 'customary chiefs') meant a drastic erosion of the old authority relations. Among the Maka there is by no means the sort of fusion between old and new dominant classes after decolonization that Rey postulates for his own research area (Rey 1971: 518). The new Maka élite of politicians and civil servants was recruited mainly from among the children of parents who had sought refuge at mission stations — these children had little choice but go to school. And this new élite maintains an extremely ambivalent relationship with the family elders, who have managed to maintain some measure of authority only within the confines of the village society.

In such circumstances we can speak of a class alliance only in the most figurative or abstract sense: as some sort of unconscious convergence of interests. In retrospect it appears that the Maka elders and the colonial civil servants did benefit, each in their own way, from the transformation of bridewealth. But the government policy lacked any awareness of such a class alliance, or even of a less distinct convergence of interests between civil servants and elders, in connection with bridewealth. And quite clearly such an alliance did not feature in the Makas' perception of the situation.

The Zambian Nkoya as a contrasting case

This issue of how the intertwining of old and new relations of exploitation became expressed in class alliances and conscious strategies is certainly still of interest. Differences in this respect may explain variations in the course of the articulation of capitalism with old modes of production leading to differing political relationships at present. For, of course, there have been considerable differences in this respect, even within Black Africa. The Nkoya, already mentioned, may serve here again as a contrasting example to the case of the Maka. In their region, part of Barotseland in western Zambia, early colonial history clearly illustrated the importance of a *conscious* class alliance (formalized in treaties and colonial legislation) between a local aristocracy and the colonial powers (e.g. Stokes 1966; Prins 1980). The two main Nkoya Chiefs, Mwenemutondo and Mwenekahare, were among the very few chiefs who, despite some vicissitudes, by and large shared in the very extensive privileges, material and otherwise, which the Barotse (Lozi) Paramount Chief enjoyed on the basis of this class alliance. Specifically, these Nkoya Chiefs are known to have issued, in their areas of jurisdiction, legislation fixing and altering the level of bridewealth ever since Nkoya bridewealth came to be monetarized (in the first decade of this century). Alternatively, these chiefs maintained relatively friendly and trustful relations with the local colonial civil servants, sharing the latter's interest in keeping the 'cheeky young natives' in their place and, with this purpose in mind, occasionally visiting the latter's places of work in the urban capitalist sector (van Binsbergen n.d., a). The explicit, conscious class alliance postulated by Rey for the Mossendjo area, and looked for in vain by Geschiere among the Maka, appears to have been present among the Nkoya during the colonial period. As a result, the contemporary political relationships are clearly different from the Maka case: the Nkoya youths' emerging consciousness after Zambia became independent took the form of persistent and violent attacks on chiefly power — the latter, however, still proved to be protected by the party and local government officials representing the post-colonial state at the district level (van Binsbergen 1975; cf. Geschiere 1982).[28]

Such essential differences in political relations and in the participants' perceptions — factors which have directly shaped the course of the articulation of modes of production — run the risk of being ignored if we focus our research too one-sidedly upon the functional requirements of the articulation process. Therefore it remains an important question, for a Marxist practice of anthropological field-work, how to link our attention to the structural logic of modes of production and their articulation, on the one hand, with political analysis in terms of acting individuals and groups, strategies and power processes, on the other.

Analysis in terms of class?

To tackle questions like these, an obvious tool for a Marxist researcher seems to be the notion of class, since it poses the relevant questions about the crystallization of class contradictions and class consciousness. For an analysis of modern conditions in Africa the concept of class has proved its utility in so far as the *analysis* of research data is concerned (see Buijtenhuijs and Geschiere 1978). But as a point of departure for the collection of data the concept often still appears to be of only indirect utility.[29]

In Africa, anthropological research still tends to take place in settings where classes and class consciousness have far from found an explicit and coherent form. In such a setting the notion of class foremost introduces the question of which factors impede the development of class consciousness and of effective class solidarity in practical politics; van Binsbergen's analysis (see chapter 6) of Nkoya consciousness is a case in point. Only if we are prepared to abstract from the actual processes of decision-making, conflict and control, is it possible to discern classes in Africa today. The way in which the French School has handled the concept of class so far would at least suggest that to employ the term 'class' does not automatically amount to detailed political analysis. Thus the youth, as an exploited class, do play an essential role in Rey's monograph (1971), but at the same time this is an extremely abstract role. The development of class relations and the transformations in the exploitation of the youth are analysed in general terms referring to the logic of the old 'lineage mode of production' and its articulation to capitalism; the young men's personal, conscious outlook, and their political reactions to their class position hardly feature in Rey's story.[30]

The extended-case method

One may well wonder whether a way out of this dilemma, also in the context of a Marxist practice of field-work, could not be found in the 'extended-case method', which has become so dear to many British and Dutch anthropologists influenced by the Manchester School (as we are ourselves). Would not the study of 'extended cases' *à la* Gluckman (1958) or van Velsen (1967), or of 'social dramas' in Victor Turner's sense (1957), provide the possibilities to link in anthropological field-work, the structural implications of modes of production with the political reality of power processes and their rapidly shifting outcomes? One obvious danger is that, with this method, theoretical premises could be smuggled in which are absolutely alien to a Marxist anthropology. Prominent trends in both British and Dutch anthropology have primarily utilized extended-case analysis in the context of an approach which could best be characterized as 'methodological individualism'.[31] But such a one-sided attention for 'Man the Entrepreneur', or even 'Man the Maximizing Animal', does not seem to be inherent to extended-case analysis, and might be avoided in the context of a different theoretical orientation. For, surely, the analysis of cases should ultimately illuminate not just individual decision-making and strategies but also the structural constraints under which the actors act.

However simple and modest the 'extended-case method' would appear to be as a point of departure for anthropological field-work, it could healthily counter-balance the tendencies towards abstraction which spring from the introduction, into our field-work, of any such Grand Theory as Marxism is. For instance, Rey's class analysis in his monograph (1971) might have been much less global, and much more convincing, perhaps, if he had offered some detailed cases in which the contradictions between elders and youth are acted out in ways that lend flesh and bones to the abstract analytical treatment. If we look at developments one-sidedly from the point of view of the structural logic of modes of production, political vicissitudes can appear only as external and superficial forms in our research. Then the perceptions of those participants with whom the anthropologist has closely associated in the course of her or his research would be treated as of only secondary importance. In an almost Lévi-Straussian fashion, the anthropologist's task would be reduced to, arrogantly, discovering the 'objective' contradictions behind these allegedly external forms. In a Marxist practice of field-work, the extended-case method may serve as some sort of antidote to such abstracting

258

tendencies. It may be a useful aid to connect, in our data collection, the determining role of the level of production and the distinct dynamics of the political level — in ways that save us from relegating to one-dimensionality the rich reality which the anthropologist was privileged enough to share in the course of field-work. Only thus can we hope to impart, in the course of our research, real meaning to such concepts as class and class struggle.

The ethnography of articulation

The problem

So far, our discussion has concentrated on the description and analysis of the inner logic of one specific mode of production, the one loosely termed 'lineage mode'. In the modern world, however, it is unlikely that a field-worker will encounter such a mode of production in a pure and independent state. Usually it will be part of a more complex social formation where it is articulated with other modes of production — with capitalism, in the first place, and often also with other non-capitalist modes, such as the tributary one. Some of the chapters of this book (see chapters 3, 4 and 6) have suggested how such articulation could be handled historiographically — capturing the significant pre-existing relations of production, and their shifts in the direction of a class alliance (between local dominant classes and capitalists) which made for such articulation. Coming to terms, as a researcher, with several articulated modes of production in a contemporary ethnographic setting is a different matter. Modes of production are models. A Marxist theory of knowledge would claim that these models are *more* real than the bric-à-brac of directly observable social surface phenomena. A more positivist methodological tradition (in which we were educated) would claim, rather, that these models are theoretical constructs, merely superimposed upon the confusing social reality, and waiting to be superseded by rival models once the latter's greater analytical power is argued convincingly. Whichever philosophical position we take, it is clear that modes of production do not present themselves in an immediately recognizable form in the social reality. Therefore, also the boundaries between articulated modes of production cannot be established by direct observation but can only be argued on the basis of a theoretical analysis of the raw ethnographic data.

Let us recall the process of articulation between the 'lineage mode of production' and capitalism, through the monetarization of bridewealth. Here we saw the *same* categories of people (the youth and the elders) being involved in two irreducibly different types of relations of production. Articulation becomes possible because a young man is subjected (simultaneously; or alternately, but within a limited period of a few years or less) both to capitalist relations of production — where he is a worker selling his labour-power — and to 'domestic' relations of production — where he is a youth trying to secure rights over a nubile woman by paying bridewealth to the elder who is her guardian. What is confusing here, from the point of view of field-work, is that articulation (which theoretically suggests some sort of distinctness, even boundaries, between the various modes of production involved) in fact is realized in the social life of an individual, who remains one and the same person, and who constantly and apparently without great effort, in his actions and conceptionalization, crosses the boundaries between the various modes.

In structural-functionalism the same problematic was often described under the heading of labour migration and urban/rural relations. In that approach,[32] the notion of boundaries between the various 'spheres' in which the actors would operate would be replaced by a sense of continuity. Both the village and the places of migrant work would be considered part of one comprehensive social field, whose constituent components would all be connected by functional and/or normative integration, by the converging interests of the various categories of people involved, the conflicts that bind them, etc. A Marxist approach in terms of the articulation of modes of production, however, would on *theoretical grounds* postulate the existence, within a social formation, of a number of more or less bounded units (modes of production), each unit with its own specific logic which revolves around the central relation of exploitation characteristic of that particular mode — while the articulation between modes would be effected whenever the spoils of exploitation in one mode were used in order to serve the reproduction of relations of exploitation in the other mode or modes involved. The structural-functionalist approach might have greater appeal, a more obvious common-sense rendering of the surface phenomena researchers would encounter in their field-work setting; and particularly that approach would do justice to the smooth movement to and fro between the two distinct spheres of life. Yet it is the lesson of a whole body of Marxist anthropological literature, including the present book, that the modes-of-production approach has greater analytical power. But how to identify, ethnographically, the various irreducible logics, and hence the various modes of production, while in fact they are closely entangled in the actions of the same set of people? A description of one ethnographic setting may suggest that, in the actual practice of field-work, concrete solutions may be found without falling into the trap of simply and blindly superimposing theoretical distinctions upon the living raw data.

Production at a Zambian chief's court

We have already referred to the chiefly courts which still exist among the Nkoya people of western Zambia. A description of these foci of the political process in the countryside may be fitting following a section on 'production and politics', even though our emphasis will now be slightly different. There our point was that the allegedly 'inescapable' logic of a mode of production is realized and actualized through the concrete and variable micro-political decisions of conscious actors. Here we want to explore how the various modes of production articulated within one social formation, the internal logic of each mode, and the mechanisms of their articulation, can be identified by describing and analysing the concrete interactions between the various actors involved.

The royal court of Mwenekahare[33] is located in Kaoma district, in a large village cluster on the Litoya stream, about 25 km south of the tar road connecting the national capital of Zambia (Lusaka) with Kaoma, capital of the district of the same name, and further west, with Mongu, the provincial capital of Western Province. In addition to the royal village itself (called by the generic name of *Lukena*, royal court), the cluster consists of some fifteen hamlets. The centre of the royal village is formed by a fenced yard, inside which are found the royal palace, a hut without walls where the royal musical instruments are kept, and finally the chiefly shrine. The chief's nuclear family lives inside the fence. Outside the fence, the royal village provides accommodation for the chief's consanguineal kin, visitors and court officials: prime minister, retainers, chief's messengers and musicians.

The prime minister, the chief's senior councillor, is a stranger from the area of the other major Nkoya Chief, Mwenemutondo, which is about 100 km away. Retainers, messengers, musicians and clients are largely recruited from among the chief's bilateral kin. Many are reputed to be of slave origin.[34] Only a minority of the court officials, however, are natives of the royal village; the majority hail from neighbouring hamlets within the larger village cluster, and reside there. Those recruited from more distant villages (like the prime minister) have established a temporary home at Lukena, while retaining a proper household in their villages of origin. The staff of the royal court number about fifteen male adults. They form only a small minority of the male householders in the central village cluster. These court officials are appointed and paid by the District Secretary in Kaoma, upon nomination by the royal council. Their salaries range from about K15 to K60 (c. £8 to £30) per month, while Mwenekahare himself receives a state subsidy of about K100 (£50). Modest though these sums may appear, they are above the level of the cash requirements of most rural households, and partly explain the keen competition that exists for posts at the court.

In addition to the fifteen hamlets in the central cluster, the Litoya valley contains some twenty villages. Kahare's area comprises over a dozen other major valleys and the extensive forest areas in between. These valleys each have their own valley chief, who presides over the valley court of headmen and other elders. In addition, the valley chief administers the valley's main rain-shrine. Valley chiefs have titles whose prestige is often equal to that of Kahare's. As hereditary members of Kahare's royal council they pay infrequent individual visits to the Lukena. These visits are prompted by the process of intrigues and changes in office that constitute (neo)-traditional politics among the Nkoya today. During those visits the valley chiefs offer tribute to Kahare, nowadays usually in the form of money. Without formal judicial powers, and with very limited ritual functions, the court activities that focus on the person of Kahare today mainly lie in the spheres of politics and of production.

Mwenekahare stands at the top of a local hierarchy of traditional political offices. Moreover, Kahare occupies a position within the traditional royal hierarchy of western Zambia, the former Barotseland, whose most exalted office is that of the Paramount Chief (Litunga) of the Lozi people, usually residing at

Limulunga near Mongu. Along with one other Nkoya Chief, Mwenemutondo, Kahare belongs to the handful of royal chiefs in western Zambia whose recognition, prestige and state subsidy directly derive from the special treaties the British South Africa Company, the British Crown, and later the Zambian state at the moment of independence (1964), made with the Litunga.[35] Contacts between Kahare's court and the Litunga's are infrequent: there is a trickle of correspondence, and official delegations from Kahare visit Limulunga (bringing tribute in cash) on the occasion of major events, such as the accession of a new Litunga. In the mid-1930s a branch of the Litunga's court was created in Kaoma district at Naliele 200 km east of Mongu, and headed by a junior member of the Litunga dynasty. Contacts are maintained similar to those with Limulunga court, but more frequently. So much for traditional politics.

On the district and national level, Kahare is also active in modern state institutions. The Kaoma District Council is a local government body which, besides elected councillors, comprises a limited number of nominated councillors who, among other local foci of power, represent the major chief's courts in the district. Mwenekahare is one of the nominated councillors. As such, he receives a further state remuneration; and he infrequently travels to Kaoma in government vehicles, in order to attend the council meetings and related functions. At the national level, Kahare is one of about twenty-five Zambian chiefs who were co-opted into the House of Chiefs, a body whose infrequent meetings in Lusaka bring these traditional rulers in close contact with the top leaders of the Zambian state. On the district and national level, as within his own chief's area, Kahare's function is largely ceremonial, and involves the maintaining of the institution of chieftainship and not the allocation of scarce financial resources and power.

Against this background we may now consider production at Kahare's court and attempt to analyse it in terms of an articulation of modes of production. Mwenekahare is involved in production in a number of ways: legally, as one controlling considerable resources of land, game and fishing sites;[36] and practically, as one supervising hunting and agricultural production at the court, and appropriating the proceeds from these activities.

Apart from that part of Kahare's realm that has been appropriated by the state for public usage (roads, a large game reserve, an agricultural development project), the chief is supposed to hold the available land area in trust for his people. The Nkoya cultivate different types of land. Wet riverside gardens (*matapa*) are permanent, scarce, and keenly controlled by villages and kin-groups; it is largely on these plots that the very limited local production of hybrid maize as a cash crop takes place. Alternatively, there is an abundance of land available for dry forest gardens, and unlimited access to such land is taken for granted once one is accepted as a member of a local village. It is here that subsistence cultivation of cassava, traditional maize, millet, sweet potatoes, and groundnuts takes place.

Village sites are frequently moved, as a result of both ecological and micro-political processes; few villages remain intact and located at the same spot for much longer than ten years. Selection of a new village site is subject to Kahare's approval. In addition, immigrants from other chiefs' areas, and from ethnic groups other than Kahare's Nkoya, often aspire to establish new villages in Kahare's area. Their settlement, however, is also subject to Kahare's approval, and he is known to have sent his own messengers, or to have demanded assistance from the police at the district capital, to oust newcomers who had failed to obtain his permission. This chiefly control over land does not affect the distribution of land among recognized inhabitants of the same valley, e.g. Litoya. Such distribution sometimes becomes problematic when kinsmen residing in different villages contest the use of *matapa*, or when an enterprising villager (e.g. the local shopkeeper) in exchange for cash mobilizes outside labour and mechanical assistance which enables him to cultivate a disproportionally large forest garden. The ensuing conflicts have no formal judicial solution; they fall outside Kahare's competence, whereas local courts among the Nkoya consider land cases obscene and not actionable. The limitations of Mwenekahare's control over land as the main production factor are also manifest when it comes to appropriation of land for the public interest. Requests are made not to the royal chief but to the Kaoma District Council. Even though Kahare is a nominated member of this body, his voice is hardly ever recorded in the Council minutes, and the Council has reallocated portions of Mwenekahare's area without formally requesting his approval.

Likewise in the sphere of control over production factors lie Mwenekahare's claims over fishing sites and proceeds from hunting. Rights over fishing in specific streams and ponds attach to hereditary princely titles, including that of Kahare; Kahare's are particularly extensive. While some headmen manage to have their claims respected by non-kin, this is no longer the case with Kahare. Fishing freely takes place in his ponds, without his permission being asked, and without the traditional tribute in kind being paid. The only vestige of his claims is that Kahare still sets the time for a day of massive, collective fishing in his ponds, when, towards the end of the dry season, catches are particularly plentiful. Part of the catch is consumed locally, but much finds its way to the district markets, normally via middlemen who belong to other ethnic groups than the Nkoya.

Western Zambia is still relatively abundant in big game, and royal chiefs used to have exclusive rights over certain animals or portions thereof. Under present-day national game legislation, most of the massive hunting that still goes on in the area would be poaching. The Department of Game and Fisheries battles ineffectively against existing practices, and particularly turns a blind eye to the conspicuous hunting activities of local chiefs. More or less as chiefly paraphernalia, Mwenekahare possesses a number of excellent licensed rifles and guns; in this again his position is similar to that of other headmen and elders. Besides being an excellent hunter himself, he sends his lesser court officials hunting, mainly in order to keep up the meat supplies at the Lukena. Besides, Kahare privately employs an elephant-hunter, who kills several elephants per year. Their meat is freely distributed among the inhabitants of Litoya and the surrounding valleys, the ivory is sold by Kahare on the black market.

On several occasions Kahare has used the proceeds from ivory sales (augmented with savings from his subsidy) in order to buy motor-cars. One landed up in the royal courtyard, immobilized for lack of spare parts; while another was appropriated by one of his urban relatives. However, during their characteristically short episode at the court, these vehicles were used not only for ceremonial visits dictated by Kahare's various offices, but also for transport runs to urban areas, where game meat and agricultural produce were marketed, and in the course of which paying passengers would be taken. While the vehicles were in running order, Kahare would employ drivers who would frequently resign on the ground of being underpaid.

Mwenekahare's main productive activity, however, lies in agriculture. He does not belong to the category, much favoured by the Zambian central government, of exemplary chiefs who combine traditional politics, representative functions within the modern state, and impressive agricultural production. Kahare's area is of old a famine danger area, and famine relief (in the form of bags of maize being freely distributed by the district authorities) was occasionally necessary in the 1970s; the recent growth of cash-crop production of hybrid maize (inevitable with the decline of cash-earning opportunities offered by labour migration) appears to have aggravated this situation. On a very limited scale (which yet exceeds that of almost all other agricultural producers in the Litoya valley) Mwenekahare cultivates both subsistence crops and marketable maize. There is no evidence of tributary labour: Kahare's subjects, even those living in the Litoya valley or in the central village cluster, do not work in his fields on some collective and unpaid basis. All labour-power used comes from people living at the Lukena: Kahare's nuclear and extended family (who are entirely dependent upon his crops), and the court officials and their wives and children (who, in addition to working in Kahare's fields, also have their own independent agricultural production in their villages of origin). All workers share, to a limited extent, in the subsistence crops produced, but the proceeds from the marketing of hybrid maize are retained by Kahare. Interestingly, Kahare's *matapa* lie outside the Litoya valley, at the Kazo stream, about 5 km from the Lukena. Therefore most of the royal establishment moves to temporary shelters at Kazo in the month of July (with picturesque effects, such as the royal musical instruments hanging in trees, and the royal guns and spears sticking out above the walls of the roofless royal shelter), only to return there shortly before the first rains, in October/November.

Just as there is no communal tributary labour in the royal fields, there is no distribution of foodstuffs by the chief among his subjects. Exchanges of foodstuffs belong, however, to the standard pattern of interaction between households, and members of the royal household are engaged in such exchanges just like anyone else. Purchases of foodstuffs (and particularly of beer) are increasingly normal phenomena, and also the royal household makes such purchases in the central village cluster and further afield. Some people stick to the custom of making tributary offerings of beer and grain to the chief, but these are exceptions which constitute only a small proportion of consumption at the Lukena, and of production in the surrounding hamlets and villages.

266

Capturing articulation in ethnographic data

Overlooking this body of descriptive data, an analysis of the patterns of labour and the appropriation of surpluses would reveal three mutually connected yet irreducible sets of relations, which sets, we argue, are modes of production.

First there is the domestic level, the 'lineage mode of production', on which Kahare, relying on the labour-force of the younger men and the women in his extended family, gains part of his agricultural production, keeps up reciprocal exchanges with other households, and in many respects is comparable to all other elders in the region. Here the basic productive unit is the extended family, co-residing in the same village. The circulation of direct producers (mainly women and youth) would be dictated by virilocal marriage in the case of married women, and by temporary attachment to elderly male consanguineal kinsmen (patrilateral or matrilateral) in the case of the youth, and of adolescent, divorced and widowed women. The youth and unmarried women normally have a choice between a number of elderly relatives with whom they can live, and to whom they can offer their labour-power in exchange for food, clothing, shelter and supernatural protection. The relation of exploitation is between elders and youth/women, and is mitigated by the fact that the latter have the option of moving to a different village if their exploitation becomes too extreme. All this applies equally to the extended kin at Kahare's court, all of whom have potential options of membership in a number of villages besides the Lukena, and many of whom have for several years lived elsewhere, or have moved away from the Lukena since the mid-1970s.

Second, there is the 'tributary mode of production', which provides the pattern and the idiom for most of the productive activities at the Lukena in so far as these involve court officials other than Kahare's nuclear and extended kin. Moreover, through the slavery connotations of many paid court officials, through rights over land, fishing sites and game, through infrequent and minor tribute (received by Kahare from lesser chiefs and subjects and given by Kahare to the Lozi courts at Naliele and Lumulunga), the tributary pattern is further worked out, in a form which suggests both the historical background of the 'tributary' mode of production, and its contemporary erosion. For the court officials, the pattern of circulation is on the surface dictated by traditional court politics: the vicissitudes of nomination to office and demotion from office; here competition can be very open, since there are no fixed rules of succession, and heredity does not play an important part. Having a slave background (i.e. descent from a royal princess and a male slave) seems slightly to increase one's chances of being nominated for the more menial court offices of musician and retainer. Formally nomination and discharge are the competence of Kahare's royal council. A perusal of relevant files at the Kaoma district capital[37] reveals, however, that these matters are ultimately decided upon by the District Secretary, on grounds of stability, political reliability and efficiency, which operate in a field of discourse totally different from that of Nkoya court politics. This is one instance where an articulation of the tributary mode of production to a third mode (capitalism as mediated through the state) can be seen. We shall come back to this. At any rate, the circulation of male court officials follows a logic radically different from the competitive kinship idiom patterning the circulation of producers in the 'lineage mode of production' among the Nkoya.

This also holds for the relations of production within the present-day tributary mode: Kahare controls the production of his court officials not because he is their elder/patron, but because he is the chief, and by virtue of his own exalted status enjoys a state subsidy on which the salaries of the court officials depend. Being paid by the state, that part of their work which yields material products is appropriated by the chief (much of their work at the courts amounts only to ceremonial or ideological production: court music, oratory, ritual). Here we encounter two moments of articulation. In the first place, all male court officials are heads of households, which are productive units in the 'lineage mode of production'. By working in the chief's fields, the wives and youths in these households generate a surplus under conditions stipulated by the 'lineage' mode (for it is under that logic that their labour power is controlled by their head of household), but appropriated by the tributary mode (under whose logic their head of household is a court official, who allows the chief to dispose of part of the labour power of his household). Second, there is a moment of articulation between the tributary and the capitalist mode, since some of the surpluses thus appropriated by chief Kahare are marketed by him for cash on distant urban produce market, or to

268

the National Agricultural Marketing Board whose lorry comes to the Lukena a few times a year.

Other examples of an articulation between the tributary mode and the 'lineage' mode can be seen in the tribute (produced under the logic of the 'lineage' mode) offered by householders and village chiefs to Kahare. The cash tribute offered by Kahare to the Limulunga and Naliele courts is circulated under a tributary logic, but when we examine its sources (state subsidy, cash tribute from valley chiefs, and cash proceeds from the production of agricultural workers, hunters, and the operation of motor vehicles) there is reason to characterize the production of this tribute as the outcome of an articulation between the 'lineage', the tributary and the capitalist modes of production.

Kahare's personal employment of hunters and drivers largely follows the logic of a capitalist mode of production: wage-labour, separation between the workers and their means of production (gun, vehicle) owned by his employer. Tributary overtones, however, can be detected in the fact that the hunter is traditionally entitled to part of the bag (ideally the upper tusk — the one that does not touch the ground when the elephant has been felled), while the driver is expected to accept subnormal wages because of the honour of being employed at court.

But while the capitalist mode of production appears in a straightforward form in Kahare's cash sales and his employment of hunters and drivers, the present data suggest that capitalism's articulation to the tributary and 'lineage' modes is much more complex and subtle than that. Kahare's state subsidy goes back to treaties (in other words, a class alliance) signed in 1900 between the British South Africa Company on the one hand, and on the other the Lozi king Lewanika, heading a tributary state which included several Nkoya chiefs. Today this subsidy is financed by the Zambian state largely from the proceeds of mineral sales, realized through the labour of Zambian mine-workers many of whom are migrants from rural areas similar to Kahare's (although few Nkoya work at the Zambian mines). The Zambian state partly finances and distantly controls traditional politics which form the motor of the tributary mode of production in present times, and while infringing on the autonomy of tributary relations of production (as is clear when we consider the chief's diminished control of land, game and fishing sites), makes ample use of the encapsulated tributary mode in order to further its own legitimation — in other words its ideological reproduction.

Thus, an analysis of the actual relations at Kahare's court may clarify especially the role of the tributary mode in the articulation of capitalism and rural modes of production in western Zambia — notably its role in legitimizing and reproducing capitalist dominance. Of course, this specific role of the tributary mode has to be analysed against the wider background of the involvement of the Nkoya, in the villages and as urban migrants, in the money-economy and capitalist relations — or, in an even wider sense, in relation to Zambia's place within capitalist economy on a world scale. Even though Kahare does receive some income from urban kinsmen, such an analysis would surpass the scope of our ethnographic example of Kahare's court. None the less, the present analysis may have given some indication of how articulation of modes of production can be detected in the practice of anthropological field-work by studying the empirical interactions of the actors within a particular setting.

Field-work on ideology, belief and ritual

Some theoretical problems

The application of the ideas of French Marxist anthropology to field-work in the sphere of ideology (which we shall here limit down to belief and ritual) poses a number of problems, which Marxist writers are only beginning to explore. But, even in general, considering the spate of descriptive anthropological publications on ideological and religious subjects, values, world-views, etc., it is amazing that the anthropological literature contains so very little on the methodology of field-work on these topics. Penetrating ideological complexes of thought and symbolic action through participant observation remains a craft that is learned not from books but by contact with experienced researchers, and by personal trial and error. This is not the place to make up for this general omission. We would rather explore how the marxist perspective on modes of production and their articulation, as presented in this chapter and throughout the present book, suggests specific questions as regards the ideological dimensions of social life — and how these questions might be approached in anthropological field-work.

270

Setting out on this course, we encounter a second difficulty. In France modern Marxist anthropology has primarily developed as an attempt to come to terms with the economic organization of local communities, especially in Africa, trying to identify the material aspects of production and reproduction, and the relations of exploitation around which these revolve; a major issue in this context has been the forms and effects of capitalist encroachment. In the works of Meillassoux, Terray and Rey, religion is either ignored or (see Terray 1979b) is treated in a way which scarcely illuminates the place of ideological elements within modes of production and their articulation. Godelier is in a different position: his short articles on religion (1975, 1977) pretend to offer a Marxist perspective, but his approach is disappointingly idealist, and, besides, a Godelierian idiom seems to contribute little that is not already contained in mainstream anthropology of religion since Robertson Smith, Tylor and Durkheim.

However, others working on the basis of a Marxist inspiration, and utilizing the concept of mode of production, have meanwhile produced a limited number of analyses of the ideological dimension within one non-capitalist mode of production; in this respect reference could be made to the works of Bonte (1975), Houtart, (1980), Houtart and Lemercinier (1977, 1979), Augé (1975), and Baré (1977). Religious analyses cast in terms of the articulation of modes of production within a social formation were offered by Schoffeleers (1978) in his historical analysis of a Malawian martyr cult, and by van Binsbergen in *Religious Change in Zambia* (1981a). That book offers an elaborate theoretical framework that enables us to interpret the complex historical succession of major religious forms in Central Africa since about 1500, and the contemporary manifestations of these forms, as the ideological counterpart of the emergence, articulation and partial decline of various modes of production. The contemporary co-existence of all these religious forms (transformed, no doubt, since they first appeared on the local scene) is explained by the fact that today's complex social formation still contains (again, in a transformed shape) the various modes of production and the structures of articulation to which these various religious forms belonged in the first place.

These studies are specific applications of a more general Marxist approach to ideology, whose classic statement is to be found, of course, in Marx's analysis of the ideological dimension of the capitalist mode of production (Marx 1973; Marx & Engels 1975). A number of leading ideas combine in this tradition. Religion is seen as the ideological projection, into the celestial and the unreal, of processes of appropriation and exploitation that constitute Man's social life. Thus religion appears as a structure of *ideological reproduction*: by reflecting existing relations of production and by endowing the phantasms thus produced with a unique, exalted sense of reality and power, these relations are underpinned and carried over to new generations (e.g. in rites of passage) and to other parts of the world (cf. the spread of Islam and Christianity). Religion, however, may take on an impetus of its own, and (in the hands of elders, kings, priests, cult leaders) may stipulate a circulation of producers and an appropriation of their surpluses which, rather than reflecting relations of production that exist outside the religious sphere, constitute relations of exploitation in their own right. In this respect (the point is also stressed in recent non-Marxist theories concerning so-called 'regional cults' or 'territorial cults'; see Werbner 1977; Schoffeleers 1979; van Binsbergen 1981: 252–5), religion may become a structure of material production and exploitation *sui generis*. Only a sophisticated materialist theory of symbolism (whose development is one of the most urgent tasks for contemporary Marxist social science) will be able to explain how the unreal is capable of imposing itself (either as a reflection, or *sui generis*) with such vehemence upon the reality of material production and exploitation. From this point of view we look at religion, primarily, as a structure of *ideological production*, and we try to classify the forms of such ideological production, and to identify the rules and laws that govern it.

Throughout, the problem of religion from a Marxist point of view might be summarized, in Bourdieu's words, as the problem of identifying

> *the transformation laws which govern the transmutation of the different forms of capital into symbolic capital*. The crucial process to be studied is the work of dissimulation and transfiguration (in a word, euphemization) which makes it possible to transfigure relations of force by getting the violence they objectively contain misrecognized/recognized, so transforming them into a symbolic power, capable of producing effects without visible expenditure of energy (Bourdieu 1979: 83, emphasis added; cf. Bourdieu 1977).

However, we must not overlook the fact that such transmutation is in principle a two-way process. For symbolic capital can also be transmuted into material capital, as is demonstrated by so many politically and economically successful ideological and religious movements, from the Roman Catholic Church to the Bolshevik Party, from the nationalist movement in colonial Africa after World War II to the Muridiyya brotherhood which is less than a century developed into a major economic force in Senegal.[38]

The dimensions of ideological reproduction, material production and exploitation, and symbolic production suggest specific sets of data which a Marxist field-worker doing religious research would primarily focus upon. The dimension of symbolic production would appear to be the most difficult to tackle from a Marxist point of view. Not only is it further removed than the other two dimensions from the processes of material production habitually studied by Marxist anthropology. Also, ideological production is by its nature innovative, and often escapes from the repetitiveness of social phenomena field-workers look for in the first place. Anthropologists engaged in religious research are now beginning to realize that the power and the appeal that are being generated in religious contexts derive not only from more or less permanent structures (which the tradition of religious anthropology has always stressed), but also from creative and unpredictable, symbolic manipulation by means of which religious actors captivate their audiences, presenting to them a new and illuminating view of their personal condition and of the world (see van Binsbergen and Schoffeleers (in press, b), and references cited there). This so-called praxeological element (which would equally be discernible in artistic production, or in political oratory in a context of mobilization for class, ethnic and racial conflict) is realized in momentaneous transactions between participants. Linking up with the language- and culture-specific processes of communication between those involved, it is eminently amenable for research by means of participant observation in the field; but it is less easily analysed in the terms that dominate structural Marxism.

Clearly, the underlying problematic here is that of the relative autonomy of the symbolic order vis-à-vis material production and exploitation. Symbolic production presupposes considerable room for experiment, free variation, unsystematic and distorted reflection of material reality, and hence a creative departure from the objective structure of social reality as anchored in relations of

273

material production. For the field-worker, this means that he or she should detachedly and attentively study symbolic phenomena in the field, before jumping to conclusions as to their repetitive, systematic nature, let alone their reflecting, in whatever dialectical way, the material structures of production and exploitation. Ultimately, of course, Marxist research into ideology should aim to reveal systematic connections between symbolic and material structures;[39] and for this purpose, the study of relations of material production should occupy a very considerable part in any such research. From an analytical and theoretical point of view, however, it would appear as if the study of ideology, belief and ritual is in a somewhat different phase from the study of exploitation, reproduction, bridewealth and related topics well covered by Marxist anthropological theorizing. Both within and outside Marxism the theoretical reflection on the ideological dimension of social life is relatively underdeveloped. One explanation for this state of affairs is that such theoretical reflection is in itself a form of ideological production, and thus when brought to bear upon other people's ideological production, raises immense philosophical problems whose solution cannot be expected to come from anthropologists alone (see chapter 6). This is no reason to sit back and refrain from Marxist field-work on religion and ideology until the theorists have finished their homework. But less than in other spheres of Marxist anthropological analysis, a break-through in the study of ideology can be expected from field-work alone.

Religious plurality and articulation of modes of production: the Nkoya case

The following example, again from the field-work of one of us in Zambia, may indicate how the French Marxist perspective of an articulation of modes of production can bring order to otherwise extremely confusing ethnographic data collected in a contemporary setting. It suggests some of the types of data a field-worker working on religous data in this approach would be advised to look for. In this case, the empirical steps can be summarized as follows.

(1) One should try to identify (through a study of symbols, participants' actions and statements, processes of recruitment and control) the underlying symbolic logic that is consciously applied by the participants in their rituals, cults and religious conceptions.

(2) Rather than assuming that in any historical social formation

one and only one symbolic logic is at work, one should make an effort to identify, in the field data, any number of such logics: mutually irreducible and contradictory, and each separately applied in a distinct cult or ritual.

(3) Analysis of non-religious data on production and reproduction within the social formation under study should lead to the identification of the various modes of production articulated (following a historical process — to be studied by additional historiographic research) within that social formation.

(4) The logics of production and reproduction identified under (3) should then be compared with the symbolic logics identified under (1) and (2), in an attempt to relegate the various symbolic sub-sets encountered in the field, to various modes of production and their articulation.

(5) It should be borne in mind that ideological reproduction (ideally resulting in a one-to-one correspondence between symbolic and material logics) is only one of the possible connections between the symbolic order and the material order — in addition, ideological production that has no clearly detectable material counterpart is to be encountered, whereas the field-worker may also come across ideological structures *sui generis*: structures which introduce an element of production and exploitation in the religious field (e.g. appropriation, by cult leaders, of surpluses produced by members of a cult in productive contexts defined by that cult), again without a detectable counterpart in structures of non-religious production and reproduction.

The contemporary religious situation among the Nkoya turned out to be extremely confusing, as a considerable number of major cult complexes existed side by side, and the same people would participate in many or all of them apparently indiscriminately. Thus the Litoya valley turned out to be the scene of (among minor other types) the following ritual forms:

— ancestral ritual, in which all members of a village would collectively take part under the direction of the headman and other elders, in cases of hunting trips, name-inheritance, and serious illness supposed to have moral implications;

— rain ritual, conducted by the valley chief and a few other headmen belonging to the Kahare dynasty, at the previous chief's burial place;

— cults of affliction, venerating not ancestors but alien spirits; these cults, treating individual diseases devoid of any moral

275

implications, would be represented by independent cult leaders who had been initiated into the cult in the course of some earlier treatment. The cultic congregations of adepts would be recruited from neighbouring and even more distant villages and valleys, according to a pattern cutting across existing units of production and reproduction;

— prophetic cults of affliction, which differed from the non-prophetic ones in that they venerated the High God, and that their cult leaders, deriving their powers from a charismatic cult founder, would belong to an interlocal cultic organization which rigidly controlled the cultic idiom and the flow of cash within the cult;

— Christian churches and sects, primarily Watchtower and the Evangelical Church of Zambia, which in many ways are comparable to prophetic cults of affliction, except for the latters' near-exclusive emphasis on healing.

This outline does not cover the whole range of symbolic expression, and particularly does not touch on divination and sorcery control as engaged in by diviners and diviner-priests (*nganga*); these activities, however, were largely of a technical and individual nature, if they were not part of the cults mentioned above.

Once the relevant ethnographic data had been collected, the five major cult complexes clearly stood out. They defined different sets of activities, organized differently. Each had its own patterns of control over people and material resources, and pursued a distinct idiom featuring different supernatural entities, interpretations of human misfortune and ways of redress. Some cults would stress morality whereas others would not. Some had a strongly communalist view of the human individual in that the misfortune of one of the members was supposed to reveal a moral crisis affecting the entire group (ancestral cult). Others would look at misfortune as a purely individual, accidental and a-moral circumstance, to be redressed by appeasing the vagrant spirit that had allegedly taken possession of the patient (non-prophetic cult of affliction). The various complexes seemed to represent, *on the symbolic level*, a number of mutually irreducible logics, whose co-occurrence within one and the same 'culture' could not be explained in structural-functionalist terms. For here the same set of people were operating, in cultic complexes which were rigidly compartmentalized rather than normatively or functionally integrated.

The pattern began to make sense once the various irreducible logics underlying this contemporary religious plurality were interpreted in terms of distinct logics of modes of production. Ancestral ritual and chiefly rain ritual could easily be identified as the ideological components of the 'lineage' mode and the tributary mode respectively. They, in other words, constituted clear-cut cases of ideological reproduction. The individual-centredness of the remaining three cultic forms, their lack of references to the processes of production (hunting, agriculture) that went on in the local community, their recruitment patterns which denied the units in which such production was organized, their veneration of invisible entities without local referents (such as chiefs and ancestors have), the more or less bureaucratic organization characterizing the prophetic and the Christian forms, and the extensive circulation of cash in all three varieties suggested a dynamic beyond the local horizon: processes of articulation, capitalist encroachment.

Only after extensive historical research and further theorizing (which led to the idea that cultic forms might reflect not just modes of production, but also the process of their articulation), was it possible to relegate the contemporary cultic varieties to specific modes of production in the articulation process of the social formation of Kaoma district, and to establish a rough periodization for the emergence and decline of the various modes of production involved. The original data, however, derived from the contradictions encountered, in the course of field-work, in the ethnographic data themselves.

Interestingly, cultic forms, which originally reflect modes of production and their articulation, turn out to replace in part the very relations of material exploitation to which they originally referred. Thus they come close to being *sui generis* exploitative structures in their own right. Non-prophetic cults of affliction, for instance, could be argued to have formed, at the time of their emergence (in Kaoma district: late nineteenth century), the ideological component of an articulation between, on the one hand, mercantile capitalism (as locally represented by alien traders), and on the other, a social formation comprising a dominant tributary mode articulated to a 'lineage' mode. The social formation today has a very different composition, and the impact of capitalism has taken new forms. Yet these cults of affliction continue to play an important part in the relations of exploitation between elders and the youth: they provide a structure through which the cash the youth earn in the capitalist sector is syphoned back to the villages, as payment for the activities of elders who are among the important cult leaders; most cult leaders are elderly women and their cultic administrations over female patients, for which the youth act as sponsors, provide a grotesquely deformed mirror-image of the relations of exploitation characteristic of the 'lineage' mode of production (van Binsbergen 1981).

Concluding remarks

It will be evident that our explorations do not yet permit any conclusive prescription of what a Marxist practice of anthropological field-work should be. Concerning the various aspects discussed above we could only offer some preliminary suggestions. And there remain many more aspects to discuss — such as, just to mention a crucial one, the practical political problems encountered by a Marxist field-worker.[40]

None the less, our argument may have shown that there is a case for a Marxist practice of field-work. The theories developed by such Marxist anthropologists as Meillassoux, Terray, Rey and Godelier do suggest original starting-points for field-work. However, the practical consequence of their ideas remain to be clarified on important points. Thus, our discussion on the concept of mode of production may have shown that further operationalization of this concept could stimulate interesting field-research. But it became equally clear that further nuancing of the concept of mode of production would be necessary in order to make that concept a useful tool for dealing with the rich variation anthropologists encounter in the field. Likewise, only further research can hope to demonstrate the value of our suggestion that the 'extended-case method' might be a proper technique in a Marxist practice of field-work in order to deal with the problematic relations between 'production' and 'politics' — in order to do justice to the autonomy of the political sphere in relation to the logic of modes of production and their articulation. The same applies to our attempts to translate this concept of articulation of modes of production and the equally problematic inter-relation of 'production' and ideology' into propositions for research and observation within a specific ethnographic setting.

Reflection on the implications of Marxist theories for anthropological field-work should have priority in present-day discussions of Marxist anthropology. Direct and systematic application of Marxist theory in field-work will enhance the value of data and their interpretation — as we hope our own future field-work in Africa will prove. But with the data, the theory also will improve on the basis of such reflection. As Reini Raatgever argues in chapter 8, stagnation of the theoretical discussions among French Marxist anthropologists has now reached a stage where a new empirical input from field-work can be expected to result in a new break-through.

Notes

1 Earlier versions of this chapter were presented at a seminar with Meillassoux, Amsterdam, 28 February 1980, organized by the Amsterdam Work-group for Marxist Anthropology, in association with the African Studies Centre, Leiden and the Free University, Amsterdam, and at a similar seminar with Terray, Leiden, 27 November 1981, similarly organized; the Anthropology seminar, University of Manchester, March 1980; and the Amsterdam Work-group for Marxist Anthropology, April 1980. We are indebted to all participants in these sessions, and particularly to Claude Meillassoux, Emmanuel Terray, and the members of our work-group, for their constructive criticism. We also gratefully acknowledge comments by the editors of the journal *Development and Change*.

2 Here lies a fundamental problem with whose implications we shall be confronted throughout this chapter. Marxist social science is often claimed to offer a total approach to all aspects of social life in its historical development — a dialectical method that is both all-encompassing, and essentially different from the methods (often with neo-positive overtones) prevalent in so-called 'bourgeois' social science. In practice we allow ourselves to be sensitized to such specific aspects of the field data as are particularly relevant in the light of our Marxist theory; yet we apply field-work techniques which belong to the anthropological discipline in general, and which imply general anthropological theories (e.g. as to the structure of kinship, symbolism, face-to-face interaction, etc.) accumulated over the past hundred years largely irrespective of Marxist debate.

3 In Rey's monograph (1971) any explicit account of his field-work is lacking. The reader is even left in the dark as to when the field-work was conducted. Only towards the end of the book may the attentive reader surmise that Rey's research topic was reformulated in the course of his field-work (Rey 1971: 23, 496, 500). Godelier in his monograph (1982) confines himself to the most general indication of the circumstances under which he conducted his research (Godelier 1982: 15–17). In his Guro monograph, Meillassoux offers somewhat

more factual details, but neither gives a real insight in the design and the development of his research (Meillassoux 1964: 7–8). Nor are the design and the conditions of Meillassoux's various field-work projects extensively dealt with in his later collection of articles (Meillassoux 1977).

4 Together with Cresswell, Godelier has edited a handbook on anthropological field-work (Cresswell & Godelier 1976). Unfortunately, the book offers hardly more, and in many ways less, than the classic anthropological methods and techniques. Godelier's own contribution to the book is extremely limited, and does not go beyond a perfunctory introduction (pp. 7–11), and a surprisingly technical piece on agricultural plots (pp. 140–51). Likewise, reactions upon French Marxist anthropology from outside France have hardly touched on the matter of field-work (see chapter 1 on the predominantly theoretical orientation of the Anglo-Saxon reactions).

5 E.g., Meillassoux's oral presentation at the Meillassoux seminar mentioned in note 1.

6 Cf., e.g., Sahlins (1972); Harris (1980).

7 See Godelier (1973): 46–52. Cf. also Meillassoux's scepticism as to the utility of detailed and quantitative data collection on production, as expressed in the oral presentation at the Meillassoux seminar mentioned in note 1.

8 Rey (1971) likewise stresses, for the Mossendjo area in Congo-Brazzaville, the importance of the circulation of young men as 'slaves'. He shows how such circulation is closely related to the elder's control over prestige goods. Rey's and Terray's views in this respect come close to Meillassoux's; the latter was the first to stress the relationship between bridewealth, prestige goods and the elders' authority (cf. Meillassoux 1960, 1975). The principal difference is that Meillassoux refuses to speak of exploitation and class contradictions in this connection (Meillassoux 1975: 121).

9 Rey (1971: 253–68) complicates this problem of how to deal with variations within the 'lineage mode of production', by arguing that even African state societies like the Ashanti did fit in with the 'lineage mode of production': the main function of the statal superstructure would have been to guarantee the reproduction of the 'lineage' system and the authority of the elders. The consequence is that Rey has to refer to 'truly segmentary' societies as a kind of subtype of the 'lineage' mode. If the concept of the 'lineage mode of production' is stretched that far, it becomes all the more necessary to refine the concept in order to deal with the considerable variation between societies like the Ashanti and the 'truly' segmentary ones. Apparently Terray would prefer to analyse the Ashanti as a formation determined by an articulation of a 'lineage' and a 'slave' mode of production (see 1974 and 1975). Meanwhile we note that the term 'lineage' in this context should be regarded as a blanket concept meant to loosely indicate societies mainly organized on a kinship basis. In Africanist anthropology since the late 1950s there is little to suggest that the concept of the segmented, unilineal descent group (cf. Fortes 1953) is all that suitable

to describe the complex and shifting patterns of social organization found in the continent, often characterized by bilateral tendencies, inchoate and optional structures and considerable local variation within a region.

10 Or, in terms later adopted by Rey (1979): among the Maka the formal subordination of the producers to the relations of exploitation was not yet fully developed into a real subordination (the immediate production was not yet reorganized in direct connection with the exploitation of the juniors by their elders). See also Geschiere (1981).

11 Cf., e.g., Bonte (1981), Kuper (1982a); the crucial role of cattle in the Diola mode of production is shown clearly by van der Klei, in chapter 3. It seems likely that in practice the monopoly of the elders over cattle is often less strict than their monopoly over inanimate prestige goods, which can be simply stored without any further investment of labour being necessary. Such variations must have different consequences for the authority position of the elders, and moreover, they appear to be of direct significance for the dynamics of 'domestic' patterns of organization under capitalist dominance. In general, inanimate bridal goods are nearly everywhere rapidly transformed into money under the modern relationships. By contrast, cattle seems to be much more resistant, as bridal goods, to modern changes; even in communities which have been involved in the money economy for a longer period, bridewealth still consists primarily of cattle. Therefore, the continuing importance of cattle as a prestige good can have a specific impact on the articulation of capitalist and pre-capitalist relations of production. Cf., e.g., the numerous compaints of modern development-specialists on the 'irrational' expansion of livestock and the 'over-grazing' in East African cattle-societies.

12 See van Binsbergen (1970, 1980, n.d., b), Geschiere (1969) and van der Klei (1971).

13 Of course, it becomes apparent here that the term 'lineage mode of production' has serious drawbacks. The general validity of the 'lineage' concept is strongly contested among anthropologists nowadays (see Kuper 1982b). The comparison of peasant communities in North Africa and in Black Africa shows in any case that patterns of organization somewhat resembling the 'lineages' of classic anthropology can function as cores of the social organization in very different economic settings. Therefore, it may be somewhat confusing to use the term 'lineage' in order to denote a specific mode of production. However, in a chapter like the present one, where we refer directly to Rey's and Terray's interpretations, it would be even more confusing to introduce a new term for this mode of production.

14 See van Binsbergen (1971, 1980, n.d., b, n.d., c). Another variation concerns the way in which the North African peasant communities were related to wider politico-economic formations. See, for an interesting Marxist analysis of the unstable relationship of the 'tribal' systems and the political centres of the states in North Africa, Seddon (1978); cf. also Seddon (1981).

15 Oral intervention by Terray at the seminar mentioned in note 1.

16 See the research project, formulated by Meillassoux in 1964, which aimed at 'identifying and characterizing the old modes of production in West Africa' (see Meillassoux 1977: 107f). Such comparative research concerning the application of the notion of mode of production on different pre-capitalist forms of organization within one area still seems very important. It is to be hoped that the results of this project may still be published.

17 Our translation. Cf. also Rey's elaboration upon Marx's statement that, for any society, it is as impossible to stop producing as it is to stop consuming. Rey continues: 'This truism is the base of the power of all dominant classes because the process of reproduction which enables societies "not to stop producing", demands social combinations which these dominant classes can control. It is by using this technical necessity of the reproduction that dominant classes maintain the social forms in which production takes place — social forms which appear as technical necessities to the dominated classes [. . .] We have shown that [. . .] the determining social relation of production never appears as a moment in the immediate process of production: it appears always as a moment of what Marx called either the "social process of production" or "the process of reproduction" [. . .]; therefore, the process of reproduction appears in the form $P \rightarrow X \rightarrow P$, in which [P is the immediate production — WvB and PG] X is the "instance" charged to accomplish the determining moment of the social production: the re-grouping of the direct producers' (Rey 1971: 160–1; our translation).

18 See Rey (1971): 450f.; as long as new economic developments (the impact of the European trade and the production of new commodities by the African communities) reinforced the old circulation patterns of the producers between the local communities, the lineage mode of production was still to be considered as dominant; in the area Rey studied, this phase continued until the second decade of this century. But about 1930, after the violent interventions by the colonial state, the impact of the money economy created new patterns in the circulation of the producers which satisfied the capitalist demand for wage-labourers. Only then the capitalist mode of production had become dominant.

19 Another problem, related to the operationalization of the notion of mode of production in anthropological fieldwork, is the issue of the unit of study which has haunted so many generations of anthropologists. Does the application of a concept such as mode of production imply a specific delimitation of the unit of study? An interesting attempt to deduce the proper unit of study from the specific characteristics of the 'domestic' (= 'lineage') mode of production is to be found in Meillassoux's use of the notion of 'matrimonial area' (1975: 73). In his view one of the characteristics of the 'domestic' community is that the relations of (biological) reproduction always have to link several communities and thus, create a wider social network than the relations of production (which demand relatively simple forms of co-operation, mostly restricted to one community).Therefore, a meaning-

ful unit of study in such a setting would be the 'matrimonial area' — i.e. the conglomerate of communities linked by the necessities of (biological) reproduction which form the basis to the widest forms of co-operation. An almost insurmountable problem seems to be, however, that, honeycomb-fashion, the matrimonial areas around individual households, or villages, seem partly to overlap and to shift from one household or village to the next, so that ultimately they do not appear as bounded socio-geographical units clearly demarcated in the landscape, but constitute statistical aggregates, in other words analytical constructs without immediate roots in observable reality. See chapter 6 for further discussion of the issue of the unit of study in a somewhat different context.

20 See Meillassoux (1964): ch. 5, notably p. 160 f.: 'The biological family[. . .] is replaced by *functional* families whose members are associated by economic obligations rather than by ties of consanguinity' [our italics — WvB and PG]. Cf. also Meillassoux (1975): 93, for a more general discussion of the topic of the necessity in the domestic patterns of organization to have the producers circulate between the units of production. As noted above (p. 249), Rey considers the 're-grouping' of the direct producers as a crucial moment in the reproduction of all modes of production.

21 Cf. Geschiere (1981); Vansina (1980); van Binsbergen (1977b), 1982 and n.d., a); and in fact virtually the whole of Zambian rural ethnography as discussed by van Binsbergen, ch. 6 above.

22 In French: 'le lien de consanguinité se transforme [. . .] en une filiation sociale' (Meillassoux 1964: 168). Further analysis is required on this point, not only in view of specific authority relations in the ethnography of the Guro, but also in the light of the very extensive discussion, in general kinship anthropology since about 1960, on 'descent and filiation', and the social functioning, and social manipulation, of genealogical and/or biological links between people.

23 Cf. Terray's warning that the somewhat trendy use of the notion of reproduction may lead to forms of analysis in which the necessities of the reproduction of the system are constantly invoked as the ultimate explanation to any relation or process, in a way which strongly reminds one of functionalist teleology (1979a): 35–6. See also Rey (1971): 242–3; there, Rey does refer, albeit very briefly, to a tension between the demographic function of the circulation of men and women in the 'lineage mode of production' and the power-politics of the elders controlling this circulation.

24 Cf. Sartre (1960): 60.

25 See Rey (1971): 48; cf. also Rey's tendency to refer to modes of production as if these were historical actors. Cf., for example Rey (1971): 459–60, where capitalism is supposed to 'create a transitional mode of production'; or Rey (1976): 55, where 'capitalism' substitutes itself to feudalism and a peasant mode of production 'offers resistance'. Such formulations make it relevant indeed, to raise the question of the relationship between the conscious strategies of the actors and

interest-groups involved on the one hand and the ultimate impact of a mode of production on the other.

26 See Rey's own criticisms of his earlier works in the epilogue to his *Les Alliances de classes* (1973: 217f.), where he stresses that closer attention should be paid to the realities of class-struggle.

27 Rey seems to suggest that in his research area at least some of the colonial administrators more or less understood the real consequences of the transformations of the old relations (for example the monetarization of the bride-'price') for the labour question (see 1971: 368, 416, 513). However, Rey's analysis remains rather vague on this point. One could suspect that here, Rey's interpretation of the motivations behind the interventions of the administrators is heavily influenced by his own views in retrospect on the real mechanisms behind the developments.

28 Of course there are many more examples in Africa of how a conscious class alliance between a local aristocracy and colonial powers directly influenced modern political developments; cf. for instance Mamdani (1976) on the development of class relations in Buganda.

29 There are of course exceptions. See for instance Konings (n.d.), who used the concept of class while doing research in a specific context of manifest, bureaucratically-organized, and more or less violently imposed capitalist relations of production in the countryside of modern Ghana.

30 Cf., e.g., Rey's extremely global analysis of the development of national politics and its effects on the local relationships and the power-balance between elders and juniors in his research area (1971: 481, 509, 513).

31 Cf. Bailey's dictum that he distrusts any explanation of social processes which is not formulated in terms of individual actions (1969). On the influence of this 'transactionalist' approach in Dutch anthropology, see chapter 1 above. For a critique of methodological individualism as applied to capitalist encroachment in Zambia, see van Binsbergen (1977a).

32 See van Binsbergen 1977a; van Binsbergen & Meilink 1978; Gerold-Scheepers & van Binsbergen 1978; and references cited there.

33 See van Binsbergen 1975, 1981, and n.d., a. The ethnographic present refers to the years 1973–4, when van Binsbergen lived at the Kahare *lukena*.

34 Domestic slavery effectively disappeared in this area only about 1930, and before that time it was customary for women of the royal family to marry slaves so that their offspring would swell the ranks of the royal village without rival residential claims being made upon them from their paternal side. This however is a point not of ethnography but of history; see van Binsbergen n.d., a.

35 Dealing here with the ethnographic present, we cannot discuss the dynamics of state formation in Zambia which, as a more or less autonomous datum, led to the special status of chiefs in western Zambia (cf. Mulford 1967; Caplan 1970; Hall 1968; Ranger 1968; chapter 6 above, and Binsbergen n.d., a; Prins 1980; Mainga 1973).

36 A useful account of these chiefly rights in western Zambia, although

largely concerned with the case of the Lozi of the Zambezi flood-plain, is Gluckman (1968).
37 Consulted by van Binsbergen in 1978 on a field-trip financed by the African Studies Centre, Leiden; for a detailed account, see van Binsbergen (n.d., a).
38 We continue, in this section, to concentrate on religion, although the problem of ideology is much wider than that, and includes, e.g., varieties of class consciousness, often appearing in a religious form. In this book, a non-religious aspect of ideological analysis, ethnicity, is treated in chapter 6.
39 We have Marx's word for it that this is even a relatively simple exercise: 'It is, in reality, much easier to discover by analysis the earthly core of the misty creations of religion, than, conversely, it is to develop from the actual relations of life the corresponding celestial forms of those relations' (1973: 372–3, as quoted approvingly by Godelier 1977: 4). Unfortunately, our task is made rather more difficult by the fact that religion is not a self-evident category in social analysis. Nor can religion (and this point is made repeatedly by Godelier: see 1978a, 1978b) always be neatly dissected from the processes of material production and reproduction in a social formation: it often forms a part of them (as stressed by Godelier — an aspect we would term 'ideological reproduction'), and sometimes generates them (under conditions we would describe as *'sui generis'*).
40 Our only excuse for not going into these practical political problems is the fact that others have already discussed them at length; see Copans 1975; Amselle 1979; Editorial 1979.

References

Amselle, J. L. (ed.) (1979), *Le Sauvage à la mode*, Paris: Le Sycamore.
Augé, M. (1975), *Théorie des pouvoirs et idéologie: Etude de cas en Côte d'Ivoire*, Paris: Hermann.
Bailey, F. G. (1969), *Stratagems and Spoils*, Oxford: Blackwell.
Baré, J. F. (1977), *Pouvoir des vivants, langage des morts: Idéologiques sakalave*, Paris: Maspero.
van Binsbergen, W. M. J. (1970), 'Verwantschap en territorialiteit in de sociale structuur van het bergland van Noordwest Tunesië', doctoraal scriptie, University of Amsterdam.
van Binsbergen, W. M. J. (1971), 'Religie en Samenleving: Een studie van het bergland van Noordwest Tunesië', doctoraal scriptie, University of Amsterdam.
van Binsbergen, W. M. J. (1975), 'Labour migration and the generation conflict: Social change in Western Zambia', paper read at 34th Annual Meeting, Society for Applied Anthropology, Amsterdam.
van Binsbergen, W. M. J. (1977a), 'Occam, Francis Bacon, and the transformation of Zambian society', *Cultures et développement*, 9: 489–520.

van Binsbergen, W. M. J. (1977b), 'Law in the context of Nkoya society', in Roberts (1977): 39–68.

van Binsbergen, W. M. J. (1980), 'Popular and formal Islam, and supra-local relations', *Middle Eastern Studies*, 16: 71–91.

van Binsbergen, W. M. J. (1981), *Religious Change in Zambia*, London: Kegan Paul International.

van Binsbergen, W. M. J. (1983), 'Rural communities in the Central African context', in *Les Communautés rurales: Receuil Jean Bodin*, no. 24, vol. 40, pp. 185–95.

van Binsbergen, W. M. J. (n.d., a) *Ritual, Class and Urban-Rural Relations: The Nkoya of Zambia*.

van Binsbergen, W. M. J. (n.d., b), *Shrines and Ecstatic Ritual in the Social Structure of Northwestern Tunisia*.

van Binsbergen, W. M. J. (n.d., c), 'The cult of saints in north-western Tunisia: An analysis of contemporary pilgrimage structures', in Gellner & Wolf (in press).

van Binsbergen, W. M. J. & Meilink, H. A. (eds) (1978), *Migration and the Transformation of Modern African Society: African Perspectives 1978/1*, Leiden: African Studies Centre.

van Binsbergen, W. M. J. & Schoffeleers, J. M. (eds) (in press, a), *Theoretical Explorations in African Religion*, London: Kegan Paul International.

van Binsbergen, W. M. J. & Schoffeleers, J. M. (in press, b), 'Theoretical explorations in African religion: Introduction', in van Binsbergen & Schoffeleers (in press, a).

Bloch, M. (ed.) (1975), *Marxist Analyses and Social Anthropology*, London: Malaby Press.

Bonte, P. (1975), 'Cattle of God: an attempt at a Marxist analysis of the religion of East African herdsmen', *Social Compass*, 22, 3–4: 381–400.

Bonte, P. (1977), 'Non-stratified social formations among pastoral nomads', in Friedman & Rowlands (1977): 173–200.

Bonte, P. (1981), 'Marxist theory and anthropological analysis: The study of nomadic pastoralist societies', in Kahn & Llobera (1981): 22–57.

Bourdieu, P. (1977), *Outline of a Theory of Practice*, Cambridge University Press.

Bourdieu, P. (1979), 'Symbolic power', *Critique of Anthropology*, 13–14: 77–85.

Buijtenhuijs, R. & Geschiere, P. (eds) (1978), *Social Stratification and Class Formation, African Perspectives 1978/2*, Leiden: African Studies Centre.

Caplan, G. L. (1970), *The Elites of Barotseland, 1878–1969*, London: Hurst.

Clammer, J. (ed.) (1978), *The New Economic Anthropology*, London: Macmillan.

Copans, J. (ed.) (1975), *Anthropologie et impérialisme*, Paris: Maspero.

Cresswell, R. & Godelier, M. (eds) (1976), *Outils d'enquête et d'analyse anthropologiques*, Paris: Maspero.

Davis, J. (1977), *People of the Mediterranean*, London: Routledge & Kegan Paul.

Dupré, G. & Rey, P.-P. (1973), 'Reflections on the pertinence of a theory of exchange', *Economy and Society*, 2: 131–63.
Editorial (1979), *Critique of Anthropology*, 13, 4: 235.
Engels, F. (1967), *The German Revolutions (The Peasant War in Germany)* (1850), Chicago University Press.
Epstein, A. L. (ed.), *The Craft of Social Anthropology*, London: Tavistock.
Fortes, M. (1953), 'The structure of unilineal descent groups', *American Anthropologist*, 55: 17–41.
Friedman, J. & Rowlands, M. (eds) (1977), *The Evolution of Social Systems*, London: Duckworth.
Gellner, E. & Wolf, E. (eds) (in press), *Religions around the Mediter-ranean*, The Hague/Paris: Mouton.
Gerold-Scheepers, T. J. F. A. & van Binsbergen, W. M. J. (1978), 'Marxist and non-Marxist approaches to migration in Africa', in van Binsbergen & Meilink (1978): 21–35.
Geschiere, P. (1969), 'Contractuele relaties in de landbouw en de veeteelt in Ouled Moussa (Noordwest Tunesië)', doctoraal-scriptie, Free University, Amsterdam.
Geschiere, P. (1978), 'The articulation of different modes of production: Old and new inequalities in Maka villages (Southeast Cameroon)' in Buijtenhuijs & Geschiere (1978): 45–69.
Geschiere, P. (1981), 'L'agriculture de subsistance, l'autonomie de la femme et l'autorité des aînés chez les Maka (Cameroun)', paper for International Colloquium of Association Française des Anthropologistes, Sèvres, November 1981 (*JABTA* 1982: 30–321).
Geschiere, P. (1982), *Village Communities and the State*, London: Kegan Paul International.
Geschiere, P. (in press, a), 'European planters, African peasants and the colonial state, alternatives in the 'mise en valeur' of Makaland during the interbellum', *African Economic History*, in press (papers of SOAS workshop 'Business Empires in West Central Africa', London, May 1982).
Geschiere, P. (in press, b), 'Bruidsprijzen en kapitalistische expansie bij de Maka, marxistische theorieën en de praktijk van antropologisch veldwerk', *Te Elfder Ure*, 33.
Gluckman, M. (1958), *Analysis of a Social Situation in Modern Zululand*, Manchester University Press for Rhodes-Livingstone Institute, Rhodes-Livingstone Paper no. 28.
Gluckman, M. (1968), *Essays on Lozi Land and Royal Property*, Rhodes-Livingstone Papers no. 10, Manchester University Press, reprint of 1953 ed.
Godelier, M. (1973), *Horizon, trajets Marxistes en anthropologie*, Paris: Maspero.
Godelier, M. (1975), 'Towards a Marxist anthropology of religion, *Dialectical Anthropology*, 1, 1: 81–5.
Godelier, M. (1977), 'Economy and religion: An evolutionary optical illusion', in Friedman & Rowlands (1977): 3–11.
Godelier, M. (1978a), 'Infrastructures, societies and history', *Current*

Anthropology, 19, 4: 763–71.

Godelier, M. (1978b), 'La part du réel, essai sur l'idéologique', *L'Homme*, 18, 3–4: 155–88.

Godelier, M. (1979), 'The appropriation of nature', *Critique of Anthropology*, 13–14: 17–29.

Godelier, M. (1982), *La Production des grands hommes*, Paris: Fayard.

Hall, R. (1968), *Zambia*, London: Pall Mall Press.

Harris, M. (1980), *Cultural Materialism: The Struggle for a Science of Culture*, New York: Random House.

Houtart, F. (1980), *Religion et modes de production précapitalistes*, Brussels: Editions de l'Université de Bruxelles.

Houtart, F. & Lemercinier, G. (1977), 'Religion et mode de production tributaire', *Social Compass*, 24, 2–3: 157–70.

Houtart, F. & Lemercinier, G. (1979), 'Religion et mode de production lignager', *Social Compass*, 26, 4: 403–16.

Kahn, J. S. & Llobera, J. R. (eds) (1981), *The Anthropology of Precapitalist Societies*, London: Macmillan.

van der Klei, J. M. (1971), 'De relatie specialist/klant, bezien binnen het normatieve raamwerk van sociale verhoudingen en zijn organizatie in 1969 (Noordwest Tunesië)', doctoraal-scriptie, University of Amsterdam.

Konings, P. J. J. (n.d.), *State and Rural Class Formation in Ghana*, in press, London/Boston: Kegan Paul International.

Kuper, A. (1982a), *Wives for Cattle: Bridewealth and Marriage in Southern Africa*, London: Routledge & Kegan Paul.

Kuper, A. (1982b), 'Lineage theory: A critical retrospect', *Annual Review of Anthropology for 1982*.

Mainga, M. (1973), *Bulozi under the Luyana Kings*, London: Longman.

Mamdani, M. (1976), *Politics and Class Formation in Uganda*, New York: Monthly Review Press.

Marx, K. (1973), *Capital*, New York: Monthly Review Press.

Marx, K. & Engels, F. (1975), *On Religion*, Moscow: Progress Publishers.

Meillassoux, C. (1960), 'Essai d'interprétation du phénomène économique dans les sociétés traditionelles d'autosubsistance', *Cahiers d'Etudes Africaines*, 1: 38–67.

Meillassoux, C. (1964), *Anthropologie économique des Gouro de Cote d'Ivoire*, Paris/The Hague: Mouton.

Meillassoux, C. (1975), *Femmes, greniers et capitaux*, Paris: Maspero.

Meillassoux, C. (1977), *Terrains et théories*, Paris: Anthropos.

Mulford, D. C. (1967), *Zambia: The Politics of Independence*, Oxford University Press.

Prins, G. (1980), *The Hidden Hippopotamus*, Cambridge University Press.

Ranger, T. O. (1968), 'Nationality and nationalism: The case of Barotseland', *Journal of the Historical Society of Nigeria*, 4, 2: 227–46.

Ranger, T. O. (1978), 'Growing from the roots: Reflexions on peasant studies in Central and Southern Africa', *Journal of Southern African Studies*, 5: 99–133.

Rey, P.-P. (1971), *Colonialisme, néo-colonialisme et transition au capitalisme*, Paris: Maspero.

Rey, P.-P. (1973), *Les Alliances de classes*, Paris: Maspero.

Rey P.-P. (1979), 'Class contradiction in lineage societies', *Critique of Anthropology*, 3: 27–79.

Rey, P.-P. (1976), *Capitalisme négrier: La marche des paysans vers le prolétariat*, (together with E. Le Bris and M. Samuel), Paris: Maspero.

Rey, P.-P. (1979), 'Class contradiction in lineage Societies', *Critique of Anthropology*, 13–14; 41–61.

Roberts, S. A. (ed.) (1977), *Law and the Family in Africa*, The Hague/Paris: Mouton.

Sahlins, M. (1972), *Stone Age Economics*, Chicago: Aldine.

Satre, J.-P. (1960), *Critique de la raison dialectique*, Paris: Gallimard.

Schoffeleers, J. M. (1978), 'A martyr cult as reflection on changes in production: The case of the lower Shire Valley, 1590–1622 A.D.', in Buijtenhuijs & Geschiere (1978): 19–35.

Schoffeleers, J. M. (ed.) (1979), *Guardians of the Land*, Gwelo: Mambo Press.

Seddon, D. (1978), 'Economic anthropology or political economy? (II): Approaches to the analysis of pre-capitalist formations in the Maghreb', in Clammer (1978): 61–110.

Seddon, D. (1981), *Moroccan Peasants: A Century of Change in the Eastern Rif, 1870–1970*, Folkestone: Dawson.

Stokes, E. (1966), 'Barotseland: The survival of an African state', in Stokes & Brown (1966): 261–301.

Stokes, E. & Brown, R. (eds) (1966), *The Zambesian Past*, Manchester University Press.

Terray, E. (1969), *Le Marxisme devant les sociétés 'primitives'*, Paris: Maspero.

Terray, E. (1974), 'Long-distance exchange and the formation of the state: The case of the Abron Kingdom of Gyaman', *Economy and Society*, 3: 315–45.

Terray, E. (1975), 'Classes and class consciousness in the Abron kingdom of Gyaman', in Bloch (1975): 85–137.

Terray, E. (1979a), 'On exploitation, elements of an autocritique', *Critique of Anthropology*, 13–14: 29–41.

Terray, E. (1979b), 'Un mouvement de reforme religieuse dans le royaume abron précolonial: Le culte de Sakrobundi', *Cahiers d'Études africaines*, 19, 73–6: 143–76.

Turner, V. W. (1957), *Schism and Continuity in an African Society*, Manchester University Press for Rhodes-Livingstone Institute.

Vansina, J. (1980), 'Lignage, idéologie et histoire en Afrique équatoriale', *Enquêtes et documents d'histoire africaine*, 4: 133–55.

van Velsen, J. (1967), 'The extended case method and situational analysis', in Epstein (1967): 129–49.

Werbner, R. . (ed.) (1977), *Regional Cults*, New York: Academic press.

Chapter 8

Analytic tools, intellectual weapons: The discussion among French Marxist anthropologists about the identification of modes of production in Africa*

Reini Raatgever

Introduction

In the preceding chapters, the ideas of prominent French Marxist anthropologists have been used to analyse empirical findings, mainly data from anthropological field-work. The present chapter will be more theoretical in scope. Resuming the line of the argument set forth in chapter 1, I intend to trace here how the discussion among French Marxist anthropologists has in fact developed. The concept of 'mode of production' has remained a central theme in this discussion. The anthropologists involved still appear to hold clearly different views as to how old, pre-capitalist modes of production should be identified and analysed. Their different views on this point, moreover, are decisive for other aspects of their theoretical thinking, and for the limitations thereof.

In chapter 1, the leading representatives of the line of thought on which we concentrate in this book were named: anthropologists such as Maurice Godelier, Claude Meillassoux, Pierre-Philippe Rey and Jean Copans; in addition such historians as Cathérine Coquery-Vidrovitch and Jean Suret-Canale can be cited. Yet it would be going too far to consider these diverse figures as though they belonged to a single school of thought. They disagree too much. However, they all address themselves to a common problematic. They are concerned above all with the potential of historical materialism for concrete analysis, rather than with

* The specialist nature of this theoretical article does not allow for the quotation of English translations of Marx's and Engels's work. Instead titles of English translations have been added in the References.

290

wrangling over tenets and dogma. In this respect they have evidently been influenced by their anthropological background. In anthropology, primary importance has always been attached to research and field-work. Anthropologists do not as a rule penetrate deeply into the epistemological, philosophical or methodological backrounds of the theories which they pursue — and in most cases they are poorly equipped to do so.

Another feature which these anthropologists and historians have in common (see chapter 1), is the influence of Louis Althusser. Here, I hope to make it clear that the essential disagreements between the French Marxist anthropologists, when applying the concept of 'mode of production', reflect difficulties inherent in the application of Althusser's premises. Their work has to be considered in the light of Althusser's thought, and of the renewal which has taken place in Marxist thought in general since de-Stalinisation in 1956. The most important characteristic of this renewal, and of Althusser's interpretations of theory, was that rigid determinism (economism) was abandoned. This made a historical-materialist approach possible in anthropology; but in its turn the marked structuralist slant of Althusser's thought has had a profound influence on Marxist anthropologists.

For a review of the discussion among French anthropologists as to how to apply the concept of 'mode of production', it is therefore necessary to consider the theoretical position of Althusser and his followers. Comment upon, and criticism of, Althusser's position within the overall field of Marxist theory, however, falls beyond the scope of this essay;[1] instead, we shall confine ourselves to the problems of field-work and of the presentation of findings, in a bid to arrive at a new scientific practice in anthropology.

A variety of questions have informed the work of the anthropologists we are dealing with — and this variety is reflected in the ways in which they have chosen to manipulate the concept of 'mode of production'. For example, Rey's principal aim is to clarify contemporary developments in the Third World, whereas Godelier is more concerned with groups which have maintained considerable isolation from the world at large. None the less they both confront the same issues: how to describe the essence of pre-capitalist societies, and how to establish a temporal sequence of the successive phases in their development. Historical materialists used to distinguish, in fairly dogmatic fashion, a limited number of fundamental types of modes of production: primitive communism, slavery, feudalism, capitalism and socialism. Dissatisfaction with this approach raised once again the question of how exactly a mode of production should be identified.[2] A related fundamental question was: what criteria should be used in order to distinguish between modes of production?

These questions are also of immediate relevance if we are to assess the analytical potential of the notion of articulation (or linkage) of modes of production — the theme of this volume. The objective behind our study of the concept of mode of production has been to acquire a better understanding of the present-day situation, in which capitalism is steadily penetrating pre-capitalist systems. The French anthropologists emphasize that the laws of capitalism on their own are incapable of explaining what is happening in this respect; such penetration can scarcely be viewed as a fulfilment of universal destiny. The capitalist system enters into specific relations with the system it encounters in a particular locality; the form which ultimately emerges represents a specific, complex union of the pre-existing systems, both the capitalist and the non-capitalist one. And this new form cannot always be described as being transitional towards capitalism in its North Atlantic trappings. The concept of an 'articulation of modes of production' has been introduced in order to denote a specific union between two or more modes of production within a more or less stable social formation.

What is the theoretical status of such a coupling mechanism? There is a danger of the concept of 'articulation of modes of production' being used in the purely descriptive sense, to denote the equivalent of 'the co-occurrence of modes of production A and B'. The growing popularity of the concept of articulation may well depend upon just such a superficial interpretation.[3] If we are to consider more deeply the concept of articulation, we ought to address ourselves to the problem of the definition and identification of modes of production — the subject of this chapter.

Apart from these introductory remarks, this chapter consists of five sections. The first one deals with the relation between anthropology and historical materialism; here I indicate the significance of Althusser's work in this context, and his initiatives towards a general theory of modes of production; the final part of this section deals with the general premises on which Godelier bases his analysis of pre-capitalist modes of production. The next section describes the attempts by three anthropologists — Meillassoux, Terray and Rey — to apply the fundamental points of Althusser's theory to various African societies. This leads, in the next section, to a review of developments and shifts of opinion in the discussion concerning the mode of production of ancient African farming communities; in this connection we shall specifically concentrate on the application of such essential concepts as 'exploitation' and 'class'. This review is again organized around the work of Terray, Meillassoux and Rey. The penultimate section contains an evaluation of this discussion. Although for the moment the discussion appears to have abated, it has not yet reached an end. The tentative conclusions offered in the final section are therefore more in the nature of suggestions as to the kinds of empirical research that now appears to be called for — if we are to emerge from the quagmire of an excessively academic exchange of views.

Historical materialism and the theory of modes of production

Anthropology and historical materialism

Historical materialism takes as its point of departure the idea that the way in which a community provides for its material needs constitutes the basis for the development of social, political and ideological forms. The history of these forms can therefore be broken into stages defined by successive systems of production and distribution. The underlying principles determining this temporal sequence are inherent in the laws which govern production and distribution, and by the mechanisms which promote the growth or dissolution of specific systems of production and distribution. Karl Marx has succinctly presented the premises which provided a guideline for his researches in the preface to *Zur Kritik der politischen Oekonomie* (1859) and in the Introduction to the *Grundrisse der Kritik der politischen Oekonomie* (1858). Friedrich Engels has done the same in his *Anti-Düring* (1879) and *Ludwig Feuerbach* (1888).

The further development of historical materialism has been characterized by a number of profound controversies about the interpretation of Marx's and Engels's ideas. Thus Bernstein's revisionism, the economism of the Second International, and Lukács's critical Marxism became the subjects of heated debate.

Yet French Marxist anthropologists were not directly inspired by these discussions taking place within the confines of historical materialism. Their interest in historical-materialist theory was, rather, aroused by the concrete political and economic problems they were dealing with: shifts in alliances between industrial countries and the Third World in the wake of decolonization, leading on to sharper opposition between these parts of the world. These anthropologists approached the conceptual framework of historical materialism with their own intellectual goals in mind. As it was, they were strongly influenced by such anthropological theories as structuralism, functionalism and symbolic anthropology.

Althusser

These anthropologists let themselves be inspired by the interpretation of historical materialism proposed by Louis Althusser, philosopher and member of the French Communist party. Althusser's work is an attempt to break with the dogmatism of official Marxist theory. Under the influence of Stalinism, this theory had grown into a closed system which did not allow for theoretical revision or growth. Althusser's contribution to the revival of theorizing must be considered in the light of significant political realignments within the communist world: the Twentieth Congress of the Communist Party of the Soviet Union, which initiated de-Stalinisation; the breach between China and the USSR; and the decision of the French Communist Party in 1966 to stimulate theoretical discussion within party ranks — a decision which kindled hopes among leftist intellectuals, only to subside in recent years. Althusser himself has constantly emphasized that theories are not ladders up in the air but they must be evaluated in their specific political context (1974: 10).

By reinterpreting Marx's major works, it was Althusser's ambition to lay the foundation for a historical materialism that would be both scientific and creative. In so doing he particularly meant to stress the relative independence of theory, thereby distancing himself not only from Stalinists but also from radical elements who exalted spontaneous, direct action. Despite the massive and severe criticism which has been levelled at his work — and including autocriticism — Althusser has had a pronounced influence on the development of thought within various scientific disciplines, including political theory, the theory of culture, literary analysis, psychology and social geography (see Karsz 1974).

In France the manner in which historical materialism should find expression in anthropology became the subject of great controversy. Most French anthropologists took great exception to the view, sketched above, of pre-capitalist communities in which human history is reduced to five invariable stages necessarily succeeding each other. In maintaining this interpretation of history, canonized by Stalin, the primary goal of scientific research was no longer an increased understanding of events but rather to find some way in which to force new facts to fit into an existing framework (see, e.g., Godelier 1973a: 15). On the other hand a number of anthropologists also opposed attempts to derive a new 'Marxist anthropology' from the fragmentary comments on pre-capitalist systems as left by Marx (the *Formen* from *Grundrisse* and notes about Morgan's *Ancient Society*).[4]

Once the orthodox scheme as a rigid evolutionary system is set aside, we run the risk that an ever-increasing number of historical stages will be distinguished, perhaps just as many as there are different historical communities. Any comparison of the various forms and of their development would then be impossible. The heuristic value of the concept of mode of production would approach zero. Recognizing this risk, the French anthropologists turned back to the source: they tried to improve their understanding of Marx's methods by studying his most mature work, the analysis of capitalism in *Capital*.

In *Pour Marx* (Althusser 1965) and *Lire 'Le Capital'* (Althusser and Balibar 1968), Althusser laid the basis for his own 'reading' of Marx.[5] He distinguished between the early Marx, still wrestling with philosophic and particularly Hegelian ideas, and the mature Marx who had arrived at the formulation of his personal scientific vision. In Marx's later work (after the epistemological break) Althusser sees a total departure from the idealistic dialectic of Hegel. Althusser attempts to reconstruct Marx's scientific outlook by making explicit the logic underlying *Capital*; and he presents this as science: as a system of thought which has general validity.

Contrary to the position held among others by Lukács and Korsch, for Althusser historical materialism is not just a critique of extant bourgeois social science; it is an independent scientific system with its own object and its own method. In his first books Althusser draws a sharp distinction between scientific knowledge and consciousness (ideology). Scientific knowledge does not constitute a reflection of reality but is rather a reconstruction of reality by means of a process of scientific labour, as a consequence of which it achieves a comparative degree of independence vis-à-vis reality (see Althusser 1965). Given this viewpoint, we can understand why Althusser and Balibar made an attempt to generalize the conceptual framework of *Capital*, forging it into a basis for the analysis of all social systems. In so doing they have stimulated many other scholars to apply historical materialism to new areas of scientific study.

The construction of a general theory of modes of production

Mode of production is a concept which occupies a central place in the Marxist interpretation of history. There exist, however, widely divergent explications of this concept. In *Lire 'Le Capital'* Althusser analyses the epistemological backgrounds of this concept, its concrete elaborations and its range. For him it remains a theoretical concept, which means that it cannot be defined in terms that are directly or indirectly verifiable; rather it brings phenomena into relation with each other, in a theoretical fashion. On the other hand, as a theoretical concept its relation to reality is very different from a Weberian ideal type. The Althusserian theoretical concept of mode of production brings out, rather than abstracts, the fundamental inter-relationships that constitute reality.

Althusser sees society as a complex whole consisting of three spheres: the economic, the political, and the ideological. Historical materialism is the theory of the history of modes of production (social forms). In this theory the concept of mode of production serves to denote the tightly interconnected combination of the three spheres: the economic as base, the political and ideological as superstructure. The superstructural aspects are relatively autonomous and have their own history but remain ultimately a function of the economic base. According to Althusser, the spheres are not layers or levels — a notion readily prompted by the metaphor of base and superstructure — but instead they constitute fields within which certain elements are bound to one another through the mechanics of specific laws.[6] He defines the connections in terms of structural causality.[7] Within the totality of the three spheres, one is always dominant, or, putting it differently, the operation of the whole is subordinate to the specific laws of the

296

dominant sphere. In the final analysis, however, it is the economic base that determines which sphere is able to occupy the dominant position. At this structural level one can thus speak of layers or levels. Within every society there exists a certain hierarchy of spheres. It is primarily confusion between the causal and the structural level, between the level which determines and the level which dominates, that has led to many errors in the interpretation of the concept of mode of production. Economic determinism is the best known example of such a misunderstanding, but we encounter similar kinds of muddled thinking in the works of many an anthropologist (see Godelier 1973).

Marx concentrated his analysis on the capitalist mode of production. He established that to an increasing degree the economic laws of capitalism had come to govern all social relations. The economic élite had acquired an ever-greater role in the leadership of society as a whole. This meant that in bourgeois society the economic sphere had achieved dominance. Oppositions in the field of production were therefore at the same time the most significant oppositions within the entire structure, not only theoretically but also in people's consciousness. Therefore, in his struggle against bourgeois society, Marx devoted himself to the study of the political economy of capitalism: the productive forces and relations of production making up that system, the history of its emergence and the signs of its dissolution.

Whereas the dominance of the economic sphere may be typical of capitalism, the determinant role of the economic sphere is — for Althusser too — a general fact which obtains in all modes of production. In order to formulate, as Althusser wishes to do, a general theory of history as a series of successive modes of production in the sense of specific articulations between three spheres, it is first necessary to provide a general analysis of the economic sphere. For this purpose Althusser generalizes the concepts of capital, labour and means of production. A short description of how Althusser sets about this generalization has been given in chapter 1. According to Althusser, the following elements are found within any system of social production: labour, object of labour, instrument of labour. Production occurs under certain material conditions and under certain social relations (the relation labourer/non-labourer).[8] The difference between various modes of production lies in different combinations of these elements.

Althusser himself, however, fails to go as far as to analyse the nature of these various combinations; this task was left to Balibar, in *Lire 'Le Capital'* (Althusser and Balibar 1968). Balibar posited that productive forces and relations of production are both combinations of three elements: labourer, non-labourer and instruments of labour. He took productive forces to mean this combination as seen from the perspective of the process of real appropriation (the labourer converts a natural object into a product for use or exchange). We deal with relations of production when we look at the same combination from the viewpoint of property relations (the non-labourer appropriates the labourer's product on the basis of a certain title of possession or ownership).

With their interpretations, Althusser and Balibar proposed to forge the internal logic of *Capital* into a general theory of modes of production. From Marx's treatise on capitalism they attempt to derive a number of elements and to construct possible connections between the elements; with such a construction accomplished, all modes of production could then be analysed. They arrive at the necessary neutral categories (e.g. non-labourer and labourer) by stripping loaded Marxist terms (e.g. capitalist and proletarian) of any specific historical reference. They then present these categories as the poles of a relation, a property relation, for example. Althusser does retain a material component in the form of conditions of production. Balibar, however, reduces even productive forces to a social relation, so that his interpretation — in *Lire 'Le Capital'* at any rate — comes close to a matrix of social relations; later, Balibar has renounced such a position (1974).

The generalization of the Marxist conceptual framework has given rise to considerable discussion and criticism by both those in favour and those against.[9] A recurrent comment is that, by placing such a strong emphasis on connections and elements within structures, one loses sight of the mechanisms which 'animate' the structures and bring about their change.[10] But however interesting and important these further ramifications of the Althusser discussion may be, they fall outside the scope of this chapter. We shall instead address ourselves to the question of how French anthropologists have employed the line of thinking sketched above.

Towards a theory of pre-capitalist modes of production

Within the ranks of French historical-materialist anthropologists, it is Maurice Godelier who makes use of the concept of mode of production in a way that conforms most closely to the insights of Althusser and Balibar. He does not, however, base his theorizing explicitly upon these two writers, but independently develops his own views as to how historical materialism should be incorporated into anthropology. He does this especially in a number of theoretical and methodological studies collected in his *Horizon: Trajets marxistes en anthropologie*.[11] In essence this volume is a plea for a new theoretical approach in anthropology, one which studies social structure as a whole by thoroughly analysing the economic foundations of society. He develops his ideas through critical reflection on current anthropological thought, especially American cultural ecology and French structuralism.

Although Godelier bases his arguments on historical materialism, he rejects any form of economic determinism. This means that he is opposed to tracing the spheres of the social superstructure (ideology, politics, kinship, etc.) back to an economic base. In Godelier's thinking, the relation between base and superstructure remains rather problematic (Godelier 1978a, 1978b). He attacks Althusser for asserting that the economic sphere stipulates (determines) which sphere in the superstructure is dominant. According to Godelier, the dominating structure is that which has the function of organizing production.[12] Within a pre-capitalist society, kinship may have such a function. The kinship organization is the base and superstructure at one and the same time, and thus reaches its dominant position. The task of the anthropologist would then consist of studying why and under which conditions a particular sphere acquires the function of ordering the relations of production, thereby becoming decisive for the reproduction of social relations in their entirety.

It is Godelier's contention that the relation between base and superstructure is not one between superimposed spheres, layers or institutions. Instead it is a functional relation. The determinant role of the economic sphere is then interpreted by Godelier in terms of its pre-eminence within a hierarchy of functions. A mode of production is an entity which comprises productive forces and relations of production, and which is capable of reproducing itself; what is more, such reproduction is the goal towards the achievement of which the productive functions (productive forces) and the management functions (relations of production) are directed. The relation between productive forces and relations of production constitutes a link between two discrete functional structures and not, as Balibar claims, merely two aspects of one and the same thing (two different ways of combining the same elements).

In his later publications, Godelier draws a less sharp distinction between base and superstructure, not only at the level of relations of production, but also in so far as productive forces are concerned. He does this by asserting that ideas and images (ideology) are an integrating component of productive forces — functioning as an '*armature interne*' (internal reinforcement), as a force which organizes the process of labour. In this fashion even magical practices designed to protect the harvest, for example, would have to be considered as part of the productive forces.[13]

However, although Godelier pointedly criticizes the base/superstructure metaphor, he clings to it at the same time. He confuses the economic sphere as a field of specific laws and relations (the domain of causal thinking such as, for example, the concept of determination) with economic institutions.

The concept of function to which Godelier resorts in order to extract himself from his theoretical muddle has more often already been pressed into service as a *deus ex machina*.[14] The teleological causality which thus intrudes into the picture completely ignores the complex interplay, autonomous development and oppositions between various spheres. Functionalism has been adequately criticized (among others by Mills, Gouldner, and Habermas). One wonders what theoretical advance Godelier still hopes to achieve by reanimating this dead horse? He has recently (1979) modified a number of his ideas, but not his interpretation of the central question of the relation between base and superstructure.

Nevertheless Godelier has certainly made a valuable contribution. He has demonstrated that historical-materialist anthropology can be more than a kind of economic anthropology. Precisely because the forms of dominance within pre-capitalist modes of production are so complex, the totality of social relations must be studied, including kinship, religion and ideology.

In search of modes of production in Africa

Discussion really began in earnest among French Marxist anthropologists only when the conceptual framework of historical materialism was applied to field-work data. This empirical orientation has had certain advantages. In the process of doing field-research it became clear which interpretations of the conceptual framework had the most to offer. A disadvantage is .that hardly any attention has been paid to the epistemological side of the various viewpoints involved. Inevitably, theoretical discussions without empirical tests soon turn into rhetorics of great vagueness and generality, while discussions that never rise above empirical data soon deteriorate into eclecticism and confusion.

In the remainder of this chapter we shall examine the contributions by Claude Meillassoux, Emmanuel Terray and Pierre-Philippe Rey. These anthropologists have been selected because they have based their argumentation on field-work carried out in West and Central Africa, and in the process have made use of different versions of the Marxist theoretical framework. In the continuing discussions among French anthropologists they have played a leading part. While working out their own ideas, they have scrutinized and challenged each other's viewpoints.

Meillassoux's deductive construction of the domestic mode of production

Various chapters in this volume have presented Meillassoux's model of the old African village communities. The main outlines of his model were set forth in a 1960 article concerning the interpretation of the economic sphere in African society. It is a theoretical reconstruction of a community based on self-sufficiency. Meillassoux concerns himself primarily with the social relations by virtue of which agriculture takes place. The most significant expression of these relations is the authority exercised by the family elders over those who are younger. The basis of the power of the elders resides in their control of social processes and of women. A younger person can achieve senior rank only once he himself has gained authority over dependants; this becomes possible only through founding a family. To marry a wife, however, he is dependent on the elders: those of his own group and those of his wife's group. This dependence is reinforced by the system of bridewealth which, according to Meillassoux, does not primarily regulate control over women themselves but rather over their offspring.

In the agricultural production of this 'subsistence community' ('*communauté d'auto-subsistance*'), those who are younger work for the elders. The harvest destined for consumption by the group is handed over to the elders for redistribution. There is a sharp distinction between these consumer goods and the prestige goods (or élite goods) which are used for exchange (marital payments and such). The prestige goods circulate exclusively among the elders, who have absolute control over them. Such goods remain outside direct consumption. Meillassoux maintains that these goods have no exchange value. Their value cannot be measured by the counter-prestation (e.g. women). At most, one can speak of their having a social value because the prestige goods are a manifestation of the relation between both parties participating in the exchange. Labour, too, has no value, for payment is an expression of the kinship relation — real or fictive — between those who perform the labour and those for whom the labour is performed.

Next, Meillassoux deals with the consequences of the penetration of trade within such communities. At first new trade products (such as iron, salt and clothing) play a rather peripheral role; later, increasing trade contacts can lead to further division of labour, and to the formation of new social categories such as smiths and merchants. The elders were successful in maintaining their position as long as they were capable of monopolizing the new flow of goods and of keeping them strictly apart from the circulation of consumer goods within their own group; and as long as they could keep members of the new occupational categories from marrying into the local group.

Meillassoux's major empirical work published in 1964 — his monograph about the Guro of the Ivory Coast — is not a direct elaboration of the theoretical groundwork he laid down in 1960. The monograph contains extensive and detailed ethnographic material about the subsistence economy of the Guro and about developments which took place under the influence of long-distance trade, colonization and the transition to a market economy. Meillassoux does not treat the Guro economic system as a special African mode of production alongside, for example, the Asian or the antique mode of production. Nor does he deal with the 'subsistence economy' as simply a preliminary stage of capitalism. Instead he attempts to capture the very singularity of that economic system in a number of distinctive features. Societies like that of the Guro, with their segmented kinship organization, are based, in Meillassoux's view, on exploitation of the land, self-sufficiency, simple technology and the use of manpower as the sole source of energy (1964: 89). There is ample land available for agriculture. The instruments of labour are rudimentary, and their preparation requires little time or expertise. The nets used for the hunt are communal property. Other instruments of labour, such as hoes, axes, knives and traps, are individually owned.

In the Guro economy command over manpower is by far the most important condition for the continuation of agricultural production. Therefore it is control over the producers and their reproduction which assures domination over the entire socio-economic system (Meillassoux 1964: 90). The system of descent and marriage alliances strengthens the elders' control of biological reproduction, and is ultimately a result of this control. Meillassoux connects control of reproduction with kinship (in the sense of real co-operative ties). This is the reason why he later uses the concept of 'domestic mode of production' (1975). Yet he does not posit any specific connection with specific forms of kinship. Thus a vast number of societies can be said to hinge on the domestic mode of production.

Meillassoux contrasts the features of this domestic mode of production with feudalism, in which control of land was decisive, and with capitalism, in which the central control mechanism is ownership of the means of production. For him it is thus the difference in emphasis in the continuous and mutual relation between object of labour, instrument of labour and the producer (seen as a socially organized group) which determines the distinction between modes of production.

Meillassoux confines himself to a theoretical use of the concept of mode of production. In his work the concept indicates a theoretical connection between social phenomena; a mode of production is not something open to direct or indirect quantitative observations.

By consequence Meillassoux's theoretical work and his empirical study remain disconnected. He even reproaches Godelier for discussing both works (1960 and 1964) in the same critique.[15] The major question is therefore how long Meillassoux will be able to uphold his global theoretical pronouncements in the light of his empirical findings which would surely suggest more specific and detailed theoretical choices.[16]

Terray's empirical identification of modes of production

The importance of the impulse provided by Meillassoux becomes obvious once we compare his work on the Guro with Emmanuel Terray's doctoral dissertation (Paris, 1966) on a neighbouring people, the Dida (1969a). In his dissertation on the social organization on the Dida, Terray concerns himself with the social sphere only, without any reference to systems of production. Too little information about production is provided to enable us to assess whether the Dida have a domestic mode of production resembling the one defined by Meillassoux. Little or nothing is reported, for example on the system of property rights and changes therein. The differences which Terray notes between the Guro and the Dida — such as the central significance of inheritance among the Dida, rather than bridewealth — are therefore left without explanation.

In a later publication — *Le Marxisme devant les sociétés 'primitives'* (1969b) — Terray deals with Meillassoux's work on the Guro. He acclaims it as the first serious attempt to apply the historical-materialist conceptual framework within anthropology. Meillassoux, however, is said to have limited himself too narrowly to a description of economic processes as though every group with the same economic characteristics also employed the same mode of production. To Terray's mind this does not do justice to the enormous diversity of social and ideological relationships which can then no longer be explained in terms of a difference in modes of production. The analysis of a mode of production cannot be identical to a general description of the economic sphere. Following in Althusser's footsteps Terray defines a mode of production as a system which consists of three spheres: an economic base, a political-juridical and an ideological superstructure (1969b). The economic base is made up of a system of productive forces and relations of production. For Terray, as for Balibar, the productive forces and the relations of production represent two aspects of the same thing. Both concepts indicate a relation between labour, instruments of labour (or means of production) and objects of labour. With the term productive forces one refers to technical relations in the form of an appropriation from nature by man. The relations of production denote social relationships within production in the form of the process of appropriation of what is produced. In the production sphere, the control structures of various forms of co-operation are the concretization of relations of production. Distribution structures are determined by relations of production. In addition, relations of production are represented in the political and ideological spheres.

How then does Terray propose to apply these historical-materialist views to an empirical study? To begin with, we should establish the number of modes of production within a particular society (or, in Terray's terms, a social formation).[17]

As his point of departure, Terray adopts Marx's proposition that the means of production constitutes a measuring-scale for the development of human labour (e.g., see Marx 1867 (1975): 341f.). In view of the varying nature of means of production, a hypothesis must first be formulated concerning which modes of production the researcher expects to encounter. Next, in correspondence with the various means of production which have been distinguished, different relations of production must be reconstructed on the basis of a study of forms of co-operation and of the structures of control and management belonging to these forms. In the last analysis, relations of production determine the specific character of the mode of production. This character lies in the connection between forces of production (indexed according to the nature of the means of production) and relations of production (indexed by forms of co-operation). This forms the economic basis of a mode of production. These relations also find expression in the political and ideological spheres. A mode of production thus does not consist merely of relations of production and productive forces, but also of ideological and political forms which correspond with the relations of production. After completing this analytical exercise for one particular mode of production, we have to establish the number of modes of production within one social formation.

Using this scheme, Terray in his analysis of Meillassoux's texts arrives at the identification of two modes of production among the Guro. The first is based on 'complex co-operation' within the 'tribe–village-system', with collective possession of the means of production and an egalitarian distribution of production; here the most important branch of production is hunting with a net. The second mode of production depends on 'simple co-operation' within the system of descent groups (*système lignager*). Here collective possession of the means of production is regulated by the elders, and the re-distribution of production is also arranged by them; branches of this mode of production are agriculture, fishing, gathering, animal husbandry, and trapping.

Among the Guro the first mode of production is dominant in ideology, while the second is dominant in politics. On this basis Terray concludes that in the Guro case at hand a hybrid dominance (*dominance croisée*) exists.[18] Although Terray regards the nature of the relations of production to be characteristic of the mode of production as a whole, his analysis virtually amounts to a description of the Guro modes of production from the sphere of productive forces. This is a consequence of his choosing to index relations of production in terms of forms of co-operation: in historical materialism, forms of co-operation are counted among productive forces.

Terray has been severely criticized on this point, especially by Godelier (1973b). Godelier stressed that a structural analysis of production processes offers no basis for an identification of modes of production. Where different modes of production exist side by side, or where they interfere with each other, the *historical process* must guide our understanding; in this context one should raise the question whether the Guro passed through a phase when their sole form of production was hunting, before they moved on to agriculture, etc. The manner in which Terray employs the concept of mode of production — at least in his earlier publications — makes it difficult, however, to arrive at a typology of historical stages.

Rey and exploitation as the backbone of modes of production

In his 1971 book dealing with the transition from colonialism to capitalism in Congo-Brazzaville, Pierre-Philippe Rey enters into the discussion concerning the ideas of Meillassoux and Terray. He considers Meillassoux's major contribution to be that he had put an end to rigid and formalistic interpretations of historical materialism as applied to pre-capitalist societies. He supports Meillassoux's conclusion that within such societies social relations are determined not by control over means of production, but rather by authority over the producers themselves, notably through control over means of *re*production. In exchange for the labour of younger men, the elders grant them wives; in this way the younger men can surround themselves with a group of dependants. According to Rey, too, the elders control the labour of younger men because the elders can allocate women. However, he takes Meillassoux to task for failing to understand the mystifying nature of the 'exchange' involved. Ultimately there is no natural reason why the elders should be the ones to allot wives. This 'exchange' obscures the fact that younger men provide labour for the benefit of the elders without any counter-prestation (Rey 1971: 34).

In Rey's view, Terray rightly paid much attention to the manner in which production takes place, and to the forms of 'complex' and 'simple' co-operation. However, Rey does not consider these forms of co-operation to be an adequate ground to distinguish various modes of production. For Terray concentrates on the direct labour process instead of on the social production process as a whole, as a coherent system fixed in time (see also Terray 1979: 29–30). Moreover, Terray sketches only one aspect of the forms of co-operation, that of mutual help. Rey, instead, focuses attention on the contrasting phenomenon of exploitative relationships.

Rey does not treat productive forces and relations of production as separate topics; instead he maintains that the specific connection between the two constitutes the distinguishing characteristic of a mode of production. In so doing he goes back to Marx's analysis of land rent. Marx's leading idea there was that every mode of production is distinguished by the special economic form in which unpaid surplus labour is appropriated from the direct producer. Once this premise is adopted, it is no longer necessary to study quantitatively the total of productive forces and relations of productions in each separate instance; on the other hand, the analyst avoids the trap of applying over-simplified labels based on a single (perhaps marginal) indicator, such as, for example, the hoe, the plough or the hunting-net.

Rey believes that a form of appropriation of surplus labour also occurs among the Guro. The elders accumulate their wealth and respect not through their own labour but through the surplus labour of younger men. Where such an exploitative relationship exists, in other words where relations of production are antagonistic, one is obliged to speak of classes. Yet Rey is not positing here a literal division between elders and younger men (as biological categories). Instead the opposition is figurative or metaphorical, at variance with ordinary usage in which the terms imply a fluid transition between the two categories and do not embrace those who are exploited on a far more permanent basis, such as women and slaves (Rey 1971: 55). Rey prefers to speak of an exploitative relation between 'elders' and 'youth' as 'social' (as distinct from biological) categories. Exploitation takes place in the following sequence: (a) production by the dependants; (b) conveyance of products and services to the elders; (c) circulation on a basis of reciprocity among the elders; (d) accumulation in the sphere of circulation, and/or destruction (Rey 1971: 68). Bride-wealth is the specific form through which exploitation is accomplished: dependants provide the wherewithal for the acquisition of prestige goods which then circulate among the elders as marriage payments.

In his study of the Kuni, Punu and Tsangui in Congo-Brazzaville, Rey analyses how such exploitative relations can function within matrilineal groups with patrilocal residence. In these 'disharmonic' societies there is no protective mimicry of exploitative relationships such as occurs among the Guro; Guro society is patrilineal and patrilocal, and younger males gradually ascend the social ladder until they finally become the elders of their own domestic group. By way of contrast, among the Kuni, Punu and Tsangui, a man can only become the elder of a different group from the one within which he has lived all his life; if a man's mother's brother dies, he may be obliged to give up his patrilocal residence and to assume the position of the elder within his localized matrilineage segment. The actual exploitative relation, however, exists between an elder and a youth within the co-residing patrilineal group. Exploitation is all the more vivid because youths provide surplus labour within a community where they themselves can never attain the position of elder. In order to acquire a wife, a young man must also rely on the mediation of an elder of the patrilineal descent group. Under the polygamous system, older men have wives, and there are few wives available for the young men. The scarcity of marriage partners, coupled with the necessity of paying bride-wealth, enhances the dependence of youths. This dependence is expressed in their offering presentations (*pawu*) in the form of services and products to the elders. The system is perpetuated by the internal logic of the bridewealth–polygamy– *pawu* chain.

Next Rey analyses the influence of colonial forced labour and the modern economy on *pawu* and the system of bridewealth. The colonial economy and neo-colonialism have been grafted on to the old system: through the perpetuation of old kinship relations, it has become possible for the new authorities to appropriate surplus labour from the village societies. Marital payments, for example, are converted into currency; they keep rising sharply. As a result younger men are obliged to earn money if they want to maintain their position within their own community. The dominant classes of the old and new order at first benefit in the process. The elders receive that part of the wages of young plantation labourers earmarked for marital payments. The plantation owners profit from the surplus labour of the younger men. But, although it may appear that the old system has remained unchanged, the independent economic mainstay of the system — *pawu* in the form of labour — has been demolished. The appropriation of surplus labour refers to the dominant relation of production, which in this case is colonial and neo-colonial exploitation.

Rey further elaborates on the conjuncture of pre-capitalist and capitalist modes of production in *Les Alliances de classes* (1973) and in *Capitalisme négrier: Le marche des paysans vers le prolétariat* (1976, with Le Bris and Samuel). In these books the ideas which Rey developed in his Congo study are applied to contemporary issues.

Although Rey does manage to avoid the problem of how to find an empirical definition for the concept of mode of production, his approach none the less invokes new difficulties. One essential question is how surplus labour should be defined for various pre-capitalist social formations. The related problem arises of how to determine the quantity of surplus labour in a self-sufficient economy with extremely low productivity and a poorly developed market system. Furthermore, it may be true that the mechanism of bridewealth as sketched by Rey explains the relation between elders and the youth, but it does not clarify the position of women and slaves. Other mechanisms will have to be invoked in order to explain why the latter categories accept their subordinate existence more or less as a means of (re-)production. The system is obviously capable of reproducing itself; force by itself is insufficient to guarantee such persistence.

Further development of viewpoints in the African context

Terray and the concept of surplus

In an article on classes and class consciousness in the Abron kingdom, published in 1975, Terray returns to the discussion on the identification of old African modes of production, and the existence of classes within such modes. He admits the inadequacy of the way in which he previously construed modes of production among the Guro (1969b). His attempt to derive the relations of production from forms of co-operation led others to conclude that, for Terray, differences between modes of production lay in the sphere of productive forces. In his 1975 article Terray accepts Rey's alternative view that a mode of production is characterized by the form in which the surplus labour of direct producers is appropriated. Accordingly, for the identification of the various modes of production within a social formation, an inventory of exploitative relations must be made. But since modes of production may not exclusively be founded on exploitation in the narrower sense, Terray proposes to redefine the concept of exploitation as 'the specific mode of appropriation, allocation and utilization of surplus' (1975: 89–90). Every form of appropriation of surplus supposes a particular superstructure as a condition for its reproduction. The growth of productive forces, however (interpreted by Terray as a growth of surplus, which makes possible new forms of appropriation and allocation of surplus labour), would explain why in historical reality a combination of two or more modes of production always exists, with one mode being dominant over the other.[19]

In his analysis of the Abron, Terray sketches the linkage between the lineage mode of production (involving the matrilineal descent groups) and the slave mode of production. While leaving relations of production in the villages unaffected, the Abron aristocracy made use of internal mechanisms of control (such as witchcraft accusations) in order to maintain their own power. Large-scale appropriation of surplus from the village population was not possible, because the Abron aristocracy needed the free men from the villages to undertake slave raids; these raids provided slaves for the aristocrats' farms and gold mines. Within the system of slave production there was no stable slave class. The second generation of slaves could no longer be traded; they were gradually integrated into the community of the free. This reduced the danger of rebellion, but it necessitated periodic slave expeditions and war. The surplus labour of the slaves was 'realized' — that is to say it was converted into valuable goods — through long-distance trade: the Abron aristocracy exchanged slave-produced

310

gold for clothing, salt, livestock, iron, slaves and, later, weapons, ammunition and alcohol. The principal aim of trade was accumulation of wealth rather than reinvestment in production; although, secondarily, such trade goods as slaves, weapons and ammunition were clearly vital to the perpetuation of slave production. By and large the slave mode of production was not autonomous but remained dependent on the lineage mode of production in the villages. Within the kingdom, villagers provided tribute and surplus labour (for slave raids); villagers residing outside the realm of the kingdom functioned as a labour reserve, from which time and again new slaves were captured. By way of contrast the lineage mode of production was autonomous to a considerable extent: the villages could keep up their production even without the aristocratic upper stratum, albeit at a somewhat lower level of productivity (without the aristocrats the supply of household slaves would probably exhaust itself).

Such perceptions about the links between these modes of production do appear illuminating, casting light, for example, upon the unstable character of pre-colonial West African states.

The weak point in Terray's argument is the shift from 'surplus labour' to 'surplus'. 'Surplus' can have different meanings. On the one hand it refers to tangible excess produce: that part of production which remains after consumption. On the other hand, more abstractly, surplus can mean that part of social production generated by uncompensated work. In the latter meaning of the term, surplus is thus the form in which surplus labour is manifest. Commenting on the relation between these two meanings, Marx says that surplus labour always generates surplus, but not every surplus implies surplus labour.[20] With Terray it remains unclear which sense of the concept of surplus he is using. From the fact that he places the growth of the surplus within the sphere of forces of production, it might be deduced that he uses surplus in the sense of excess produce; but in that case he would imply that there is such a thing as a natural level of consumption. Products which are not directly needed or which fall outside the sphere of 'basic needs' constitute surplus in this interpretation; they can be appropriated by the elders without exploitation being involved.

Forms of production and distribution, however, have a historical dimension.They do not follow from any standard level of consumption that is invariable for all societies (stipulating, for instance, a particular minimum, which can be expressed in quantitative units, such as the joule). Rather, forms of production and distribution constitute a subsistence level which is specific for a certain time and a certain social organization. When the elders lay claim to the best meat procured during the hunt, it can be established objectively that the youths can go on living without these delicacies. Nevertheless this meat, too, is part of the group's total means of subsistence; and that part is monopolized by the elders. As a part of collective production, it may not be equated with surplus in the sense of excess produce, even if it approaches the form of 'useless' prestige goods, such as leopard-skins, gold and ivory. With his use of the concept of surplus, Terray undermines Rey's argument. Rey's analysis does not imply that exploitation as appropriation of surplus labour always occurs in every society. According to Marx, the development of surplus labour depends on two objective conditions: the soil must be so fertile that producers have extra time after attending to their own food needs; and the social organization of labour must lend itself to the exploitation of surplus labour (Marx 1894 (1974): 647–8). It is also possible that exploitation in the theoretical sense occurs in societies where, subjectively, it is not or hardly perceived as such by the participants; such a situation might particularly obtain in systems where production is geared towards the making of consumer goods. Only after the beginning of production for the market (i.e. for profit) can the appropriation of surplus labour increase rapidly.

In an autocritical article 'On exploitation', Terray (1979) once again replies to criticism launched against his analysis of the Guro: the way he used the concept of mode of production, his neglect of reproduction, and his standpoint in relation to exploitation and classes. With regard to the first and last points, in 1979 he offers an elaboration of the stance which he has already assumed in 1975. What is new in 1979 is that Terray admits he ignored the importance of reproduction, leading to a distorted view of dominance in Guro society. He asserts now that that mode of production within a social formation is dominant which succeeds in making the other modes of production subservient to its own reproduction.

Alternatively, Terray cautions that emphasis on reproduction must never be allowed to go so far as to analyse the economic sphere exclusively from the perspective of reproduction (control over the allocation of wives to younger men). For such a view would erroneously grant primacy to the sphere of circulation (in

312

this case the circulation of persons) instead of production. Also we would run the risk of viewing reproduction as a social goal: the society would then be considered as a system organized so as to perpetuate the existing order. It is Terray's belief that society as such has no goal; only individuals and groups have goals. From a historical-materialist viewpoint, what is being reproduced is an opposition, such as a relation of exploitation. The group which exploits tries to maintain its own privileged position; the exploited group tries to bring an end to the exploitation. Reproduction has to do with inter-group relations and their consequences.

Meillassoux's interpretation of surplus labour

In 1975 Meillassoux's *Femmes, greniers et capitaux* was published. In the first part of the book he sketches the theoretical transition from 'bands' to a 'domestic community' of farmers; in the second part he turns to the influence of colonialism and capitalism upon these domestic communities. In the context of this chapter it is especially important how Meillassoux deals with the production system of the domestic mode of production and with the forms of exploitation therein. It is interesting to see that despite major differences in emphasis his view corresponds in certain respects with Terray's.

As discussed above, Meillassoux asserted in earlier publications that the domestic mode of production differed from other modes of production in that control over production took place through means of reproduction and not through means of production. To control the total production process one requires command over the labour-force; therefore the central point in a domestic economy is to have a grip on the means of reproduction of that labour-force through food, seed and women. The elders exercise such control. Therefore the kinship system becomes socially dominant. Relations between people are expressed in the idiom of kinship, and this applies to production, inter-group politics, conflict regulations and also ideology (ancestor worship and fertility rituals).

Raising control over reproduction to the status of a distinctive feature of the domestic mode of production produces, however, an inconsistency: from the perspective of reproduction, the vertical kinship relation of father and son is the most significant, but in the production sphere the lateral kinship relation between older and younger brother is of decisive importance. In fact one observes that the political system is regulated through lateral kinship relations, whereas Meillassoux maintains that political power is based on exercising supremacy over the means of reproduction. He attempts to escape from this contradiction by stating that reproduction remains subordinate to production as the ultimately determining factor (1975: 78). In distinguishing between vertical and lateral kinship, Meillassoux takes issue with Godelier, who interprets both these relations merely as kinship relations which in one manner or another generate their own determination (so that kinship appears as an infrastructure).

Although Meillassoux has a point here, it remains unclear how he himself sees the connection between reproduction and production. He writes that reproduction is the 'dominant preoccupation' of the domestic community; thus he appears to link this domination with the sphere of ideology (1975: 78). On the other hand he makes an attempt to analyse reproduction as a component of economic circulation. Because of the confusion indicated here with regard to the concept of reproduction, Meillassoux ignores the discrepancy between the factual level of reproduction and maximal reproduction as a significant value orientation (see chapter 2).

It is also entirely from the perspective of reproduction that Meillassoux deals with the concept of surplus labour. He says that in a domestic community there is no such thing as surplus because supplies are needed for the reproduction of the group over time. One can speak of surplus labour, however, in the sense that a quantity of energy is available above that required for the production of basic needs under conditions of a stationary reproduction (1975: 91). Meillassoux's formulation translates surplus labour into terms of free time. The members of the domestic community work to meet their direct material needs and the elders lay a claim to their leisure hours. Reasoning further along these lines, Meillassoux also argues that both the feudal form of surplus labour (land rent) and the appropriation of surplus value in capitalism are based on an appropriation of free time (1975: 91, n.; cf. Marx 1894 (1974): 827). Here Meillassoux makes the same mistake as Terray: both seem to assume a natural level of consumption. Meillassoux's analysis hinges on control over the means of reproduction; the appropriation of surplus labour — in the sense of a residue of time and energy — is treated as a means to preserve such control. Therefore he can arrive at the conclusion that within the domestic mode of production there is no continuing exploitation of one group by another. For Meillassoux, exploitation takes place only if available food and human energy are redistributed in such a manner that one category receives systematically less than its fair share (1975: 122).

If we compare Meillassoux's and Rey's interpretations it emerges that Rey reasons in precisely the opposite way. According to Rey, the elders control the means of (re)production in order to perpetuate the appropriation of surplus labour. Where surplus labour is appropriated there is, by definition, exploitation as well as classes. Therefore Rey distinguishes two classes in the Guro mode of production: the elders on the one hand, the youth, slaves and women on the other. Meillassoux does not turn a blind eye to the subordinate position in which these groups find themselves, but he denies the existence of any class relation. Elders and youth do not constitute distinct classes because every young man can become one of the elders; there is thus no question of self-perpetuating groups. Here, too, the accent appears to fall on biological reproduction; if a category involved in the economic process is not capable of physically reproducing itself, the concept of class is said not to be applicable.

Rey's further thoughts on exploitation: Varieties of subordination

In a 1979 article Rey, too, has worked out his ideas about exploitation and the appropriation of surplus labour from direct producers. In Rey's view one cannot speak of modes of production without at the same time bringing in social classes and exploitation. He does, however, concede that not all societies can be analysed within this conceptual framework. He proceeds to revise some of his former ideas. Of central importance is his assertion, in agreement with Marx's stance in *Grundrisse*, that the social production process is a unified whole that also comprises, in addition to the production process in the limited meaning of the term (as process of manufacture), the process of value formation (as proces of the realization of surplus value). Now, in a departure from his earlier analyses, Rey finds the process of appropriation of surplus labour in itself an inadequate base for distinguishing between different types of relations of production. A number of forms of exploitation are possible which involve a more or less regular appropriation of surplus labour, forms such as plunder and extortion. Yet in such instances it would be erroneous to speak in terms of relations of production because the exploitation does not actually take place within the sphere of the production process but in the sphere of distribution, or of plain and simple theft. Only if the exploitation is interwoven with forms of labour and co-operation does an enduring system, based in a relation of production, exist.

For Rey, the brutality of exploitation is not the important issue, but rather whether the appropriation of surplus labour is connected with the total social production process in such a way that, should it disappear, production as a whole would cease. Societies which are subject to pillaging raids carried out by outsiders, or even by their own aristocracy, stand to gain if these raids are discontinued. From a technical and organizational point of view, the continuation of the production process does not depend on the raiders. In his 1971 study Rey confined himself to demonstrating the appropriation of surplus labour as such; he did not go as far as to consider whether the producers themselves were already subordinate in the production process. In 1979, making up for this earlier omission, Rey differentiates, as Marx had done, between 'formal' and 'real' subordination of producers. In *formal* subordination the form in which appropriation of surplus labour takes place determines the structure of the distribution of labour and the organization of production. *Real* subordination means that in addition technical aspects of the labour process and technical innovations are also determined by the subordination. From among African social forms based on kinship ('systèmes lignagers') Rey uses examples from Congo-Brazzaville and north Togo. For these places, in any event, he claims formal subordination to exist in the distribution of labour between men and women. The next question to ask would be whether real subordination is also found; only then does it become possible to speak of true exploitation and social classes. Rey suggests that in the societies he analyses real subordination exists. Innovations in agriculture (the importation of new crop varieties, for example) are tolerated by the elders only to the extent that such change does not ultimately diminish their power. On the other hand the subordinate groups of younger men and women are constantly attempting to cultivate new crops which do not fall under the traditional control of the elders. Rey concludes that thus one may speak confidently of a lineage mode of production and therefore also of exploitation.

316

A purely academic discussion?

Subsuming French historical-materialist anthropologists under a single label is no easy task. The preceding section does not reflect a discussion which has ever actually taken place. Instead, it attempts to reconstruct a debate running through the works of the authors involved. Some of the controversies have been more explicit than others. In this chapter the social-psychological and political-economic backgrounds of the French anthropologists are ignored; it does not therefore pretend to be an exercise in the 'sociology of knowledge'. Neither was it my intention to lump all these authors together. Their standpoints are too diverse and the tone of the exchanges between them has too much of an edge, partly as a reflection of differences in their political practice. At the same time, however, they appear to be in agreement about essential matters. All select material aspects of life as their starting-point for the study of society as a whole; all establish a temporal sequence on the basis of different modes of production; all maintain the possibility of an articulation of modes of production at a given moment. They share the opinion that the history of Africa, and current developments within African countries, can be better understood through the analysis of ancient African modes of production and of the linkage of such modes with various forms of capitalism.

In reviewing the discussion among the anthropologists, it appears that the application of historical materialism in anthropology continues to encounter fundamental problems of the first order. First there remains the question of precisely how we are to think about economic determination in societies without clear-cut economic institutions. Some, preferring to use the concept of determination more loosely, speak readily of regulation (Pouillon 1976: 64). In this connection Godelier, as has been pointed out, sharply criticizes the base/superstructure metaphor itself, detecting in it the reflection of a strongly ethnocentric interpretation of society. Yet others regard determination in the last analysis as more of a general principle, one that does not require any further elaboration or demonstration.

A second problem is the confrontation between historical-materialist thought and field-work data. Here the difficulty is how the mode of production of a particular society can be described with the help of the concepts of mode of production, productive

317

forces and relations of production. Terray made at first a rather empiricist use of the conceptual framework. Alternatively, Meillassoux regards it as a theoretical apparatus that defies definition in terms of what can be observed — directly or indirectly. Rey has no desire to manipulate the framework of ideas as some kind of formal prescription, but instead wants to capture its central essence as his starting-point; this, he feels, was also Marx's objective. For Rey this essence lies in the way in which surplus labour is appropriated from the direct producer.

Althusser's and Balibar's premise was that modes of production can be interpreted as so many combinations of the invariable constituent elements of the production system, whereby in the last analysis the material basis of the society determines which social sphere is dominant. This view has not proved to be very helpful in attempts to solve the problems outlined above. The major value of the work of Althusser and his followers lies in the fact that it has enabled a connection to be established between historical-materialism theory and anthropological field-work. Yet the high level of abstraction of Althusser's writing has prompted a multitude of interpretations. The discussion among the anthropologists concerned, despite areas of heated controversy, nevertheless displays a certain common orientation. Especially since the late 1960s these anthropologists have undergone a similar development, moving away from a more or less formal application of historical-materialist concepts and towards the derivation of a new theory capable of explaining the coherence of pre-capitalist modes of production. The convergence of their interests emerges most distinctly from the fact that all have paid increasing attention to the concept of surplus labour.

Nevertheless they have certainly not reached anything like a consensus as to what is surplus labour in an African subsistence economy, how the appropriation of surplus labour takes place, or what its significance is for the totality of social processes and for the related problem of classes and class conflict in such a society. A recent contribution by Meillassoux suggests that the debate over these issues has implications which go beyond African modes of production. Having earlier distinguished between energy expended on work to meet one's own material needs and energy spent on work for others (1975: 89f.), in his 1979 article Meillassoux tries to establish the distinctive forms of exploitation within widely diverse modes of production through an analysis of the kinds of

318

demographic manipulation belonging to these different modes.

A further convergence in the recent work of these French anthropologists is the concept of ideology.[21] This is all the more welcome since initially the discussion remained too narrowly constricted to the economic.

The last word has not yet been spoken in the debate on identification of modes of production and the articulation of these modes. Without a doubt the debate so far has generated considerable confusion, but it would be a pity were this to discourage other participants from making analyses of concrete problems. The principal danger is that the discussion, without new empirical input, will be swamped in an academic quicksand.

The discussion traced in this chapter calls for some more general critical comments. Let us first reconsider the relation between theory and research practice. In terms of theory, there are certainly objections to be raised against the ideas of French anthropologists at various levels: their derivation of concepts, their interpretation of the conceptual framework, and the extent to which they fail to free themselves from rigid economic determinism. Since our primary objective, however, remains the formulation of a new research paradigm for the analysis of current social problems in Africa, it seems more meaningful to concentrate here on errors committed by the French School in the empirical application of their theories.

The beginning of every historical-materialist analysis consists of a thorough Marxist analysis of the systems of production and distribution. Meillassoux and Terray, however, map out these systems using concepts proper to bourgeois economics; only in their subsequent interpretation do they apply Marxist concepts such as productive forces and relations of production. The reasoning of these writers goes as follows. Younger men and women work on the land. The product (P), the harvest, is handed over to the elders. The elders redistribute part of the product directly among the households (P_h). Another part is used to acquire prestige goods which serve as bridewealth (P_b). Younger men recover this part in the form of a wife (W). (see Figure 8.1.) This diagram would justify the conclusion that no exploitation occurs ($P = P_h + W$). Terray's later differentiation between production necessary for consumption and surplus production (P becomes $P_c + P_s$) does not alter this schema essentially. Nor do Meillassoux's corrections make any appreciable difference, when

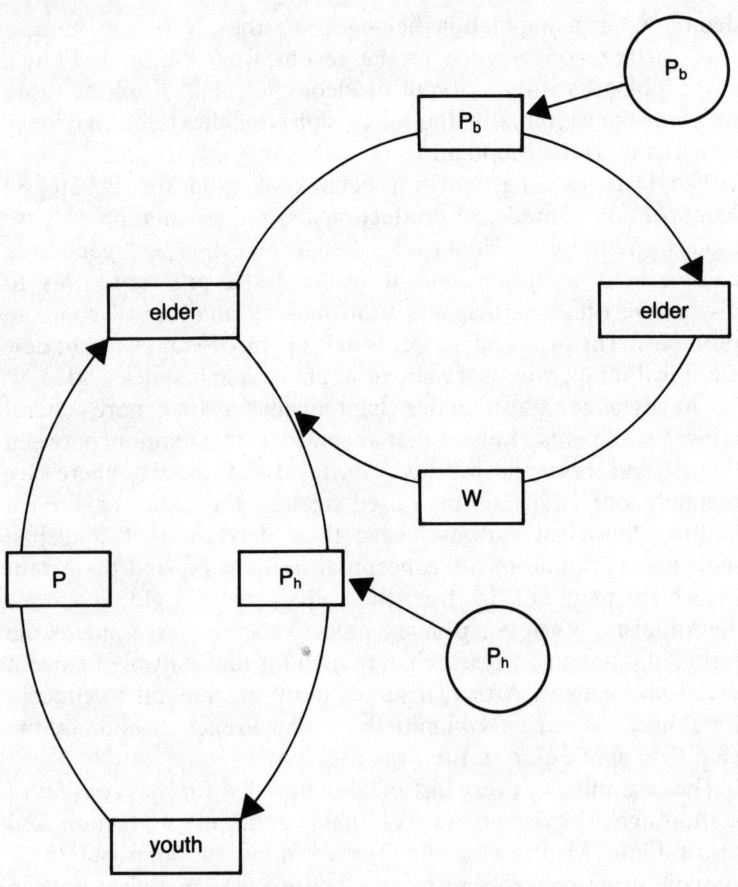

Figure 8.1 Relations between elders and youth in the domestic community. P = product; P_h = part of the product that is redistributed over the household; P_b = part of the product that is circulated as bridewealth; W = wife

he distinguishes between necessary labour and labour during the producer's free time.

Rey emphasizes that the wives which the younger men receive are no true payment, so that a description in terms of exchange and reciprocity would obscure the exploitation that takes place. The part of production designated for the acquisition of élite goods (P_b) is appropriated from the younger men as a form of surplus labour. Although this perception of Rey's is a significant step forward, his further analysis conforms to Figure 8.1. In their economic analysis, all these writers take as their starting-point the product that has already been produced; they deal merely with its distribution. The production process is regarded as a system of activities (Terray provides the clearest illustration of this line of thought); its underlying economic laws are not studied. As a result the concept of surplus labour cannot find an economic derivation cast in terms from the production sphere itself, but rather assumes some meaning such as 'a quantity of energy' or 'a unit of harvested produce', that is to say, a derivation in terms of the sphere of distribution.

A historical-materialist analysis must involve a consistent study of the underlying economic laws of the entire system of production and distribution. When the agricultural systems of a domestic community are the object of study, the starting-point should be the differentiation and analysis of productive factors: questions related to the allocation of land and the alignment of the labour force. Then we should assess who supplies the constant 'capital' (means of production such as seed, axes and hoes) and who supplies the variable 'capital' (food to keep the producers alive). Next comes the phase of production; here we must study how much time the producers spend in order to produce the equivalent of the amount of food which is furnished to them throughout the season of cultivation. The product which is harvested can be divided into two portions: one part is to be seen as the equivalent of the capital which has been invested — an amount sufficient to keep the group alive until the following harvest, and to provide seed for the next cycle; the other part constitutes the surplus product. The percentage of surplus product should not be calculated against the total product but rather against that part of the total product which embodies necessary labour time.

The next question is what happens with the surplus product. The surplus product in itself is of little use to the group which appropriates it. The surplus product, and the surplus labour which it embodies, acquire value (in the form of prestige goods) only in the exchange system. Where there is a low level of economic development, trade plays a minor role within the village; and if trade occurs it will at most take place between villages and between different regions engaged in long-distance trade. In such circumstances the exchange value of élite goods cannot be derived from the internal production. It is therefore understandable that

Meillassoux, when examining the village community in isolation, is unable to state the connection between the internal production of use-value, and the value of prestige goods. He then derives the exchange value of these goods from their symbolic function as marital payments. Exchange value never exists, however, without an ultimate use-value.

For a proper understanding of the value of prestige goods, more than a study of internal production is necessary; research must also explore whence prestige goods derive their character as commodities.[22] In some instances they derive this character from the fact that they are used as an equivalent form; Godelier gives this explanation in his article on salt among the Baruya. When the market system is still largely undeveloped, equivalent form is extremely complicated; a package of various goods can serve as the equivalent of another commodity or for another package of commodities (see Marx 1894 (1974): 340, 348–9). Another possibility is that prestige goods have their final use-value outside the area of production; this would hold true, for example, for gold, ivory or ostrich-feathers. It can also happen that particular prestige goods (salt, iron, textiles) do have a certain use-value within the community itself, but that this use is monopolized by a specific group.

However this may be, the conclusion remains that an essential part of the economic system in the domestic or lineage mode of production — notably the exchange value of prestige goods and concomitantly the realization of surplus labour — cannot be understood on the exclusive basis of the study of the internal production system within the villages. From its inception the economic system, via the sphere of circulation, extends far beyond the boundaries of the domestic community. That the commodity character of certain goods must be derived from the sphere of circulation and not that of production is certainly not in conflict with historical-materialist premises. In economies with a low level of development there exists a comparative autonomy of circulation with respect to production. The production of goods in such an economy is no direct guarantee that these goods will reach the market. Circulation then depends on many more factors, including politics (protection from war, theft), geography (the distance that must be travelled) and financial conditions (the level of development of credit systems). Only under the system of capitalism does trade become an extension of production and can one maintain that the commodity character is already created during production (see Marx 1894 (1974): 342).

Conclusion

The above discussion only suggests the large amount of preparatory work that is necessary before we can analyse the economic base. Even then little will have been clarified concerning social relations. Yet it has become clear that one needs to exercise caution in using the concepts of 'productive forces' and 'relations of production' to analyse African social structures. Exchange structures appear to be of primary importance in understanding political relations. Personally I am not inclined to go as far as Coquery-Vidrovitch (e.g. as reprinted in 1977) who posits the existence of an African mode of production characterized by long-distance trade. Her position has been challenged by Terray on the grounds that instead of building her argument on the principle of production, she chose circulation as her point of departure (Terray 1974: 340). In the practice of research this means that one is required to carry out an analysis through a wide-angle lens, encompassing all the geographical ramifications of trade networks etc.; such an increase of scope conflicts with the field-work requirement of focusing in sharply upon one's subject (see above chapters 6 and 7).

The brilliant way in which Marx derived distribution, exchange and consumption from production, which is to be found in the Introduction to *Zur Kritik der politischen Oekonomie* (Marx 1859 (1972)), was never meant to be emulated by anthropologists carrying out village or regional studies. Whether one works along the West African coast, in the Sahel or in East Africa, one invariably finds significant volumes of trade transacted with areas far afield. Goods which are exchanged are of major importance for internal political relations within the community (e.g. prestige goods, weapons). Exchange intervenes in relations of distribution, not only as far as the redistribution of finished products is concerned, but also with respect to the allocation of producers and production instruments, factors which are antecedent to production itself. Because of the fact that the anthropologists' research area is habitually restricted in geographical scope, it is well-nigh impossible to deal with the mutual derivation of relations of production and relations of exchange. Instead of persisting in the somewhat infertile view that the economic relations exclusively consist of relations of production, it may be preferable to acknowledge, instead, the relative autonomy of exchange relations alongside relations of production.

If one pursues this train of thought with an eye on practical research, we should also consider its consequences at the theoretical level. Recognition of the significance of exchange relations is nothing new; entire generations of anthropologists have performed spadework here. Does one desert the hallmark of historical materialism if one looks at distribution as well as production, and no longer identifies modes of production solely on the basis of the linkage between productive forces and relations of production? Recognition of the importance of exchange relations must be afforded its proper place within an historical-materialist theory concerning the lineage mode of production. This has no direct consequences for the Marxist analysis of capitalism. It does mean, however, that we must abandon the interpretation of different modes of production as various combinations of the same elements (a position held by Althusser and Balibar, among others). Another consequence is that we may no longer consider economic oppositions within the sphere of production as the only basis for social oppositions. In the sphere of production a split into two classes at odds with each other is impossible within the lineage mode of production, but that does not rule out underlying exploitative relations which have to do with distribution.[23]

We are still in the pioneering period of drafting a historical-materialist theory of the lineage mode of production. In this attempt, Pierre-Philippe Rey has gone the furthest, it seems to me (Rey 1979). Yet even he proceeds too rapidly from the observation that surplus labour is appropriated from the producer, to the invocation of class theory: appropriation of surplus labour implies in his view, *ipso facto* a dichotomy of classes (elders–youth).

The historical-materialist input in anthropology has proved of great critical value vis-à-vis extant anthropological theories. Historical materialism itself, however, has not offered easy solutions to theoretical or practical problems in anthropology — nor should it be expected to do so. In his letters, Engels time and again emphasized that historical materialism provided 'above all a guideline for further study and not a lever for Hegelian constructions'.[24] Before theoretical advances become possible it may well be necessary to discard certain Marxist premises should they prove a hindrance. Historical materialism is, after all, but a theory. If we still insist dogmatically on the wholesale preservation of the received conceptual framework, our tools may turn into weapons pointed at ourselves.

Notes

1 Sound general commentary concerning Althusser's work is provided by Seminar Althusser (1977) and by Karsz (1974). For more critical evaluations, see Projekt Klassenanalyse (1975) and Thompson (1978).
2 The idea that these five basic types constitute necessary phases in social development comes not from Marx, but from Stalin. The forms of the antique and feudal modes of production, confined to specific historical periods, are generalized, and the Asiatic mode of production, confined to a specific part of the world, is omitted. Marx rejected a universal philosophy of history as detached from history itself, even should it be founded on his own work; see Marx 1877 (1974): 107–12.
3 A rather superficial and mechanical application of the concept of articulation of modes of production can be found, for example, in the introduction to Wolpe (1980).
4 See Marx: *Formen die der kapitalistische Produktion Vorhergehen*; this is a part of *Grundrisse* (Marx 1857–8 (1972): 375–413) and thus not a definitive text. In addition, see Krader (1972). Further, see Meillassoux's criticism of Suret-Canale (1974): 'Beaucoup d'anthropologues marxistes semblent avoir suivi Marx dans les zones les plus faibles de ses analyses: l'interminable réconstruction d'une succession hypothétique de modes de production précapitalistes à demi-imaginaires ou mal définis' (Meillassoux 1977: 321).
5 In the 1968 edition of *Lire 'Le Capital'* only the contributions by Althusser and Balibar are included. The original edition, prepared by a collective, appeared in 1965. Among the contributions omitted in 1968 was that of Jacques Rancière; it was omitted because of his deviant position with respect to the events of 1968 in Paris; see Rancière (1975: 56–75).
6 For a more extensive account, see Karsz (1974).
7 In addition to linear causality (the effect of one element on another) and expressive causality (the effect of the whole on the parts as expressions of that whole), both of which appear in bourgeois theory, Althusser posits structural causality. With this term he, also, designates a relation between the whole and its parts, but it is an extremely complex relation, which could be summarized in the following terms. The cause of the effects is the complex organization of the whole. This whole is not an entity in itself, nor an essence which lies behind its manifestations. The whole is present only in the effects, not all of which form part of the complex structure. To give an example: a Marxist would not be interested in the question of whether social

theatre is a simple representation of reality, nor is he interested in the transcendant truth which radiates from the play, but he is intent on analysing the mechanism that causes the events that take place on the stage. 'The object of his science is the mechanism which produces the stage effects' (Althusser & Balibar 1968, quoted from the English translation (1975): 310).

8 This is to interpret the relation labourer/non-labourer as the equivalent of the relation between, on the one hand, producer (as well as his or her dependents) and, on the other, non-producers profiting from the labour of producers.

9 Althusser replied to his critics in *Eléments d'autocritique* (1974). He concedes that he has approached his work too theoretically but denies the allegation that he has gone over to structuralism. He maintains that there is at most a flirtation with structuralist terminology, in *Lire 'Le Capital'* (Althusser & Balibar 1968).

10 For a critique of Althusser's, Balibar's and Godelier's structuralist tendencies, see Goodfriend (1978).

11 Godelier 1973b.

12 Marx acknowledged explicitly that in non-capitalist social formations institutions other than economic ones are dominant on the plane of the social structure; the Church during the middle ages in Europe is a case in point. At the same time he stated that this in no way detracts from the premise of materialism that in the causal sphere the mode of production of material needs is ultimately the determining factor: for one does not stay alive by the manipulation of symbols alone. See Marx 1867 (1975): 96, n. 33: 'Soviel ist klar, das das Mittelalter nicht vom Katholizismus und die antieke Welt nicht von der Politik leben konnte. Die Art und Weise, wie sie ihr Leben gewannen, erklärt umgekehrt, warum dort die Politik, hier der Katholizismus die Hauptrolle spielte'.

13 Godelier (1978a: 160): 'Nous trouvons *donc à l'intérieur* même de toute activité matérielle de l'homme sur la nature un ensemble complexe de réalités *idéelles* dont la présence et l'intervention sont nécessaires pour que cette activité ait lieu' (Godelier's emphasis).

14 The same confusion of 'function' and 'institution' has for several decades now dominated the discussion between 'substantivists' and 'formalists' in economic anthropology; see for example, the Introduction in Sahlins (1974).

15 See Deluz & Godelier (1967), and Meillassoux's reply (1967).

16 In the monograph on the Guro numerous empirical findings can be found which are not altogether consistent with Meillassoux's theoretical statements. Meillassoux, for example, sketches the lineage and kinship system as the sphere which organizes production. Among the Guro this function is primarily attended to by the *goniwuo*, the patrilineal kinship group. Meillassoux comments, however, that this system is observed only by the Guro who live in the forest. Among the Guro who live in the savanna, the *goniwuo* is more often made up of a combination of different kinship groups without a common ancestor. In production there are also forms of co-operation which are

territorially-based (the village, 'le *bo* communal'); or which do not fit into the hierarchical structure of the patrilineage and instead are reciprocal or temporary by nature (*klala*). A similar discrepancy between theoretical statement and empirical findings appears in Meillassoux's treatment of the relation between the elders and the young men. He asserts that in general this is a fundamental distinction; but among the Guro he observed 'shifting' ('glissant') kinship relations with elders having no direct authority over their married sons (Meillassoux 1964: 169, 176).

17 For Terray, just as Godelier, a socio-economic formation is a concrete historic society.

18 What is more, Terray's (1969b) interpretation of the concept of domination is a marked departure from Althusser. In this chapter there is no opportunity to pursue the subject further; suffice it to say that in his later publications, Terray abandons his earlier interpretation. See Terray (1979).

19 By the term 'dominance' here, Terray means the dominance of one mode of production over other modes. Thus he uses the concept of dominance in a sense different from his earlier work. For further explanation of the relation between the concepts of determination and domination, see Raatgever (1982), and note 18 above.

20 That not every surplus product represents surplus labour is illustrated, for example, by sharply increasing harvests in a market economy. The surplus does increase, but the percentage of surplus labour may decrease as the result of a drop in prices.

21 Compare the contributions of Godelier, Augé and Terray in a special issue of the French anthropological journal *L'Homme* devoted to the concept of ideology (*L'Homme*, 18, nos 3–4 (1978)).

22 Cf. the concept *Wertbildung* in Marx; see, for example, Marx (1867, 1975): 76.

23 For an elaboration of the class analysis of the lineage mode of production, see Raatgever (1982, and forthcoming).

24 Engels, letter to Joseph Bloch, Koningsbergen, 5 August 1890 in *Marx-Engels Werke* (MEW), vol. 21.

References

Althusser, L. (1965), *Pour Marx*, Paris: Maspero.

Althusser, L. (1974), *Eléments d'autocritique*, Paris: Hachette.

Althusser, L. & Balibar, E. (1968), *Lire 'Le Capital'*, Paris: Maspero (English translation, *Reading 'Capital'*, 1975, London: NLB).

Balibar, E. (1974), *Cinq Etudes du matérialisme historique*, Paris: Maspero.

Bloch, M. (ed.) (1975), *Marxist Analysis and Social Anthropology*, London: Malaby.

Coquery-Vidrovitch, C. (1977), 'Research on an African mode of production', in Gutkind & Waterman (1977): 77–92.

Deluz, A. & Godelier, M. (1967), *Apropos de deux textes d'anthropologie économique'*, *L'Homme*, 7, 3: 78–91.

Engels, F. (1879), *Herrn Eugen Dürings Umwälzung der Wissenschaft, Marx-Engels Werke*, vol. 20, Berlin: Dietz Verlag, 1975 (*Anti-Dühring*, London: Lawrence & Wishart, 1969).

Engels, F. (1884), *Der Ursprung der Familie, des Privateigentums und des Staats, Marx-Engels Werke*, vol. 21, Berlin: Dietz, 1976 (*The Origin of the Family Private Property and the State*, Moscow: Progress Publishers, Marx and Engels Selected Works III, 1969).

Engels, F. (1888), *Ludwig Feuerbach und das Ende der klassischen deutsche philosophie, Marx-Engels Werke*, vol. 21, Berlin: Dietz, 1976 (*Ludwig Feuerbach and the End of Classical German Philosophy*, Moscow: Progress Publishers, Marx and Engels Selected Works III, 1969).

Godelier, M. (ed.) (1973a), *Sur les sociétes précapitalistes, Textes choisis de Marx, Engels, Lénine*, Paris: Editions Sociales.

Godelier, M. (1973b), *Horizon, trajets marxistes en anthropologie*, Paris: Maspero.

Godelier, M. (1973c), 'Modes de production, rapports de parenté et structures démographiques', *La Pensée*, 172: 7–31.

Godelier, M. (1978a), 'La Part idéelle du réel, Essai sur l'idéologique', *L'Homme*, 18, 3–4: 155–88.

Godelier, M. (1978b), 'Infrastructures, societies, and history', *Current Anthropology*, 19, 4: 763–8.

Godelier, M. (1979), 'La Notion de formation sociale économique', unpublished lecture, Amsterdam: Free University.

Goodfriend, D. E. (1978), '*Plus ça change, plus c'est la même chose*: the dilemma of the French Structural Marxists', *Dialectical Anthropology*, 3: 105–27.

Gouldner, A. (1970), *The Coming Crisis of Western Sociology*, New York: Basic Books.

Gutkind, P. C. W. & Waterman P., (eds) (1977), *African Social Studies*, London: Heinemann.

Habermas, J. (1970), *Zur Logik der Sozialwissenschaften*, Frankfurt a. M.: Suhrkamp.

Karsz, S. (1974), *Théorie et politique: Louis Althusser*, Paris: Fayard.

Korsch, K. (1923), *Marxismus und Philosophie*, Frankfurt: Europäische Verlangsanstalt, 1966 repr.

Krader, L. (ed.) (1972), *The Ethnological Notebooks of Karl Marx*, Assen: Van Gorcum.

Lukács, G. (1923), *Geschichte und klassenbewusstsein: G. Lukács Werke 2*, Frankfurt: Europaische Verlagsanstalt, 1968 repr., pp. 171–98.

Marx, K. (1857–8), *Grundrisse der Kritik der politischen Oekonomie* (Rohenturf), the part entitled *Formen die der kapitalistischen Produktion vorgehen, Marx-Engels Werke*, vol. 42, Berlin: Dietz Verlag, 1982 (*Grundrisse, Foundations of the Critique of Political Economy*, contains the part *Forms which Precede Capitalist Production*, Harmondsworth: Penguin, 1973).

Marx, K. (1859), *Zur Kritik der politischen Oekonomie, Marx-Engels*

Werke, vol. 13, Berlin: Dietz Verlag, 1968 (*A Contribution to the Critique of Political Economy*, London: Lawrence & Wishart, 1959).

Marx, K. (1867), *Das Kapital*, Band 1, *Marx-Engels Werke*, Berlin: Dietz Verlag, 1975 (*Capital*, vol. I, Harmondsworth: Penguin, 1976).

Marx, K. (1877), 'Brief an die Redaktion der *Otetschestwennyje Sapiski*', *Marx-Engels Werke*, vol. 19, Berlin: Dietz Verlag, 1974: 107–13.

Marx, K. (1885), *Das Kapital*, Band II (ed. F. Engels), *Marx-Engels Werke*, Berlin: Dietz Verlag, 1975 (*Capital*, vol. II, Harmondsworth: Penguin, 1978).

Marx, K. (1894), *Das Kapital*, Band III (ed. F. Engels), *Marx-Engels Werke*, Berlin: Dietz Verlag, 1974 (*Capital*, vol. III, Harmondsworth: Penguin, 1981).

Meillassoux, C. (1960), 'Essai d'interpretation du phénomène économique dans les sociétés traditionelles d'auto-subsistance', *Cahiers d'etudes africaines*, 4: 38–67.

Meillassoux, C. (1964), *Anthropologie économique des Gouro de Côte-d'Ivoire*, Paris/The Hague: Mouton.

Meillassoux, C. (1967), (Rejoinder to Deluz & Godelier), *L'Homme*, 7, 3: 91–7.

Meillassoux, C. (1975), *Femmes, greniers et capitaux*, Paris: Maspero.

Meillassoux, C. (1977), *Terrains et théories*, Paris: Maspero.

Meillassoux, C. (1979), 'Historical modalities of the exploitation of labour', *Critique of Anthropology*, 13–14: 7–27.

Mills, C. W. (1959), *The Sociological Imagination*, Oxford University Press.

Pouillon, F. (ed.) (1976), *L'Anthropologie économique*, Paris: Maspero.

Projekt Klassenanalyse (1975), *Louis Althusser: Marxistische Kritik am Stalinismus?* West-Berlin: Verlag für das Studium der Arbeiterbewegung.

Raatgever, J. H. (1982), 'Geëchte arbeid: Uitbuiting onder de dominantie van de verwantschap, *Te Elfder Ure* 32: 736–71, Nijmegen: Socialistiese Uitgeverij Nijmegen (SUN).

Raatgever, J. H. (forthcoming), 'De waarde van vrouwen: Economische en sociale status van vrouwen in Kameroen en Senegal'.

Rancière, J. (1975), *Wider den akademischen Marxismus*, Berlin: Merve Verlag.

Rey, P.-P. (1971), *Colonialisme, néo-colonialisme et transition au capitalisme: example du 'Comilog' au Congo-Brazzaville*, Paris: Maspero.

Rey, P.-P. (1973), *Les Alliances de classes*, Paris: Maspero.

Rey, P.-P. (ed.) (1976), *Capitalisme négrier*, Paris: Maspero.

Rey, P.-P. (1979), 'Class contradiction in lineage societies', *Critique of Anthropology*, 13–14: 41–60.

Sahlins, M. (1974), *Stone Age Economics*, London: Tavistock.

Seminar Althusser (1977), *Seminar Althusser: de Marxistiese Filosofie en haar Verhouding tot Spinoza, en Hegel, Bachelard en Lacan*, Nijmegen: Socialistiese Uitgeverij Nijmegen (SUN).

Suret-Canale, J. (ed.) (1974), *Sur le 'mode de production asiatique'*, Paris: Editions Sociales.

Terray, E. (1969a), *L'Organisation sociale des Dida de Côte-d'Ivoire*,

Annales de l'Université d'Abidjan, série F, vol. i, part 2.
Terray, E. (1969b), *Le Marxisme devant les sociétés 'primitives'*, Paris: Maspero.
Terray, E. (1974), 'Long-distance exchange and the formation of the state: the case of the Abron kingdom of Gyaman', *Economy and Society*.
Terray, E. (1975), 'Classes and class consciousness in the Abron kingdom of Gyaman', in Bloch (1975): 85–137.
Terray, E. (1979), 'On exploitation: elements of an autocritique', *Critique of Anthropology*, 13–14: 29–41.
Thompson, E. P. (1978), *The Poverty of Theory and other Essays*, London: Merlin Press.
Wolpe, H. (ed.) (1980), *The Articulation of Modes of Production: Essays from 'Economy and Society'*, London: Routledge & Kegan Paul.

Author index

Subject index

336

340

MORE ABOUT KPI BOOKS

If you would like further information about books available from KPI
please write to

>The Marketing Department
>KPI Limited
>Routledge & Kegan Paul Plc
>14 Leicester Square
>London WC2H 7PH

In the USA write to

>The Marketing Department
>KPI Limited
>Routledge & Kegan Paul
>9 Park Street
>Boston
>Mass. 02108

In Australia write to

>The Marketing Department
>KPI Limited
>Routledge & Kegan Paul
>464 St. Kilda Road
>Melbourne
>Victoria 3004

KPI